DISABLED JUSTICE

Lacking Equity Within The Justice System,
" i, am not an attorn'ey "
by Adam- Daniel – for the family of borsotti

~~Non-Esquire~~

A Humble Man
Inside The Legal [1]***, There Are Idiots***
With The Law [2]***, There Is Life***
To Trust Government Is Stupidity
God & Jesus, Is What Is True

vi et armis [3]**.**

AF699900

Borsotti Issuing,
Integrated God

Disabled Justice,
Lacking Equity Within the Justice System,
"i: am not an Attorn'ey "

---

[1] LEGAL: defined as L.E.G.A.L Lawbreakers Exercise Govern ment Artificial Law (includes no periods to separate) and LEGAL: under colour of rules, regulations, statutes and codes but not LAW and a part of a systemic monopoly game played against all wo/mankind.
[2] LAW: L.A.W. Land Air & Water: under god's laws there is the right to the Land for which all wo/mankind shall live and flourish for their family posterity; No woman, man or govern ment agent can ever stop any wo/mankind from breathing air as it is the first essential substance to sustain life itself. Water is the second most essential element for all life sources to sustain life itself. Without Land Air and Water nothing on this planet or in this universe can sustain life as we know it. It is the LAW from god that sustains all life force on this earth. In contrast to manmade statute and code.
[3]"vi et armis: with force and arms—used of a trespass to person or property which is the immediate cause of damage" https://www.merriam-webster.com/dictionary/vi%20et%20armis

Volume 1, One, I

Issued by:
Borsotti Issuing, Integrated God,
5152 Sepulveda Boulevard Suite 175;
Sherman Oaks California [91406-9998]

www.DisabledJustice.org

Available by Borsotti Issuing, Integrated God**,**

ISBN: 978-1-972000-00-7 (Paperback)

Library of Congress Control Number: ~~0000000000000000~~

Available simultaneously On Mother Earth and In the Spiritual Realm of Heaven's Intent;

Tradenames:

Borsotti, Borsotti Issuing, Integrated God., logo, "Disabled Justice, Lacking Equity Within the Justice System, "i: am not an Attorn'ey". logo, Borsotti Issuing, Integrated God, logo, Disabled Justice , Lacking Equity Within the Justice System, "i: am not an Attorn'ey", Disabledjustice.org , related trade dress are trademarks or registered trademarks of Borsotti Issuing, Integrated God., and/or its affiliates in/on the United States and other countries, and may not be used without written permission. All other trademarks, pictures, names are not copyrighted are the property of their respective owners. Borsotti Issuing, Integrated God., is not associated with any product or vendor mentioned in this *Living Missive*;

Limit Of Lawful and Responsibility/Requirement Of Guarantee: The Issuer Make No Representations Or Guarantees With Admiration To The Accuracy Or Completeness Of The Contents Of This Work And Specifically Disclaim All Guarantees, Including Without Limitation Guarantees Of Truths For A Particular use;

No Warranty May Be Created Or Extended By Sales Or Promotional Materials. The Information And Facts Contained Herein May Not Be Suitable For Every Situation Nor Woman, Man or Child. This Work Is offered With The Comprehension That The Issuer Is Not Engaged In Rendering Legal, Account, Or Other Professional Services; "This Living Missive Is A Claim For Which Relief Shall Be Granted;" "Shall" is obligatory as natural vitality;

If Professional Assistance Is Required, The Services Of An Experienced Professional Non-Title Should Be Sought. Neither The Issuer Nor The Author Shall Be Liable For Damages Arising W/herefrom; This claim are causes of actions for the public to decide as the fourth form of supervision above all agencies;

Because All Facts Stated Herein Are What The Author and by two or more witness, Knows to be (2-B) True From Personal

Firsthand Knowledge And Experience. The Facts And Names Will Not Be Changed To Protect The Guilty, it is to expose those who know for what they do and do it anyways without care to share what is God's Wisdom as wise;

The Fact That An Organization Or Website Is Referred To In This Work As A Reference And/Or A Potential Source Of Further Information Does Not Mean That The Author Or The Issuer Endorses The Information The Organization Or Website May Provide Or Recommendations It May Make;

Further, Readers Should Be Aware That Internet Websites Listed Here On This Living Missive May Have Changed Or Without Notice Disappeared Between When This Work Was Written And When It Is Read. As Enquiring Minds Do Not Want Readers To Know What Is *True* Verses What Is *Truth*;

The Author, Is a man; adam – daniels – of the borsotti family, That Do Accept Full Responsibility For Everything Written Within This Living Missive. It Is The Author's Intent To Expose Perpetrators, Evil-Wrongdoers, Debtors, Sinners, And Those Who Do Trespass;

To Encourage Other Wo/Mankind To Heal Themselves In The Same Manner As This *Living Missive* As It Is Created For The Full Purpose Of Healing, For A Long Awaited, Therapy Sought And Received In The Final Days Of This Living Missive as open thoughtfulness;

God Bless the Readers and wo/mankind throughout the World!

For technical support, please visit DisabledJustice.org or Disabledjusticeasking@proton.me
Borsotti also proffers its missives in a variety of electronic formats. Some content appears in print may not be available electronically.

Library of Congress Control Number: ~~0000000000000000000000~~
Manufactured on [~~the United States~~] God's soil: 0 9 8 7 6 5 4 3 2 10
Legal Is Not Normally Moral or Ethical: Do not follow l.e.g.a.l. when in conflict of God's l.a.w. of comity and reciprocity;

The Mission of Author

The man: Adam – Daniel Of The Borsotti Family

The Mission of the man; adam –daniel, is to support the effective and expeditious supervision of integrity and for the safeguard in all fairness as a watchful eye and ear over the govern mental's[4] on behalf of all wo/mankind and against those that act as pubic[5] serpent.

Not just without but also within and at the courts, of the courts throughout all of the States of America united. To do so, i, will encourage the fair and prompt resolution of disputes to ensure the effective expulsion of all corrupt pubic serpents and to stop the erroneous fraudulent court business that is and has been perpetrated upon all wo/mankind for too many years. i, shall follow up with a measured volume five in how to encourage change for wo/mankind throughout the world when i, am finished with these four volumes as *living missives* as claims.

i, do what i, write to prevent any form of undesirable action in equity, and enhance public and private understanding[6] of, confidence in, wo/mankind that enforce all rights to safeguard

---

[4] Government: Government equals govern mental (mental or mentals) I defined for this living missive as the agent that acts for said pieces of paper know by titles of agency(s).

[5] **PUBIC SERPANT**: for this missive each time the word Pubic(no matter upper or lower case) comes up, it is defined hereinafter as PUBIC as in a pubic-hair that is infected by a strange demonic source of energy that has no morals, ethics, or integrity nor can it be a living wo/mankind because it has taken on an agency as its lord and savior. It is an inflamed pubic hair /pubic servant where eventually it becomes infected and either need to be eradicated by cutting off its source or have a surgeon (we of wo/mankind) extract it B-4 it takes over the body/world. So the rest of the body or world can heal, we get tweezers of righteousness to take it out, which was long overdue. We extract it and then B-4 it/they get infected. This is why wo/mankind must be aware of the potential plagues spreading too many pubic hairs or servants to control the wo/mankind on this earth, which has gone on for years. For too long have the pubic servants known by the titles of the U.S. and State, County and City agents act as pubic servants known by agencies or corp[s]orations of the dejure, public and private fictions of every type.

[6] **UNDERSTAND** OR **UNDERSTANDING**: understand or understanding and all lower/upper case only means full comprehension and not to stand under any authority of another wo/mankind or fiction;

comity, reciprocity[7], honor and the lack thereof, to promote public awareness from all wo/mankind that are exposed for their corrupt acts as pubic serpents at all judiciaries and beyond created and run by agents not agencies.

To my knowledge there's no *living missive* of this type obtainable anywhere, and the reason is simple; this writer has the balls (testicular) and fears not what this country agents may do to he, as much as he can do for the wo/mankind when applied with Jesus Christ's tenacity. The information is very well uncovered by personal firsthand knowledge and those who do know it generally wouldn't fathom of making it public knowledge as they are very likely to be ridiculed in many ways as they are scared pubic agents, evil wrongdoer satanic in nature's form.

Disclosure of Right

i: a man; daniel- adam – of the family borsotti, non-esquire, non corporate entity will discuss life trends regarding how woman and mankind (wo/mankind) become of the age of majority. Not many people[8] actually ever reach this age of majority, regardless their tenure. i, am not an attorn'ey so this piece of writing is a *living missive* that should not be considered as l.e.g.a.l. advice, but can be construed as information about L.A.W.: [9]
Land, Air and Water as well as fire which are the basic elements of life. Just like this *living missive* as it is a catalyst for readers to ponder, to differentiate between what is true[10] verses what truth[11]is.

---

[7] **RECIPROCITY:** 2 Timothy 4:3-4ESV / 2 helpful votes
For the time is coming when people will not endure sound teaching, but having itching ears they will accumulate for themselves teachers to suit their own passions, and will turn away from listening to the truth and wander off into myths.
https://www.openbible.info/topics/reciprocity

[8] **PEOPLE**: herein is defined as wo/mankind and not defined as for the govern ment purposes because woman and man is on a higher totem pole closest to god, therefore, no agent, pubic servants judge, or any other created title is higher than mankind therefore, no created govern ment, which creates its own agents as pubic servants on behalf of all wo/mankind or as herein known forever more as people… And the wo/mankind is sovereign the highest source just below god…and God is the highest sovereign known to all mankind.

[9] **L.A.W.:** Land Air & Water; there is law of the land, law of air and law of Water…(Singularly not plural)

[10] **TRUE:** What is true is not compared to what is True or False it is backed up by indisputable facts with proof of claim otherwise there can be nothing that is true; The sense of "consistent with fact" https://www.etymonline.com/search?q=true.

This *living missive* is intended to separate reality from fiction and for all readers to actually intercept the reality and strip it out from fiction in order to discover that mainstream govern mental's do not want anyone to know. This writing is a *living missive* and a benefit from i, pains, trials, tribulations as an experience of one mankind's true story aimed to assist all wo/mankind; sometimes altered by titles known of people of this country verses the people ***of*** the United States of America. i, wish is for all wo/mankind to find their own inner spiritual journey and to share personal stories with the world. (i, will assist you writing your story);

It is only through stories of the past that the future can evolve and to not make the same mistakes of the past creates a safer place to learn, to grow and to live in harmony for all wo/mankind.
This is why it is crucial that all wo/mankind do not allow any govern-mental's to destroy the books, statues, or monuments of the past. It is because of the past that who we were heightens what we will become which can only be up to i, and you personally and collectively.

The full purpose of this *living missive* is truly for the healing, and benefit as it do state claims of trespass, crimes, conspiracies, facts backed by evidence and by witness of living wo/mankind that do witness said facts, evidence, and in the eyes of "his-story";
The ancient principals of life is not to go backwards but forwards with comprehension of how far we have come to unlimited potential for a future. It is all about preserving wo/mankind on this unique planet.

i, *free will* gifted by the creator of all creation requires free choice to work, live or die, to barter, without dependency and to live wherever and with whomever i, wish; trespass is forbidden. The past is a roadmap out of the present into (N-2) the future from which we all will go;

i: a man; Adam –
daniel of family borsotti .

---

[11]**TRUTH:** is not always what is true backed by facts. What is true can be restricted to what a wo/mankind believe to be true in fact is what one wishes to be true and is not true. Let [*Truth*] and Falsehood grapple; who ever knew *Truth* put to the worse, in a free and open encounter. [Milton, "Areopagitica," 1644]

B-4 We Begin

There Are Lots Of Things You Need To Know

Some of the inscriptions are written with no deliberate or incomprehension of any improper or proper etiquette, (such as using a semi colon " ; " instead of a period " . ") or (and the lower case "i," followed by a colon or comma depicting a wo/mankind instead of an "I" meaning a title of a corp(s)oration[12] as titled fiction).

This writing is considered a *living missive*; it is an affidavit in the private that stepped over the line between natural and fiction like a memo to god, a man's journey, thoughts and feelings. It is forever living like in God we trust. What man knows to be true and should be free from perceived judgment or mistake. It is free from mankind's judgment and only to answer to god almighty only. It is written to encourage to never ceasing from having an impact on the present and future generations or what should be the norm. That mainstream public needs to get used to as only God can judge any wo/mankind. And i, as man; "for i, know not what i, do, even though i, do knowingly..." This is Jesus' tenacity guided by god's grace. i, searched extensive and rigid at every stop to get out of other writings, from books, magazines and discovered the reality that they are all filled with nothing more than people exercising their own opinions with some resolutions to some of the problems. i, will do resolution text when finished with four volumes;

That resolution is fundamental to offer creative ways to carry on with the same old place and same old ways of living scenarios. To continue to obfuscate and hypothecate the wealth and natural rights of all wo/mankind must stop and either revert back to the commandments or make certain that the long forgotten morals and ethics still reign supremacy. Paying karma forward is to not allow

---

[12] **CORPORATION**: a Corp(s)oration is basically a corporation, a fiction, not real, under the game of monopoly, which is a dead entity, not real not natural but was created in the 1930's wherein a corp[s]oration can sue and be sued. I, forget the court case action that created a fiction can from then on allegedly sue a wo/mankind under a certain auspice only. Only a living wo/mankind can be sued only by another living wo/mankind; rather a person citizen, resident or the like- kind is under the title with a corpsoration. A corpsoration can never lawfully sue against a natural wo/mankind without an agent by a privilege only under the 14th Amendment, etcetera...

govern mental's and their bank-sters that try to control all aspects of all wo/mankind's rights to title of land and *free will*. It is done through controlling the narrative by agents of agencies –that are supposed to enhance and protect, rather than control and enslave through fear tactics known to men like Stalin, Hitler, Mussolini, George and all Bushians, Clintonians, Obama-ians, Biden'ians, all the way back even B-4 FDR and many others known in here as Satan's Minions.

It is time to stop agreeing to contract away one's rights to life, freedom and the protection of property. For some kind of deal for protections of nothingness, which is what we truly receive when all wo/mankind consummate with satan itself.

Political Porn Through The Courts

This *living missive* is the explanation about pornography[13] of govern mentals [14] by all judiciary. It shows how attorn'eys, ~~judges~~ and politicians rape the wealth of wo/mankind and a child's innocence, even at 90 years young. This *living missive* uncovers how pubic serpents share with their own kin while exploiting the public as wo/mankind's ignorance. It is unadulterated, uncut, in your face, no-holds-barred, direct at times and with i, normal indirect everyday humor, that will test the readers patience, comprehension, questioning the writers meanings, giving tolerance for said vernacular when intolerance is the norm.

---

[13] PORNOGRAPHY: 1842, "ancient obscene painting, especially in temples of Bacchus," from French pornographie, from Greek pornographos "(one) depicting prostitutes," from graphein "to write" (see -graphy) + pornē "prostitute," originally "bought, purchased" (with an original notion, probably of "female [but males too] slave sold for prostitution"), related to pernanai "to sell" (from PIE *perə-, variant of root *per- (5) "to traffic in, to sell"). **Pornocracy** (1860) is "the dominating influence of harlots," used specifically of the control of the government of Rome and the election to the Papacy during the first half of the 10th century by the noble…"
https://www.etymonline.com/search?q=porn

[14] **GOVERNMENT**: Govern mentals; the original purpose of a created govern ment is to protect wo/mankind's property and rights. It is set up by wo/mankind and run by agents called pubic serpants, who are supposed to take on an overwhelming servitude to all wo/mankind. All wo/mankind are supposed to let they be known as a wo/mankind verses any title to all pubic servants at the very beginning, of every interaction, on every occasion, regardless whether we leave a room use the labonio (bathroom) and re-enter a room or venue.

Seeing that not all whom read this *living missive* will comprehend, nor appreciate this style from the author who is nothing more than a man who writes from a fifth grade level; having graduated from the streets of Hard Knox. So give this writing a little slack while you continue down his path to healing, and possibly your journey towards god. The author's pinnacle is in transforming his life free from fear of govern mental interaction or as little govern mental pornography as possible.

If you feel this content is too obscure, over the top, not appropriate for you, your young or maybe you feel it is not educational, by your societal driven judgment, not up to par. We know you could do better. So, why did you not write something better?

However, the aspects of judgment of what is proper writing etiquette, is not the effect the author is searching. The author hopes you and your young people, who will soon grow 2-B outstanding citizens, residents, persons, individuals, or pubic serpents, will actually evolve into a moral and ethical wo/mankind, by moving closer to god.

If your intentions are to move closer to god then hold this *living missive* until you or your youth are old enough to comprehend what is true because sooner or later you will search for the writings within this *living missive* which is compelling for a wandering mind; it is necessary and proper for the heart to evolve with the soul, to see and hear from another's discernment.

If you think because of your own view that you, will never give this to your children, nor share this *living missive* with a friend, then i, feel compassion for you in a way that you are either a govern mental agent, work for a contractor for the govern mental's or just ignorant, scared, live a life of enslavement or fear.

Only a slave will refuse to accept what is true, and hide it from the young and your own inner circle and worse from your sense of all-knowing subconscious medium. However, if your inner sense of all-knowing, knows that i, feel compassion for your unwillingness to allow you and your young eager minds to figure out what you or millions of wo/mankind have known for centuries, or are about to dis-cover, then continue to read on as it gets better B-4 it gets unfathomable. It cannot get any worse than you have lived to this juncture in your life as a slave.

For those of you readers, who have no patience? Hold on to your hat or shorts and for those of you who wear panties who are afraid to tell your friends, be prepared for i, sphincter humor because there is something for you too. This writing is not a precarious mystery novel, or a testicular grabbing, nail biting horror script, or a heart dropping, tear jerking love story or even a passive sugar coated documentary. This is a no-holds-barred, get in theirs and your face, tell it like it is, Nock'em Sock'em Robot; a fearless *living missive* by a living man. Fearless, as i, fear not any wo/mankind as what is for to speak, that what is true.

May The Birds Of Paradise Fly Up Your Nose

For the political birds who wish i, did not write this *living missive* and for those birds, who wish you were courageous enough to write like this, i, write this for you. i, wish you to fully comprehend, when you are too ignorant to fathom or when you do get a small inclination of what is being enlightened herein. Keep on...

You can tell your legal court (cluck),[15] secretaries, assistants and colleagues of what you have read herein; especially when yours or their name pops up like a 4:30 a.m. erection. For the scared govern mental agent-birds out there, you can have your children read this *living missive* and tell you what it says about you and your workforce, because you will not like what i, do expose of you, your cronies and your genre.

Yet, it is crucial to tell it like it is and was for i, to grow as a man, and to become free from all tyranny, free from govern mental's' constraints, and as free as a "...freebird yah... as lord knows i [cant] wont change...[16]" flying high to meet God through Jesus Christ the one savior and lord of all kings, presidents of all corp(s)orations, master of all the universe and the lord over all pubic serpents.

---

[15] **CLUCK**: define Cluck is like defining herein a chicken that clucks its ass off hereinafter clerk is defined as cluck

[16] Freebird: By Lynard Skynard : https://www.youtube.com/watch?v=0LwcvjNJTuM

There is no fear herein because where i, come from is with purpose, other than it being for i, own healing, like natural gold, as god gifted medicine, to test to see if you the reader will show patience and enjoy what there is to suffer and suffer what there is to enjoy. Leaving Satan's stone unturned from hiding snakes of no light.

For this *living missive* is not just another mankind's view. This alone is where your patience is necessary and proper in order for you to learn, realize, liberate your enslaved thinking that is embedded deep within your subconscious marrow, or that place where you might hide when you are masturbating, when you think no one is around watching as the wrinkles on your face crinkle when you reach orgasm.

Somebody Is Always Watching You

Remember, god is always watching you and it is you that must honor i, accordingly. The unscrupulous bones of govern mental's has been around for centuries and now is the time to release the hounds of trueness, morals and ethics for all wo/mankind's integrity for creating value for society, instead of lies and deceit that plague society for centuries by those wo/mankind that acts as attorn'eys, [~~judge~~]s, actors on the never ending unscrupulous stage of politics.

It is for those past to present pubic serpents, whom work for the banks, the state and federal govern mental's, and all agencies from the dog catchers, to the C.E.O's of any corp(s)orations. i, write for you along with your cronies. :) . So, i, say as i, heard for years on the 70's tell-us-lie-vision [17] show… however, i, do not use the quote by: Mister T: "I pity the…[woman or mankind] the nabal[18]

[17] Tell-us-lie-vision: Is a Television System and the lies that are created to control the public which will only give 10 % of what is true and 90% falsehood. Brainwashing is crucial to a govern ment in order to control the narrative. What is the narrative? It is what is necessary at the time of the agenda to brainwash the weak, stupid, ignorant, emotionally distraught, mentally challenged such as (politicians judges, and other titles)… in wanton, wo/mankind who act like a title with an agenda. "It's a simple question with a surprisingly complex answer. At its core, a "television" is a device that takes electrical input to produce moving images and sound for us to view. A "television system" would be both what we now call television and the camera/producing equipment that captured the original images." https://historycooperative.org/the-first-tv-a-complete-history-of-television/, the tell-us-lies-vision is the contraption for which to spew propaganda of lies and deceit.

[18] **NABAL:** Fool, foolish

However, i, do pit[t]y the nabal that does not read this *living missive* from start to finish and then share it with others. Therefore i, do not pity any nabal that acts as wo/mankind whom know for what they do because the bible speaks of pity and fools. It speaks enough for all wo/mankind to feel foolish and to share pity, for then we can have pity by compassion on some other wo/mankind for their ignorance when we personally experience foolishness. It is not for their malicious intent to cause harm to another fellow wo/mankind and claim a foolish mistake, repent and move past the acts, all awhile to invoke to create more on others.

What about an attorn'ey that tries to represent the ignorant, infant, or those who have not become the age of majority at a court action? Do these ignorant whom might be pro-se-cuted for no certain cause of action whereby the ignorant has not truly harmed anyone except maybe an allegation of not following a statute, code, or regulation deserve the penalty. And how about an attorn'ey that is accused of and re-presents[19] her/himself as a client [20] ? Do we pity this foolishness and is there actually a fool for a client? Do not forget it is only fiction that the public consents by overbearing mongrel govern mental's that seeks to destroy the American dream through fines, fees, penalties and assessments that creates the false narrative.

There is no such thing as l.a.w. that starts with the words: code, statute, regulations, ordinance or acts. But for pubic serpents to try to fool wo/mankind that are aware of what is true to the facts of l.a.w., foolishness must be learned the hard way. Any new upcoming adolescent will learn how some court actors are s.l.u.t.-s[21] and other attorn'eys that try to run the show. What about an attorn'ey and equally for each govern mental agent wanting to be

[19] **RE-PRESENT:**" also be a representative of" (the authority of another). late 14c., representen, "show, display, express; bring to mind by description," also "to symbolize, serve as a sign or symbol of (something else, something abstract); serve as the type or embodiment of;" also be a representative of" (the authority of another). https://www.etymonline.com/search?q=represent

[20] **CLIENT:** late 14c., "one who lives under the patronage of another," from Anglo-French clyent (c. 1300), from Latin clientem (nominative cliens) "follower, retainer" and "The notion apparently is "one who leans on another for protection." In ancient Rome, a plebeian under the guardianship and protection of a patrician (who was called patronus in this relationship; see patron). The meaning "a lawyer's customer" is attested from c. 1400, and by c. 1600 the word was extended to any customer who puts a particular interest in the care and management of another. Related: Cliency. https://www.etymonline.com/search?q=client

[21] S.L.U.T.: student lawyer under training…

liberated by a colleague for which she/he protects from the shire [22] of despair. This public wants to know what they already know and that is the actors (serpents) act to protect them and the privateers.

When brotherhood of govern mental's do anything to rock the boat of the enslavement mentality, which has shaped this great country into another unethical galaxy. The agents with the most hierarchy take control of their lower minions and seem to always protect their blueblood, next-to-kin (colleagues) that has sworn the oath to an allegiance to devilish functions. These functions all wo/mankind posses naturally and does not keep the moral and ethics of god's grace because the pubic serpent [23] end up swimming with skunks, skunks once reviled to change.

Introduction by i: a man;

i: a man; adam- daniel– of family by borsotti, do state as true of the statements made herein are by i, as man, in witness of i, genuine firsthand experience as to what i, know 2-B true, in witness of i, own eyes, ears and hands with full faith and honor in god, and to the glory of Jesus Christ, Joseph Smith, Gandhi, Mother Theresa, Nichiren Daishonin, Jehovah, and all other past, present and future wo/mankind that believe them moral and ethical. At the fore to uphold to what is true with facts and evidence is up to the readers own discretion to revere in spirit.

What happened to character Martin Luther King Jr. once spoke about? For what is 2-B will be, and for the facts 2-B discovered and exposed herein have already been released to the hounds of despair by those who are attorn'eys, politicians, and their like kind. Hence forth, only god will be the ultimate judge with the assistance of all of God's caretakers to continue to feel free to expose. For

---

[22]**SHIRE:** Middle English *shire*, from Old English scir, scyr "administrative office, jurisdiction, stewardship, authority," also in particular use ("care, official charge"). https://www.etymonline.com/search?q=shire+

[23] **CIVIL SERVICE OR NOW CALLED PUBLIC SERVANT** : Used to be called civil service and now i, do use the title **pubic servant**. Civil service reform in the United States was a major issue in the late 19th century at the national level, and in the early 20th century at the state level. Proponents denounced the distribution of government offices—the "spoils"—by the winners of elections to their supporters as corrupt and inefficient. They demanded nonpartisan scientific methods and credential be used to select civil servants.... Wikipedia and i, use the terms pubic servants

eternity of repentance is on the heart of the scorched and frail, but healed from no pain can wither what is to unfold, no spark can enflame the righteousness of the tame and no agent or scholar will ever retain; as this is a *living missive* of no turning back;

Lord's Prayer:

Our father, who art in heaven, hallowed be thy name,
thy kingdom come, thy will be done, on earth as it is in heaven,
give us this day, our daily bread and forgive us our debts
as we forgive our [debtors…] [sinners…] trespass,
as we forgive those who trespass against us],
and lead us not in to temptation, but deliver us from the evils of this earth; for thine is the kingdom, the power and the glory forever,

Amen;

Nam Myoho Renge Kyo:

It is by the devotion to the mystic law of cause and effect, through the teaching of the sound that vibration moves the wandering spirit. To encourage it will take to form by action when necessary and to have compassion at the same time for others when all fear comes over one's inner thoughts. It is through the challenge to the learning and realization of life's trials and triumphs in order to overcome all obstacles. i, do hope that thee who reads this *living missive* will grow to become better than you once were, open new thought process and encourage all readers to run a new race towards God's will to create harmonious world for all wo/mankind.

It is by way of always having an attitude of gratitude no matter the circumstances, and never 2-B disparaging no matter what. Then we will achieve our greatest test and fulfill our forever dreams through learning and realization of life's experience. It is by this scheme linking law that specifically is a reminder to govern mental agents and all bank-sters that you can run but you cannot hide, because i, and others are coming for you.

We shall not harm you physically, however, we will take away what you have stolen from i, and all wo/mankind over the years. It is meant to govern the actions of *all* govern mental agents and their assisted banks and finance organization that allow themselves to be thwarted away from morals and ethics.

These laws i, do speak of are still in place, but have been displaced by titles of the courts such as [~~judge~~]s, commissioners, magistrates and court clucks, which seem to have somewhat abandoned or evaded the true laws over the years - one might say aggressively dejected by those who benefit as i, will prove by this *alive missive* that all agents are stealing with thoughts of immunity with impunity revealed.

i, intent is to present true factual information regarding what is true in this *living missive* so that you the reader can use i, experiences and with hope in God that you know Jesus Christ and the will of god that has given i, the strength so you might apply the info. On how to or why not to deal with the govern ment agents and get constructive results that may duplicate repeatedly for all posterity.

Explanation:

When i, write "or use the expression "true" [24] it is for i, personal cause that not only do i, believe it 2-B true, it is true because i, can back it up with actual verified proof, facts and evidence. It is only by firsthand experience or by two or more wo/mankind who verify as witness, which validates all things 2-B true. In contrast, compared to "what is truth"[25] is contrast to what is not backed by factual evidence, such as what can only be verified by woman and mankind belief and not who do witness the particulars by way of personal encounters, video, audio, and other tangible irrefutable evidence. Even though the truth may set one free, it is not always what is true;

When i, underline (_) a word this means that i, will elaborate further in this missive, (or look under definitions in the glossary for meanings) for variety of terms of expressions;

---

[24] True: what is true can always be validated, and backed by proof of facts and evidence and is different that truth.

[25] Truth: (a meaning of personal belief) does not necessarily have facts to validate its authenticity…

As to each woman or man named herein whom i, also place their names, and standing to verify everything that is written herein, as i, do place what is true and not just belief and not in the way of judgment of any wo/mankind [26]. Rather i, forward it to the one ultimate judge of all wo/mankind, once this *living missive* is released to at least one million of the public to determine.

As God almighty is king the superior judge over all things, i, as a mere man, although made in the image of god, am only here on this plane to assist god as one of god's students and caretakers of this great earth. i, do inscribe everything herein tangible and intangible for perpetual memorial for the proper era to summon retribution for the disabled, illiterate, unknowing, once distraught wo/mankind, and for those who do not have the courage, yet, but wished they do find the courage to write what they think and know backed by facts on their own. For all posterity deserves your hands to create from what is true and bring your missives too, as i, do to print.

Govern mentals Caught in its Own Dragnet

This story you are about to read is true, only the names have been changed to protect the innocent (Dragnet the tell-us-lies-vision) as far as the guilty, their names are clear as sin and not changed to expose the guilty. You will follow step by step with a lawful man, who tells what is true, from crime to punishment, from the enlightened to the corrupt actions of criminals like certain wo/mankind, that have stood the watchful eyes over your homes, children, land and over you and your property. Remember, you put trust in them and got burned by the unfathomable trusting structure of a system less honest than once believed. This is true not truth.

For the next few hundred pages, you will follow step by step a courageous man; that of adam - daniel – borsotti, who do refuse to give N-2 the women and men that are named herein for their crimes, unethical and immoral actions against his life caused by a dragnet that all wo/mankind find themselves ignorant to what is true. A dragnet of govern mental's, acting a part in a fictional play.

---

[26] wo/mankind: is as living woman and a living man that of all mankind spoken about in the bible

It is through educational brainwashing at public schools, by governing habitual infrastructures between agents of govern ments and the public wo/mankind that sets a part the constructive fraud upon wo/mankind. i, would rather not have been forced to do this documenting of official cases[27], and by official public notices. i, am forced to unveil all names and faces from beginning of i, journey of learning l.a.w. to the end without beginning.

The crimes of many wo/mankind herein are true as i, do speak of the suggested punishments. This *living missive* is for thee who reads and for all Americans, all wo/mankind everywhere on mother earth, who are ignorant of the law[28]. This is i, story, it was not meant to become a discovery of i, lifetime, therefore, it is as it shall be written.

Temporarily Skip To The Effect

It was March 2006, in Los Angeles California, a cold [29] fairly bright day, i, remember it well, as if it were yesteryear. As i, finally received what i, thought was justice in albeit unjust judiciary world, by way of a settlement from the County of San Luis Obispo California and various insurance companies;

i, do sustain multiple physical, mental, emotional, intellectual, social and spiritual harm on that third day, May 2001. It was an auto accident out on a semi-desolate road that crossed from San Luis

---

[27] CASE/COURT CASE: Court Action, Action At Law Or Action…

[28]LAW: is not a statute, codes, rules, regulation or acts, LAW is Land Air Water (do not forge this terms)

"…There are multiple types of rules of mankind to live by titled that use the word "LAW" however, are not truly the original LAW. L.A.W. and are as follows: Animal Law, Admiralty Law, Bankruptcy Law, Banking and Finance Law, Civil Rights Law, Constitutional Law, Corporate Law, Criminal Law, Education Law, Entertainment Law, Employment Law, Environmental & Natural Resources Law, Family Law, Health Law, Immigration Law, International Law, Intellectual Property Law, Military Law, Personal Injury Law, Real Estate Law, Tax Law…" https://www.collegesoflaw.edu/blog/2018/11/06/different-fields-of-law-explained/

"Legal" redirects here. For other uses, see Legal (disambiguation).

Law is a set of rules that are created and are enforceable by social or governmental institutions to regulate behavior,[1] with its precise definition a matter of longstanding debate.[2][3][4] It has been variously described as a science[5][6] and as the art of justice…"

[29] https://weatherspark.com/h/m/1705/2006/3/Historical-Weather-in-March-2006-in-Los-Angeles-California-United-States

Obispo up to highway 101. i, did not know what was truly to come, yet the repercussions affect i. Although, i, have and do always retain an attitude of gratitude, and never disparaging, it was not as easily said then than done. These recoveries do take many years that still affect i, to this day 2025;

After i, fought tooth and nail to recover i, compensation for the harm caused by other wo/men, for their negligence, not only by the county of San Luis Obispo, the driver and the registered owner of the driven property.

i, thought a little respite from the struggles which effect most wo/mankind after a traumatic experience such as being knocked unconscious, in and out of rehabilitation institutes, such as the Brain Institute at Midlothian Virginia and many others. Boy was i, wrong that i, would be healed in a few months as i, did not know what was to come nor how injured i, truly was;

Interception for the reader

Have you the reader ever thought, "If I do not do something today then the present will repeat until I do something different? Or I can and will make a difference to create value for society? Ask yourself what have [you] "I" done to make this world a better place for the future of the children whom are being berthed/born today? Do you leave lasting impressions when its necessary?

The Healing Do Begin

Will the bird of Paradise fly up your nose? Or will time wasted be full of joy? Let us put on our seatbelt, grab some buttered popcorn, milk duds and a Yoohoo!

The following writing will and do uncover many things about wo/mankind, govern mental agents, banking institutions among many other commercial monopolistic structures dealing with this commercial world. The fraud portrayed against the nation, by corporate entities and those who have become age of majority is endless.

Screech, Smash, Bing, Bang, Boom, Lights Out 3rd Day May 2001

Although it was early and September 11th 2001 had not yet occurred, a man would be tested for more than just his self worth, he would be tested in faith alone. On a semi-clear afternoon, as usual i, turn on the signal, slowed to a stop, and sat waiting for the oncoming traffic to clear to make a left turn. i, was headed over to the storage before i, usual long run on the mountain at San Luis Obispo California.

With only a moment's notice to barely grasp i, hands on the steering wheel, it happened; Screech, Smash, lights out. i, was knocked unconscious, coma-like state, as i, wavered in and out of consciousness for which seemed like forever ending.

As i, lay on a hospital bed, i, was woken up by an officer. It was blurry, i, kind of recall that the officer(s) was asking i, questions. i, did not know what he was asking but soon realized, i, was in a hospital [30].

One thing piloted to another. Moments of conscience awareness turned N-2 days of the unknowing. The unknowing of what will be of i, life. Will i, be back as i, was B-4 this incident or succumb to the unrelenting injuries.

Then weeks turned to months churning like i, life was dropped N-2 a blender and turned on. As i, head and bodily injuries worsen, time spun away from months to years.

There were many trying situations and many attempts to receive lawful assistance. Things like the right doctors to treat the multiple symptoms and to finally receive proper diagnoses for i, injuries. i, finally found what i, thought were i, hero's and shero's. [31]

---

[30] Hospital: a contracting word for "Hostel" performance as in an entrainment house, such as theater performing on (you) patient, in a form of practicing on other people, Doctor: church father, and "Nurse" means mother as going to a hospital B-4 a practicing former mother…"
[31] Shero: is a woman hero…

Like Mighty Mouse

After many unethical and unsettled matters with many doctors and l.e.g.a.l. firms, i, captured the Mighty Mouse of all law firms about two hundred miles south.

i, remember thinking that god has heard i, prayers to the issues. i, must have interviewed over one hundred and fifty attorn'eys [32] and paralegals from various l.e.g.a.l. firms. i, did not know the difference between the types of attorn'eys there were. It appears that there are as many types, similar to the multiple types of medical professionals there are for every part of the body. Thereto, there is a different type of attorn'ey for every different court action.

i, did not know that hiring an attorn'ey is to give up all personal rights to the attorn'ey who is actually an actor that *practices* in the courts and re-presents i, (or its client) in the best interest of the courts, which truly is owned by the B.A.R.[33].

An attorn'ey is not just wo/mankind who do re-present their trade in the best interest of their client. The attorn'ey is actually an officer of the courts. The association of attorn'ey themselves, thereby leaving the wo/mankind who do hire the attorn'ey at the bottom of the totem pole of morals and ethics to succumb to whatever the court actors serpent instruct the attorn'ey to do. (More on this later)

When i, finally established the legal firm whom turned out 2-B Masry & Vititoe. Many people i, know, were telling i, how lucky i, was. Once, i, realized who they were, and that they actually would accept i, personal injury case, i, was so appreciative, i, allowed what was left of i, inner common sense, logic and other reasoning mechanisms, 2-B thwarted by their prestige. Eventually i, became stunned as if i, were knocked unconscious again when i, found out

---

[32] Attorn: attorn (v.): late 13c., Anglo-French, "to turn over to another," from Old French atorner "to turn, turn to, assign, attribute, dispose," from a- "to" (see ad-) + tourner "to turn," In feudal law, "to transfer homage or allegiance to another lord."
In English law, a private attorney (attorney in fact) was one appointed to act for another in business or legal affairs (usually for pay); an attorney at law or public attorney was a qualified legal agent in the courts of Common Law who prepared the cases for a barrister, who pleaded them (the equivalent of a solicitor in Chancery). So much a term of contempt in England that it was abolished by the Judicature Act of 1873 and merged with solicitor.
https://www.etymonline.com/search?q=attorn

[33] B.A.R. Association: is a group of private for hire agents of banks/corporations: Bank Authorized Representative.

who they were and what they wanted i, to do. i, am not proud for succumbing to their pressure.

This legal firm attorn'eys, are very well known all over the planet as in throughout every judicial system as they all know their name. You the reader might even have heard of them, Masry & Vititoe? The famous case settled in 1996 for $333 plus million. The largest settlement ever paid in a direct-action lawsuit [34] in American history, whereby Julia Roberts played Erin Brockovich in the movie. i, do remember being introduced to Erin in her office, however, because i, was recouping from injuries and repercussions of the incident, i, did not talk to her more than an introduction. i, do recall her being a beautiful woman.

Blinded By The Light

i, know i, do not have to explain who Erin is. When i, was able to meet Erin in her office, she worked in the same building where Ed Masry & James Wilson Vititoe have their offices. James Vititoe acted as if i, should be star stricken as he was towards Erin. i, was truly side blinded by their status, and of the judiciary world, media, and movie industry. i, had succumb to the tactics of l.e.g.a.l. authoritarianism; orchestrated and directed by James Wilson Vititoe and his cronies. At first everything was a feeling of, finally i, can relax and not worry about having to do anything but try to heal i, body, mind, and spirit. Little did i, know at the time, i, hero's and shero's would transform N-2 villains hidden in sheep's clothing. As

---

[34] Direct-action lawsuit" is brought directly against an insurance company for a wrong done by the insured… "

In a lawsuit that is not direct-action, a wo/mankind brings the claim against the wrongdoer, who actually wronged the wo/mankind. Once judgment or decree has been rendered against the wrongdoer(s), there are a number of ways that the wrongdoer might later be made to pay the victorious wo/mankind who was wronged.

If the wo/mankind who file claim wants to avoid the extra time and process required to eventually be compensated by the wrongdoer(s), the action can be brought directly against the wrongdoer as the claim. The wo/mankind who filed claim must still prove all of the same facts that would be the burden by the claim, had the action been brought against the insurance company as a direct-action lawsuit. Also: The wo/mankind who filed claim must prove that the wrongdoer caused harm, and that the wrongdoer was in dishonor, the kind of wrong for which the wo/mankind claim support the sought after remedy. There is also a direct action activism. "One example can be a customer suing a company to repeal an action deemed an infringement on the rights of the customer as a citizen and thus a subject to federal or state law. The largest direct-action lawsuit in history ($333 million) was the subject matter of the motion picture *Erin Brockovich*.[1]" https://en.wikipedia.org/wiki/Direct-action_lawsuit Masry & Vititoe law firm is victor.

time and the court action at law [35] had progressed, i, was dumbfounded by the unethical demands made to i, by the so-called well known and famous attorn'eys. It was not Edward Louis Masry who was the villain, rather it was James Wilson Vititoe, and his cronies whom begun to treat i, in a manner conducive to an enslaved servant by threat and coercion.

To this day i, question i, own morals and ethics, however, at the time, i, was in a dream-skate [36] not fully comprehending the difference between demands made on behalf of the court case, and the morals and ethics of life in the moral and ethical, god's world. Although, i, do have opportunity to write about i, personal experience with this legal firm of Masry & Vititoe, particularly James Wilson Vititoe and others associated with they. For now, i, leave this one to god and their karma. (In the future, i, may direct i, focus on their story. For now, i, give this free advertisement to this law firm as follows) :

Law Offices of Masry & Vititoe
5707 Corsa Avenue 2nd Floor
Westlake Village, California 91362
818 991 8900

James Wilson Vititoe

---

[35] Action at law (action): the court case filed at any court of law…

[36] Dream-skate: "sequence of sensations or images passing through the mind of a sleeping person," even while the mind is awake. It is as in a daze skating from one situation, of fear, wandering thoughts, uncertainty and with many high and emotional lows without the feeling to "seek to harm, injure," and to glide or slide from one emotion or situation to another always searching for a way out; a way 2-B healed… https://www.etymonline.com/search?q=dream/skate

Chapter 1, One, I

Men Of Martial Arts & William Wagener's Interview

Adam-Daniel-of Borsotti family. My entire life has been a journey to look at where i, have been to know what i, have overcome. Although the future is unknown, i, realize, it is in my own control , as to how far i, can go when i, never give up on i, greatest potential.

William Wagener, journalist turned friend that without his experience quick response with a camera i, could not have captured crucial evidence. i, owe William Wagener a debt of gratitude for his experience and willingness to support i, in all i, court process and endeavors. He is a gentleman and a scholar.

Young thriving martial artist reaches level of 3rd degree It is an honor for i, 2-b able 2 be a part of the year 2000 Men of Martial Arts Calendar i, dedicate all of i, hard work to Master Sayed Qubadi. As a man he taught i, all of the attributes of the true meaning of self-defense .

The Road to Recovery

There is a certain road to recovery for most injured wo/mankind that has experienced a Traumatic Brain Injury. Sometimes, the recovery itself becomes a change in one's life for the better.
Yet, most that are actually going through the transformation cannot see the signs at the time and when looking back on the experience, the light shines brightest down the healing path.

When God is the healing path, there is never any loss that is not rewarded by and in the grace of god through Jesus Christ. Contrary to customs of America, or that express or signify political ideological tendencies, the states united, individually or collectively, are nothing more than a cartel [37].

[37] Cartel: A cartel is a criminal organization composed of independent bankers, politicians who collude with each other in order to improve their profits and dominate the enslavement of wo/mankind by trade.

The states and federal govern mentals as is noted herein, is a cartel, used to push the destruction of the principles of freedom, honesty, integrity, constitutions, and declaration of independence. Yet within reality, this U.S. and State Corporate cartel, politically really stab the public and private sectors in the immorality, unethical back, leaving scars on wo/mankind from mother earth to hell and beyond a galaxy far, …far away.

This Caveat Is For The Wrongdoers

i, do not change the names to protect the innocent, as each named wo/mankind, who take on title as a person, citizen, agent, pubic serpent, individual, entity, corporation, ens legis fictitious entity, or animal, that act as a titled agent are not innocent by far. What is stated herein is true, uncut, factual, cannot be disputed with a higher claim than that of i, adam- daniel– borsotti family as a man. Therefore, it is counterproductive to change names of Evil-wrongdoers to protect the likes of scoundrels, scorpions, rattlers, vipers, rodents or the acts of pirates whom act as an unlawful, dishonest, immoral, unethical pubic serpent or titled person.

When an Evil-wrongdoer is amoral, unethical and do unscrupulous acts against the rights and property of wo/mankind, which is against god's laws, it is by the obligation of all wo/mankind to name Evil-wrongdoers as is done herein. In order to expose them for their malicious intent, a wo/mankind must grab the bull by the horns [38] and wrestle it to the ground after riding it and breaking its will to fight back. It is a malicious intent when a pubic serpent do rape, steal, threaten, collude, and commit champerty, maintenance, conversion, vexatious progression, coercion, extortion, identity theft, with intentional infliction of emotional harm against another wo/mankind. In wanton a committed trespass against another mankind.

Reassure What You Read Is True

Not only do i, validate the facts, i, do state as true to you, the reader, that i, do send to those agencies, agents, pubic serpents, employees, and all of the wo/mankind in their personal capacity who are exposed in this writing notice. As a *living missive* by giving full

[38]**GRAB THE BULL BY THE HORNS:** "…Bulls in a crystal shop…" Disabledjustice.org

disclosure,[39] prior to this edict, therefore, you can move forward to read to discover what is true with confidence that i, take full control and accountability for what i, do place on paper.

If what is written is not true, then why have the Evil-wrongdoers not filed or lashed back against a man, that only tells what is true? i, say whether any known Evil-wrongdoer herein were going to file anything, which i, care not if they do so, which is the validation that it is all true. Then i, do say, what are and ~~is~~ they waiting for?
i, already do send all claims directly to each Evil-wrongdoer's (hereinafter wrongdoer[s]) last known post location, and always place the facts on file which is what i, do herein. Get it on file.

i, do affirm what is stated herein and so far, there is no surprise, no caveat and no bond necessary in case someone's little ego, pride, or anus orphus clinches too tight from their frustration and anger. Or maybe it is that their little girlie panties were placed too tight and their anus no longer needs 2-B flossed as strings of their ego and pride are "…reunited and it feels so good, reunited as it's understood… Peaches & Herb…" just get over it.

Exposure to what is true about them has been disclosed to the entire world. It is not like they do not know or care of what is true. The entirety of this *living missive* goes beyond all commercial worlds. *It is the claim for which relief shall be granted through Jesus Christ as in by god almighty.*

Besides when wrongdoers do not like what is written, they should exercise what i, and all wo/mankind learn growing up, that is to recite: "Sticks And Stones May Break My Bones, But Words Will Never Hurt…" To this ever-changing calendared day in the year

[39] Full disclosure: Define Full Disclosure: Everything You Need to Know;
To define full disclosure, it's important to examine its purpose or function in different areas…accounting, patenting, in business, stock exchange, Securities and Exchange Commission, contracts.
Contracts: in order to receive a lawful contract there must always be: A. Meetings of the minds, B. Offer and acceptance, C. Equal consideration, D. Mutuality of agreement. It is also the general requirement for all parties to open up about any issue concerning their transaction with honesty. https://www.upcounsel.com/define-full-disclosure

2025, not one of the informed named evil-wrongdoers[40] herein, rebutted anything they do receive notice to date.

Healing Is A Process So i, Continue

In order for i, or any wo/mankind to fully recover from any type of traumatic brain injury, post traumatic stress disorder, fraud, theft, threat, assault, collusion, coercion, vexatious progressions, champerty, assault and or battery, rape or any situation such as legal abuse syndrome; not to 4-get facts that do cause a trespass upon another wo/mankind, is important to receive compensation for the harm committed. After having gone through every known lawful process and i, have been denied all lawful juridical processes, i, so choose this *living missive* as the previous alternative to receive i, healing. It is the first/fourth form of protections known.

For And On The Record

On and for the record, it is important as a part of healing also to not get angry for those things that others deliberately do to interfere to receive self healing. i, do not ever encourage or insight violence unless it is to protect life, and then it really is not violence when done in self-defense of life, freedom or property. All life is more precious beyond any value on this planet. No gold, silver, diamonds, land, guns, cars, clothing or ego is more valuable than that of the *Land* we live on, *Air* we breathe or *Water* we hydrate cells with. The last 3 issue is termed L.A.W. ;

Of course, the life we protect is governed by the LAW of Land Air and Water. The food we nourish our health is for wellbeing as one life is not worth more than that of a life of any other wo/mankind. This is why Law was originally created by God to protect all life. The Commandments are the laws given to all wo/mankind.
In the healing process, many wo/mankind need only one certain type of law in order to receive compensation for whatever harm has been committed against them. It can only be one law that can make anyone whole.

---

[40] Wrongdoer(s): Scoundrel, Criminal, sinner, good-for-nothing, malefactor, troublemaker… you choose

As in prior to any certain type of trespass, i, intend to repeat what i, have already distributed with public newspapers, on multiple forums such as on social media, and on the streets of Los-t Ange-less Californifi-cation [41], filed onto many open court records, on several occasions; whereby i, was forced to take all issues to the streets. As i, did and will continue.

It is by those wo/mankind such as pubic serpent actors: Hilda Lucia Solis; Kamala Devi Harris; Barrack Obama; magistrates like, Michael John O'Gara; Melvin Douglas Sandvig; Stephen Peter Pfahler; Tricia Jane Taylor , policy enforcers (police officers) Michael Moore; commissioner such as, Mark S. Priver; court officers and their crony- clucks, likes of Sherri R. Carter, Adrina Chebishyan; Maria Salmaron; as well as some strife bankers C.E.O.'s such as Jamie (James) Dimon; Jay Bray, Stripes Mark Grier; David Brickman and attorn'eys, such as Mathew Brian Learned; Mellissa Maria Hernandez; David A. Lee; just to name a few evil-wrongdoers that continue to rape the public, have sexual intercourse [42] with its own kind; similar to their next to kin,[43] in wanton, they act with devilish functions .[44]

---

[41]**CALIFORNI-FICATION**: is termed herein as the agents who act as pubic servants for California state government who fornicate their unethical tendencies to rape, and have commercial intercourse against the public with no morals or ethics by disregarding the spiritual sense of forsaking God and worshiping the false gods (i.e. worship the state government over god) at whatever stakes it matters not to thee who justify…" . Examples of fornication can be found in 1 Corinthians 5:1 a male has sex with his step-mother, or a prostitute (1 Corinthians 6:13, 15-16),…

[42]**SEXUAL RELATIONS**/Commerce: Sense of "frequent and habitual meeting and contact, social communication between persons" is from 1540s. Meaning "mental or spiritual exchange or intercommunication" is from 1560s. Meaning "sexual relations" (1798) probably is a shortening of euphemistic sexual *intercourse* (1771) with *intercourse* in its sense "social contact and relations."
[connection or dealings between persons or groups]…https://www.etymonline.com/search?q=intercourse+

[43]**KIN**: Family or social relations…

[44]**DEVILISH FUNCTIONS**: naturally arise to assail those who practice the correct teaching…, and "Those who let themselves be influenced by devilish functions will be drawn toward the evil paths of existence, …" and "the wisdom to see devilish functions for what they are and not be swayed by them and the courage to stand up to them without fear. (*The Teachings for Victory*, vol. 1, p. 100)…" https://www.worldtribune.org/2022/remaining-undaunted-by-devilish-functions/#:~:text=Obstacles%20and%20devilish%20functions%20naturally%20arise%20to%20assail,us%20to%20realize%20our%20own%20inner%20transformation.%20%E2%80%A6

i, also filed well-over twenty-five state and federal court actions at law (cases listed at within these 5 volumes) against multiple pubic serpents, agents, even some of i, own family are on the list. i, did not file to cause them harm, or to disrupt their lives, that i, am angry, egotistical nor do i, have any vendetta.

i, recently realize that i, do file with over 100 wo/mankind actors as agents and the agencies to inform their, top brass or, supervisors for the sole purpose to expose each pubic serpent for the harm each cause. i, do it with intent to preserve what is true, moral, ethical and to suppress their desire to continue devilish functions towards i, and other wo/mankind. Trueness is to discover what is proper to you. When one wo/man make a stand then all wo/mankind feel like they too can make a difference. Making a difference is sometimes the difference to be made.

Bible, Koran, Ideology, Philosophy, Etcetera

B-4 reasserting i, belief in something outside of mankind and allowing god to find i; i, in turn found god and not by any mistake. In finding god once again in i, life, or albeit truly for the first time, i, realize that there are certain teachings, at certain times, a wo/man is either introduced, to like a path, crossed to become enriched by such teachings or it falls in their timely lap.

Although, i, was a long time practitioner and student of Nichiren Daishonin Buddhism, had it not been for certain issues to transpire, i, may not have crossed the road to Jesus Christ. It is through court satanic affairs, that cause much benefit in time to embrace i, love of God and i, life today when god desires, we can see the cross.

To this day, i, continue to assert certain teachings of Nichiren Daishonin Buddhism as the teachings have become imbedded in who i, am. Even though i, study the Bible, and continue to believe in god, by not forgetting what has brought i, to where i, am in life today, i, most likely would not have seen this side of life. Certain traits or teachings are imbedded in i, bone marrow, therefore, i, become a mix breed of knowledge, educations philosophy by compassion and love and in turn, topped off by experience of life that propels i, forward with no fear and hope with jesus' tenacity.

This is the sole reason that "*i, can see clearly now the rain is gone…*" (By: Johnny Nash); and in order to "*…get all obstacles out of i, way….*" and oh, when i, am finished herein writing this *living missive*, "*… it is gonna be a bright, bright, bright, sun shining day….*" Of course not all evil-wrongdoers will feel the same. And as to those who do commit a trespass against i, as man, some knowingly and others unknowingly, i, am able to forgive such atrocities and yet, never want to forget. It is because the wrongdoers are ignorant, blind, malicious, or just uncaring for the effects each cause by their actions. i, can still forgive them and to never forget. For if i, were to forget, then i, lessons of the past will surely poke up its weary-Karmic-head in the future; this i, know for sure. It is the way of prophets oh, yah and wise wo/men.

It is those who do know for what they do and do it anyway, whom are usually the alleged well educated, scholars of a society. For wo/men that cause their own demise, by the devilish functions for which they commit to i, reason, do proffer full disclosure through exposure and for a perpetual memorial. Alternatively, when i, and all other wo/mankind do not memorialize the wrongs of pubic serpents N-2 the public record, it is the same thing to encourage, all wo/mankind to become an accessory to their sin.

It is for that reason and more, that no one should allow obstruction by devilish functions to go unnoticed. It is when we allow devilish functions to go noticed and shrug it off as if this is the way life is… in essence, it is this type of manifestations of a fundamental darkness, ends up creating more negative adverse effects. To determine, is necessary and proper to expose EVIL-wrongdoers for their wrongs is the ultimate adjudication. Therefore, i, do reprint herein and state the names and issues: so it is said: "So let it be written, So let it be done, here on earth to kingdom come"[45];

Who Is This Precarious & Tenacious Man?

Who is adam - daniel, borsotti? Or the man without a title, without an ens legis fictitious persona, as a non-resident, non-person, and

---

[45] The phrase is actually, "So let it be written. So let it be done." This is said by King Rameses to Baka in the 1956 movie The Ten Commandments. https://www.answers.com/american-government/Who_said_%27so_it_was_said_so_it_will_be_written%27

non- agent or employee for any said govern mental institute. A society as a group of citizens, who chooses not to take on any titles of corporate status in life is no other than that of mankind. A name of a man, under god almighty, the only one and true god of this universe and beyond; will you speak the words “i, love almighty god forever and a day”?

First, let i, tell you, readers who adam-daniel – borsotti, is not. adam-daniel – borsotti, is not a hu-man being [46] as a colorable subject that can take any S.H.I.T.[47], from any power hungry, (Forever Under Kangaroo Court) F.U.K.C.-ing pubic serpent that act as [~~judge~~]. He do not take any S.H.I.T. off officers that operate through K.U.N.T.-s (Korruption Understands Nothing True) that act on just-if-ication for their title or job[48] as an individual. Nor a group of agents, pubic serpents, citizen, resident, or employee for any state or federal govern mental agency. Those who take on a job believing they are immune from the crimes to steal or control other wo/mankind, while each pervert their public service to gain for agency and self for private growth [49] have found their way herein. i, think i, just described above what an attorn'ey is again. However is it you who i, do describe and are you offended by your title? [If so write to: adam- daniel – borsotti, general delivery, Van Nuys California [91406-9998];

Wo/mankind Are Pubic Serpent s' Masters

i, can never describe an attorn'ey too many times because the more i, illustrate the more wo/mankind will desire to get rid of this genre

---

[46] Hu-man: Hue: early 13c., "skin color, complexion," from Anglo-French culur, coulour, Old French color "color, complexion, appearance" … "color of the skin; color https://www.etymonline.com/word/hued#etymonline_v_51188 and man: created…

[47] S.H.I.T.: P.O.O.O.P. (Pubic Obstruction of Other People)… pubic servants obstruct the public by stealing their rights, through enslavement without full disclosure of the true rights of law verses legal statutes codes, and regulations which are not true law.

[48] Job: 1660s, "to buy and sell as a broker" (intransitive), from *job* (n.). Meaning "deal in pubic stocks on one's own account" is from 1721. Meaning "to cheat, betray" is from 1903; earlier "pervert pubic service to private advantage" (1732). Related: Jobbed; jobbing. https://www.etymonline.com/word/Job#etymonline_v_6472 …"

[49] Private gain means any interest or benefit, in any form, received by a city employee or official. Private gain is specifically defined as a use for the principal purposes of making a profit not pledged 2-B used for pubic or charitable purposes. https://search.yahoo.com/yhs/search?hspart=pty&hsimp=yhs-ext-ff_freetestnow&param1=20220527&param3=speedtest_%7EUS%7Eappfocus1%7E&param4=%7Efirefox%7E%7E&type=yhs-ext-ff_freetestnow_appfocus1_ff&grd=1&p=define+private+gain+

for good. Within society 95% of attorn'eys are unnecessary. When we reinstate civics to the local schools, thus; to abolish attorn'eys from the planet, this is the aspiration for people as the fictions masters.

From 1850 through the turn of the 19th / 20th century, civics was the crux syllabus for all public schools. From the time children could read and write, they learned laws of the land; mostly biblical. However, B-4 govern mental's took civics, american government (which is not all true) and then the bible teachings out of the schools, L.A.W. was only taught through bible scholars who taught children at home, and in certain ethical disciplines.

Children had to learn the bible, constitutions, declarations of independence treaties, and other writings that instill a republic form of life. It was not obligatory, yet is crucial for a growing society to know the laws of the land. The ten commandments, constitutions, declarations, ordinances, the basics of reading, writing and arithmetic was and should still be the bedrock [50] of every society. "*i, shall reiterate l8er about the old doctrines...*"

i, therefore do not [~~judge~~] critique others for which i, expose. i, expose others in order to not be criticized by god. A hypocrite is a wo/mankind that does say to others to do certain things then not follow the heed by actions to its karmic demise.

When a wo/mankind take on certain titles, with alleged authority, to implement certain laws for society and do not follow the same laws themselves; each turns into a hypocrite. It is similar to when i, were to point one finger at others for not following certain ethics, morals to reprimand them, all awhile the lower three fingers are pointing back at i, for not doing as i, say rather than i, do syndrome.

---

[50] **MATTHEW 7, NEW LIVING TRANSLATION, DO NOT JUDGE OTHERS:**24 "Anyone who listens to my teaching and follows it is wise, like a person who builds a house on solid rock. 25 Though the rain comes in torrents and the floodwaters rise and the winds beat against that house, it won't collapse because it is built on bedrock. 26 But anyone who hears my teaching and doesn't obey it is foolish, like a person who builds a house on sand. 27 When the rains and floods come and the winds beat against that house, it will collapse with a mighty crash."
https://www.biblegateway.com/passage/?search=Matthew%207&version=NLT

i, have no godly power to [~~judge~~] another wo/mankind for their wrongs done to i, or others. Rather to expose is to disclose others wrongs, is not judgment when they do harm as it is also important to expose others for learning and applying the Ten Commandments. It creates value for all others who are aware of said wrongdoing.
It is because of the commandments that we do not allow others to get away with their mischief, lies, deceit and crimes against other wo/mankind. As it is today, the courts and govern mental's have continuously tried to rebuild a society premised on the state and federal govern mental's as the highest authority; as the lord over all of the wo/mankind. As "***if***" the State or United States or Supreme titled court-justices are the authority over all wo/mankind? They do not and it is their opinion at best and that is all they have… opinion!

As all wo/mankind must stop allowing pubic serpents to rain terror of fear, extortion, coercion, theft of land, rape, of a minimum our labor, through the threat of some order against them in the name of a State's agencies. Otherwise the house of our society, as it seems 2-B burdened today, will crumble in the winds and floods of govern mental's and pubic serpents attempt to enslave all wo/mankind by taking away the bedrock of these great Americas. A bedrock founding's which is and always have been the stronghold to the social order called America.

Look Back To Move Forward
Therefore, i, say to you, who read this *living missive*, go back to the basics. Take control of who you have become, and change the way you look at things back to the real law, gods laws, by comity and reciprocity. Because "*when you change the way you look at things, the way you look at things change.*" By: Dr. Wayne Dyer.
Just Google any school curriculum for the late 1800's, 1920's up to the 1930's. You will see what children were taught.[51] It will blow your mind and make you feel flat out dumb compared to how and what those generations instilled as ethics and morals and how many less f.u.k.c.-ing attorn'ers there were compared to today. i, am man [52] do instruct i, pubic serpents, who are woman or mankind

---

[51] **8TH GRADE EXAMINATION: https://www.huffpost.com/entry/1912-eighth-grade-exam_n_3744163**
[52]**man:** Genesis 1:26-28 defines man as having the image and likeness of God. In the verse, man is said to have been made as identical to God as possible. This has been assumed to mean

who act. To act and call themselves agents, servants, employee, individual, citizen or resident, for any govern mental is not the same as private entities. In wanton, for a pubic serpent to take on duties of public position, each must follow real law. To instruct their likeminded colleagues, that are also actors, that might have originally had good intentions, in the end, take on a bad title. Yet it is for the wrong reasons when any wo/mankind go against god's laws themselves in name of a State.

In order to move ahead, many times we must review the past to see how we got somewhere B-4 we move forward. Just because a wo/mankind take on a clothe [53], which looks like a tree that bears nourishing fruit, does not mean that the clothe or title have authority, power or jurisdiction.[54], Any right to order you, i, or anyone around to do any bidding; when it is a wolf in sheep's clothe-ing is not real nor law; a fiction at best, a fiction nevertheless.

It is only when wo\mankind give up their own power for another authority, that give full consent to those who dress as sheep in wolves clothe-ing, wrongs are committed. Like Casper the friendly ghost. When a kind and gentle wo/man, act as a public servant, with a title, this is where your guard must be raised high in regards of one giving away their rights. When a wo/man actually believes that a title has more authority than they do, the hierarchy becomes society's crux of blame and shame. Because repercussions of a trust for wolves in sheep clothe-ing, in the unknowing and the ignorance

---

that although God is said 2-B spiritual, He bears the exact resemblance to man. The same verse defines man as having authority over all the other creatures, and then authority... https://search.yahoo.com/yhs/search?hspart=pty&hsimp=yhs-ext-ff_freetestnow&param1=20220527&param3=speedtest_%7EUS%7Eappfocus1%7E&param4=%7Efirefox%7E%7E&type=yhs-ext-ff_freetestnow_appfocus1_ff&grd=1&p=where+does+the+word+man+show+up+in+the+bible+ "

[53]**THE TREE AND ITS FRUIT:**[15] "Beware of false prophets who come disguised as harmless sheep but are really vicious wolves.[16] You can identify them by their fruit, that is, by the way they act. Can you pick grapes from thorn bushes, or figs from thistles?[17] A good tree produces good fruit, and a bad tree produces bad fruit.[18] A good tree can't produce bad fruit, and a bad tree can't produce good fruit, yet, wear a clothe one of the same. https://www.biblegateway.com/passage/?search=Matthew%207&version=NLT

[54] **JURISDICTION:** Personal, Subject Matter, General, or Territorial (i, will go over jurisdiction later)

of what is called law, is actually called colour of law actually called (L.E.G.A.L.[55]) and society loses when allowing others to rule.

Retain Da Power You Always Have To The End

This ignorance of law causes effects of loss of morals and ethics of a society. It is almost 100 % of the time a result in wo/mankind being chopped up and placed onto a fire 2-B the next meal for those wolves in sheep's clothing. To take on a title of attorn'ey, [~~judge~~], officer, politicians and their kin folk that care not for the masses over the few is satanic.

Because of the public school system, the tell-us-lie-vision, media, our parents (pay-rents) and grand-pay-rents who dropped the ball on instilling god's true laws of the Land Air and Water to their posterity, society now lacks original consistency with the forefather and mothers' comprehension. God's laws have always been the most important for a society to flourish, to grow in a moral and ethical manner.

It is up to this generation to retain the power of god's original intent and pull the reins back on the horse/buggy, put their Fred Flintstone brakes on, B-4 the runaway train or court as govern mental corruption races too far out of control. The rights of wo/mankind will certainly go completely off the moral tracks for a period, *almost* impossible to retract it back on the ethical rail. To hold god long enough for wo/mankind to see and know it B-4 (god's) primary ethical train is eternally derailed, will change life 4-ever.

You Should Have Given Up Your Day Job?

There is still time to take back what was once called the greatest country on the planet. Know what a *rite* is, know how to retain your *rights*, and start to implement your *write* in the correct way, similar to this *living missive*.

It is expressed to those pubic serpents that might now be wishing she/he had stayed in college, or sports, became a plumber, chef, school teacher, computer tech, or sewer cleaner, or some other artistic genre. Instead you, pubic serpent's opted 2-B a police (policy tax collector) enforcement officer, enforcing unlawful taxes

[55] L.E.G.A.L.: Lawbreakers Exercising Govern ment(als) Artificial Law

and unlawful codes, statutes, rules regulations, ordinances acts or unnatural restrictions on your alleged fellow wo/mankind.
This *living missive,* by i, a man, pubic serpents should have known would become visible within their lifetime. As it is at this time, every wo/mankind from within society from as far east as China, to the far west of California, should either get on board or get out of i, way because i, am coming, and i, am coming to expose all of you for what you do, do. Maybe your original desire was to do well for society and create value as a [~~judge~~], commissioner, magistrate, or an employee for the fiction govern mental's. Govern mental's who have converted into a custom of ignorance from and by wo/mankind who call themselves The People Of….," or as titles.

"The people…" should know those who call themselves a [~~judge~~], officer of a court, that think they have complete judicial immunity with impunity[56] to rape, steal, and abuse a position as a pubic serpent are all wrong. You titles are supposed 2-B unbiased referees or in better term a witness, to listen to both sides and not ~~judge~~, but allow trials by a jury, that of one's own peers to determine both law and fact.[57] Today's statutory system is no less than land piracy. "Laws are made for us; we are not made for the laws." [William Milonoff]"Juris precepta sunt haec: honeste vivere, alterum non laedere, suum cuique." [These are the precepts of Law: To live honorably, to hurt no one, to render everyone their due.] not of you.

This previous paragraph tells a tale of what has become a long and drawn out battle for justice, in albeit an unjust govern mental system. Instead politicians, govern mental agents, acting for some offshore corp(s)oration, pharmaceutical or oil cartel, or for some narcissistic authoritarian, agent hired by an agency called the Los Angeles Police or Sheriff's Department, Superior court of…,United States District court of…, or Supreme Court of…, (DOJ) Department Of Justice, (FBI) Federal Bureau of Investigation, (CIA) Central Intelligence Agency, (IRS) Internal Revenue Service, or any of the other hundreds of alphabet soup groups, act that all

---

[56] **IMPUNITY**: Freedom from unpleasant consequences; exemption from punishment, harm, or recrimination
[57] **JURY OF ONE'S PEERS:** Determine both law and fact:

wo/mankind are slaves and must submit to the serpents demands. As in State this Bitch!

When i, am through, with this *living missive*, i, will make certain that, you, and you know who you are, you pubic serpent you; for one, you will need to take all kind of pills, to get all types of thrills, not any thrills you have ever known, and will not want to buy five copies of this *living missive* for your mother or father; nor will you, as you are directly named and exposed herein will hide behind what is true. You will not have found your picture on the cover of the rolling stone [58] magazine, but on the Banner called "*Hall of shame…*" It was set in stone, in the local newspapers, sent to you at your last known post location. It was posted up at every local united states post office as a lawful public notice; see it posted on the disabledjustice.org for the entire world. Go to the website (still under construction).

It was a lawful recorded trial where you were invited 2-B present at the Daniel – Adam- Borsotti Open Court of Record at 9425 Penfield Avenue, Chatsworth California Courthouse, [91311-9998] on that windy day of 24th day March 2023. [59] Not one of you was present and for that evasion, a decree followed against you evil-wrongdoers and for i, the man. The compensation for the harm that you do cause for the said trespass you commit against i, is being billed to you to date.

To Do Wrong Is Easy To Do Right Is Not

i, am with great hope, and do wish for you, the reader, 2-B on the side of i. Not because i, am begging, nor am i, trying to get you on i, side to believe in what i, think or believe as if i, were running for some office. Rather because what i, do, herein is right and not wrong, is moral and ethical, not fraudulent or in dishonor and most of all is for the posterity for all wo/mankind's future to know what is true through and true.

---

[58] **"COVER OF THE ROLLING STONES…"** : Dr. Hook: Single by Dr. Hook & the Medicine Show…

[59] https://disabledjustice.org/

It is easy to not do what is moral, ethical within the laws for all mankind. The pubic serpents think they have the right and the power to inflict monetary fines, fees, penalties, assessments for codes, rules, statutes and regulations against the mainstream of the state and federal society. Yes, this conflicting words and meanings. This last statement is only the truth when a people claim to be a citizen, resident, state and federal slave attached to the society that has authority over. Actually i, can and you can be a citizen or a resident for some purposes and not for other reasons. You must learn self preservation laws to control your namesake.

It is to know the difference of who, what, why, where, when and how "to be or not to be that is the answer." When any wo/mankind allows them to be enslaved within a society as a citizen, resident or by contract, they have contracted away their entire god willed rite. The wo/mankind verses a citizen or resident gives away comity and reciprocity to some policy enforcement that wo/mankind allow themselves to succumb by threats of said pubic serpents; known by titles of policy enforcement. Whether an agent for a state or federal agency, wo/mankind has all of their natural berth/birth rite to not contract away certain power to any all capital enslaved entity known by the "CITIZEN OF UNITED STATES" ...OR "STATE OF... CITIZEN OR RESIDENT"... thereof.

It is the "OF..., of..." that places the wo/mankind into an enslaved body to be governed, yet not for life. Read any states constitutions and United States constitutions for clarity. Read this *living missive* to its end for transformation;

So, to do what is wrong is always easier than to do what is true, fair and just. Because it deals with years of brainwashing a society of misfits, halfwits and well, most people fall into this category; even i, did and yet i, have been set free of enslavement that as long as i, do no harm; i, do no harm! And Vis Vie to thee. What i, place on the line, depends, not the diapers that pubic serpents use to catch the S.H.I.T. that spews out their mouth when they talk, rather on what is integrative, honest, moral and ethical, with no personal motive. No pubic serpent can ever claim they are integrative when they come for your wealth or freedoms dictated by a code.

Unless the pubic serpents tell what is true, under oath on the witness stand, at an *open court of record*, serpents will never be able to be honorable. At the same time, to enforce their statutes, codes, rules, ordinance, regulations, acts and the like; they cannot be in honor as l.a.w. is not a code, statute, rules, regulation, ordinance or acts attached with fines, fees, penalties, assessments, or charges. Ninety-nine percent of all govern mental agents are trained to control, threaten, coerce, and extort something that they believe is l.a.w.

When in reality, like all of historical monarchs proves, as long as there is not an injured wo/mankind/property, (bring up the body), which cause a loss of something tangible, then there is not an l.a.w. being enforced. There is only a policy placed on society of wo/mankind. It is meant to steal and control one mode or other by agencies agents and not god. Call it roman empires and imperialists.

To Continue Is Easy To Stop Is Difficult

As i, continue to expose and stop wandering on about how bad govern mental agents are towards all people, maybe i, could give some examples. It is the exact reason that all of the wo/mankind, that act as pubic serpents who take on a title, have deliberately cause a trespass against i, and as man, as i, write their names herein this *living missive*. i, who do cause your name erected up in lights, on banners, billboards as the world turns [60] or that you thought the world was your Oyster [61], you must remember that you cannot keep stealing from go[o]d-ly wo/men of this world. As you were supposed to work hard and diligently to receive the gooses golden eggs and instead, you abuse your titles for which i, do not allow and for that "you have got another thing comin."[62] "Judas Priest." However, after you do to i, that for which you knew was amoral, i, have a diaper for you, to catch all that S.H.I.T. that spews from your

---

[60] **HISTORY OF AS THE WORLD TURNS:** https://en.wikipedia.org/wiki/History_of_As_the_World_Turns

[61] **THE WORLD IS YOUR OYSTER**: https://english.stackexchange.com/questions/21713/what-is-the-meaning-and-origin-of-the-common-phrase-the-world-is-your-oyster

THE MERRY WIVES OF WINDSOR: http://shakespeare.mit.edu/merry_wives/merry_wives.2.2.html

[62] **YOU'VE GOT ANOTHER THING COMIN**: Judas Priest - You've Got Another Thing Comin' (Official Audio) https://www.youtube.com/watch?v=XJMgveYdO-M

mouth because you could not clam it shut and with it your political careers shall swirl down the drainpipes, which attach your mind to your anus, back up to your mouth to where your bullshit flows.

Message To The Public At Large
It is the type of wo/mankind who act as a pubic serpent, that call themselves a good honest, ethical, caring compassionate hu-man being, that is also the type that says one thing (under color of law) as a hu-man being, but never follow through with their honesty or contractual agreements. Whether on paper or orally, for whatever reason can be thought of; it is this type of hu-man who always justifies why they do not fulfill their integrity to the public that we expose.

You know who you are. You are the type of hu-man beings that we expose herein as a trader to wo/mankind race and for those of you wo/mankind who always procrastinate "why not put off today what could be done tomorrow? Because your tomorrow rarely ever becomes fulfilled. This *Living missive* is also for you!
You procrastinator you, you need to get off your fuckwit [63] Pot-smoking, potato chip, donut gorging, soda pop washing down candy-bar eaten, lazy asses. Change your life for the better. Either way, you get what you put N-2 your body, mind and spirit. The karma you create for not being in honor with your body, mind and spirit, knows that you do not give your word to god. To fulfill integrity to other wo/men is important, you create negative karma as integrity unfilled when you say you are god fearing and do otherwise.

i, know it sounds like i, do a bit of pubic serpent or agent bashing. It is time someone does place them all on the moral and ethical chopping block. i, promise this *living missive* gets worse B-4 it gets better. Remember this is for i, healing for their trespass fulfilled.

Pubic Serpents Are Known Criminals
This *living missive* is for wo/mankind to learn and for i, next *open court of record* when compulsory. It will be properly spoken; as a

---

[63] fuckwit (n.): fool idiot," slang, c. 1970, originally British or Australian English, from *fuck* + wit (n.).

verdict reads in. Is there a nexus between pubic serpents that operate behind the guise of protection called immunity with impunity [64] and a wo/mankind that takes on said title? The real criminals rarely operate with any fear of being caught, as each is disguised as a pubic serpent and use the system to protect them from any criminal prosecution. At the same time, the pubic serpents use tools of media and standing armies called "The [Los Angeles]… Police Department (P.D.'s) or "The [Los Angeles] … Sherriff's Department or FOX, CNN, CBS, KNBC (in your geographical area who have your own titles) etcetera, as hired guns. A standing army, to do their bidding, to go out and collect and enforce tolls upon its local wo/mankind. Oh what a racket they have contrived when they so steal jewels of all our lives.

It is rare but sometimes it transpires whereby one rogue outcast (such as an attorn'ey, [~~judge~~], or officer) from within their own genre is used as an example. Sometimes the agency will use one of their own kind to show the public that if you are going to do something so blatant and not hide it good enough, then you will get caught and we are forced, not because we want to, to expose you too and pro-se-cute you as we do the mainstream public because you were not discrete enough.

However, this idea using their own kind as an example rarely happens. And when it do happen, there is an excuse or falsified papers, destroying of evidence or miraculously certain body cam was accidently turned off, lost, stolen or erased. They know how to use their means to protect colleagues of their operation. Rarely but once in a blue-moon, agents will sacrifice one or more of their own kind.

There own kind: herein refers to their blue blood brotherhood, good old girls and boys clubs. We encourage the readers to compare your local Police Department actors that act as enforcement to the wo/mankind that are smeared all over the media; such as you, or

---

[64] Immunity with Impunity: immunity (n.): late 14c., "exemption from service or obligation," from Old French immunité "privilege; *immunity* from attack, inviolability" …"exemption from performing public service or charge, privilege," from immunis "exempt, free, not paying a share" https://www.etymonline.com/search?q=immumity
Impunity:

your average citizen, resident or employee for the agencies. They do use different words, terms, when going after one of their own mistakes.

This *Living Missive* Has Multiple Benefits

One benefit of this *living missive* is that we encourage exposing all criminals and evil-wrongdoers, by taking pictures, video, and audio of all pubic serpents whenever you can. This is a crucial task so that wo/mankind will govern all agents and pubic serpents for all with the sole purpose to protect justice no matter real wo/mankind or govern mental's. It is for the benefit to the public, to uncover serpents and their agencies and label them with colorless-collar-crimes (not of the colour of their skin) that are public figures. It is fact that their own kind tries to suppress sacrificing in order to prejudice them to the public B-4 they get a chance 2-B exposed by the average wo/mankind.

In similar words, the agents abuse their system and make billions of dollars against the wo/mankind's ignorance of what the true laws are verses codes, statutes, rules, ordinances, regulations and acts. It is in this time *we* govern the govern mentals.

When the public uncovers what has been going on for hundreds of years, as many are already realizing when an agency gives up one of their own, it is as if they are cutting off the toe that has gangrene, to save the rest of the body. The rest of the body keeps the public ignorant to the whole picture of what govern mentals were originally intended to do, which is not what is being done to you or i, on the stage of public service.

When the entire body is plagued, as in the cancer has metastasized through the entire body, it must be metaphorically killed off, or used as an example so others do not follow in its footsteps. i, bet the govern mental's want to do this tactic to i, again? i, already have endured their wrath. i, did not worry then nor do i, worry now. i, say "be gone Satan; go back to your govern mental's' lair; Satan be gone."

This is why wo/mankind who are watchful eyes and ears of this nation, must get rid of all of the bad seeds B-4 the entire body deteriorates the rest of the population or in this case, all of us non-pubic serpents that live life by comity and with reciprocity created through the ten commandments and other credos.

Therefore, we must get rid of the entire flock or agents, so it can continue to flourish for whatever time it takes for the rest of the body 2-B healed from the same political gangrene for which started at the top. The end result is govern mental's will continue as it has until we get rid of all bad seeds; which is achievable now.

i, Will Make You Famous

The meaning of the phrase is not "i, will make you famous" because U want 2-B famous or because your morals and ethics are such as those like Jesus Christ, Mother Theresa, Mary Magdalene, Gandhi, or Martin Luther King Junior, famous. Because those previous mentioned five well-known famous women and men are so well-known, so well admired that any other wo/mankind could never stand up to this level of making you famous.

Rather, i, shall make you famous. Not like Angus and Andy,[65] or Michael Tyson, (don't tell mike i, said this i, do not want to have to kick his ass) and besides, i, am a vegan not a carnivore. ☺
i, could make you famous like Donald John Trump who is so famous that it will most likely get him reelected again. But no one knows until it is time to know.

It is those pubic serpents that do not seek fame only fortune and the fortune they seek, is off of the backs of good moral and ethical hard working Americanos. It is by wo/mankind, known by agents as attorn'ers, that brings forth controversies at several levels. It is the pubic serpents i, name in this *living missive* that are being made famous; famous, for their unethical, amoral and unlawful acts [66]

---

[65] https://cindymarcolina.medium.com/a-bit-of-angus-andy-cedd8a2b1b58

[66] **ACT:** The verb agere had a broad range of meaning in Latin, including "*act* on stage, play the part of; plead a cause at law; chase; carry off, steal." The theatrical ("part of a play," 1510s) and legislative (early 15c.) senses of the noun also were in Latin. https://www.etymonline.com/search?q=act

against another wo/mankind. Each pubic serpent named herein do act on their stage at the *open court of record*.
Knowing each pubic serpent could not afford 2-B placed N-2 the public media; it is that i, will make you famous in the manner for which you deserve, but does not mean you are famous in a good sense, moreover it is meant to expose what is true.

Instead, it is more like "i, will make you famous…" as Jesse Woodsen James or Frank James, John Dilling, (Dalton Gang) Robert, Emmet, Gratton, Robert Leroy Parker (Butch Cassidy) Edward Ned Kelley, El Torpedo, Kutay Duzel, or (Cole Younger) Thomas Coleman Younger , or El Chapo as these are well known historical wrongdoers in the opinion of govern mentals who made them famous.

Intermission:
What is the difference between govern mental criminals, drug cartel and mafia? The one that calls themselves government … :)
Maybe the evil-wrongdoers i, name herein wanted 2-B famous in more of a humanitarian aspect and i, as a man will make each wrongdoer herein; just like Emilio Estevez in Young Guns 2 – stated: "*I'll make U famous like…*", so famous that it puts a stent in the heart of the word famous. Famous, such as: Manuel Noriega Moreno, The Wild Bunch, Stacy Torrance, The Desperadoes, (Cattle Russlin) Dan Rawhide Hersam, Sodom Husain, Ramiro De La Torre, Osama Bin Laden, Belle Starr, Apache Kid, or even Billy the Kid. And those are just named mankind that people know as a household name, "*make you famous*."

It is possible i, will make the evil-wrongdoers as famous as: Elizabeth Báthory, of Hungary, (Countess Elizabeth Bathory killed over 600 young girls) Bonnie of Bonnie And Clyde, Andrea Yates, who drowned all five of her children, or Aileen Wuornos who went on a killing spree in Florida. Maybe you want 2-B more like Evelyn Dick named the "Torso Killer," or Susan Atkins, one of the women who killed for Charles Manson.

It could be that i, make you famous like Jane Toppan who was a nurse whose patients became her victims, or like Amy Archer-

Gilligan who ran a nursing home and killed many of her patients. (Some say she was acting like Doctor Kevorkian) even though Kevorkian did not exist in society yet. Still, the concept is everending. Although, is it wrong to assist the patience who either were terminally ill, did not want to live any longer, or could not speak and were already dead in their bodies? There are too many wo/mankind that live like prisoners within their own bodies and minds that no one knows how much trouble or pain they feel, or nobody cares?

It is this famous type of celebrated actions that memorialize past wo/mankind who act as criminals disguised as pubic serpents. i, will record them N-2 history books for all generations to know. What happens to serpents that commit crimes, against fellow wo/mankind or their property? Some crimes seem minor, and others seem to cause catastrophic repercussions. A small lie is the same as a big lie, as the same to contrast crimes is to not fess up for personal wrongs each of us commit. Repent! Repent! Repent!

i, Swear To Tell The Truth…

What about pubic serpent known by politicians, [~~judge~~]s, police officers who are duty bound that allegedly sworn and oath to do no harm to their fellow wo/mankind or country? The pubic serpent who are just other wo/mankind whom take on the clothe, and act as … "they put their hands in the air as they just don't care…[67] And yet almost every wo/mankind, who do act as a [~~judge~~], policy enforcement, and politicians, commit crimes every day from their non-protected seat, on a bench or in the proverbial work place/office.

The crimes stem from theft, rape and extortion, to champerty, threats, kidnap, and an entire host of other atrocities against the private wo/mankind. It happens at every courthouse-ship by pubic serpents and politicians across America and the world is without awareness.

---

[67] **WORD UP:** By Cameo "…Put your hands in the air like you just don't care…"

Wo/Mankind Verse Corp(s)orations

It is fact, not conjecture or hearsay, whenever a wo/mankind is involved with a court action, state or federal, where the wo/man handles their own court action, the wo/mankind rarely if ever will receive the lawful hand of justice. When banks, govern mental's agencies, state, federal, or any corp(s)oration is involved within the court action, the agents rarely are forced to show their cards. Cards (are their facts/evidence) if ever. Thereby, pubic serpents rarely act against the agents or agencies which is why there should be no bench trials; always, always… trial by juries.

In as much too, when wo/mankind goes to court against another wo/mankind and an attorn'ey is hired to re-present one wo/mankind, the one with the attorn'ey almost always is victorious within the l.e.g.a.l. system and yet, not the lawful one.

Unbeknown of how the courts operate, is a mystery to the average wo/mankind, because civics was stripped from all public school systems between 1850 and 1950. Civics of the days of yester-year are almost never heard of, unless you are a s.l.u.t. that go to the legal schools, which knowledge of legal, is only for the blueblood collar workers as the secrets of true juridical knowledge is hidden from the public schools.

However, when a wo/mankind wants to enter the commercial world of monopoly and wants to sell their soul to the corp(s)orate devils, of course, <u>Satan</u>'s [68] agents, you know them as pubic serpents that act as [~~Judge~~]s, officers, attorn'eys and the like kind. Serpents will flat out deny wo/mankind compensation and all rites known of l.a.w. especially when they are not a part of the B.A.R. associated assemblage.

The Schools of Devilish Functions

All ~~Law~~, rather all schools that indoctrinate teachings that used to have an honorable impact for true and honest lawyers to apply the l.a.w. has long been destroyed by the l.e.g.a.l. system of statutory

---

[68] **SATAN:** n Christianity, the enemy of God, the lord of evil, and the tempter of human beings. He is sometimes identified with Lucifer, the leader of the fallen angels. "i, define Satan: as Bankers and their like kind"

schema. Such schools as Harvard, Yale, Georgetown, Columbia as the top four of ten, are no longer teaching honorable l.a.w. If they are, attorn'eys that are not applying moral l.a.w., or the agents for banks, known as B.A.R., refuse law to be applied everending.
In similar words attorn'eys nowadays are only puppets on a string to do the bidding of the B.A.R., which are owned by Banks, George Sorrows or whomever controls the banks. It is wo/mankind that act as [~~judge~~]s, court officers/serpents, tell all attorn'ers what they can and cannot do. This is why i, say all, but not ALL attorn'eys [~~judge~~]s are unethical, amoral, dirty, and need 2-B abolished by the means for which is taught to the s.l.u.t. as l.e.g.a.l. students which is not l.a.w. rather l.e.g.a.l. If wo/mankind will ever have a chance to survive on this planet, we must abolish the statutory system and go back to l.a.w., real law.

This deception created by the schools of l.e.g.a.l., are not law rather is statutory. Cases used to determine another wo/mankind's judgments are not lawful. Rules regulations and codes that were created in a few circumstances for a certain purpose can work for citizens, residents agents and only for those who acquiesce to the facts that those codes, rules, regulations are not true law unless each wo/mankind consents to those judicial and govern mental systems. The purpose of attorn'ers through the statutory schema is to trick, as in fool the average wo/mankind to submit their private power. However, there are none less important than that of the name game. In the name game the pubic serpent must get the opponent or any wo/mankind that stands at court, to admit it is the same her/him as the corporate name which is on the paper in front of the pubic serpent at the time.

Once the living wo/mankind gives up their name to the producer [~~judge~~] of the name game, it is lights out. The wo/mankind may as well bend over, turn around and just smile, while the [~~judge~~] serpent places its penis or fingers up your anus.

Remember all [law] schools teach a system of statutory schemes [69] and not l.a.w. It does sound like the same homophone [70]

---

[69] Statutory Scheme: Congressional Research Service: https://sgp.fas.org/crs/misc/97-589.pdf

heterograph, homonym or heteronym, but it is not. Such as l.a.w.s verses l.e.g.a.l. which is actually spelled differently. Almost every wo/mankind believes their name means the same. It is not. As a matter of a fact it is ~~non fiction verse fiction~~, if it is not spelled the same, then it is not the same regardless of it sounds like. To know the game is to know the rules. By what rules the moving wo/mankind brings to their *open court of record* and not the generic rules of the court, the pubic serpents try to force down the public's throats. What type of court are you on or in? Is it a court for basketball, tennis, or are you playing a game of monopoly, or actually on a chess board?

The govern mentals and especially at court's of l.a.w. and l.e.g.a.l. are operated by pubic serpents who must get control or authority over the wo/mankind in order to have lawful or legal power to throw any wo/mankind in jail, charge or steal the labor (their monetary worth) from the wo/mankind bank, property, land or nest eggs. This is the name game and the statutory game that every court serpent acts. This is called theft by consent; however, is it theft when a wo/mankind actually is ignorant and consents to non-full disclosure by the [~~judge~~] and court clucks, is it by consent?

Volunteering Names Has Many Meanings

When a wo/mankind voluntarily consents to become a subject of the issue it really is not theft per se rather it is a situation whereby there is not complete honesty by the parties involved. Take a pubic serpent, who acts as a [~~judge~~], when a [~~judge~~] asks you for your name, she/he is acting as-king (as king[71]) for something you are not. "*May I have Your Name*"? You say the *name,* case closed you are enslaved.

This is not acting as-king such as a sleep number bed, "…OR YOUR MATTRESS IS FREE…" this is a pubic serpent actually acting as-a-king to rule over you as a subject, slave, popper or animal. Whereby U will submit (like tapping out MMA style) to

---

70 Homophone: https://www.thoughtco.com/homonyms-homophones-and-homographs-a-b-1692660

71 Asking… As King: not like the king of rock and roll, or Elvis Presley, or the king of pop, king of jazz, or the king of sleep day beds, nor the king author, or even Jesus Christ the King, rather as king, the pubic servant transform by your consent N-2 your king.

their authority or you will be given a rest (arrested) in a private room, where you may or may not have a special roommate, who will have her/his way with you any time she/he desires to slap your ass and take it for their own. They take you whenever she/he decides to fondle, stick its penis, tong or finger N-2 your ass or N-2 your vagina. Although the last one may not be by consent, but it occurs, when you consent to agents.

The consent that is given at court has many consequences. So next time you go to court, know the language and intent of the alleged officer who acts (as-king) for certain things of you. Be prepared so this queen/king that you consent to, does not get consent so she/he may have her/his own way with you by uninformed coercion.

What Appears On Papyrus, Is Not Always True

In addition, do not forget the prize they seek. They are going after your offspring, cars, and homes, all of your property, especially your body and your nest eggs. If you do not have much to get, they will also tap N-2 govern mental created accounts, created at the time of your berth/birth by way of the Certificate of live berth/birth. (i, shall explain further down within this *Living missive* about certificate of birth/berth).

On the papyrus in front of the pubic serpent, it reads a name in all Caps and sometimes it can also be in upper and lower case. What is crucial is what is in the mind of the pubic serpent and its interpretation. Does the pubic serpent believe it to be, a wo/man or citizen. The name may not be the same as yours. Even though it sounds like, or it looks like a name that does not mean it is the same. It also may even be spelled like, but do not sound the same as the name game for interpretations or definition purposes. Be smart, do not consent. Be a wo/man as it is a key point of every court action.

Consensual Sex/Commerce By Consent

Giving sex is not just penetration of the vagina or anus by a penis or having copulation via oral suction and discharge. It is also giving up your rite/right as a wo/mankind to another wo/mankind that acts like a policy enforcer, attorn'ey or [~~judge~~], i.e., pubic serpent that acts like the govern mental's court witness known as magistrate.

Once this authority over the wo/mankind is achieved, the pubic serpent then transfers to any attorn'ey that is hired for a fee, rate for hire that receives such author-ity [72], by the attorn'ey/client contract; this is also game over. The authority as in jurisdiction is taken from wo/mankind, conveyed to attorn'eys that perceives to transform N-2 the author of your life, whereby you have submitted to the courts. Because all attorn'eys are owned by the B.A.R. for the association, employed as pubic serpent, that acts [~~judge~~] whereby the actual wo/mankind that acts as [~~judge~~] serpent must control the attorn'ey that stands B-4 the court witness. The attorn'ey will submit to what the B.A.R. serpent is trained to do at the will of the B.A.R. .

Next, the B.A.R. serpent enforces and passes its authority to an actual policy enforcer (Sheriff) to take your wealth, your body or your offspring by lien/levy. It is mind blowing that all or a portion of your property is 2-B transferred N-2 their banks, holding- tanks, (jails)/stockade or Child Protected Services to take your offspring by impound.

As sick as it is, it is very ingenious and simple to achieve and is why and how every wo/mankind that walks N-2 a state or federal court submits all their rite/right to the court's jurisdiction. By their own ignorance, unless certain words and more importantly their knowledge expressed as honorable actions on the fly is achieved. In wanton, picture yourself walking N-2 a court room backwards, with your ass up in the air, while your hands are wrapped around your ankles, no underwear on and yelling "*just fuck me up my ass your honor*; *just stick it in without any Vaseline...*" because in reality, this scenario is truly what the B.A.R. serpents are doing to you.

Now albeit, it is not that dramatic as the previous sentence, however, the same result is achieved which is what the court serpent truly desire from anyone. You or i, walk in as a walking dollar sign. The young (your children) as in a dollar sign, and list of your

---

[72] Author-ity: word-forming element making abstract nouns from adjectives and meaning "condition or quality of being ______," from Middle English -ite, from Old French -ete (Modern French -ité) and directly from Latin -itatem (nominative -itas), suffix denoting state or condition, composed of -i- (from the stem or else a connective) + the common abstract suffix -tas (see -ty (2)). https://www.etymonline.com/search?q=ity+

property, i.e., cars, land, bank account balance, stocks, bonds which they already have a list because they have investigated your wealth B-4 you enter. One of the first questions almost every attorn'ey asks is "*do you have a job*?" "How can you pay for my service if I am going to re-present you?" If the attorn'ey is not hired, yet, the pubic serpent will ask you similar questions. At last resort, they will get you to confirm your wealth, on courthouse-ship, at Satan's trone.

Harm To Another Wo/Mankind Or Property

After all, there must be some law and order on the land, by air and water. When there is facts, evidence and other wo/mankind who do witness you cause injury or harm to another wo/mankind or property, whether by accident or on purpose, then the tables may have changed. Only when there is honor concerning the actual proof of any injury or harm to another wo/mankind will the law and legal apply. When no harm present it is all their game to control and steal, plunder what you will allow them to get away with; you or your offspring is the prize for the serpent.

It is the acts of you that authorizes to attorn jurisdiction and right to rule over you to the corporate agents such as policy enforcers, pro-se-cuters, (~~judges~~) because this is the statutory L.E.G.A.L. not lawful juridical system, is it not? As stated, once, any wo/mankind cause injury loss or harm to another, the game is all over and virtually impossible to reestablish self professed right and authority to establish your own power to govern thyself.[73]

It is by the consent of the wo/mankind that does not know how to stand on their own wo/manhood that all wo/mankind lose their own power to another wo/mankind that acts as an agent for a corp(s)oration B.A.R. Serpent , STATE OF… SUPERIOR COURT OF…. FEDERAL DISTRICT COURT OF….

---

[73]**CONSENT OF THE GOVERN**: Simply put, *consent of the governed* means that a government exists only because the people freely allow it to and have given their consent. The idea of *consent of the governed* came from political philosopher John Locke (1632–1704), Locke argued that a government exists to serve the people, who are all equal citizens, and the people have the right to rebel if the government fails at this duty. Locke's ideas inspired Thomas Jefferson, would put Locke's philosophy in the second paragraph of the Declaration of Independence.

Democracies and repubics, both of which operate under *consent of the governed*, are two of the most common forms of government in modern times…"

https://www.dictionary.com/browse/consent-of-the-governed

This is how the state or serpent will have jurisdiction but only to administer your rights away from the lawful trial by a jury of one's peers. Never give up the rite/right to a trial by jury of one's peers.

How Did We Get Here?

The way we got here starts a long, long time ago. The previous wo/mankind of society allowed there delegates such as John Jay, William Samuel Johnson, Rufus King, Alexander Hamilton, and James Madison, who were the primary authors of the Constitution. These three mankind were influential mankind who worked up there writing magic, known as The Federalist Papers. Along with several other men and i, am certain their wives had influential tendencies to inspire the final drafts. All of our grandparents and parents dropped the ball because they thought they were citizens, residents, as "*we the people of…*" It is not as wo/mankind for these Americas whom worked up to finally build a public support for the Constitutions. The wo/mankind back a hundred to four hundred years ago was a lot more intelligent than people (wo/man) of today.

Yet our parents and grand-parents (pay-rents) to even fathom a fight for a constitution, declaration of independence had no clue what their elders knew. It has taken several generations to dumb down Americans and truly the entire world. It is all the more reason to give credence of the intelligence, lack of fear and the courage it takes to move for a future posterity as those writers' foreseen coming. What did they foresee and do their best to give us of today in order to govern the pubic serpents? What we have today is not reassuring to state as said by the spider to the fly without a tear to cry.

The wo/mankind of today, are complacent, have a sense of entitlement, do not know what it is like for the most part to struggle. Think about it, wo/mankind on the Americas have it made. Most of us have homes and cars with heaters and air-conditioning, toilets, dishwashers, washers and dryers, can go to any local street corner or food bank and get some type of food, if that is what you want to call it. Whereby, most Americans are not starving. Just look how other country officials treat their public; although there is disengagement to our homeless population.

See how the homeless on streets all over the states of the states united, whom can receive general relief, food stamps, housing, (if they want it) get massive handouts from food banks, emergency medical and dental etc… i, know for a fact that not all, but many people who are on the streets refuse to accept county services. Spoiled ?, Entitled ?, Pride ?, Ego ?, or just flat out lazy;

Complacent, Lazy Or Ignorant?

Over time, wo/mankind became ignorant to the belief that govern mentals are their friend and on their side. Govern mentals have never been on the side of the people. Or even if it were at any point, they are not now! And to this day what we have now from this state and federal government is over taxation, suppression of almost every rite/right. Sneeze in front of a parking enforcement, dog catcher, politician, policy enforcer (officer) and you will find yourself locked up for assault and battery or some other [Donald] Daffy-dick-trumped up charges.

The alleged wo/mankind used to cherish, such a right to free speech, (which is never free) right to make your own decision for your posterity. Try to tell that to (CPS) Child Protective Services that you have rite/rights for protections of your property (tell that to the Sheriffs), right to own and protect your own private property. i, do see the entire world now seems 2-B scared or living in F.E.A.R.[74].

F.E.A.R., is an emotional mechanism to control the weak minded, faint hearted, and or ignorant. i, used to ride a bike, skateboard, swim when i, could, get to a watering hole, roller skate to work down the middle of the streets at 3:30 a.m., and run, hike, play basketball, tennis and other recreational sports. Periodically when i, was growing up, i, was able to do many things without fearing the repercussions of what if this or what if that… . As an adult, i, still do many things to stay fit. These are the average things that young people used to do when they are three years old on up. Now, everyone is living in fear of being sued by the state or agents on behalf of some alleged lawful but truly illegal enclave statutory agencies agents.

[74]**F.E.A.R.**; False Expectation Appearing Real and it being the fear only appears in one's own mind first always.

The laziness i, now see with this 2025 society, is electric or motorized skateboards, bicycles, mountain bikes. The youth do not go to the local roller rink, or bowling alleys. All of the local dirt bike trails, car racing parks and fun places are banned from public. And what about those brainwashing, mesmerizing babysitters called cell phones, computers, and the longtime running tell-us-lies-vision (T.V.).

As young as 16 year olds are driving cars and motorcycles, do not dance as much as years gone past, do not play much sports, eat too many junk foods that can be found on every street corner, such as 11-7, and at the local little gas station convenient stores. There is Jocksdtrap-in-the Crap, McDoofers, Staco Snail, Dill Staco, and a whole host of places to receive pasteurized, salted and sugar infested, synthetic-infested laboratory created preservative foods that are harming people.

Of course, just like smoking cigarettes, marijuana, drinking forms of alcohol, vaping, chewing tobacco and other harmful substance that does not usually kill anyone right away, however, the fall out of the repercussions do and will cost money that is over taxed, and tolerated mostly resulting in death substances.

The end result is when it can be regulated and overtaxed, therefore, regardless that it sometimes takes years of habitual abuse using the list above, just like the abuse of habitual binge eating or not eating can and do cause medical problems. The govern mentals that cares so much about their public citizens, truly care more about the commercial gain regardless that to regulate it can slow or all together eradicate any immediate fatal problems; whereby most wo/mankind live a relative long productive tax-healthy life. (i, will talk about hereditary issues further down).

Back To The Founding Papers

The Constitution, Declaration of Independence, Bill Of Rights, Articles and other alleged protections that many wo/mankind think to this day and thought had authority or protections, never applied to a wo/mankind. It is true that those doctrines were meant to give wo/mankind a sense of security created for their posterity. The posterity of today has fallen asleep and most are brain dead. They only applied to a citizen, resident and never a living wo/mankind unless each voluntarily consents regardless of what people think otherwise; they are wrong. i, shall prove what i, say above about the constitution and declaration of independence is true and backed up by fact and evidence throughout this *living missive*. You must keep your brain engaged, and activate your common sense, logic and reasoning mechanisms in order to find the nuggets herein.

For now, i, shall move on about the previous doctrines being unnecessary in today's and even back in the days of James Madison, Jon Jay, Alexander Hamilton the writers of those doctrine to have had any power but for themselves. All wo/mankind are governed by their actions or intent to do no harm. This is why even those pubic serpent that think they have jurisdiction, venue or authority to make decisions on or in your court action are f.u.k.c.-ing out to lunch and have or do usurp the *open court of record* against the average ignorant wo/mankind's silent consent. The laws of reciprocity by the ten commandments is all that is, all that was, has and will ever be necessary and proper for all societies to live in honor among other wo/mankind. Your silent consent lack of knowledge is your demise.

No wo/mankind can release or give up their authority to another wo/mankind's control. Every wo/mankind has their own rite/rights to breathe air, to drink and have the use of water, and food to nourish and for the protection for self and family. These are fundamental rite/rights and are a necessity for survival that no pubic serpent may ever lawfully impede. Yet lawful and legal are not the same. Awareness and ignorance are two separate sides on the same coin. Do not stop being stupid!

However, the agents as pubic serpent operate on a different premise. The govern mental's have devised a simple plan to control the populace as a mass, in order to enslave a nation. It is always and will always be that the right to contract no one can encumber. Even if the U.S. or your States Constitutions says there are certain rights unalienable, those doctrines were written for slaves who claim 2-B under the power of contract as a 14th amendment citizen, resident, individual or one of the people. Any agent for agencies which the constitution was written is fraudulent. It really is very simple and ingenious how this United States and State govern mental's have perpetrated against all wo/mankind. Some control by contract other by just ignorance that gives up their rite/rights by using certain titles. A woman or man who knows their standing, status and character does not need to claim they are anything but a woman or man period. Do you get the true picture readers?

No wo/mankind need to become an American National, Citizen, Resident individual, Govern mental employee, write letters of intent to the Pope, Queen or King of England, to the Secretary of State or the President of the united states, or rescind or authenticate their berth/birth certificate in order to inform the pubic serpent of some status. At the same time, none of the wo/mankind ever needs to not contract N-2 a jurisdiction which is not easy in today's society. (I will give tips later on how to stay out of their jurisdiction). One quick tip, you do not have to consent into their monopoly game, Shuuush do not tell anyyyybodyyyyy, okay? Did You Know, there are two separate systems that exist and only one is real?

Law is the original system created by the creator, through Moses Ten Commandments. Legal is a counterfeit system created by Romans to control wo/mankind. L.a.w. will always be far more powerful than l.e.g.a.l., hands down; "we the people" this isn't just a catchphrase—it's a statement of the l.a.w. and right of free will. Govern mental is simply public service that is supposed to work for all wo/mankind. A wo/mankind is the authority, and pubic serpents are here to support us with whatever we desire. The crisis is as stated previously, you as a wo/mankind the creation of the original creator God has forgotten, never knew or refuse to believe what i, say is *true*. What is *truth*? What you believe without fact!

Transform From Wo/Mankind To B.A.R. Agent

It is at the time of graduating from that alleged prestigious [law] l.e.g.a.l. school Transformer of…. time runs short thereafter an oath is taken where the point of no turning back begins. It is at that very point right B-4 the transformation from wo/mankind N-2 a corporate entity, agent or employee, and the wo/mankind becomes controlled by the agents for the [B.A.R.] Association as the agency. This is not some type of metamorphism like going into a phone booth as a newspaper reporter and coming out as Superman, or placing some bracelets on one's wrists, a place on a cape, with some special rope and all of a sudden you become a wonder woman. However, it is similar, to you, as a slave mind, to learn, realize and transform your mind back to your celestial or natural selves.

The above explanation is why it is crucial to know one's rite/right, therefore, the court system will not be able to unlawfully engineer you and your property N-2 their jurisdiction. Whereby all your [rights] as to *free will*, property and freedoms are lost to the malicious intent to be deceived against your ignorance which the state and federal govern mental's have monopolized against all wo/mankind.

Knowing The Game Is To Function On The Board
The true reason someone is forced to have an attorn'ey to re-present[75] them in a court is not because of ignorance of the law. It is that pubic serpents, at court, cannot see or hear you because the system of court is rigged in such a way that no wo/mankind can ever have a lawful chance 2-B present to act as self. The courts operate only within the fiction statutory scheme under statute, codes, ordinance, regulations, acts and rarely, albeit sometimes with case-law, not real and true l.a.w.

Case-law really is not l.a.w., even though it sounds like l.a.w. because the word law is in it. The courts for the past 90 years N-2 today, 2025, can only see a wo/mankind as a corp(s)oration, citizen, person, individual, subject to, instead of a wo/mankind. The court agents, who act as a [~~judge~~] etcetera, cannot see the wo/mankind without a representative. Because there is no parity/nexus between a fiction and non-fiction; the non-fiction being the reality, must have an attorn'ey.

[75] Re-present: "… also be a representative of" (the authority of another)." https://www.etymonline.com/search?q=represent

The end result is almost always corp(s)orations/banks win and wo/mankind will lose hands down as i, have observed this repeatedly with over 28 personal court actions, and hundreds of other citizens and wo/mankind's court actions.

On or about March 24th 2023, i: a man; adam-daniel of the borsotti family was able to change the entire multiple years of fiction non-fiction rhetoric when i, held i, "*Open Court of Record*" at the Chatsworth Courthouse whereby a jury of peers, and of the evil-wrongdoers with other wo/mankind that do witness the *trial by jury* and a magistrate as witness were present. Resulting with a final decree for i, the man; daniel – adam- of the family borsotti for the amount of twenty-five, million, six-hundred-forty-three thousand dollars and no cents ($25,643,000.00), which is now in the process of being noticed, billed and collected while interest continues to accrue. (More about this decree later);

Wo/mankind Transform N-2 Sharks

This *living missive* is all about sharing i, experience, and knowledge with the readers to better their lives, to become more empowered, and with hope, others will join the history books by creating their own hue-wo/man revolution in order to transform what once was enslavement N-2 something more beautiful and forever encouraging to move 4-ward create value for society for all wo/mankind.

It is the types of wo/mankind who transform from god abiding women and men that i, expose herein, who have no care of harming other wo/mankind. While hiding behind the masks of pubic serpent, backed by govern mental's, that is truly not a lawful government, unless you and i, allow those wo/mankind that are as actors/agents for the government to continue to trespass upon the world.

To transform from a wo/mankind into a land shark is very simple. We bring the pubic serpent from their private capacity, hiding behind a corporate veil, N-2 the forefront of their public community by placing a badge, give them a gun, place a title over their living name and give them a shot of arrogance, ignorance, false courage and a paycheck. [There i, said it, what are you gonna do about it rocko?] "Rocko is all of the pubic serpents called govern mentals…"

It has been long known as long as the agenda is followed by the serpent that sets out to achieve, for whatever reason, and it is fulfilled, the world will continue to spiral into devilish functions. As pubic serpents act under Satan's control, by the name of govern mentals will not stop until you and i, stop them from the rape. Contrary to what most people believe, Satan is not an evil spirit with horns, per say, or with a serpent snake-like body or any of the other pictures which have depict Satan for hundreds of years. Satan is similar to that of a thought manifesting to an act as a devilish function that comes to be famous from minds and souls of wo/men who have gone rogue against Jesus and Gods laws that function in a devilish manner. (Simple more on this later; stay tuned because i, can talk for years on this).

What Is It 2-B Famous

i, said when i, am through herein i, shall make all named wo/mankind a part of the family called Evil-wrongdoers. The status of wrongdoers will be so famous, they will make Annie Oakley, Princess Dianna, or Jesus Christ, not less than, but more of a household name than they already are.

The evil-wrongdoers herein will definitely not receive any awards for the arts, entertainment, sports and hobbies, nor for the humanities, science, technology, business, or service to society depicting self as a shero or hero. Rather by exposing the wrongdoer i, will assist to reset morals and ethics with honor and integrity back within all of the courts, political arenas, and with help of others, share with the entire world and bring it into your homes and hearts.

Moderately, i will make absolute certain each wrongdoer, will at the least, find their picture and name on the *wall of shame*, in multiple newspapers and on many forms of social media all over the internet. And for each participated act of theft, rape, threat, corruption, kidnap, coercion, conversion of property, including unlawful incarceration, identity theft, defamation of charter, champerty, maintenance and vexation progression, that wrongdoers do commit, each already received notice, when they heard of or read i, name.

i, public notice is not like that of a conventional, Grammy or Music award, rather of a historical proportion as they should have already found their name on the hall of shame on 24th day, March 2023. And, of course they should be honored i, write them down in this *living missive* for all eternity.

When the wrongdoers decide to file an ad with the Los Angeles and New York Times newspapers to negate what i, say, first they must give i, notice B-4 they take such drastic measures and give i, the same opportunity i, do give all of the wrongdoers by notice B-4 they take it public. When the wrongdoers do not stand by honor, then the opposite of honor affects their causes of dishonor. Nah, i, do not think i, want to waste i, money, that they owe to i, for such a trespass that continue to this day against i, nor do i, have to.

Notice Of Intent

i, do not wish 2-B famous just doing the right and honorable part for society as this is similar to a notice of intent. It is i, intent who will depict that in every known unethical, amoral, unjust, malicious award for each evil-wrongdoer, like those criminals of the past, who do wage war by way of: rape, theft, threat, extortion, coercion, barratry, champerty and maintenance that do effect vexatious progression and the murder of the souls of other wo/mankind. It is by actual act or attempts to murder souls of innocent and ignorant wo/mankind i, move to protect.

It is by evil-wrongdoers who have stripped or attempted to strip out honor from hard working, moral and ethical families across this globe by monopolistic materialistic media world for which agents for govern mentals create their own names imbedded in the ether of god, whom already knows of their journals of their past. i, thrush B-4 god on the thrown that of God's world so that i, do not need to [~~judge~~] give to another wo/mankind. For it is not up to i, to judge another wo/mankind, it is always left for God to do as she/he pleases.

Born or Berthed On the North American Land

The fact that i, might have been born or berthed on these North American lands i, am not owned by any name, whether all capital or upper and lower case. Because a man cannot be a title a fiction without of the UNITED STATES, STATE OF … or STATE OF (CALIFORNIA), or any incorp(s)oration. A man cannot be contracted by false pretenses, nor have i, knowingly contracted with full disclosure from berth/birth to date, regardless of whether the biological vagina that i, fell from, (mother) signed any paper as an informant which is what happens to every single baby that is born or berthed at a hospital across the world; or at least these U.S. of A.

It is a fact that most govern mental's assume and presume, as they treat all wo/mankind as citizens, residents, individuals, employees or agents, are under the jurisdiction of their administration; this is far from what is true. Just because a child received digits called Social Security Number and a NAME at berth/birth on a document called the Certificate of Live Berth/Birth, or nationalized, that wo/man or child is owned by such a monopolistic created genre, called County of…, State of…., or United States regardless of how it is spelled upper or lower cased.

From i, experience, it is true that not one pay-rent, child, or student from a public school system have ever received full disclosure. It is now time the county, States and United States govern mental's must come clean to all wo/mankind with complete full disclosure. And not whether it is true, as much as it is whether it is not true. This is a challenge to all politicians and all pubic serpents to come clean.

The Age Of Majority

It is said, once the pay-rent has informed on the child and a child has the number, registered with the county recorder, secretary of state, or has received public assistance, it is virtually impossible 2-B able to rescind the birth/berth number or certificate of live birth for a wo/man's entire life to actually be slavery free. Not i, said the fly. It is from birth/berth through aging, sickness to death that all wo/mankind do evolve with such a number, however, until the child to adulthood becomes the age of major-ity, the *will* of the child never grows up. All wo/mankind up to the age of 90 sometimes never realize what the age of majority truly is. Take your right of *free will* to be wo/mankind and to free yourselves from the tyranny of the enslavement that governs, you into the court, and see whether you are treated with any respect.

The age of majori-ty is not a number rather a comprehension of one's own status on earth and in their character in how one handles life in the public compared to how a child actually handles their selves at a court of l.a.w. Once one gets to a court of l.a.w. where the spam hits the griddle, of course, when the griddle gets too hot it can burn. Rather than allow a court to decide your conflicts, how to act honorably that one truly becomes the age of majori-ty.
Such as Matthew 5:25. "*Settle matters quickly with your adversary who is taking you to court. Do it while you are still with him on the way, or he may hand you over to the [~~judge~~], and the [~~judge~~] may hand you over to the officer, and you may be thrown into prison.*"

Always Give Notice B-4 You Enter Court
The notice i, do give to all evil-wrongdoers is the process here of discussion to avoid conflict is derived from the teachings of Jesus Christ. While religion and god are a dialogue for another time and place, the fact is Jesus had momentous understanding of l.a.w., and how the courts work. This is why dialogue is significant in universal l.a.w. All disagreement can be avoided through honorable dialogue and open and honest interactions. Using these notices in universal l.a.w. one acts as sui juris, is of one's own l.a.w. and perceptive, being the age of majori-ty and not always of the full lawful age of consent as an adult.

Court Of L.e.g.a.l.
Giving Notice gives comity, reciprocity, until the other side dishonors the lawful process of comity and reciprocity. Then when there is no comity or reciprocity this is the time one is forced to give a final notice B-4 the honorable will bring the issues to the courts of public opinion. However, the courts of public opinion are not the same as a court of neither l.e.g.a.l. or a court of l.a.w.
LEGAL: defined as L.E.G.A.L: Lawbreakers Exercising Govern mental Artificial Law (includes no periods to separate) and LEGAL: under colour of rules, regulations, ordinances, statutes and codes but

not LAW. A part of a systemic monopoly game played against wo/mankind on a board; "the board is mother earth".

This L.e.g.a.l. system is what all superior courts and federal, as well as circuit courts operate (like doing surgery) "under", "within" or "on" and even "at". They have a [~~judge~~], ~~judge~~ pro-temp or magistrate and sometimes a commissioner. There is a cluck of court, a cluck assistant, and sometimes a delegate [deputy] to keep the peace. The l.e.g.a.l. courts follow statutes, codes, court rules, ordinances and regulations for citizens, residents, PERSONS, and any infant, indigent or idiot that do not know the difference.

Court Of Law

LAW: Land, Air & Water: under god's laws where there is the right to the Land for which all wo/mankind shall live and flourish for their family posterity; No woman, man or govern mental agent can ever stop any wo/mankind from breathing Air as it is the first essential substance to sustain life itself. Water is the second most essential element for all living sources to sustain life itself and the third part of the LAW. Without Land, Air and Water nothing on this planet or in this universe can sustain life as we know it. It is the LAW from god that sustains all life force on this earth. In contrast to wo/man-made statute, codes, court rules directive, ordinances and sometimes acts is the disconnect between wo/mankind and you.

Courts Are Games With Certain Rules

Chess is the most prevalent game for people to learn to figure out the monopolistic control that govern mental's try to control by the word commerce. However, monopoly is truly the board for which all of this fictional life operates.

Yes this life is a Chess game that we all need to learn how to play. It is not so much Universal law as it is common to a geographical area of discussion. Because most people have heard of Common law, i, shall stay with this terminology.

What levels the playing field in the game of chess is not the rules per say as it is to know what the pieces on the board are able to do. The pawn is equal to the citizen, resident and all govern mentals controlled entities. Then you have the castle/rook which has certain movements such as North and South only. Then we have the horse /knight which can only move in an "L" shape movement. However, the horse/knight can jump over the space one to two or two to one whenever there is either an opened space or to capture one of the opponent's game pieces.

Then we have the bishop which can move only diagonally as far as there is an open space or to capture one of the opponents game pieces. Then we have the King which must be protected at all times. However, other than the very first move such as a pawn, the king can only move one space at a time and it like the bishop and the castle/rook and pawn, the king can move forward and backwards only one space at a time. The queen however, is the second to most powerful piece on the board. The queen can move North, South East and West. She can also move diagonally as many spaces as she wants that are opened and to capture one of the opponent's game pieces.

As i, do state the queen is the Second most important/powerful piece on the chess board. The most important is not the king, is not the bishop, night or rook. It is the pawn. The reason the pawn is the most powerful piece on this chess board is because there are more of them than the other game pieces and without the pawns none of the other pieces can survive. It is the same in real life chess games.

Face it, without the people the others will have to do their own bidding, wash their own clothes, till their own fields, prepare their own meals, and do everything on their own as if they are worthy even though they are not worth a brass farthing. All pawns sometimes become other pieces. Some agent-pieces of s.h.i.t., others just pawns for the game of life.

Remember it is the pawn that begins to move towards the opponents' kingdom. It is the pawn so to speak that works the fields, builds the roads, bridges, furniture, cars, runs the power lines, pays the taxes, moves mountains and begins the movement towards an enemies army, air force, marines, or coastguard.

It is and always has been a pawn that is also dumb down to the point of being used as a slave rather than the most powerful piece on the board as each is under god. When the pawn becomes educated, and knows her/his self-worth, it is the pawn that the other controlling pieces which want the masses of pawns to believe that a king or queen is the most needed, or the bishop because the bishops are the ones that give spiritual advisements to all of the pawns.

Or it is the knights as policy enforcers who protect the pawn from intruders. Or that the castles of the queens and kings who certainly are the fictional rulers that are to be protected because it is the queens and kings that know all and dictate to the pawns who, what where and how to act and be within a society of other dumb down pawns. You get it reader?

When it is and always has been the pawns all along that already know how to protect their own castle, their own families, and to till their own fruits, vegetables and livestock and to build their own castles and to build their own armies to protect their own livestock, cars, monetary wealth and all of the things that the kings, queens, bishops and knights want the pawns to believe is the way of life.

When in reality, brainwashing has only caused a lifetime of distrust, and allowed the chess masters to control most pawns in order to take what is not theirs to take and to threaten those pawns for things that the kings and queens have no right to encroach upon another wo/mankind as a pawn.

When will this game of chess turn on queens and kings, bishops, rooks and knights? i, say the time is now, and the time is long overdue. This is to say that the pawns have a choice to receive this understanding and take back control of their own lives and stop allowing their hard earned labor to be stolen, threatened away by the chess master bureaucrats (govern mental agents) that think they have a right to continue to threaten pawns into submission.

Now is the time to govern thyself because govern-ments are not set up for discussion. You will rarely or never receive a response to your notices, but always be able to evidence an attempt to offer discussion, to stand in honor, to avoid conflict and maintain your honor, which is what court is or was suppose to be all about.

Direct Message To The Readers

Using common sense logic, and reason with the court actors most often will have positive outcomes when the numbers are more than one. Because "One is the loneliest number that you will ever see..". But one hundred or one thousand is much more ensuring and gets the attention of the queens, kings and bishop masters.

When it is you that cause the harm to another wo/mankind, then "come to terms quickly with your accuser" while you are going with her or him to their court.

A direct message from the inscriber to the public and private sectors of this world: i, speak only what is true, and appreciate the opportunity given that i, received from God to allow i, to share this *living missive* with the world. It is through this *living missive* i, will heal from past wrongs by the named criminals named herein as evil-wrongdoers.

May the lord be with i, in these times, as i, continue 2-B homeless at the hands of those who rather place all non-slaved wo/mankind out in the streets, in order to justify how and why they do what they do for the rewards for which they steal.

Because i, like challenges, this is a challenge to all wo/mankind, to learn, listen, educate, and take back who you are as a wo/mankind because you are not a slave, you are not a pawn and leave the slave behind; so become aware and transform the life, as in your life into a new era.

Even when evil-wrongdoers and the likes of them, who perpetrate against other wo/mankind are without knowing, with the notion that they are doing what is l.e.g.a.l. By their ignorance, these wo/mankind are only one step shy of constructing the crimes, are as guilty by association, guilty as their employer, when each acts against god's laws of reciprocity, moral, and ethics especially when...
"Yee do know for what you do and do it anyways;
Amen.

Until Death Due Do Us Part
It seems 2-B more like a marriage, till death do us part, or do us all part and only those to forever be reunited in the kingdom of God, will never truly die. We know that even when we physically expire what was due is still due by the posterity to said govern mental monarchs. Therefore, to know god, Jesus, Buddha, Jehovah, or to have seen the light is to make such changes.

It is while we are aware and alive, B-4 the time we meet our maker, the opportunity to repent, to learn, realize, and change karmas. It is for which we have created today's world, individually, globally and karmically throughout the world, why it is crucial in order to be free of all govern mental constraints and of course free from Satan itself.

The following is a picture of a man. A man who has come a very long way from the days of watching the tail end of I Love Lucy, Leave It To Beaver, Partridge Family, Eight Is Enough, Brady Bunch, Kimba The White Lion, Speed Racer, Scooby Doo (Where are you?) not to 4-get The Flintstones, and many other society altering, mind-changing, and brainwashing tell-us-lies-vision shows. Yes, humorous they were, still with brainwashing intent.

Each was a futuristic portal to what the future would soon transform from then to the present society of today as the public became brainwashed like walking zombies.

Over the time growing up i, learned that a beaver is not just a tel-us-lies-vision show, nor a large rat that creates damns and survives out on the plains' of God's green earth. Nor is a bear limited to Yogi, or Smoky, but is also a wo/mankind that takes on the persona of a [~~judge~~] or in this case, a persona of a title and a female private area.

The saying "do not poke the bear…" is one that i, do not learn until recently when i, make it i, own duty as one of the wo/mankind on this earth and of this mainstream commercial private world; a world that i, was born onto this land, as i, breath free air and use the rain water for survival, so with it i, do learn how to poke the bear while never allowing it to sleep for the winter; with or without a robe.

i, will be damned to allow any such façade known by a title of [~~judge~~], any pubic serpent to tell i, what i, can and cannot do with i, wealth, the air i, do breath and the land i, so wish to till and the good-ol H2o that sustains i, and all life.

i, Said It Many Times B-4 As i, Say It Hereinto:
" i, a man; do not wish harm on anyone; i, do speak only what is true backed by factual proof that what i, do write herein is of i, personal firsthand knowledge " And "It is i, who heal from the scars of yesteryear. i, do wish the greatest of healing for those who do trespass knowingly and unknowingly regardless of their title" as " no wo/mankind ever has the authority to control by threat, duress, or coercion unless you have placed your dishonor into the realm of man-made legal system"

" when in doubt go to god and Jesus for advice as no titled-man is worthy of the advice that is necessary and proper for all mankind but the creator her/his or itself "

" do not answer the questions but question the answers of those who seek to strip others of their power, wealth, character, or property, as property is never theirs "

" Know the right to contract, to voluntary involuntary servitude that is from false prophets that portray a status of hierarchy, willing to trespass without honor "

"Learn to realize, then adjust, create dialogue that seeks harmony, always repeat what there is to be in the grace in the presence of Jesus Christ and God Almighty"

One does not always have to believe in Jesus Christ, Buddha, Jehovah or God to know what is right or wrong. This *Living Missive* is a reminder that all wo/mankind are good in nature at berth/birth that all things are not created equal, rather are innocent until brainwashed to indifference. A key to life's journey is about the will you succumb or to win over it?

WORDS FROM THE AUTHOR = Man

" LIFE "

"Life Is Of Reality, It Is Here For Us To See,
If We Are 2-B You And Me,
Life Is Of Reality,
And To Find What Is Eternity,
Then Our Lives Will Be Free,
Life Should Not Be Time Wasted On This Earth,
For If We Do, We Won't See, The Next Part Of Reality Of Life."

adam — daniel of the family Borsotti
One of Gods Disciples

Here is i, message to all of you pubic serpent across the globe: "When you seen me coming, you should have stepped aside, a lot of you didn't and your name will forever perish in society by your political wayside," end quote;

By i: a man; Adam – Daniel .

WITH FRIENDS LIKE THEM WHO NEEDS ENEMIES

SCOTT, ROBIN & RONALD NINER'S
CRIMINAL GANG 2006-2025

Scott Alan Niner

(Ass-wipe [76] Niner)

Scott Alan Niner. Not a very honest man nevertheless

a man made by god, yet even satan was made by god as well?

It is not so much whether that scott niner was an ex-drug attic, alcoholic, and adulterer, or whether he is one of those now. As much as it is that he was and is a liar, a thief, and a dishonest man that had taken advantage of i: daniel - adam – of the family borsotti, a once severely unearthed man; hereafter having been deemed disabled by medical practitioners.

Although scott allan niner (ass-wipe niner) always needed to control his game, the game scott played on i, his own family, and especially his now ex-wife robin elizabeth, lillian nigretto/osborne aka niner.

---

[76] **ASS-WIPE :** In Spain, Toilet paper/Papel higiénico is the usual word to use but "el papel del culo" (i think is Ass-wipe) is a slang term to use with friends. It happen the same in US with Ass-wipe ?
https://forum.wordreference.com/threads/toilet-paper-Ass-wipe .606340/

2000 through 2025

At, the time of his mischief between 2000 through 2014, Scott is not the only one who had abandoned all moral compasses to achieve his end result. The result that scott sought after, and did complete and even to this day 2025, i, do not know of his character changing. The result of knowingly, willfully and disgustingly having taken advantage of another man, he incorporated his ex-wife, that scott cheated on, his brother jim or james niner and his own father ronald george niner, whom all aid and abetted Scott to pull off his immoral and unethical acts against i. It was there about February to March 2006, when i, finally accepted the final amount from the law offices of Masry & Vititoe whom received a substantial settlement from all of the injuries that i, sustained at the May 3rd 2001 car mishap. Because i, was unable to drive and i, wanted to have someone with i, to witness the ongoing between James Wilson Vititoe and i-self, i, asked James (Jim) Niner, Ass-wipe's brother to give i, a ride to the law office of Masry & Vititoe and Jim Niner did witness some of the interactions between James Wilson Vititoe and i, concerning the final settlement. Therefore, Jim Niner new exactly how much i, was going to receive B-4 Robin Niner and Ass-wipe Niner new.

Promiscuous With Another Woman

At the time, ass-wipe was on his way back from Georgia, where ass-wipe was having an affair with his last wife, which at the time, whereas he was committing adultery. i, know ass-wipe was committing adultery because i, had taken a trip back east and traveled to Georgia, where after i, do witness ass-wipe's mischievous deeds, then i, flew back to California.

However, B-4 i, left Georgia, i, made it i, duty to protect i, best friend at that time, robin niner. i, ended up going to ass-wipes apartment, whereas i, seen him with some (as robin niner described she to i, as a cocaine whore (na)) young blonde gal. However, robin's definition of whore, is not abbreviated, as the same as i, use herein as (w.h.o.r.e.). [77]

---

[77]**WHORE**:Whore, whore, w.h.o.r.e. all upper/lower caps w/without (.) Without Honor Openly Refusing Evidence.

Is The Brother At All The Same

This gal was very skinny almost like an anorexic. i, figured he was cheating on Robin and as it turned out he was. As i, waited in the living room, i, observed crack pipes, torches, and residual of cocaine (na) on the counter of the kitchen. i, know they were crack pipes etcetera because i, too used to have a problem with the coca.

One day, i, received some phone calls from ass-wipe, asking i, to loan him some money. Now, i, had not told Ass-wipe anything about any settlement, how much or when i, was to receive it. Although, everyone knew i, was going to receive some settlement. Yet, i, nor anyone knew how much until jim/james niner, ass-wipes brother told them. It was the next day after the meeting with james vititoe, when ass-wipe really started to hound i, for a loan of $50,000.00. Then the amount went up to $100,000.00.

i, asked Robin how did ass-wipe know i, was going to receive i, settlement and Robin told i, that Jim Niner told his brother ass-wipe, which i, already preserved what i, thought was confidentiality from James Niner. Who knows how many other people Ass-wipe‘s brother Jim told that i, was going to receive settlement and how much. Jim had an oral confidentiality agreement not to talk to anyone about i, settlement and he broke i, trust and the agreement as via robins statements to i.

i, did realize it on i, own anyways because it made sense that no one else new, not even robin knew when or how much settlement i, was going to receive except ass-wipe's brother jim/james niner.

After, i, turned ass-wipe down for the loan, of course the loan was attached to all kinds of promises. Ass-wipe was going to make sure i, received all the money back. One deal lead to another and then ass-wipe all of sudden, came up with this plan, whereby ass-wipe wanted the money for some patents ass-wipe was creating. Some type of roller machine for these huge half a million dollar printer machines. There were actually two separate types of patents ass-wipe wanted to manufacture and they were as he stated a sure thing to make *him* millions.

i, told Ass-wipe no because i, personally did not know anything about what ass-wipe was doing and i, did not want to trust him because of what i, seen and new about his committing adultery against, at that time, i, best friend in the entire world. At that time, ass-wipe was on the out and was in bad standing having many problems with his brother Jim, father Ronald and his entire family, not to forget the adultery. Of course his brother, mother and father were very moral and ethical wo/mankind. They definitely would not approve of his adultery, even though the family wanted Ass-wipe to have children that Robin was not eager to give.

A Falling Out With Family

Ass-wipe even quit the business, at Creative Graphics Services and ass-wipe eventually started to work for other printing shops. One Print shop was down in North Hollywood California, which fell out because ass-wipe did not get the owner of that shop to go into business with ass-wipe. He eventually ended up working for some shop in Georgia where ass-wipe met the cocaine whore. i, gathered by i, keen private "I" intelligence, as it does not take a brain scientist to figure out when a woman or man is cheating, therefore it was this time when ass-wipe met that Floozy as Robin Called she and committed adultery.

Because of the falling out ass-wipe had with his family, ass-wipe's brother and father would not loan any money for ass-wipe's inventions, or what he had planned because his brother and father and especially ass-wipe's mom seemed to know him obviously his entire life. It was ass-wipe who was always the deadbeat of the clan. And when ass-wipe did not get his way, ass-wipe had semi tantrums as ass-wipe would go off the amoral and unethical cliffs of life, such arguments, drinking sprees and abuse of his now ex-wife Robin and other family.

A Call For What Reason

It seemed like just a few days had gone by and ass-wipe called i, again and said he was coming back from Georgia and wanted to meet with i. Ass-wipe made it sound really urgent. So as usual, i, made time for him, however, in-between his arrival, i, was able to get a hold of an old family friend who was a lawyer by the name of

Jeff Bright.... After explaining to Jeff what ass-wipe wanted of i, Jeff suggested that whatever i, do, to get everything in writing, especially pertaining to patents, and inventions etcetera. Jeff also said that i, should always hold 51 % and give 49 % ownership to ass-wipe if i, were to give into ass-wipe's blitz of ideas for i, money.

After i, expressed to Ass-wipe about the 51% to 49 % Ass-wipe became a little angry and completely turned down the entire issue of the Inventions and patents. A couple of days had gone by and Ass-wipe approached i, again. This time, he was very frank. Ass-wipe begun first telling i, how much he loved Robin and would never do anything to harm Robin.

Now, i, knew this story ass-wipe begun telling i, was a bold face lie. It was a lie because he was already cheating on Robin. Robin also knew and did not tell i, because she was allegedly trying hide it from i, because she thought i, might actually do harm to ass-wipe. After all, Robin had been i, best friend for several years. Actually we first met when we were about 17/18 years young, with a long history.

Sometimes Friends Are Better Than Lovers

Although we did date for a few years, over time, i, knew it would be better for she and i, to remain best friends. And our friendship turned into an everlasting bond similar to how brothers and sister are with each other, or are supposed to be. A sibling's love is something to adore which i, have not ever had with any of i, biological siblings. Yet i, had found it with Robin; an everlasting lifetime of always being there for each other no matter what; so i, thought?

So ass-wipe finally gets to the home, at that time his and Robin's home at 27508 Sycamore Creek Drive, Santa Clarita California; [91354]. And the first things out of ass-wipe's mouth to i, was "I am sorry that this relationship has come to this...." I love Robin and I always will Love Robin.... We are going to lose our house to a foreclosure and I need your help to save the house from foreclosure."

i, was stunned for two reasons: One, he was telling i, that he was getting a divorce from i, best friend in the entire world, because ass-wipe was then living with another woman, and two, ass-wipe wanted i, to help him save ass-wipe's home from a foreclosure. The world's smallest violin was playing on ass-wipe fingers right B-4 i, own eyes and ears and it sounded very convincing and amorally loud.

Ass-wipe continued how he will always take care of Robin and would never do anything to hurt Robin. At the same time, he told i, that his family will not help him with money to save the house and that i, have to save the home for Robin. Ass-wipe continued to inform i, that i, cannot tell Robin that i, know that Robin has cancer and it would kill her if she were to lose the house while she has to undergo chemo or radiation treatments.

A Wolf In Sheep's Garments

So here i, am listening to all of these heartbreaking issues from ass-wipe, at the same time, by a man who is cheating on i, best friend. robin was right, i, wanted to wring his freaken neck with i, bear hands. i, did everything i, could to refrain from violent behavior and while trying to hold back tears of the news about i, friend's cancer and losing her home. To this day, i, do not know how i, did not harm him.

A day had gone by, and i, contemplated going to i, friend Robin to confront she about the cancer, about ass-wipe's adultery, and about the foreclosing of her home. Yet, i, did not know how to approach her because ass-wipe asked i, not to tell her, that i, know. Of course when ass-wipe said not to tell her, this was his way of working i, into his confidence while he was playing i, heart like a viola; plucking each string as if he was controlling i, feelings towards Robin like a orchestra leader at a symphony. It is the real reason why ass-wipe said things the way he said them. His own family knows of ass-wipe's manipulations for years.

i, did not ever give ass-wipe i, word that i, would not talk to robin about his alleged secret, which turned out not to be a secret. However, i, did not know how to or when to approach robin because ass-wipe said there is no time as the home will be foreclosed at an auction sale within a few days. Therefore time was of the essence; so i, believed.

One thing led to another, and i, finally broke i, guard and all logic, reasoning and common sense had gone out the window. i, was already deemed permanently disabled by multiple social security medical practitioners along with many non-govern mental medical doctors.

Mind you, robin niner was i, Social Security Representative Payee, and acting in a fiduciary capacity as a conservator representative along with ass-wipe Niner because i, was not capable to handle i, own money, and other basic daily tasks.

There was supposed to be a fiduciary responsibility as in *trust* whereby a trustee (wo/mankind placed in a trust position) has certain duties to abide by strict standards of l.a.w. and l.e.g.a.l. Trust law is one of the, if not the highest law on earth or laws of the land in private and public commerce. Air is trust law and water admiralty maritime law. It is the law as in Land, Air & Water that equals L.A.W. and it is the trust [78] law that no wo/mankind should ever breach. In God we trust! However, Ass-wipe and Robin Niner both breached all law not to mention morals and ethics pertaining to how they dealt with i, money and i, life.

The Final Deal

After ass-wipe Niner worked on pulling or playing the strings to i, heart towards Robin; ass-wipe finally talked i, into a deal that was supposed to be iron clad. i, can remember it as if it was yesterday.

Ass-wipe told i, that if i, were to save their home from foreclosure for what was owed on it, ass-wipe and robin would pay i, two years of house payments, in advance, and then buy the home back from i, at the end of the two years for no less than what i, put down and i, would have no out of pocket loss. Then ass-wipe will buy the home back at the fair market value but never less than what i, put out of i, pocket. "i, do state that last paragraph is what is true and all what is

[78] **TRUST:** "reliance on the veracity, integrity, sound principles of someone; religious faith,"

true Under Penalty of Perjury and attest under witness of God"; i, finally agreed and ass-wipe ran with it so fast, metaphorically of course, and pushed all the papers through as fast as he could. Ass-wipe had i, call his broker, who he had it already set up, and eventually worked all the escrow papers with their colleagues.

Everything that was transpiring was delegated to i, from ass-wipe. When i, would receive a call from the broker, or the closing escrow people about i, needing to send certain papers, i, called ass-wipe and he told i, what to do. He even set it up with his Brother Jim and Ronald Niner to allow i, to go to Creative Graphics Services (CGS) to use their fax machine because one, i, did not have one, and two i, did not know how to use one so the papers would immediately be received by the escrow agents. Ass-wipe's father Ronald attested to this fact under oath.

i, would go to CGS and ask bonnie or ass-wipe's best friend matt and brother jim or james as he is conveniently called, who all worked at CGS and they would show i, how to use the fax. Eventually i, learned how to fax on i, own. So, i, would show up there and fax papers, and then say hello, talk to matt, cody or bonnie and another gal sarah and then leave.

What You Know Can Set You Free

i, know to this day they all know what ass-wipe was doing, because they all do witness that ass-wipe had a falling out with his family, none of them liked that ass-wipe was committing adultery and his actions were not coinciding with god's laws.

The main issues that ass-wipe did not like was the fact that Jim had more control over the business than ass-wipe, Which is why ass-wipe left the business and stole i, money to start the business "Dangling Carrot Creative". It does not matter whether any of the family or workers would ever come forward, the facts are true, regardless of whether they would ever come clean and tell what is true, does not matter. i, know what is true so does Robin, and especially ass-wipe Scumbag[79] Niner and its sperm-doner father.

[79] SCUMBAG: a contemptible or objectionable person

It Was Time To Consummate The Deal

So it was on that one day, where the papers were to be signed by a witness notary, and ass-wipe was there at this point, robin's home, because robin would not allow ass-wipe to sleep at the house because of his adultery issues.

When ass-wipe did make an issue of the fact that it is still ass-wipe's house and ass-wipe will sleep anywhere ass-wipe wants to. Ass-wipe definitely slept in one of the spare rooms as far as i, know.

i, asked ass-wipe to write up the agreement and ass-wipe said he would. One thing led to another and ass-wipe kept putting i, off with multiple excuses that he was out of town, or would write up the agreement tomorrow. And as you guessed it, tomorrow never came. Finally, i, put i, foot down (even though i, should have placed it up ass-wipe's ass) and told ass-wipe i, am not going to go through with saving your home from foreclosure if you do not write an agreement.

Let Cancer Heal On Its Own

At this point, i, was trying to not bother robin about the home because of the alleged cancer. This is when robin begun to cry to i, and tell i, how much she loves this house, and that she does not want to lose it.

She pointed to all of the animals, cats, dogs, all of her knickknacks, furniture, pictures on the walls; it was her and it was actually her first house she ever owned. The home was Robin's personality, it was created for her, so of course i, heart fell for i, best friend's tears and ass-wipe Niner's bullshit lies. Tears and Bullshit do not mix but get results.

Now, i, found out later that robin's name was taken off of the deed. Of course ass-wipe had robin convinced that she was to be taken off of the deed by telling robin that ass-wipe needed to be the only name on the house for tax purposes.   It was so like ass-wipe to file in a certain manner to evade income taxes. Ass-wipe actually convinced robin that they both would be able to save on not having to pay as much taxes contrast to both of their names on the deed.

Robin and i, was lead to believe that ass-wipe's mother was also not on their deed to the family home.

A quit claim deed is easy to do and has fast results. Why do it when you love someone and you have made a pact or oath to be with that wo/mankind till death do us part. i, wonder what those wo/mankind who do not follow God's laws feel when once oath given, and then for personal reasons go back on the oath and move on to another relationship. Obviously each individual has their own justification. i, think whatever the issues arise, an oath is an oath and nothing should break that covenant with God, let alone with a significant other.

Robin fell for it. The lies continued and even became worst. The problem was that i, was being dragged into their web of lies and it was i, to be the next man caught in their web, ready to be devoured by ass-wipe allan and robin niner's deceit.

SCOTT & ROBIN, NINER CRIMINAL GANG 2006-2025

Robin Elizabeth Lillian ~~Nigretto/Osborne~~ Niner

Robin Elizabeth Lillian~~Nigretto/Osborn~~-Niner

A woman made by god who should be ashamed of herself

It was about April 23rd 2006 when i, had a long talk with who i, thought was i, best friend in the entire world; a woman who i, would have done anything she asked. We were morally and emotionally inseparable even when i, was miles away. i, loved her with all of i, being, with every waking moment, with every fiber in i, body and with every breadth i, could take. i, never imagined what was to come from robin.

i, was always ready to come to robin's side to do whatever she asked of i, as she was truly the first love of i, life, and the connection was beyond anything i, could have ever imagined. However, a friendship beyond lovers, beyond brother and sister, beyond mother and son, because we knew we were not meant for the relationship, better to stay as family type friends.

Then she comes clean about everything she knows about ass-wipe committing adultery. How long she suspected him cheating, drinking, doing cocaine and just treating her like a piece of shit. i, asked robin, Do you want me to take care of him? (the old fashion way)" She would not have it, because she knew i, was serious at that time. Robin knew of not only i, ability but i, craziness and willingness to hurt people really bad. Remember, i, had known she since, 1981-82 therefore, we had been through many years of trust, friendship ups and downs; that once thought forever bond.

Robin and i, had not only grown up together, Robin has known of things i, had done, what i, was capable of doing, and willing to do when necessary. Robin reassured i, that ass-wipe will do what he said. He will not rip i, off, because "this is my house", as she believed that ass-wipe was going to allow her to continue to live in the house, as this is what ass-wipe had told she and i, separately.

The Infamous Foreclosure Statements

Robin left the room and came back and showed i, the foreclosure statements that allegedly ass-wipe did not show her until recently. Obviously she was being lied to for several months. Robin did not handle the moneys for their family.

Ass-wipe was the bread winner, and handled all of the bills. Robin did everything by taking care of all the dogs and cats, keeping the house clean, and food shopping all the housewife things.

i, looked at the foreclosure statements and read Quality Loan Service Corporation. However, i, did not realize the name until many years later. i, explained that i, do not have a job, i, do not have income, i, do not have good credit, i, cannot get a loan, and robin reassured i, that ass-wipe says he will get the loan through it will go through because ass-wipe has it all set up through ass-wipe's realtor connection.

Brotherly Love

i, asked robin, "how did ass-wipe find out about i, settlement" she told i, "jim told [scott] ass-wipe." i, figured it out on, i, own anyways, but if one cannot trust ass-wipe i, guess the brother was not far from who ass-wipe is either. Maybe one day they will all repent to god even though god already knows what is true. Maybe one day they will apologize to i, but i, am not wasting one second of time waiting for that either. i, have a better chance winning the lottery, i, do hope for their remorse.

It was about a week to ten days B-4 the escrow papers were to be consummated. The house needed to be tented and ass-wipe was nowhere to be found and, only by his mistress of the dark, c.o.c.a.i.n.e-w.h.o.r.e. soon to be new wife and robin was sick in bed, as she used to be, sickly, depressed and not very sociable at that time. i, head was spinning with fear for her unknowing, ass-wipe's deceitful bullshit and i, was still healing from i, injuries to be pressured like this was too much.

House needed tenting as usual when transfer of title. Ass-wipe always delegated chores to others, as he could not fathom getting his own hand dirty or doing any real physical labour. Therefore, i, once again was left with the tasks of cleaning everything up as usual. i, just bagged everything. The foods, plants, animals all had to be removed so the home could be gassed from any varmints. Now, i, just wish he reads everything herein and sulks it all in. Of course i, was angry at the time even writing this, but under God's auspice, i, do not ever wish harm on anyone or anything. It makes for funny writing, even though it was not funny at time it was all transpiring revolutionary and then the time came to consummate niner's deceit.

Here i, continued to be scared for robin's cancer. Robin worked i, about not losing the home to foreclosure, ass-wipe reiterating that he will write everything down on a contract. i, was forced to stay on him about the contract. Finally ass-wipe said he would write up a complete agreement tomorrow, which was 24th day April 2006.

It was Tuesday the 25th day of April 2006, i, recall it perfectly. A lady showed up with papers for i, and ass-wipe to sign for escrow. i, do not remember what the papers said as there were so many and i, was not allowed to read them because ass-wipe kept hurrying i, up to sign them. Hurry sign here, initial there, and there on and on and that i, do not need to read them just sign them.

Because i, felt pressure, i, was also hesitant because ass-wipe did not write up the full agreement, only a partial agreement, and the Lady that day seemed to be in a hurry too. i, do not know if ass-wipe knew she, but it seemed like he did by their eye contact and energy together. i, recall asking the lady, "where is John the notary," she said "I am his wife and I will bring the papers to john to sign; john is at home sick in bed with the flue and could not make it. (More on this later)

Signing The Escrow Papers

It was not even more than 30 seconds once, i, do sign the papers, and the notary's wife left, ass-wipe immediately walked over to Robin's bedroom door and said in a clear, loud and precise voice, "it is done" and then turned and ass-wipe brushed by i, in the hallway as ass-wipe ran out of the house for a while seeming excited.

i, then turned from feeling like a savior to feeling like a fool. Not so much for i, as i, did not truly know what i, had gotten i, self into. i, felt like a fool for robin and she was truly not as upset as i, thought she would be. i, suppose she knew all along that ass-wipe was cheating, was not going to give she any house, no money from the house, nor truly take care of she as ass-wipe promised i, he would. i, did not know how much money was owed. i, did not know if ass-wipe was going to fulfill his indenture to i, or robin. All i, knew is that i, helped alleged friends from foreclosure, and i, was out approximately $105,000.00 for helping people that were supposed to be i, friends. And i, was prepared to take a two month reprieve into the woods of the East Coast to heal i, body, mind, emotions and spirit. However, i, was reassured B-4 i, left, that ass-wipe would not back out on ass-wipe's original agreement.

Get Away To Heal I, Body, Mind, Emotions & Spirit
It was about June of 2006, whereby i, planned to go away to heal from the surgeries sustained from the 2001 accident. Years of litigation, fighting to survive from day to day and repercussions caused by the traumatic brain injury (TBI), the post traumatic stress disorder (PTSD), the chronic depression, sleep deprivation, obesity, high blood pressure, ulcers and an entire list of effects caused by the issues sustained from the May 3rd 2001 car accident.

Although the first mortgage payment was not due for two months, it was not long after i, flew to the East Coast. i, was visiting friends, family and took a few weeks and eventually found i, self out in the boondocks [80]alone. With i, self, and only the memory of i, love for a lady i, thought was a friend, i, worked on self healing. i, will make this short because it truly is three months of writing, but the just of it is that i, locked i, self far away from society. i, was out on a farmland, where the only things i, seen were Silos, massive cattle ranches, Beaver dams, Elk, Deer, Moose, Bear, Wolves, lots of snow and some big wild cats. i, do not know if they were huge bobcats or mountain lions.

The evening and nighttime natures shows were nothing i, had ever seen B-4. The Northern lights, with such brilliant and outrageous swirls of colours the skies would open up and poor buckets of water, that i, called god's tears. The lighting storms that i, have never experienced B-4 in all i, life. All i, did was chant, eat, walk, sleep and write into all of i, journals which i, had kept via writing and audio taped records.

Now, i, was not completely alone. i, rented a second story three bedroom apartment high up near the Canadian Border. Although, i,

---

[80] DOWN IN THE BOONDOCKS: By Billy Joe Royal and I did love Robin and I did never feel I ever fit into society… so I concur with this song…

did buy a Honda Accord from a native friend. It lasted i, long enough for the purpose i, was there. The main purpose was so i, needed a quiet place to heal and to get i, self around.

So, i, also bought a used mountain bicycle, and begun to walk the mountains, then ride the bike and eventually i, begun to lose weight, and started to *look like* i, old self again.
It was a long road to recovery, however, i, do not stop and continue for the rest of i, life. When a wo/mankind become complacent, we resort back to our childhood; we should always strive forever until the days we perish.

MEN OF MARTIAL ARTS CALENDAR

December 2000 Special Edition

There were a family with one child living downstairs, and although, i, did not see them often unless we crossed paths. Usually when i, had gone down to the basement to do laundry, i, would say hello, and they replied with the same. But this is the extent of interacting as i, was there to be alone with i, tape recorder, pencils, paper, computer and time alone.

Deceit From The Start

It was not more than a few weeks, that i, would check i, bank account by telephone. i, did not have a cell phone as i, still had a pager. i, used the phone that was set up at the apartment to make all calls, therefore, no one could get a hold of i, but i, would check in with robin every few days or so and that is what i, did.

It was June 2006, which is when ass-wipe was supposed to make the first mortgage payment which was a part of the indenture. i, was not supposed to have to pay one red cent for anything, and is why i, was ready to keep to i, integrity as i, was not supposed have to do anything.

No closing costs, no mortgage payments, for two years, no upkeep in case anything broke, nothing. It was around the end of June 2006, where i, begun to call robin every other day, and ask where ass-wipe was and why is ass-wipe not making any of the mortgage (death pledge) payments. i, asked robin to make certain that ass-wipe paid i, as he said he would.

Like always, robin begun to make excuses for ass-wipe. She played the runaround game with i, as so did ass-wipe when i, would call and leave messages on his cell phone because ass-wipe refused to answer his phone. This was the first issues for i, when i, wanted to focus on healing, and i, had to shift gears by moving into acting like a collection agent and find out why ass-wipe was not wiping his own ass and making certain that his integrity was solid unlike his bowels runny and slimy as he.

i, begun to leave multiple messages. Then i, begun to ask ass-wipe's family why ass-wipe is not keeping to his integrity. They had no answers except that they would talk to ass-wipe. They know ass-wipe better than anyone, they are his mother, brother; father and sister all have known ass-wipe and robin knew that ass-wipe's modus operandi, "M.O." Because ass-wipe had his own particular way of doing things and his family all knew his M.O., but did not

tell i. Once ass-wipe approached i, for money, ass-wipe left the family and friends alone from pressure.
Finally it dawned on i, why ass-wipe wanted i, to set up automatic withdrawal from i, new bank account. It was not enough that i, placed i, name on papers and that i, pulled out over $105,000.00 dollars of i, medical fund from the settlement that was to be for i, lifetime injuries which were supposed to assist i, in getting well.

Setting up the automatic withdrawal meant cash would be taken directly out of i, account, therefore, ass-wipe did not have worry about any death-pledge payments because he played my heart and ignorance as cords to have the land payments come right out of i, account.

Ass-wipe did not need to worry about anything but f***ing his new c.o.c.a.i.n.e.-w.h.o.r.e., stealing all of i, money which he was supposed to pay i, direct for two years of land payments.

Instead, ass-wipe stole this money, lied to i, cheated on his now ex-wife robin niner, and then he used i, money to start up his or truly i, new business, Dangling Carrot Creative at Santa Clarita California and in Georgia.

Scott Allan Niner (Ass-wipe Niner) stole from a man, who had been deemed severely disabled, who only received up to a fifth grade education, had multiple issues, and then used the stolen funds to start up the business, so ass-wipe could live happily ever after with his cocaine-whore.

The new family, (good for you ass-wipe) and now has at least two children who do not know about their scumbag father ass-wipe niner.

Of course ass-wipe's wishes or the repercussions of ass-wipe's actions are all in the past. But they are not in the past because they are still present to this day and there has been no resolution fulfilled to date. The auspicious thing for i, and many people, there is no statute of limitations with the laws for mankind nor on a trespass.

Trespass Has No Statute Of Limitations

Scott (ass-wipe) allan and robin niner with others have continuously, to this very day, 2025, commit a trespass against i, a once severely disabled man. A man that is still harmed by scott niner and his family's actions is still ongoing. All the effects of ass-wipe, robin and ronald niner's actions, to this day 2025, are trespass.

Ass-wipe and robin had fiduciary relationships, duty by l.a.w. (consider God's laws) not to forget or leave out moral ethical duties to i, a man and to god to never do harm.

Robin elizabeth, lillian nigretto osborne, eventually became aka notorious robin niner one of the niner clans most dishonest family gang member, once she took a vow to the niner family. Robin would throw away all moral compasses in order 2-B lead astray from god's word, trust of i, for some back door deal.

After robin elizabeth, lillian, osborne/nigretto was married to scott allan niner, robin niner became the worst friend that anyone could ever call a friend. As far as someone who did unscrupulous things like she. Obviously i, would be so ashamed of i, self that i, would never lift i, head up out of the hole for which she dug so deep that the thought of her name brings ethereal slivers of razorblades through i, dermis, epithelium layers of i, integumentary system.

The deceitful actions and inactions for selfish gains by robin niner is the crowbar that severed all relations between a best friend that was once thought of as a pair of friends spiritually and inseparable for life, to robin's abandonment by abuse, traitorous lies, and took advantage of someone who loved she more than himself, more than God, more than anyone he had ever known.

i, think at that time robin new things she did not tell i, such as ass-wipe never had any intentions of paying i, one dime, nor to keep up to his original indenture, his adultery and inner satanic traits. Maybe his family knew him to the same? i, do not know. i, only know from i, own personal experiences.

Betrayal Started Its Engine Long B-4
It was the October/November months of the year 2006, that robin made up lies unforgivable to cover up not only for ass-wipe but for herself as well. i, thought as she told i, to leave, go and heal yourself on the East Coast, that she knew i, truly believed that ass-wipe was going to keep up to his end of the indenture and that she cared about i, and wanted i, to be safe and get well.

Robin knew how i, changed since that 2001 accident with all of the physical, mental, emotional and spiritual transformations that occurred.

i, could not stay away any longer because i, was continuously being lied to by all of ass-wipe's family and robin. i, made a pact with i, self to return to California and deal with whatever, i, need to deal with as to i, responsibility as the new land holder.

Once i, flew back to Los Angeles, i, immediately had gone straight to robin's home at 27508 Sycamore Creek Drive, Santa Clarita California [91355-9998]. i, knocked on the door. No one answered. i, had gone around the back, and banged on the wall and window. No one answered. i, called and called and robin refused to answer.

Finally, hours later, i, got robin to open up the door. Robin new i, had nowhere to stay. Robin tried to tell i, that i, could not stay at her house, even though it was really i, home. At that point, robin still had possession of it. Here i, am the man who saved the home from foreclosure, and was being lied to repeatedly by everyone around this scene, and i, was not allowed to stay at the home i, paid for?

Then, i, was treated as if i, was not their friend. Ass-wipe and robin both started to treat i, as if, they never knew i. This was i, best friend and she begun to treat i, this way. i, knew something was really wrong. Once, i, was able to get robin by herself without ass-wipe around, which was not too difficult because ass-wipe was spending most of his time at i, newfound business: Dangling Carrot Creative
[http://www.Danglingcarrotcreative.com or scott1@danglingcarrotcreative.com]

Recall, he used i, funds that he misappropriated from the lies and deceit ass-wipe conjured up to get i, to save their home. Ass-wipe continued making with his new life with his cocaine whore, as robin called she. His new and current wife. Robin told i, that i, could not stay at the house with she even though ass-wipe was with his new gal sometimes in Georgia and sometimes at Santa Clarita. i, could not fathom what was going on, and soon realized i, was truly duped.

It came down to i, giving ass-wipe ultimatums; he was to pay i, all the back moneys owed, and give i, all the difference of the two years which was approximately $43,000.00 and ass-wipe was still supposed to buy the house back at the end of two years being April to June 2008.

Ass-wipe told i, to get out of his house, as he tried to kick i, out of i, house even though they had possession. It was around the same time, robin told i, that i, cannot stay with she at all ever in the house and if, i, was going to press the issue of receiving payment for ass-wipe's indenture, that she would move out to another house. This was devastating news to i, heart because i, best friend was no more.

The Search For Honest Attorn'ey, Yah Right!

i, begun to search for attorn'eys and paralegals to do an Unlawful Detainer because i, was forced to throw out i, friend from the house. Now granted, i, knew absolutely nothing about law, L.A.W. or legal, statutes, codes, rules, regulations. Nothing about how the court systems operate; other than ~~whatever a judge says is the law~~!

i, actually thought like everyone else do about the courts. What i, believed (past tense) is that the courts where run by people where one goes to get their disputes adjudicated. i, thought a ~~judge~~ was the court, and whatever the ~~judge~~ says is the final decision. i, thought that i, did not need an attorn'ey and had a right to be heard on i, own. i, thought that if i, lost at the courts, i, lost forever.

i, did not know about any appeals, nor about discovery, Motions, Subpoenas, Summons, Complaints, or Claims. i, truly did not know anything about the courts, only what i, seen on tell-us-lies-vision shows.

However, i, did what i, could to stand in honor and to hold niner's to it as well. So i, gave robin and ass-wipe more time, pleaded with ass-wipe's father ronald, his brother james/jim, and talked to matt, ass-wipe's best friend and others at CGS to find out why ass-wipe was not fulfilling his word.

i, asked everyone why is ass-wipe doing this to i, and everyone begun to treat i, as if i, was a bad guy, or that they did not want to get involved. It was obvious that everyone already knows how ass-wipe is as each of them have dealt with ass-wipe for years.

Although, ronald niner kept telling i, that ass-wipe would pay i, yet, neither ronald, jim, nor his best friend matt were willing to loan ass-wipe any money to pay i, just like no one was willing to assist ass-wipe to create his patents, nor to save their home from foreclosure. Why would they, ass-wipe had i, as a disabled fool and gave all i, trust and faith with hope to i, best friend and husband ass-wipe.

i, did all i, could and finally i, gave a letter to Ass-wipe called "a pay or quit" demand. This was when ass-wipe said: "GO F*** YOURSELF AND GET THE F*** OUT OF MY HOUSE." Right after that, ass-wipe walked over to robin's room, slightly kicked open the door and said "*ROBIN, I WANT A DIVORCE ...*" Some friend ass-wipe turned out to be that would never do anything to harm robin?

i, can comprehend why i, was taken advantage of, but it seemed that ass-wipe was wrecking many lives all because of ass-wipe's self-centered, lying irresponsible and selfish ways. His lies to i, about saving their home from foreclosure. 2. Lies about not harming his ex-wife from causing the woman who allegedly had cancer. 3. Lies from his new divorce notice in the moment of anger. Some character this ass-wipe has hah? Cheating on his wife with a cocaine-whore as it was stated: oh, se la vie;

Unlawful Detainer To File

There was nothing i, could do at this point, as i, knew that i, was going to have to take ass-wipe to court. So, i, had gone to talk with i, best friend. Robin was not very receiving of i, and actually told i, that she would not tell the truth about what happened and begun to claim that she did not know anything about the indenture between ass-wipe and i.

She begun to claim that she was never in any rooms whereby ass-wipe and i, made the agreement that i, would not have to pay for one thing and that they ass-wipe and robin would buy back the house after two years and pay everything for two years up front; robin begun to lie to protect ass-wipe.

Why? i, could not fathom? It was at this point that i, really knew that robin was not going to be a willing witness, nor honest. Therefore, i, gave a last ultimatum that i, would have to file against she and ass-wipe because they were both in possession of the house, they were married still; this is what i, was instructed to do by a lawyer, not an attorn'ey.

Betrayal Feels Worse Than Death Appears

i, recall feeling sick to i, stomach as if i, was going to throw up when robin told i, that she was going to move out. i, felt as if, i, had just lost everything but even worst, i, could not believe that i, best friend through away all of the years, of friendship for ass-wipe who had committed adultery on she and all of the trouble ass-wipe caused. It truly was as if someone just died. All i, could think of doing is walk away and go into another room.

However, it really set into i, bones when, a couple of weeks had gone by and robin and ass-wipe had already been moving things out of the house and the master bedroom was empty. Robin still had Tazman the dog. His name was actually Taz which is short for Tasmanian Devil. And he was just that.

i, loved tazman as it was i, who brought him into all of our lives. i, did not know what to say, or do. i, walked over and walked tazman into the empty master bedroom to say goodbye to him. It was then i, was overwhelmed by emotion.

i, crouched down into the corner of the room, where i, begun to leak tears down i, face. i, gut begun to tighten up and i, entire body began to shake. i, did not know if i, was having a stroke, heart attack or what was happening. As i, stayed crouched down i, grabbed i, hands around i, shins all the way to the ground and i, felt like long knives stabbing in i, stomach and then i, begun to profusely leak streams of water like a rushing river to where i, could not see out of i, eyes.

Tazman walked over to i, and begun to lick i, face and try to give i, comfort even though tazman was slightly Psycho dog in his brain, he knew i, was not doing well. At that point robin and ass-wipe without telling i, had left the house together. i, and Tazman were left in the half empty house, which was an eerie feeling.

It was not as much as it was empty, it was more that i, was feeling empty, betrayed and not by ass-wipe because i, have always known he was a deadbeat. It was more that i, had been betrayed by i, own friend. Of all wo/mankind on this planet, i, thought she was the one friend that would never betray and never cause i, harm.

Time To Get A Lawful Degree

There was a lot i, did not know about lawsuits, Superior Courts, Federal Courts, Attorn'eys, ~~Judges~~, nor the political arena. i, truly did not know anything about much other than street life, drugs, how to fight, to bust i, ass doing labour.

In wanton, i, knew how to survive because i, did not receive any formal education, by only reaching barely the sixth grade. Back in the day, the only reason i, actually reach the sixth grade was by i, age transfer and not by being academically inclined.

Forgiveness, Not Easy Is Necessary & Proper

On or about February 2007, i, finally was forced to file an action at law against robin and scott allan niner: action Borsotti V. Niner, court # PC04224, at the Superior Court of California Chatsworth Courthouse, which i, did just that.

It was not easy, and i, dealt with a lot of roller coaster emotions dealing with robin, however, i, did not have any problem filing against scott ass-wipe niner.

Reader, enjoy i, road to search for justice, honor and integrity from the courts. A ride long and difficult, yet one i, would not ever change or wonder if i, should have turned back, as i, have received the greatest gift between 2007 through 2025.

This journey has brought i, closer to God, closer to comprehension of life, knowing what is right and wrong, knowing how to summon up the strengths and courage in order to allow the past to heal and then when the time is correct, be in the past.

i, learned recently and only after i, have been writing this *living missive*, when i, ask for forgiveness from any bitterness towards others, still sourness do rise towards others. Whether it is family dealings or with govern mentals or whatever i, am doing, i, remind i, self not to forget that we are all brothers and sisters and that each of us is loved by God equally. As much as i, feel that god loves i, too, i, still must learn to forgive and will once this *living missive* is final.

i, state as true fact, that i, offer a healing as forgiveness to all evil-wrongdoers herein and to date i, have not received a response or claim from any of the evil-wrongdoers.

i, state that i, have not conveyed any interest rights, titles nor have i, received compensation by way of property to i, land commonly known at 27508 Sycamore Creek Drive Santa Clarita California "Rancho Santa Clarita." For this i, applaud i, self for never giving up, for believing in i, self and for i, keeping i, integrity from start to date, once i, do expose what is true to the world.

Readers use the following lines for your notes and questions for author: ____

____

____

____

____

____

____

____

Chapter 2, II, Two

L.A.W. OF WO/MAN V. PUBIC SERPENT, R.I.C.O. & CORPORATE CORRUPTION

This is i, journey. Continue to sit back and enjoy as i, continue to expose those who do cause harm by way of trespass. A trespass a most egregious form of crime. Those wo/mankind that act as pubic serpents; some are old friends and family that do know for what they do and they continue to do it anyways. For a minimum i, pray for a healing by, not by them asking i, for forgiveness; therefore, i, must continue to expose otherwise all pain is lost to Satan's' minions. Healing is said to be received through mercy and that of god's grace.

L.A.W. Land Air and Water, is the law of wo/mankind within the universe which has been proffered to all mankind by god. In contrast to this L.A.W., the l.e.g.a.l. system is not very difficult to comprehend, however, it is said that law is equal to, if not more complex, that brain surgery. In reality it is the l.e.g.a.l. that is equal to brain surgery, as it is not always easy to follow compared to L.A.W. which is simplicity.

The reason l.e.g.a.l. is not easy to follow or even apply is because each woman or mankind has to govern themselves according to the fairy tale fiction. It sounds easy, but in reality to govern oneself, each (woman or man kind) wo/mankind, must be aware consciously to laws of God first, the laws of the Land, Air and Water, the laws of gravity, inertia, and even hydraulics. Yet, each law is similarly and different, each holds to and under god's laws first that precede all l.e.g.a.l. .

The laws of all courts start and end with god which are the most fundamental laws to know because in order to apply god's laws wo/mankind must see, hear, feel, touch, taste and smell all laws of god. When i, or you, as a part of wo/mankind are aware of what is moral and ethical, what it is to be in honor verse vile, what is true and not true, heightens insight of the legal system of courts which is a no brainer.

However, the State govern mental's believe statutes and codes are laws of the State. And they are not unless you are a citizen, resident or contracted away all of your inherent rights. Actually when i, as a man implement god's laws it feels right because it is what is right. This, not to say, many pubic serpent especially serpent who act as attorn'ey and [~~judge~~]s constantly try to justify within their own minds, without souls, to achieve their own objective. What is true is true through and through. There is no justifying what is not true. It puts an end of having had to decide the facts and evidence as anything but what is true.

To achieve the level of god's law, this all-knowing law, wo/mankind must be consciously aware of their actions on many levels, such as thoughts, word-speech, actions and reactions. To instill this all knowing law is not difficult to those who are aware of certain basic elements of communication between all wo/mankind, which is to govern one's own heart and soul.

To govern oneself, a wo/man must instill from within their heart and soul what is true, B-4 any law can be integrated N-2 one's body, mind and spirit. It is after this integration of what is true is consciously comprehended, thereafter, law will be transformed N-2 the soul to apply on an every-day awareness to govern. It is a process from senses into soul.

Pubic Serpent Do not Act In Honor
Once, the process of an administrative statute, code or regulation is achieved, whereby a wo/mankind has allowed an attorn'ey or a court actor to usurp the *open court of record*, only then will a wo/mankind need to regroup and change its process from the off course statutory world back to real law for wo/mankind.

The signs of courts running a stray, by the wo/mankind that act as [~~judge~~]'s, attorn'eys, pro-se-cuters, or court personnel is prevalent when actors refuse wo/mankind to move its *open court of record* forward. Being in dishonor is present when one pubic serpent will try to consciously get away from the L.A.W. by not applying laws of god and change to man's l.e.g.a.l. process which are inferior to god's laws. These traits wo/mankind possesses are instilled from centuries ago and for love of mankind. It is time to change the administrative fake l.e.g.a.l. statutory schemas back, B-4 any wo/mankind actually enter a court if entering one at all. It is a daily conscious awareness of how to and when to apply l.a.w. of reciprocity verses the l.e.g.a.l. satanic statutory world.

Statutory court is a game to take advantage of all wo/mankind's ignorance of law and legal process. Attorn'eys are great at thwarting what is true in order to achieve certain outcomes for theirs and benefit of their clients known as citizens. Because no wo/mankind will ever be allowed to present their self as their own counsel, the entire executive courts are not lawful in fact are completely against law.

The statutory game is one of monopoly. It is known best by pubic serpents, which are mostly made up of attorn'eys, pubic officials, and those secretive society driven mongrels whom would rather hide true knowledge from the public in order 2-B able to justify and control wo/mankind. These are manmade legal structures and subparts set to control non serpent whom have not taken an oath to the corporate gods called the States of… and United States of…. To take advantage of wo/mankind who do not have the wherewithal to know the difference between l.a.w. and l.e.g.a.l., that pubic serpent and their kind apply codes, statutes, court rules and regulation.

These corporate gods are known as fictions, agents, citizens, residents, individuals, persons, and defendants, named titles created by Roman Empire. How do i, know this last statement to be true. Just look at the judicial schema and how it operates. It is traced back to the Roman Empire. Also, Jesus was murdered by Romans, while the execution was directed by Jews. How much more corrupt today?

To Dis-cover Is To Unearth What Is New

Up to now, i, have expressed i, true stories and how bad the courts and govern mental actors are in contrast to wo/mankind. The following *living missive* will uncover more for the reader, as it is a transformation along a journey of reading which is no different than that of i, journey or any wo/mankind's life. It is through time, trials, triumphs, N-2 i, achievements do not coincide with average wo/mankind.

This *living missive* is intended not to hinder, discredit, to displace or exaggerate anything or to lesson any one wo/mankind's understanding or personal views. This *living missive* is to discover, unearth, in order to expose, within the kindest manner the writer can muster up, as a healing of life and to bring some old and renewed knowledge, experiences and so-called-wisdom attained to the general public.
To the evil-wrongdoers named herein, it is from the compassion of i, heart that i, share with the world what is true in this albeit unconventional writing.

Rather than be a judgmental or bureaucratic associated writing, to achieve what is true, this *living missive* continues to find healing, not just for daniel-adam-of the family borsotti, but all named here involved. i, know the wrongdoers listed herein will not like this *living missive* as a constructive knowledgeable writing, and so what if they do not, get over it, as i, will not take the red or blue pill.
It is for all involved to receive some healing because adam-daniel could not bear the guilt that he has carried all of these years. For those who have done wrong, for their own salvation, daniel releases the hounds of guilt, unto those who are named that need healing the most.

Once all evil-wrongdoers are named and exposed they are released back to take another crack at transforming their own lives. With hope all evil-wrongdoers will not continue down a desolate path for which each is a part of conspiring to suppress what is true, hide from god's laws, and find their own repentance.

Sometimes wo/mankind needs a little push of encouragement in an honorable direction to begin. All wo/mankind named herein have portrayed a part in society which has brought them and i, to where we are today. For the acts played, like on a stage, for those key components of life and to what is proper, it is released for all wo/mankind to receive as a *gift*, from a man as i, am, daniel – adam – of the family borsotti to adam daniels for this living missive.

A gift from one of god's beloved servants, a care taker of this great mother earth, and always ever-adjusting, recipient of life's trials and triumphs as a servant. It is the one true god almighty for which i, have the gift 2-B compelled by karma, what i, reap i, sew. This gift of penitence is given to the entire world. When the entire world receives opportunity, as it is a fortune for the recipient of the process of realization to transform from their ego, greed, or hate N-2 their heart.

i, proffer this *living missive* to the lord of all lords, the king of all kings, Jesus Christ, Buddha, Joseph Smith, Hare Krishna, Mohammed, Jehovah, Mother Theresa, Princess Diana, Martin Luther King Junior, and all of the thousands of saints who were named and recognized. i, proffer to all the saints, that of i, recognition who have been recognized by God and not mainstream Lord of any State in and of our world in time in memorial.

Hidden No Names Saints

There are saints who act as mothers and fathers, uncles and aunts, brothers and sisters, friends and foe of those strangers known as wanderers. Wanderers who walk(ed) god's green earth and made a difference whether positive or negative in another wo/mankind's life; as in the father, son and wholly spirit. We may not all be perfect only as perfect as god made us all in the image Yet, "they" say nobody is perfect, and i, am a nobody!

If anyone's feelings are not in harmony of what is written, you may contact the writer [~~Disabledjustice@yahoo.com~~], to share your views, to start a dialogue, or to file a claim against i, the writer for speaking out.

i, shall stand in honor from here to kingdom come. i, do encourage anyone who wishes 2-B able to move forward in life, each of us must fulfill our unfilled prophecies, in order to heal, mature, and embrace to receive gods rapture through his grace and the will is for all wo/mankind. It is in this time that you, evil-wrongdoer to get over what you have done. Because you cannot tell another wo/mankind what they feel, what they believe and by all facts presented, which are documented and undisputed to this day, to you the reader. i, the writer and almighty god know what is true herein.

So it is 2-B said, so it is 2-B written in annals herein on earth until kingdom come! i: a man; daniel- adam- borsotti.
Read on shall we?

Freed Mind is Freed Spirit & Fearful Mind is Fearful Spirit
The wo/mankind who make the attempt to handle their own court action, you, will find out very quickly, that the courts do not operate morally, ethically nor do the court actors follow any oath to any wo/mankind; the oath is only to their own kind.

When you readers move into the realm of a statutory court, you must go with a freed mind and spirit without any fear whatsoever. No fear of being held in contempt, or doing some jail time for standing up for what you know is true, honorable and forthright. Remember, a fearless heart with a wary soul, is God like soul.

The pubic serpent that act as [~~judge~~]s, attorn'eys, court clucks have their own kin, being other actors, such as: attorn'eys, [~~judge~~]'s, court employees, deputies, bank-sters, politicians and many others behind the scenes they protect. There are other pubic serpents that operate like physicians within their field. Regardless of any alleged oath taken or given, the oath is not to you or me as wo/mankind, nor is it to god, at least not any god i, have ever heard of, unless their god is Satanic.[81]

The oath to Satan is the same oath to the corp(s)orations, bankers, and Federal Reserve and all [~~judge~~]s as pubic serpent and

---

[81] Satan (n.):proper name of the supreme evil spirit and great adversary of humanity in Christianity, Old English *Satan*, from Late Latin Satan (in Vulgate in the Old Testament only), from Greek Satanas, from Hebrew *satan* "adversary, one who plots against another," from *satan* "to show enmity to, oppose, plot against," from root s-t-n "one who opposes, obstructs, or acts as an adversary." In the Septuagint usually translated N-2 Greek as diabolos "slanderer," literally "one who throws (something) across" the path of another (see devil (n.)), though epiboulos "plotter" is once used. https://www.etymonline.com/search?q=satan

attorn'eys, which is a society of their likeminded titles. As far as the institutions, it is not so much wo/mankind who work for the banks, courts, State and federal govern mental that are satanic, rather it is the wo/mankind who allow themselves to throw away their morals and ethics for the paycheck. It is for bonuses and all the perks in the name of the corporate banks, courts, and govern mentals and B.A.R. Associations wo/mankind fall short.

It always seems that wo/mankind at large, are always last ones that are treated with respect, dignity and ethically by govern mental serpent at the courts. When pubic serpent are put on the spot as to why they are taking i, or you, children, college tuitions, freedoms or wealth they have no answer except because they can. They do not care whether we saved years for a vacation or surgery for one of our children. It seems that pubic serpent do not care about anything but feeding the beast that they serve. When wo/mankind challenges the integrity of any pubic serpent, some serpent become combative, others i, have witness run away from sight as if they will melt when an honest light hits their skin when being tested by a wo/mankind.

It is pubic serpent who proffers excuses, "*I am only doing my job…*" when they know for what they do is wrong and going to harm another wo/mankind. Just like in times of war, going to court is a type of war. It is such as a war against all wo/mankind verses corporate agents whom work for govern mental agencies.

The Nuremburg trials uncovered, such ignorance. It seems that all pubic agents have taken as adopted a Nuremberg philosophy. "*i, am only doing my job or as "i, am only fulfilling orders…*" or "*i, do what i, do because it is in the name of the State or a word called justice, democracy, or the UNITED STATES*".

This excuse did not fly then and it will never fly today or in any future. Do not 4-get, god reigns with a spirit of god within each and every wo/mankind who liberates their heart and soul through their mind, body and spirit without fear.

First, all wo/mankind need to be aware B-4 anything can change. However, Doctor Wayne Dyer stated: "*When we change the way we look at things, the way we look at things changes*." To follow law of god must supersede the statutory schema.

Where did those morals and ethics that were instilled N-2 the moral thread of society go from years ago? The days when, a woman or man could give a handshake and be trusted on their word alone?

The days when the Ten Commandments or the l.a.w. of the land was trustworthy unto itself as a trust? i, tell you, the morals and ethics did not go anywhere; they are still within each and every wo/mankind.

Yet, in most wo/mankind morals and ethics lay dormant, until they are awoken to what is true. i, hope to awaken yours, you do not need a catastrophe to happen. In turn, all pubic serpents will have to get back on the catch and ride train to comity as reciprocity.

A Memory From The Lane

i, remember a trust not so long ago, as it is how i, live i, life today, when i, stepped outside i, front door, or i, opened up i, car door, and walked up to another wo/mankind; i, knew what she or he truly meant when they said "good morning…" or have a great day…" and when a wo/mankind says "I mean what I say and I say what I mean." This truly was worth its weight of integrity.

When someone do say what they mean, followed by actions, it is agreed and acknowledged, it is consummated that one can contract and trust. The days of old are soon 2-B reincarnated N-2 the days of today and tomorrow. This will be the new norm of wo/mankind awaken to law of wo/mankind not govern mentals.

Is it bedrock or sand, one builds a life on? Remember the bible quotes states[82]: "*Anyone who listens to my teachings*….." however,

---

[82] **Matthew 7:24-27:** 24 "Anyone who listens to my teaching and follows it is wise, like a person who builds a house on solid rock. 25 Though the rain comes in torrents and the floodwaters rise and the winds beat against that house, it won't collapse because it is built on **bedrock**. 26 But anyone who hears my teaching and doesn't obey it is foolish, like a person who builds a house on sand. 27 When the rains and floods come and the winds beat against that house, it will collapse with a mighty crash."
https://search.yahoo.com/yhs/search?hspart=pty&hsimp=yhs-ext-ff_freetestnow&param1=20220527&param3=speedtest_%7EUS%7Eappfocus1%7E&param4

a lawful society is based on law and not l.e.g.a.l., where claims are solid backed by facts and evidence and to the point. Whereas a complaint [83] is just someone complaining about something she or he should have taken care of B-4 going to court.

With a statutory world, when in dishonor, one goes to court and asks Mommy/Daddy, as Misses/Mister [~~Judge~~] to decide who is right or wrong; Mommy or Daddy [~~judge~~] to tell little jimmy or mary to stop doing what they complain about when in dishonor. However, this is not the case with a claim.

A claim is backed by facts and evidence and other wo/mankind who do witness. The only time a claim comes B-4 a court is when one side dishonors the other and enforcement is needed. This last one is a moral society's way to handle issues of harm to a fellow wo/mankind. This previous process of a claim is honor, strips the need for a court of legal. This is not how the judiciary system is set up today.

Outside Of Court Is Where Honor Is!

It has long been decided that when any issue arise, we should first go to our subject of the issue. This concept to communication, i, think, is what all wo/mankind comprehend. Go to your brother or sister when you have issue with they and work it out. And if or when you cannot work the issue out cordially, bring two or three wo/mankind to witness said issue and what remedy one proffer to resolve any controversy that may arise. This is simple, all biblical; it is not any new concept.

=%7Efirefox%7E%7E&type=yhs-ext-ff_freetestnow_appfocus1_ff&grd=1&p=bible+statement+%22...bedrock+on+sand+

[83] **COMPLAINT**: complaint (n.):late 14c., "lamentation, expression of grief," also "grief, sorrow, anguish" itself; also "expression of dissatisfaction or disapproval; statement of grievances, formal accusation; a plaintive poem," from Old French complainte (12c.) "*complaint*, lament," noun use of fem. past participle of complaindre "to lament" (see complain). Meaning "that which is complained of" is from 1745; specific meaning "bodily ailment, cause of pain or uneasiness" is from 1705 (often in U.S. colloquial use generalized as complaints)." https://www.etymonline.com/search?q=COMPLAINT"

Where the decorum of a courtroom was (past tense) in past is a place that people go when they used up all their other moral and ethical options privately and administratively and only when no resolution could be received outside the courts? The laws that governed society were set by lady justice, Juris prudence, the law of reciprocity, comity that can never leave the average wo/mankind.

On the American soil, titles are down on the bottom of the totem pole. A defendant, plaintiff or other title, takes over once any wo/mankind enter a courtroom. Yet the ~~judge~~ pubic serpent is not the court of law for wo/mankind, only for those who do not know. Since, the 1990's, it seems like when any wo/mankind go N-2 a court setting, they are scared, even when they themselves have not done wrong.

People have begun to fear the court pubic serpent that ACTS like court officers. The fear, to a point that people would rather place their own power outside of them, and give their power over to another woman or mankind, who acts as an attorn'ey, rather to take control of their own lives. This leaves wo/mankind at a loss of all rite and rights of law.

In reality, few people say wo/man get what is deserved by lacking knowledge. It is true the systems that have sprung up all over the states united operate more like revolving money laundering banks, instead of a place to receive compensation for a level of remedy for a harm that is caused to a wo/man by another wo/mankind, pubic serpent or agents. Think there is no such thing as fictions.

What you readers will learn herein is that you have all the power to handle your own affairs from your heart to your brain, from your toes through your lips.

When wo/mankind gives up their power, they become an indigent, an infant and an idiot in the eyes of the wo/mankind who act as [~~judge~~]s, court clucks, or other perceived court officers, especially magistrates that do witness facts and evidence. There are a few fine line, we must ponder B-4 court. It is not so difficult.

What is a court?
i, a man; will give i, interpretation of what i, learned and know from experience of what a court is and quote others' ideas and add them herein for benefit of readers.

A court is a place where games are played, whereby there are referees, some basic rules, and guidelines to be enforced by deputies with guns. The perceived authority which is delegated from court clucks, to a wo/mankind that act as an official, magistrate or [~~judge~~]. In wanton, a court is a stage for which actors put on a show.

Although, i, always invoke an *Open Court of Record* as i, court whenever i, have gone to apply the law. i, found out very fast, that the courts do not operate lawfully by an *open court of record*. However, the court actors do operate like surgeons that operate on wo/mankind who do not know any better of law. It is under Colour of law that is inferior to an open court of record. See 1215.org for definitions. [84]

What Is An Actor?
An actor is an entertainer and all they do is perform. Although many people do act and portray them as something they are not, in real life or on the big movie screen, down at the box office and on tell-us-lies-vision and call themselves stars.

A huge problem within society is that members of the public live inside their phones, computers, play stations, and do not comprehend the magnitude of how far away from what is true, fiction and reality of life has transformed. Their logic, reason and common sense have strayed away from reality itself.

These disconnects between actors on the screen and the actors whom act as pubic serpent are no different as a fiction in the courts compared to on tell-us-lie-visions. Many wo/mankind are either dragged N-2 a jail or court by the pubic serpent or each volunteers by consent through F.E.A.R. or ignorance of the law. It is when pubic serpent makes an average wo/mankind feel fearful of what

[84] **COURT/COURT OF RECORD:**
https://www.1215.org/lawnotes/lawnotes/courtrec.htm

might happen if the wo/mankind do not follow orders given. What if this or that?

Each wo/mankind and child do succumb to the thought of threat of harm or the takings of one's freedoms, possessions, or god forbid levy their bank accounts. Most wo/mankind would rather sit in a jail cell than have their nest eggs, as in their labour taken away or placed in jeopardy of being levied by the same pubic serpent threats. The pubic serpent portrayed to serve and protect have become the pirates.

Most wo/mankind, not knowing anything but what they have been brainwashed to believe by teachers, peers, pay-rents, tell-us-lies-vision, as authority over their lives. Fiction-state, federal titles known as police officers, (not police men or wo/mankind) ~~judges~~, ~~attorn'eys~~, ~~politicians~~, ~~IRS~~, ~~FBI~~, ~~CIA~~ or even ~~dog catchers~~, as agents who masquerade around as pubic serpent with titles to control narratives whereby loss of all rights incur.

Nothing can prepare a wo/mankind for what is revealed while litigating one's own court action especially with no training. Without a quick lawful course in law, or even the basics B-4 entering this realm of the judiciary system, most wo/mankind will lose. Law is not rocket science. Readers need to do some internal brain surgery on self-realization that anyone can apply law. Law verse legal is knowledge pubic agents don't want you to know.

Tell-Us-Lies-Vision Is Not What Is True

A huge problem is that tell-us-lies-vision, the big screen theatre has done a great disservice to wo/mankind on one hand and a great benefit to those who perform as pubic serpent at the courts; govern mental's and corp(s)orations' sole purpose is to control. On the other hand, even words have been changed to disparage the average wo/mankind. Words mean things. Know the lingo and win the war against you.

Although there are multiple meanings of certain words from the English and many other dictionaries, thesaurus and etymology, as well, there are multiple authors of words by definitions, as there is no different from within this *living missive.* i, the author have i, own language similar to the courts compared to what the average wo/mankind learn from public schools or on the streets. The key is to follow god's laws and not manmade l.e.g.a.l. false system, by never wavering into the matrix.

What is great for this *living missive* is that i, daniel-adam- or adam-daniel of the family borsotti have not created a personal vocabulary just like the united states, and state govern mentals have. i, apply factual law for all wo/mankind from god.

It must be construed for this *living missive* outside of the mainstream vernacular, or out on the streets, that the words used herein are not the same as used on the streets, and is no different than the l.e.g.a.l. jargon that is used against the wo/mankind by govern mentals especially at the courts across America.

The difference is with govern mentals, especially courts that use excuse or word magic to suppress, control, and take advantage of the less informed, unintelligible, low educated, or with some type of disability; the unknowing wo/mankind to suppress the wo/mankind's comprehension while at the court's bailiwick.[85] The difference between this *living missive's* definitions is the reaction, for which is meant to receive and achieve from the writer to the reader, and even the named evil-wrongdoers herein. It is for i, to heal from the wrongs committed against the man: daniel-adam- of the family borsotti. i, do accept all responsibilities for such creation of words only for this *living missive* as it is for i, healing only and to expose the evil-wrongdoers for which they do commit as trespass.

Ignorance Of The Law Is The Excuse

It is also not ignorance of the law for each wo/mankind that walk N-2 a court proceeding to honestly answer or interact with court personnel while being moral, ethical, and honest all awhile the court

---

[85] **BAILIWICK**: 1. one's sphere of operations or particular area of interest: "you never give the presentations—that's my bailiwick"
2. the district or jurisdiction of a bailie or bailiff: "the warden had the right to arrest all poachers found within his bailiwick"

personnel are knowingly, with mal intent, using the lack of comprehension of certain l.e.g.a.l. jargon to steal your rites/rights away. It is their definitions by not giving full disclosure. Rather than just call it ignorance of the l.a.w. their word magic is not l.a.w. It is l.e.g.a.l. and why i, write this *living missive* to expose these satanic minions for what they know they do.

First of all, there is no ignorance of the l.a.w. when there is no honor by the court actors. i, have not once, ever received any honorable, moral, ethical, or common decency from any of the court actors that portrays to play the role of pubic serpent concerning defining terms for i. When i, so required them to answer i, questions, not one, serpent as a matter of honor, when asked, shall define words to be defined and each flat out refuse to answer. Some have made record that they not only will not they cannot answer certain questions. It is they refuse to answer, leaving injustice to continue against wo/men.

The wo/mankind, actors at court, divert answering i, questions by asking a question to i, demand for certainty for the proper terms be defined. The Actors have little to zero court etiquette or in other words, the actors apply word magic, threats against the wo/mankind and call it moral, ethical or a lawful court proceeding. In reality, the pubic serpent tell, i, they say "*I cannot give legal advice.*" i, never ask for anything of the sort. There are certain things that need clarification and pubic serpent refuse to engage honorably to answer i, questions.

The terms are <u>required</u>, as i, do not ever require actors to give any guidance of law. Because l.e.g.a.l. advice is not l.a.w., therefore, i, never require it. However, the actors still move forward as if, i, comprehend what foreign language they speak like playing an old record player backwards. What the f.u.k.c.[86], do they, as in the pubic serpents, think they are playing by not answering i, lawful questions? No wo/mankind can comprehend what the backwards record is saying unless they are on LSD, Mushrooms or Peyote. Even then, words are not going to mean the same what they know it to be at executive courts. Sometimes if not always, i, wonder if all

[86]**FUKC**: Forever Under Kangaroo Court

court personnel are all ingesting LSD, Mushrooms, Marijuana, or Peyote Buttons by the way they act against i, you and true l.a.w.

Bait & Switch Monopoly

The court actors of today run a bait and switch game of monopoly and the average wo/mankind haven't a clue as it was designed this way since B-4 Abraham Lincoln was the man who do act as president of the United States of America. Of course most wo/mankind knows what monopoly means and for those who do not, monopoly means: a type of cartel that dominates all narrative by controlling the game. Therefore, when a court actor asks one thing that the average wo/mankind thinks they know the meaning, in reality, it actually means something totally different. For instance, (understand)-ing is a certain impression or statement or even terminology, that actually does not mean that: "i, understand what you are saying or mean…" at all. There is bait like a fishing line with a hook. The participant gets hooked into their word game, once the answer is "yes i, understand…" and then without notice, the court actor switches the meaning to actually mean understand as to stand under their authority.

A similar example is when the court actor asks for the name of the wo/mankind that stands at the court such as "The state of California verses Adam Daniels. "Are you Adam Daniels…"? (There are many replies i, will give later), but the issue here is that the actor is trying to get consent that the wo/mankind that stands at the court, at that moment is the citizen, resident, driver's licenses recipient, or title under their jurisdiction in order to continue the court action.

To operate by the auspice of actually knowing how to reply between you and court actors as the wo/mankind, is to know how to handle one's self within the confinements of any given institution for which wo/mankind find themselves "at." It is not "in" whereby a govern mental agent is trying to get jurisdiction over the wo/mankind. Where disconnect begins and where it ends is why i, a man have gone to great lengths to take all of i, experiences, to benefit the greater of the wo/mankind at i, own expense and time. i, make it i, life's journey to share with the world, what gifts i, do receive from those named as evil-wrongdoers herein.

It is the govern mentals fault, so blame the evil-wrongdoers named herein for this *living missive* and for the knowledge i, do share with the wo/mankind that do read this *living missive.* The problem is that all court actors do not allow or once, they know that you know their monopoly game; they either play the hold you for last, so no one can hear you, or will not allow you at their court at all game.

Full Disclosure What is That?

Unless each wo/mankind has been given full disclosure from the onset, prior to going to the court, i, would write questions to require the actors to define by definitions and offer a list of words so that both the evil-wrongdoer and the wo/mankind that stand on honor know how to interact.

Otherwise, it is a one sided game of integrated process whereby only one side has the advantage and actually knows all the definitions and with nothing to reply or defend one's self which is where the courts and govern mentals have already gone. They always hate when i, am at their bailiwicks as i, do not give into their sadistic dishonorable hobby.

In this previous instance all wo/mankind that walk on to a court ship (which i, would not voluntarily succumb to that invitation or threat) to allow self to be forced by invitation to any govern mentals parties (which is always by summons) is like being invited to a barbeque and you are the main course. Just bring the BB-Q ketchup, A-1 sauce, unless vegan (Beyond Meat) as you will be the main course.

From the actors of the courts, there is no full disclosure, thereby causing a one sided court proceeding. Each time i, do and did enter courts, i, never received the answers to i, questions with any trueness. The court actors whom have not and will never answer any of i, questions, continue to move forward as if it is just another day at the office. These court actors are f.u.k.c.-ing s.l.u.t.-s that are c.l.i.t.-s by getting you or i, to agree that you and or i, am one of their slaves by title.

The statement "*ignorance of the law…*" can never apply from a statutory schemed court, when it is the court actors who are supposed to operate by the law for wo/mankind. There business model is that of a statutory world, not a world of law. It is an immoral crew of serpent as agents that are a group of women/men that act as serpent-agents for corp(s)rations. i, do expose them all for what they do.

This type of fraud can only be construed as a criminal gang that is operating, like a group of surgeons, on wo/mankind who are ignorant. The court surgeons do not care towards those who expose them either for what they know they do maliciously. (more on this later…) the arrogance is beyond anything on this earth. In reality it can only be found in a fictional theatre.

The theatre is that the title gets the wo/men to acquiesce into their realm as venue and it is just another day of trickery, deceit, by consent of the governed; you the unwittingly wo/man period.

i, a man: daniel- of family borsotti do state as true, i, did not know the difference of the meaning between law v. legal, man v. person, citizen, individual, hue-man, pro se, pro per, re-present or to present, claim v. complaint and many other words that need to be defined B-4 i, ever walk back on to a court of any form of public monopoly. From i, experiences there is no court of L.A.W. or agents left.

This image is compared to a man being present verses a man that appears (like Casper the friendly ghost), as being whole verses the cut umbilical cable and an entire host of other definitions that encompass i, journey through the Wizard of Oz, Alice and Wonderland, Matrix-Court systems.

Therefore, as this *living missive* unfolds, i, terminology skills changed from 2001 to 2025. i, also have heightened i, knowledge and ability to control courts, instead of courts running all over i. You do not act as a person, citizen, resident, individual, employee, or self-employed, Plaintiff or Defendant unless you knowingly contract into their realm.

We can knowingly, but it needs to be knowingly by full disclosure. It is a scam upon wo/mankind by the court actors that knowingly do not give you full disclosure even when they use the terms… “ *I cannot give legal advice…*”, but they can apply the law correctly.

Do not accept statements by the actors… “*i, cannot give legal advice.* ” Apply your law correctly. We do not ask for l.e.g.a.l. only require what is true of the law; (Read on will you):

It is the wo/man who is the author–ity over one’s own life,
It was the days from B-4 Jesus that keep us from strife.

It is the land that is free for our home of thee who is brave,
As wo/mankind traveled long trails since days of the cave.

And govern mentals have no author-ity, to those who do not waver,
And stand tall in honor do need not to beg, borrow or slaver.

Join what is true and instill hope, faith in our only one lord,
As we sever the ties of the wholeness to the umbilical cord.

As i, am present and whole from fertilization to i, last breadth,
It is not that in life rather what is accord, in what is i, death.
As man from day one, to - day seven then rest, this is i, bequest.

By: i: a man; Adam .

Come join the rollercoaster rides between i, resolve to apply morals, ethics and honor, verses pubic serpent, lies and deceit, theft, extortion, conversion, barratry, champerty and vexatious progression.

Any wo/mankind recipient on the wrong side of the l.e.g.a.l. instead of on the right side of the l.a.w. will certainly feel the wrath of the colour of the l.e.g.a.l. which is not dejure.

It is supposed to be by the people for the people unless people speak about are the govern mentals’ people who operate by surgical instruments called statutes, codes, and regulations, dishonor, unethical, amoral acts of devilment. i, journey has yet to start!

SATAN'S NO.1, TRONE CHATSWORTH COURTHOUSE
<u>CRIMINAL GANGS</u> OF 2007 – 2025

9425 Penfield Avenue, Chatsworth California. [91311]

Owned and Operated By Satan's minions

&

Satan's Minions For The Saga Of
Scott Allan Niner's <u>Criminal Gang</u>

The Clucks at this court also have cause a great deal of trespass against the man, adam – daniel of the borsotti family.

It is by their demise that i, do uncover to discover what malicious acts by:

Osana, Maria, Renee, Mary, Carter, Henderson, Chebishyan, Salmaron, Claussen and many others over the years and it is within this *living missive* i, do expose them herein for life as a perpetual memorial.

SATAN'S 1ST MINION, (<u>B.I.T.C.H</u>.- MLO[87]) <u>CRIMINAL GANG</u>
OF 2007 – 2025

(Scott Alan & Robin Niner Criminal Gang)

Superior Court Chatsworth Calif. Case # PC04224 - 2007
Margaret Lynn Oldendorf BAR # **116069**

Margaret Lynn Oldendorf
Satan's 1st Minion
[Pubic Serpent]
(B.I.T.C.H.-MLO)

Superior Court Chatsworth California
Borsotti V. Niners PC040224 – 2007 through 2009
Margaret Lynn Oldendorf The Woman who act as judge

i, find this woman Margaret Lynn Oldendorf, hereinafter, "The B.I.T.C.H.[ibid f.n.60] MLO" the tip and the epitome of the iceberg of all other wo/mankind that do act as ~~judges~~, court witness, or magistrates to be as dirty as all the rest of the [~~judge~~] named evil-wrongdoers herein. Each wo/mankind that do take on rolls is truly no more than a pubic serpent that do act are……. (place title here)

[87] B.I.T.C.H.: <u>Barraters</u> Inside The Court House: early 15c., "sale of ecclesiastical or state offices," from Old French baraterie "deceit, guile, trickery," from barat "malpractice, fraud, deceit, trickery," ... "In marine law, "wrongful conduct by a ship's crew or officer, resulting in loss to owners," it is attested from 1620s. The meaning "offense of habitually starting legal suits" is from 1640s. The sense of the word has been somewhat confused with that of Middle English baratri "combat, fighting" or Spanish baratear "to cheat, deceive," https://www.etymonline.com/search?q=barrater

and are duty bound by gods laws towards all mankind. To justify anything less than what is moral and ethical is beyond the scope and duty to wo/mankind's trust. This serpent can only be one of satan's minions that has not sworn a correct oath to the wo/mankind known by the name "people of… ***Place your enclave herein***".

Even though i, court action first begun with a public servant, Barbara M. Scheper, who continuously denied everything, i, had filed. It was from the original complaint, the Default Judgment, statement of damages, case management statement, Forcing a First Amendment Complaint and Demurrer was found in the Niner's favor. In reality, it was in favor to an attorn'ey Joseph Ramin Kerrendian hereinafter "Top-Ramin" who niner's hired as almost all ~~judges~~ find towards the litigant who has an attorn'ey.[88]

Then about ten months of games had gone by and then the action was transferred to Margaret Lynn Oldendorf (Bitch-MLO). Therefore, i, shall give the B.I.T.C.H. Barbara M. Scheper a break and leave she out of this *living missive* for the most part only to say, i, filed everything correctly, gave proof of service, and yet i, was denied the default judgment against robin and ass-wipe niner anyways. i, could see it coming after the first denial.

After the fact, i, l.e.g.a.l. team expressed that almost all courts will give either side an opportunity to defend a court action regardless of whether a default is proper or not. It doesn't mean a default will not order, as it is the way court actors operate.

Although, in order 2-B an actor, these pubic serpents, not just like those actors on a stage or big screen at the box office, rather these serpent are wo/mankind whom are supposed to take an oath to do no harm to their fellow wo/man or country. Most importantly, court serpents are supposed to not be bias towards any one side.

Transfer Was Imminent And Do Issue

As stated, after a few months, the court action was transferred to this b.i.t.c.h.-mlo who, in i, outlook had taken advantage, lied and mocked i, daniel – Adam of the family Borsotti who was medically

[88] **STATISTICS OF ATTORNEYS WINS VERSES NON-ATTORNEY WINS**

determined disabled. In addition, b.i.t.c.h.-mlo was therefore, required to apply federal laws pertaining to Americans with Disability Act and Amendments Acts. Why has any protection for wo/mankind interest or estate? And not to the state or to a private unethical man that had hired attorn'eys that are dishonest. (i, shall explain what makes attorn'eys corrupt later), as if you do not know.

The three attorn'eys were not just doing their job, in a way like honest wo/mankind that would make a mistake unknowingly. Corruption, because the court system is corrupt and it is a B.A.R. Association [~~judges~~,] who encourage attorn'eys to lie, commit perjury, cheat and steal in the name of an oath to the B.A.R. Association. Pubic serpent! Attorn'ey = a license to lie; and lie they do at will. The perjury rule or ethics has long gone out the window. Of course it do make a difference when a wo/mankind might make a mistake and the letter of the l.e.g.a.l. will be applied without fail, but not against attorn'ers. Attorn'eys are licensed to tell all lies.

i, Thought Officers Were Bound To Honesty

i, thought as an attorn'ey by duty and oath, each was to not act, but actually be moral and ethical while re-presenting a court action for their clients. i, found out very quickly, what pubic serpent do is justify their means in the name of the corp(s)oration, in the name of their job, and in the name their clients ability to pay, and in the name of Satan. It is not an oath which each serpent is alleged to have fore taken to the people. The oath that a majority of all wo/mankind believes is an honorable oath is actually an oath to the B.A.R. However, the oath is not to all wo/mankind, just to whoever and whatever the attorn'ey decides to be loyal. It is a fact regardless of morals and ethics, attorn'eys are bound to whatever a court instructs of they to do regardless of right or wrong; this i, know to be true.

B.i.t.c.h.-mlo, the three attorn'eys Richard Thomas Miller, hereafter (Dick-em) , Top-ramin (top-ramin) and Thomas Wanner, hereinafter (Weiner-dog) all failed the duties under god's laws by playing court games that cause a trespass by way of harm against another mankind, to this very day 2025. As stated B-4, trespass has no statute ceiling, therefore they still do trespass against i, to 2-day.

Maybe that previous oath above is not the oath to god, instead a Hippocratic Oath received and given by medical practitioners or by pubic serpent to the STATE and COUNTRY Incorporated. No matter whether l.e.g.a.l. practitioners (attorn'ey or ~~judge~~) do have their own private oath, an oath to submit to the minions and not to people of each State, regardless of whether one takes on a title of citizen, resident, person, or said agent. When a wo/mankind hires one of these pubic serpents, the attorn'eys have signed on as an agent for wo/mankind. The duty above all else, is supposed to be to god, then wo/mankind who hired the attorn'ey (This oath is not what happens). The hierarchy of oath is to the B.A.R., the [~~judge~~], the State, themselves and lastly then to the client. God is not an issue for attorn'eys. This is why there is controversy between god and state, which is not church v. State.

It was not long after i, filed the original claim also known as (aka), [Complaint], as a normal process. i, filed the on point answer as to Proof of Service. A [Default] or by evasion from any reply culpability is by final [~~Judg~~ment] decree opposition to ass-wipe niner's Demurrer. Then a Motion for Request for Interrogatories and Special Interrogatories, Request for Production of Documents, which are always ongoing. Then i, do file Motions for Discovery. i, did not know other forms of law. i, had to learn on the fly…

i, was also denied an x-parte, Motion to Shorten Time to Compel Form and Special Interrogatories, Admissions, Supplemental Briefs, along with all Memorandum Points Authorities. i, did not file them i, self i, had a well-known and very experienced lawyer and paralegal who knows State and Federal juridical process. i, was beginning to feel that i, was never going to be able to receive any justice regardless of how good i, writers were doing. It did not matter that i, get a lawyer and paralegals to write for i, which i, did. No matter…, denied, denied, and again denied.

i, Recall The Subpoena Runaround

Then on or about October 2008, i, was forced to deal with ass-wipe niner's attorn'ey *land sharks* filing Motions to Quash i, Subpoenas Duces Tecum. As i, was moving Subpoenas and all of i, evidence to support the facts i, required for trial.

By this time, i, had already dealt with b.i.t.c.h.-mlo giving i, orders at 11:00 a.m. at the x-parte hearing to file and serve certain papers to ass-wipe niner's attorn'eys B-4 five (5:00) o'clock that same day. This seemed almost impossible and do place massive stress or bitch-mlo was going to deny i, x-parte concerning taking a deposition of robin and ass-wipe scott niner. Bitch-MLO gave i, 4 hours to serve.

After i, ran around like a chicken with no head to get everything written and filed down town Los Angeles which was a task in of itself dealing with afternoon traffic, i, mission was accomplished, fulfilled and caused massive stress on i. Then i, received a Motion to Quash the Subpoenas Duces Tecum which i, needed many papers to bring forth to prove all facts and evidence for i, court action at trial. i, recall to this very day, as i, memory is keen and i, shall never forget who did what to whom.

October 2008, i, had gone to the court and filled out all of the Subpoenas and brought them to the courthouse to have the court clucks stamp and sign them. B.i.t.c.h.-mlo's court assistant Cluck told i, that she does not sign the Subpoenas that i, had to go downstairs to the court cluck's window unlimited civil desk and that court cluck will sign and stamp the subpoenas duces tecum.

After walking downstairs, i, met with Osana (dark haired chunky woman) a known court cluck who has given i, a world of trouble. Osana always talked down to i, was short in demeanor, and rude by always telling i, lies, sending i, back and forth to the [~~judge~~]s clucks upstairs. She always made i, wait on average 40 minutes to several hours. That f.u.k.c.-ing Osana, she is w.h.o.r.e. to come back to instruct i, where to get papers signed i, required, or not allowing i, to review court docket folders.

This time was no different. Osana k.u.n.t. told i, that i, had to go back upstairs to get the [~~judge~~]s cluck to sign the subpoenas because she does not do them. i, had gone back and forth at least four times, telling each court cluck what the other said.

i, am certain the f.u.k.c.-ing clucks were getting a kick out of what they were doing, however, i, was through with the games and i, left without the subpoenas being signed nor stamped by the court clucks. Regardless because i, was told by that Bitch-mlo that the court must treat i, with the same respect as an attorn'ey and hold i, to the same honor and standard as an attorn'ey. This gave i, the author-ity and i, signed the subpoenas i-self. Not prejudice right?

After all i, am being held to the same standard as an attorn'ey. i, do file the subpoenas anyways and this is when ass-wipe niner's land shark top-ramin filed DEFENDANT'S NOTICE OF MOTION AND MOTION TO QUASH PLAINTIFF'S SUBPOENAS DUCES TECUM; ETC. Volume 1-5.

The hearing on motion came and Bitch-mlo asked the attorn'ey to speak first. Always the attorn'ey had gone first to talk even when i, was the moving party, which always shows bias as this is what all court actors do to a non attorn'er. Regardless i, was the man that filed claim (sometimes known in the statutory world as [plaintiff]) as the moving party, multiple times. i, was forced to speak last the majority of the times. They call it f.u.k.c. the pro se, or pro per in wanton, it means special bias as courtesy to all attorn'ers.

After, i, stepped up and expressed the runaround game, and required b.i.t.c.h.-mlo to sign the subpoenas and stamp them, bitch-mlo denied i, subpoenas and then told i, to go down stairs to the court clucks window on the first floor and get them signed. The same place i, already was hoodwinked by Osana over three times.

Bitch-mlo, knew what was going on, and she did not reprimand the court clucks, this should have been done in i, eyes; as in i, mind's-eye as i, demanded she do. The problem was that i, was denied those subpoenas, then bitch-mlo denied the corrected stamped subpoenas as untimely. It was too close to trial rendering the subpoenas invalid and i, did everything i, was instructed to do to receive the crucial information necessary for this court action, yet i, was denied over-and-again. A trespass to this very day still occurs.

Bitch-mlo, completely denied i, the right to ADA accommodations as well and all of the Motions to Compel Discovery, regardless of what i, reasons were. Then they played a switch and bait game by incorporating this short, chubby, balding man, who took on the title as [~~Judge~~] a man with a name of Melvin Douglas Sandvig hereinafter, (Richard-cranium).

Richard-cranium stepped in on a one time hearing to fill in for bitch-mlo in order that Richard-cranium could and did shut down i, rights to discovery without cause. Richard-cranium knew what it was doing to i, rights without a care, regardless of all despair denied, denied and again denied.

This was i, first encounter but not the last time i, would have run ins with melvin douglas sandvig the infamous richard-cranium. Richard-cranium not only refused a postponement of the hearing, he stepped all over i, disability rights, the right to a fair process, which i, required of Richard-cranium since Richard-cranium did not know anything about i, court action. This was a setup as you will review?

Yet, Richard-cranium knew enough to find in favor of the ass-wipe niner's attorn'ey, top-ramin.

> This is only one of the unethical things the pubic serpent do to all wo/mankind regardless of whether you have an attorn'ey or not. When they are given orders to shut your case down as fast as possible, especially, when they are playing the monopoly game, the amoral and unethical satanic ritual-games against a litigant they know is unknowing about all of the court corruptive process. They f.u.k.c. you.

Bring In Another[~~Judge~~] Pubic Serpent

Without knowing anything about the action, or i, disabilities, due to the filed MOTION TO RECONSIDER THE MOTION TO COMPEL DISCOVERY, Richard-cranium flat out denied the motion to reconsider the motion to compel discovery too that resulted in collapsing i, right to crucial discovery.

i, was forced to move the matter closer to trial without the crucial facts and evidence necessary to prove all that the scoundrel ass-wipe/scott alan niner and his then wife robin are thieves and liars.

Up to that point of the court action, i, was losing the opportunity to prove i, court action. Due to i, lack of knowing the statutory scheme, i, was at a disadvantage like a guppy in a pool of piranha. After bitch-mlo regained her presence within the court action, bitch-mlo moved the action N-2 the pre-trial faze forever closing the discovery for i, court action.

FYI: (So you readers look for this to happen if ever you are in your own court action where you handle your own case with/without a land shark attorn'ey). i, did not have an attorn'ey, however, i, was able to secure some writers of l.e.g.a.l. and not law papers who had over 30 years experience between them. It was not that i, papers were not well written, it is the deception by court actor's malice.

As i, had all the statutes, codes, court rules, regulations, case law, declarations, timeliness, and con-stitutional issues when necessary. Along with proof of services, everything that any l.e.g.a.l. scholar would write and do. It has taken i, years to learn variations between l.e.g.a.l. and true law. It was of no concern to shut i, down.

Although, these types of interactions with all of i, papers, continued no matter what i, had submitted on i, own behalf. No matter how much i, do object, which was very difficult for i, because i, did not know how or why to object in the beginning.

All i, knew is something did not seem right in Denmark by way of the legal writers expressing to i, what was in the papers, who should prevail, and what i, was working toward achieving for that stated hearings motion. i, was flat out denied every step of the way.

i, recall after i, returned to court from the previous motions hearing, that b.i.t.c.h.-mlo made a condescending comment about i, Buddhist practice. i, had made a reference to b.i.t.c.h.-mlo about i, do not fully comprehend the l.e.g.a.l. process and that i, am disabled, hard of hearing, dealing with the repercussions of a head injury, T.B.I., P.T.S.D., and multiple surgeries and more.

i, do continue that i, have been diagnosed with dyslexia and that i, had a right to subpoenas duces tecum and all of the discovery. i, also sight the written case law and rules of court to support all contentions of receiving discovery. i, recall that i, was denied when i, do reiterate the courts own words… b.i.t.c.h.-mlo expressed that "*…the court will have to hold you to the same standards as an attorn'ey…*"

i, was presenting i-self and that courts cannot give any special treatments, yet allows court clucks to deliberately do runaround games to suppress i, every attempt for a lawful juridical process! i, proceeded as if i, was able to do the same as an attorn'ey and is why after the court clucks played their games on i. i, signed the subpoenas just as an attorn'ey is authorized to do.

Yet, an attorn'ey can sign their own subpoenas, and sign their own papers, for their client, but, even when all court clucks Osana-k.u.n.t. and w.h.o.r.e. played games with i, it did not matter, everything i, required of the court was denied without any good cause to suppress.

So there truly is no camaraderie's with court actions other than an attorn'ey can say, lie and do whatever it wants. Although a wo/mankind who presents their own court action is being held to the same standards as an attorn'ey. No one who presents their own court action is ever treated with any respect as an attorn'ey.

Not being held to the same bullshit: honor, ethics, morals integrity and canons of law, because there is a double standard for i, and all wo/mankind that choose to present their own court actions. i, dealt with so many different types of runaround games, so many demands placed on i, by bitch-mlo, and its court clucks. i, felt like i, was in a movie, that was being scripted by pubic serpent actors reminding i, of, [Nightmare On Elm Street][89]. Instead it was Nightmare on the Chatsworth Courthouse-ship; 9425 Penfield Ave,. From the first motion filed throughout every paper, forward, i, was denied by that woman Barbara M. Scheper, all the court clucks and pubic serpents,

---

[89]**NIGHTMARE AT 9425 PENFIELD STREET**: is a 1984 American supernaturalslasher film written and directed by Wes Craven and produced by Robert Shaye. https://en.wikipedia.org/wiki/A_Nightmare_on_Elm_Street

that act as [~~judge~~] "b.i.t.c.h.-mlo" as in margaret lynn oldendorf and richard-cranium … Sandvig.

FYI: For the reader to learn who, what, why, where, when and how to do certain court actions, go to **1215.org** for all of your real history on LAW and how to handle your lawful court action according to common law and stop using state and federal statutory schema, which is executive l.e.g.a.l. process and not real LAW.

When you want to stand inside their matrix learn "Jurisdictionary"
https://www.howtowinincourt.com/coursebrochure.pdf
"Tell Hargraves i, sent you…"

Also, when you want to truly learn about the laws for mankind, go to Greg-Paul & Jon-Little at:

https://thesovereignsway.com/get-law-for-mankind-foundations/
or go directly to Jennifer Goodwin at:

https://jenniferhgoodwin.com/home;

1215.ORG is one hundred percent totally free: the other two (tell them all Adam Daniels sent you) you might receive a 10% discount. i, do not refer for rewards. If you receive any discount it is yours. The honest man sayeth to those who inspire against Satan's corrupted courts by pubic serpents, attorn'ers, [~~judge~~] and their like kind.

FYI: It is easier than you think when you have the correct lawful teachings. Please take notes, If you like: ____________________

SATAN'S 2ND MINION OF THE BITCH M.L.O. CHATSWORTH
CRIMINAL GANG OF 2007 – 2025

Superior Court Chatsworth Calif. Case # PC04224 -2009 Ramin Joseph Kerendian B.A.R. #186343

Joseph Ramin Kerendian
Satan's 2nd Minion
(Top-ramin)
Scott & Robin Niner's attorn'er
2007 through 2009

Attorn'ey joseph ramin kerendian (top-ramin) is your typical attorn'ey who ass-wipe scott alan niner hired to do one thing. To file everything he knew how in order to stop what is true from making on the record, and minimize the damages as much as possible. Top-ramin was not a very accomplished attorn'ey, at this point, that i, could find out doing research on his life. However, i, know that top-ramin, knows only two things; win at all costs regardless and to play the dishonest monopoly game.

Top-ramin, who is not famous until now, a man that acts as an attorn'ey, handled the ass-wipe niner case PC040224, filed February 2007, whereas a false judgment was rendered on 05/18/2009 by a pubic serpent that act [~~judge~~] for the Superior Court Chatsworth California. Not only was the original action originally mislabeled as a "Breach Rental/Lease" action when it was actually Breach of Contract, Fraud, Breach of Fiduciary Duty et al., whereby top-ramin did everything he was hired to do against a disabled man in favor of crooks, liars and thieves by the names of ass-wipe and robin niner… criminal gang.

Top-ramin acted as if he was litigating against a world renowned scholar of law or rather l.e.g.a.l. or someone who had more credentials than Gloria Allred, who is stated to stand for women and has the prestige over almost any other female attorn'ey. Allred brought cases against many high-profile men and celebrities including President Donald Trump, Bill Cosby, Roy Moore- while managing the media narrative which surrounded her clients in order to control the outcome for her cases.

Maybe top-ramin thought he was litigating against an attorn'ey such as Clarence Jones who played an important role not only for doctor martin luther king jr., for the civil rights movement as a whole.

Perhaps top-ramin thought he was litigating against the mind of sandra day o'connor, the First female justice to serve on the supreme court or the man with the heart of the lion, thurgood marshall, the attorn'ey and first african american supreme court justice who appeared to stand on morals and ethics only from within their own personal venue. Each 2-B judged in the end by god almighty only.

To leave those attorn'eys that came B-4 and to those attorn'eys who will come after top-ramin, each should never forget the history of international law without mentioning the 17th–century Dutch jurist, l.e.g.a.l. scholar, and philosopher Hugo Grotius who was an attorn'ey general, legal scholar and philosopher.

Top-ramin, is as far as i, know, only famous for assisting a thief and a liar of the likes of robin and ass-wipe scott alan niner, which i, am convinced that top-ramin has taken on many clients as the likes of niner's criminal gang. As a man, who follows a system of sleaze, such as the State and Federal govern mentals of today, corruption is what they eat for breakfast, lunch and maybe supper too.

Not a very rewarding achievement for an attorn'ey such as top-ramin, or maybe the more corrupt the attorn'eys are, the higher status this individual receives from its colleagues. As i, will say with certainty, top-ramin will never receive any awards from i, said the spider to the fly as he is eaten spiritually alive by god almighty along with all of the other attorn'ers that act from a satanic realm.

What Was The Achievement For?

i, always wonder to this day, what top-ramin felt like after he received his name on the list from ass-wipe scott allan niner's bankruptcy. By the actions of ass-wipes criminal gang, ass-wipe never intended to pay his own attorn'eys that worked a disabled man like he was fighting Mike Tyson at the courts. Ass-wipe placed top-ramin on his B.K. list of creditors and did not pay top-ramin one dime after the court action was over. As far as i, know, ronald niner paid top-ramin.

As a creditor and knowing ass-wipe, his father ronald george niner (sperm-doner) paid for the BK too. Ass-wipe refused to pay top-ramin for his mischievous deeds against i, a once severely disabled man. However, top-ramin actually accepted payment from (sperm-doner) who aided/abetted its son ass-wipe to file bankruptcy.

It was sperm-doner and its other offspring james niner that also helped hide ass-wipe's ass-ets, (whatever he had) transfer ass-wipe's or truly i, business "Dangling Carrot Creative" that ass-wipe used i, money he stole from i, into ass-wipe's brother Jim/James's and sperm-doner niner's name and the sham transfer begun.

It Is Called Unlawful Conveyance

Unlawful or unfair transfer of property: Not a lawful conveyance, also known as a fraudulent transfer, is an l.e.g.a.l. term referring to the unlawful or unfair transfer of property, often in the context of bankruptcy proceedings.

The legal battle and outcomes when not-lawful transfer is suspect, it generally leads to l.e.g.a.l. procedures intended at shaping legitimacy of the asset(s) conveyed. The discoveries will have different outcomes, for both deadbeat-debtors and creditors.

In cases where creditors suspect unlawful conveyance, they can initiate l.e.g.a.l. and lawful actions to recover the transferred assets. This process involves gathering evidence, such as financial records, communication trails, and expert testimonies, to prove the fraudulent intent behind the transfers.

When successful, the court shall order the return of the assets to the creditor or the equivalent monetary value. On the other hand, deadbeat-debtors who have transferred assets need to answer certain questions against allegations of fraudulent conveyance. They may argue that the transfer was made for legitimate reasons unrelated to fraud. In such cases, the burden of proof often shifts to the deadbeat-debtor to establish all operation's legitimacy. i, know and all of the niner criminal gang knows the transfers were not lawful. Instead they aid and abet ass-wipe.

Fraudulent conveyance is an l.e.g.a.l. concept with significant implications in bankruptcy and asset protection. It encompasses both actual and constructive fraud, each with its unique criteria and l.e.g.a.l. contemplation. It is very easy to prove intent to defraud an unlawful conveyance. Yet, the pubic serpents, ass-wipe's then attorn'er, the B.K trustee and ass-wipe's criminal gang assisted in the deception to suppress i, rite/rights to the information as facts.

Whether you are creditor or deadbeat-debtor, deceptive transfer is necessary and proper for making informed decisions protecting your interests. i, was repudiated. It is not called illegal conveyance for a reason. Because when doing something against god's laws it is against *the law* and when doing things against the matrix made up statutory schema, it is il-l.e.g.a.l. as in ill will on mankind. i, am man.

i, was not going to stop until i, fulfill i, integrity to i, and i, word i, gave to god that not if, but when i, start this battle, i, must go all the way and file the papers at the post judgment debtor hearings against scott alan and robin niner. i, filed to receive liens, levies for post decree litigation, which is entirely different type of action.

i, will never forget the look on sperm-doner ronald george niner's face and his body language when sperm-doner walked into the Chatsworth Courthouse-ship deck while i, was there ready to fulfill i, integrity with post judgment/decree collection issues.

With top-ramin right by sperm-doner, niner's side who filed the notice of bankruptcy stay. It was all of the actions of ass-wipe's father sperm-doner who was filing the B.K. for ass-wipe, that stopped all superior court collections. Now, i, cannot tell a lie as "i, always tell what is true even when i, lie". When sperm-doner niner entered that courtroom, i, was kind of taken back for a moment. Of course i, did not know at that time what was going on.

i, had no idea that even when a wo/man loses a court case at the county/state court level, or at any level federal or state, that the deadbeat-debtors can file for bankruptcy and place a private debt onto a commercial bankruptcy. At least this is what bitch-mlo told to i, and this is what bitch-mlo did. It applied the automatic stay pending the B.K. court.

i, stood there while sperm-doner niner and top-ramin stared at i, as if they both had just stopped i, heart from beating or that i, life would stop from living. It totally seemed that bitch-mlo already knew because of the reaction which she was not surprised at all. Maybe it, as in bitch-mlo just as the others wanted to see i, face expression as if to say, "*you are not going to get one dime, even though you won a decree...for over $22,000 grand.*"

All of them looked at i, and waited for i, to react as if they knew that this was the end of the road for i, because sperm-doner truly was gloating in a way, i, only have seen one other man act so childish, which is a satanic and sickening gleeful gaze.

It really was disgusting to see a grown elder man that used to be in i, mind's eyes and heart a very moral and ethical upstanding member of this world. It only bothered i, for a very short period like about one or two days. Then i, remember i, vow to i-self and to god and then i, did some research and moved to the next chapter of fulfilling this saga of "*Must go all the way...*"

Then after ~~judge~~ bitch-mlo expressed that the case was on a stay while the bankruptcy is pending, i, looked in the eyes of ass-wipe's scumbag attorn'ey top-ramin and i, did not know it at the time, but he did not look like he had won any case. Top-ramin actually appeared disappointed and embarrassed.

As a matter of fact, top-ramin looked so disappointed and even the bitch-mlo looked a bit perplexed as to top-ramin being there and filing those bankruptcy papers. i, know i, would if i, were top-ramin because top-ramin fulfilled theft for ass-wipe niner and his clans-wo/mankind. It is as if they pulled off a brinks theft.

Sleep Well Satan Sleep Well

i, know, i, could never sleep at night knowing it was i, as in top-ramin, who assisted liars and thief's as in ass-wipe niner's family to receive a semi-win against a well under educated disabled man. It is hardly a moral or ethical consolation prize.

Even though top-ramin and his assistant attorn'ey thomas wanner (weiner-dog) had conspired with the - attorn'ey richard thomas miller (dick-em) in order to minimize i, ability to actually receive justice against the niner criminal family. Either way he did it!

Kudos and hats off to you, top-ramin, weiner dog and dick-em, for your great achievement and throwing yourselves under the unethical, amoral Satanism bus. (More to come in this *living missive* on the three minions above); you all assisted ass-wipe and robin niner to take advantage of their once long time friend. Kudos to you.

A man who the niners had a fiduciary responsibility to not ever mix money with their duty as the social security representative payees, acting in a trusted position. The key rule is to not take advantage of daniel's physical and disabled condition. Kudos to you all ?

SATAN'S 3RD MINION OF THE B.I.T.C.H. M.L.O. CHATSWORTH <u>CRIMINAL GANG</u> OF 2007 – 2025

Superior Court Chatsworth Calif. Case # PC04224 -2009 Thomas Edward Wanner BAR # 195300

Thomas Edward Wanner, ("**Weiner-dog**") and not like the Oscar Myer Weiner, nor like the Dodger dog, as in a wiener more like as in P.e.n.i.s.-head, seemed 2-B a decent man, however, as an acting attorn'ey, he is like most of the rest of attorn'eys i, do encounter. Weiner-dog[90] appeared 2-B pleasant to talk to, knows a lot of about health and wellness, as we did chat for short intervals. He was hired by the niner criminal gang/family to assist the theft, lies, and steal

[90]**WIENER**: A wiener is a type of sausage or anything that superficially resembles one, particularly a penis or a dachshund breed of dog. https://www.dictionary.com/e/slang/wiener/

from i, a man. Except when hired 2-B a pubic serpent, and act as an attorn'ey for its client [91] he is as ruthless, conniving, and a mischievous snake as all the rest i, have ever met; and i, have met a lot of snakes, i, mean attorn'ers/attorn'eys as actors of courts.

i, do recall when i, first encountered the man: weiner-dog who was polite, cleaned shaved, well dressed. He seemed not like an average scum sucking suite wearing, land shark attorn'ey. Although, wiener-dog do appear normal, he did everything he could to work i's ex-best friend, robin niner to lie, cheat and steal against i.

i, actually believed in i, heart and soul that once, robin was under the deposition, there was trust to reconcile with the friendship we once attained. i, was wrong. i, knew then as i, do know to this very day, robin was being coerced to go all the way through with whatever lies and deceit niners needed she to in order to fulfill niner's quest to bankrupt, i.

Niner's have stood in dishonor nonstop, in order to get back at i, for holding ass-wipe scott alan niner to his original indenture. Weiner-dog was by all means unethical coercing and slightly forcing robin, (at her own will) to be amoral at the attorn'ey play book.

Yes, wiener-dog did try to charm, i, with his short comments about health and wellness. Wiener-dog even made statements directly to i, "*I like you adam* …" The true meaning of a lawyer,[92] is not of itself an attorn'ey that sometimes <u>practices</u> law, rather one who applies devilish functions to attorn every penny or material possession from

---

[91]**CLIENT**: (" The notion apparently is "one who leans on another for protection." In ancient Rome, a plebeian under the guardianship and protection of a patrician (who was called patronus in this relationship; see <u>patron</u>).),

[92]**<u>Luke 11:45-52</u>ESV / 105 helpful votes. LAWYER:**
One of the lawyers answered him, "Teacher, in saying these things you insult us also." And he said, "Woe to you lawyers also! For you load people with burdens hard to bear, and you yourselves do not touch the burdens with one of your fingers. Woe to you! For you build the tombs of the prophets whom your fathers killed. So you are witnesses and you consent to the deeds of your fathers, for they killed them, and you build their tombs. Therefore also the Wisdom of God said, 'I will send them prophets and apostles, some of whom they will kill and persecute,' ...
https://www.openbible.info/topics/lawyers

an opponent. Then it will transfer all immoral, ignorant servitude to itself, the courts and or its patrons.

However, i, personally experienced something that was very disturbing as the day robin sat in front of i, with ass-wipe's second attorn'ey, wiener-dog at the deposition. Instead of robin answering the deposed questions, robin made fun of i, as she and wiener-dog mocked every question i, asked to build i, court action.

Here i, am doing i, best to depose this f.u.k.c.-ing k.u.n.t defendant robin niner w.h.o.r.e. and all they both did was make fun of i, the entire time. i, was deposing the w.h.o.r.e. and k.u.n.t.; i, am heartfelt, very serious, yet not them; it was a game for them.

i, literally was not emotionally ready to depose i, ex-best friend. i, did not know how to depose anyone. Actually i, cried many times B-4 the day of deposition because i, did not want to go through with this deposition.

The pain of the thought of this action made i, sick to i, stomach at times. However, the more i, realized that ass-wipe and robin niner were all in on stealing i, compensation from the May 3rd 2001 car accident, something continued to give i, strength to move forward and fulfill i, word to self and to god. i, suppose it was God all along.

Crazy Mad Woman Downstairs

i, am not going to go through the entire event, as i, shall just summarize how it had gone. i, remember it well. i, was waiting upstairs with a friend regina and we all heard a woman screaming. i, have recordings of the entire event, because i, did hire a stenographer who was there to witness via transcripts of the entire interaction.

i, being the man who was moving the action in deposition, was able to set up an empty apartment in the building On Magnolia Street in North Hollywood California. Regina's daughter was a manager and allowed i, to rent a unit for a day, for the deposition.

Regina's daughter called i, and said, "There is some woman screaming at the top of her lungs causing the tenants to call in a disturbance" and "would you please go and investigate it or i, will need to call the police". i, looked out the balcony and observed robin and some man crossing the street. As i, watched robin was creaming; "I, DO NOT WANT TO DO THIS" and "I, AM NOT GOING TO DO THIS, HE IS MY BEST FRIEND..." She actually repeated those exact words several times. This notion did give i, a little bit of strength, but did not change the fact that robin was there to discredit what was true against i. i, need to be strong and faithful to i, god that gives i, everlasting courage.

It did not dawn on i, at the time, rather i, forced i,-self to continue even though i, heard those words. It made i, stronger because i, knew robin was not lying for she-self, rather ass-wipe and papa sperm-doner niner's criminal gang.

i, then ran out of the unit and down the stairs to greet them at the building entrance. There was a glass door with sections opened so i, could hear everything on the street outside. i, waited behind the wall as i, listened to wiener-dog and robin in conversation long enough to hear all i, needed to feel with i, heart.

Weiner-dog told robin, "don't worry, i, will not let him harass you, and you have to do this remember the agreement." This is very important because "*Remember the agreement*" "*Remember the agreement*" "*Remember the Agreement*" was the term for robin. As she must do what she said she would because of the *divorce agreement* ass-wipe and sperm-doner set up for robin.

i, found out later within the case that the agreement weiner-dog was pressing on robin was: scott and ronald niner promised that when, robin testi-fied (i, say lied about what she knows) against her best friend, there is a divorce decree that will set robin up for many years.

No matter what, as long as robin lies and suppresses what i, state as true of the original decree, robin would receive X amount of divorce money, for a certain length of time, with her Jeep fully paid, medical insurance, cell phone paid; the whole kitten caboodle. All i, do receive was the caboose, and yes it was dry without any humor.

She Sold Friendship For Divorce Decree

i, left and hurried up to the unit where the deposition took place. i, immediately asked i, friend's daughter to buzz robin and weiner-dog into the building as i, hurried back up to the unit. As i, waited with the reporter, at the door of the unit, i, felt almost an urge to release the water works, especially when i, seen robin.

Here they are, this man and woman, the woman who i, had known for so long. The idea i, even needed to fulfill this deposition was one of the most difficult things i, have ever done. i, do not know how i, did it, other than it was the sheer will of god directing i, and with god's grace giving i, all the courage and inner strength to fulfill what i, do when i, give i, integrity.

Weiner-dog introduced himself as the attorn'ey for the ass-wipe niner's action and robin needed no introduction. As robin sat on her side of the table i, begun with the introduction of the court action, wiener-dog immediately tried to take control and interjected as to what is appropriate and not appropriate for the deposition.

Now, i, was very well versed on how to make the environment suitable for a deposition. i, made certain the unit was very clean, it had several tables and chairs for more than five people, in case more than just robin and her wiener-dog were present.

i, knew that i, needed to get started and that is exactly what i, did. i, offered water, snacks, directed them where the de baño (bathrooms) are and then i, was ready to begin. The fact that i, was going to fulfill the deposition towards, i, long time friend completely ripped every fiber of any love i, ever had by the betrayal by robin, ass-wipe and sperm-doner; the created divorce decree of betrayal.

i, gave instructions as to the court action name, number, and pre rules for the deposition. i, continued that if we did not get through today, then i, will have to continue the deposition for another day.

Averting Answers To The Questions

The entire time, from start to finish, all robin would do, is not answer anything direct even when i, said: "for the record, please state your name…" and robin answered, "*You know my name …*" and when i, began to get stronger and threaten with contempt, robin would say, "*oh who do you think you are Perry Mason…*" or "*an attorn'ey…*"

It was very clear weiner-dog was not going to force her to answer. Most of the other questions i, asked, robin flat out denied answering by saying; '*I am not going to answer that, you already know…*" or "*ask scott i, was not there…*" even though she was there. She just completely derailed telling what is true, avoided answering, or made fun of, i.

Towards the end, when i, realized that i, would have to depose she in front of the court, to force robin to answer, i, closed the current session with extending the time to reset a new deposition date.

Weiner-dog, said "*i, will let you know what days she is available…*" The entire event was very taxing, costly, as i, had to pay for the reporter, the venue, etcetera, and had taken most of i, energy, at that time.

Because, i, was forcing i, self to fulfill this endeavor, the picture was clear on the wall. No matter what i, would file, say or do, robin and ass-wipe already made a deal to lie, cheat, conspire with others to deter and derail every effort i, made to bring what is true to a lawful court.

Instead it turned out to be a court by the (D.O.J.) deprivations-for-just-us, as in those who have attorn'eys and pay [~~judge~~] off; the pubic serpent as this is a known fact, [~~judge~~]s receive backdoor cash, gifts, or special favors and some get land loans onto their pre-existing homes and they never have to pay them back.

i, was determined at the cost of i, own life, to make certain these two niners would never harm another wo/mankind as they do to i, and i, was even more determined now in 2025 by sheer passion to share this with the world regardless as it is the proof of service of the upcoming court action.

And as ass-wipe once had written to i, therefore, i, will not stop until i, expose what they and all the other evil-wrongdoers continue to do. And i, will share it with the entire world. This is i, vow today to god as it is from when Jesus was here and i, do believe jesus would do in existence on this God's green earth.

SATAN'S 4TH MINION OF THE BITCH M.L.O.
CHATSWORTH CRIMINAL GANG OF 2007 – 2025

SUPERIOR COURT CHATSWORTH CASE # PC04224 -2009
DAVID EARL WOODRUFF BAR # 137416

David Woodruff Mediator-prator For The Ass-wipe Niner Action

Going forward a couple months. It was a few days B-4 the trial was to begin, whereas i, was requested to attend mediation with the mediator David Woodruff. i, had already found a mediator which i, was going to pay half and i, expected ass-wipe too or it should have paid the other half.

Being as ass-wipe was, of course, being a tight wad not wanting to meet i, half way, he denied mediating unless we were to take advantage of the courts referral mediator. i, emphatically declined the offer as i, wanted an unbiased mediator.

The fact that ass-wipe's attorn'ey weiner-dog, top-ramin and even bitch-mlo wanted i, to use mediator-praetor, i, did not like the idea. Hence, i, did finally agree only as to a non-binding mediation, which means if, i, do not like what goes on, i, can stop, and would move into the trial phase as if mediation never occurred. That is what i, did. i, am not saying that all court appointed mediators are corrupt like most of the [~~judge~~]s, attorn'eys, pro-se-cuters and court clucks towards i, as a man. However, from i, vast experience and after chatting with many attorn'ers, i, was instructed to use a third party mediator/arbitrator.

This third party mediator would eliminate bias and would not be attached to any court system. i, did as instructed, i, called mediators; one who was a retired ~~judge~~ pubic serpent that apparently knew all three: l.a.w., l.e.g.a.l. and the original court process. The inevitable had occurred.

Mediation had come and gone, and the end result was ass-wipe and robin, tried to get i, to drop the entire court action. Ass-wipe was going to give i, $20,000.00 cash and call it a day. Although, their mediation was in the crews quarters area of the Chatsworth courthouse-ship, i, recall it kind of a cold and damp dungeon terrain.

i, did try to make another opportunity to get robin to come to her senses and tell what is true and stop the habitual lies and deceit. Once there, i, sat in one room and ass-wipe and robin sat in another part of the area.

The mediator did his part by acting like a ping pong ball going back and forth between the rooms to express all offers and non-acceptances. After the mediation was through, i, began to walk out; i, stated, "*robin, you and ass-wipe need to hold to your original integrity*." It was and is not about money for i. It never is about money ever. It was as it is to this very day and always will be about integrity. Principals are god preserved and i, do not waver on i, word. When i, give i, word it is better than gold, silver, or any mineral on this earth. i, go to i, grave upholding honor of i, and god's grace.

Court Is A State With Many Actors

The actors at courts know very little about integrity to god. The courts especially all of the one's i, have been at over forty-five years, only care about the numbers.

At the end of the day, it is always business and there is zero morals, ethics or god's laws in the courts. i, should actually state that it is the court actors who run the game, through rules, codes, statutes, regulations, ordinances and acts which they do not follow themselves. Hypocrites, i, suppose they all are?

However, i, do expect the average wo/mankind to abide by laws, and not only when it is convenient for the actors involved. They only apply l.e.g.a.l. not l.a.w. Morals, ethics and what is true should always prevail over any offers to settle, for less than what is true. This is why courts are satanic and not in god's grace.

To not tell what is true, or allow others to get away with lies, threats, theft, and deceit, to receive payouts, to shut one's mouth or offer more than what was asked to not tell what is true is an abomination of all gods laws and portrays sin. Whoever does not abide by gods laws over manmade legal statutory schema might as well be one of the evil-wrongdoers from the onset.

The problems that most attorn'eys has are the deals by corporate and especially govern mentals that would rather pay millions to billions of dollars to someone to shut their mouth and take a gag agreement. All govern mentals for the states united are jack-ass backwards in i, heart and soul as well as under Gods world in contrast to biblical integrity.

To suppress exposure is not what this great nation nor the founders stood and lived on. To expose those who are cheats or think they can just write a check and all their sins are forgiven is not a life i, have ever desired to live. Certainly, i, am not perfect, and i, have had i, share of mischief in life, but when wo/mankind finally do grow up and become the age of major-ity, it is as it has always been.

The commandments inspired by god through mans' hands should always be memorized and more importantly put to practice at every court across this nation. As i, demand it!

If you, the reader need a mediator see below, i, did not say that david earl woodruff is not a nice guy, so use him at your own risk, i, therefore give him free advertisement.

See: Address: Woodruff Arbitration & Mediation, Inc., 4227 Abbington Ct, Westlake Village, CA 91361-4504;

137416 Westlake Village California December 1988; Phone: 818-422-6629
| Fax: Not Available

Email: dwoodruff64@yahoo.com |
Website: www.woodruffadr.com

SATAN'S 5TH MINION OF THE BITCH M.L.O. CHATSWORTH <u>CRIMINAL GANG</u> OF 2007 – 2025

Superior Court Chatsworth Calif. Case #PC04224 -2009
Richard Thomas Miller BAR # 155522

Richard Thomas Miller
Satan's 5th Minion
(Dick-em)
Borsotti V. Scott & Robin Niner
2007, 2009, 2010 through 2025

Hiring an attorn'ey takes some planning. One does not just go and hire any tom, dick, or mary knucklehead attorn'ey. It must be the right knucklehead attorn'ey for your type of action at law. The problem, i, had was that i, rushed hiring and that i, had already started i, own action. Most attorn'eys do not favor getting involved unless they are number one or two inline. This means that they either started the original court action or the first attorn'ey really did not know what she/he was doing and there is not too much damage done. This happens all the time.

i, remember when i, interviewed to hire the man, that act as an attorn'ey, richard thomas miller hereinafter, "dick" thomas miller or "dick-em" for the trial of i, action against the niner family. Dick-em seemed 2-B very sin-<u>cere</u> about how, who, where, and what he was able to and going to do for i, court action. i, had gone to dick-em's office on roscoe boulevard near woodley street at van nuys california adjacent to the van nuys airport.

Dick-em immediately showed i, pictures of his wife, as he continued to express how many years of experience he has been practicing his profession. i, believe he tried to build confidence with i. Dick-em told i, the story about his wife, who was also disabled. Not disabled like i, was, she was portrayed to have multiple physical, mental or some neurological disorder.

This story put a wrench in i, heart for this man, as i, felt that he must truly be very compassionate to be able to take care of another wo/mankind in this manner. i, figured that he might be compassionate to i, who is also severely disabled at the time.

i, left the first visit feeling overwhelmed and desperate to hire help. Having already moved the case with assistance of good paralegals, and other lawyers research and writing skills, i, wanted to do the entire action, on i, own, but have never handled any court action to this point. As far as i, was concerned, being left alone, to actually do a full blown trial, overwhelmed i, mind, heart and soul. However, now i, encourage all wo/mankind to never hire an attorner, unless *they* or *it* will sign on as co-counsel. See how many attorn'eys will refuse your offer.

i, asked for advice from certain paralegals, other attorn'eys i, already knew, and many people whom have gone through their own court actions for input. Court actions from criminal, to probate, from infractions, DUI's, drug possessions, civil action, to contract stuff, child protective service, administrative, to constitutional, law. No case is exactly the same too to another court action only similar.

All i, had ever seen up to that point was trials on tell-us-lies-vision. Finally after a few days and as the trial date moved ever so closer, i, ended up getting sick with a bad headache and in i, stomach. With a lot of anxiety, sleep depression, ulceration in i, gut, i, felt i, could not handle a full blown trial in i, condition. i, succumb to hiring attorn'ey dick-em. i, called dick-em again and then allowed i, inner gut (instinct) 2-B sidelined as i, had gone against, i, original belief that, i, was capable of handling i, own court action and that this guy dick-em is not the right advocate for i. All i, knew is that it was i, that must go all the way through a *Trial By Jury*.

Against i, better judgment i, allowed dick-em to sign on to, i, court action. i, distinctly remember dick-em wanted around ten thousand dollars of real federal reserve notes as payment to handle a trial, which was supposed to be a *trial by jury.*

Dick-em went on to express his tactics in how dick-em was going to stick it to the niners. Then dick-em began to express how he will employ his paralegals, secretary, and his vast experience at taking other actions to trial. This was more attorn'ey bullshit. Dick-em reassured i, he will fight for me. Although, i, papers were not perfect, of course, as perfect as dick-em could do. Dick-em stated he would have created the papers slightly different. Because dick-em was not a disabled man and dick-em truly built himself up 2-B a well-educated l.a.w. man, who fights for his clients to the end. i, learned after the fact, that all dick-em do, is the legal statutory schema and was not ethical to i, nor ethical nor moral to god.

Dick-em expressed that he will take a no prisoner attitude. i, believe, at first i, gave Dick-em $ 2,000.00 down. Then i, made another payment and dick-em kept asking for more, but something told i, not to completely pay dick-em everything until i, reviewed some of his work and until i, actually seen some work effort from him.

Great Lawyers Ask Important Questions

The closer it came to the trial date, the stress had become so elevated, to the point that i, was unable to sleep, eat, or think clearly. PTSD kicked into high gear. To handle the already difficult everyday tasks of life, and being that i, had never been in this type of court proceeding and against i, now ex-best friend and her deadbeat ex-husband ass-wipe and criminal niners gang. i, gave dick-em $2,500 more. Dick-em begun the strategies for the complete trial, yet refused to tell i, anything.

Although, i, did question things along the way, as to his tactics, how he was going to posture the action and other inner workings. i, wanted to be a part of everything so, i, could learn and know where i, could be of the most benefit to assist dick-em. After all, no one knows their own court action better than thee who experienced it.

i, also figured it was possible that this is Dick-em's way to release stress. The stress i, felt was beyond words. However, dick-em talked himself up a storm. A storm that "*I am a long time attorn'ey and have X amount of year's experience.*" And "*I will fight for you,*" And "*I am an ATTORN'EY, I (Dick-em) have been through this type of trial so many times no one can ever beat me…*" attitude.

i, thought this is peculiar, because up to this date, all dick-em was worried about was luring i, in to his confidence speech. He asked very little about my story. Then it was all about i, money and he kept trying to get i, to pay him up front B-4 the trial. Once, i, became adamant that the $5,000.00 was all he would receive up to this point, his attitude slightly changed.

However, days continued closer and it was two days B-4 trial. Dick-em wanted to meet with some of i, wo/mankind who were going to be called as witness. We all met at the Black Angus Steak house on in Northridge California. Everyone ordered their drinks, food and i, being vegan did not get more than a dry baked potato with chives and Olive oil. Everyone else ordered their juicy salivating carnivore plates with all the trimmings. Some ordered a beer. After all, i, was paying the bill.

Dick-em learned of what everyone was going to testify to, and he did not take much notes, nor did he talk too much to instruct them as what to expect, as i, figured he would. i, do know a little bit that B-4 a trial everyone is to be on the same or similar pages up front and center. The attorn'ey or rather, i, shall say a great or even a good lawyer will go over all of the questions and important factual issues B-4 any trial. Dick-em was only interested in eating lunch.
It is crucial to all court hearings of every type, whether a trial or deposition etcetera in order to make certain the attorn'ey knows how to and when to and where to receive the most factual true statements at Open Court for their own client.

All dick-em wanted to know was who they are, where do they live, and only a tiny bit, like maybe one or two questions as to what they knew. However, dick-em rarely ever actually gave anyone any eye contact. The rest of the questions were about what they were going to eat, drink, and what time the witnesses were going to be at court. This was not an open and shut court action. i, have lots of facts.

i, also found it odd that each time i, would bring up things about certain issues that were crucial to i, court action, dick-em changed the subject. Dick-em did this which to i, seemed as if he did not want to actually hear anything from i, witnesses that would benefit i.

Finally the first day of the trial was upon us. i, was just a nervous wreck inside. Dick-em hardly asked any of the witnesses any questions while on the witness stand as dick-em said he would previously to i, hiring him. i, mean, if dick-em asked more than one or two questions for each witness, while they were on the stand and under oath, which is the time to ask the correct questions. i, would be shocked and i, would bet i, penis would fall off i, pelvic if he even asked three of anyone. This was a pre set to F.u.k.c. Adam-over unknowingly by niner criminal gang.

Where Do They Go To Lunch Dick-em?

On the second day of the trial, at the break, dick-em was supposed to meet with i, and other witnesses to stay focused on the action. Dick-em was nowhere to be found.

There were a lot of exhibits, facts and evidence that i, was able to retrieve, however, there was also much that was suppressed from i, getting on the record by that w.h.o.r.e. bitch-mlo, that F.U.K.C.-ing richard-cranium, many court clucks and by ass-wipe's attorn'ey top-ramin and weiner-dog as each filed frivolous motions to strike, suppress, quash or deny i, every movement.

When i, asked one of the deputies have you seen the attorn'eys that were just here? The deputy seemed to know what was going on. If he didn't i, can only presume that the deputy knew as deputy told i, that he seen i, attorn'ey and ass-wipe's attorn'eys going towards the cafeteria area together. And because i, was with other witnesses, i, did not go to investigate nor did i, think anything negative about this action at the time. i, did call dick-em on his cell phone, but he would not answer. i, eventually became very suspicious and so did some of i, friends and family who were there for i, benefit.

Dick-em never even objected to any of the things ass-wipe was saying, robin was saying, ass-wipe's sperm-doner was saying either. It was as if dick-em was ass-wipe's attorn'ey and not i, attorn'ey.

Stoned Out Of One's Mind

i, remember this next issue as if it were yesterday. i, biological brother Paul Andrew Cohen (although he actually is not a ~~Cohen~~ but a Troy) was there to testify on i, behalf. One, he was very late, two he was fu**ing stoned out of his mind. Paul could barely hold his eyes open, whereas Paul actually looked as if he was sleepwalking. i, asked him if he needed toothpicks to hold open his eye lids.

Once Paul was up on the witness stand and sworn in, even the woman who acts as [~~judge~~] margaret lynn oldendorf (bitch-mlo) asked Paul if he was alright. Paul said i, have been taking medication (yah right all he was ever doing was smoking dope, snorting cocaine(na) and crank, ice and drinking booze). It did not take Paul very long when he started to try to make flirtatious acts towards b.i.t.c.h.-mlo making stupid statements that not only embarrassed i, and all i, other witnesses. Ass-wipe and robin loved it that paul was wasted out of his mind on the witness stand.

It was like a comedy show, only i, was not laughing. However, ass-wipe and robin were smiling from ear to ear with shit eaten grins all over their faces. They knew paul was stoned out of his freaking mind which did not help i, side at all, especially when he was flirting with the bitch-mlo. Paul was so embarrassing to the point that i, told the attorn'ey to get him off the witness stand and call him on a different day. The attorn'ey refused to recall him so i, could sober him up. i, was furious that dick-em refused to take a recess too and get paul for the next day's examinations.

There were thousands or at least hundreds of questions that i, attorn'ey should have asked, not only of i, witnesses, but especially ass-wipe, robin and scott's father sperm-doner niner who was lying out of their asses on the witness stand too.

At the time, sperm-doner would answer scott's attorney's questions, sperm-doner glared down at i. All i, could do was sit there and listen to what seemed to be lie after lie from one niner to another niner. After i, attorn'ey had his opportunity to cross the witnesses, dick-em totally, not only fell way short of what attorn'eys are supposed to do and ask in cross-examination, again, by asking only one or two questions. Dick-em also asked questions in a way that was passive, and actually assisted ass-wipe's attorn'ey in his case against i.

One thing led to another, as dick-em actually began leading the opposition and getting them to state things that helped them instead of i. It felt as if i, was in a nightmare.

i, did not know what to do except stop dick-em and ask him "what is your problem? Dick-em became angry with i, as if i, was causing trouble and he made it clear in front of everyone, when all i, was doing was reminding dick-em about all the evidence and facts we have and to stay on point with questioning.

Combative Attorn'ey Game Over For Your Action

i, head begun to swirl like berries in a blender, and i, got dizzy from all of the disbelief as i, sat there, witness after witness, was dismissed with few to no questions asked. Then it was i, turn to get up and give facts and evidence. As i, did tell what was all true, i, did the best i, could even though, i, was in what seemed like a nightmare. Wherein, i, could not at times, speak, think of the facts and evidence that was crucial to i, court action. i, have multiple folders with all the facts written down as evidence to place and i, did place them all on the record.

Even when i, was trying to assist the attorn'ey dick-em with certain parts of the action, the attorn'ey knew what points were crucial to i, action, and he refused to raise those key issues at open court.

Throughout the court hearings, bitch-mlo had to tell ass-wipe several times to stop talking aloud to his attorn'ey. Ass-wipe was acting as the attorn'ey trying to control everything in the courtroom while i, and all of the other witnesses testified. It even was worst when i, was on the witness stand as ass-wipe, at one point, was asked basically to leave if he is not going to shut his mouth.

End Of This Chapter Of Trial

It came time for the trial to be over and on that Friday, May 15th, 2009, we were all to leave and come back on Monday 18th day May 2009.

i, had to go another weekend not knowing what was going to happen. And dick-em was nowhere to be found. Although i, knew after dick-em's display of crossing the ethics boundary of assisting the other side, and that i, do make a mistake hiring dick-em. Nothing would prepare i, for what was to come. Dick-em was not good for i, court action, and i, felt the outcome B-4 it was even presented. i, was somewhat glad this part was almost over because the entire issues of trial and court were tiring to i, heart, mind and soul all the way down to i, toes.

Monday had come and gone and as i, suspected, i, did not receive what i, had worked so hard to achieve on i, own. Here, ass-wipe and robin niner was able to afford two attorn'eys for their attempts to lie cheat, steal and to suppress all of the facts and evidence from i, actions. Yet all i, do know is that god knows what is true and in the end, god will sort them all out. In the meantime, i, continue to expose.

There is a saying that most people have heard. It is not ever appropriate, however, i, shall say it herein, because i, am not of an angry man only a man that knows the difference between right and wrong and to show the amount of anger i, did hold for some time and where that anger comes from is not wrong just honorable.

"KILL THEM ALL AND LET GOD SORT THEM OUT."

The Origins of "kill Them All and Let God Sort It Out" —"In 1209, Pope Innocent III decided it was time to crack down on followers of a religious sect that had become popular in Southern France. Originally called Albigensians, they came to be more widely known as the Cathars.

Cathars were Christians. But they rejected the authority of the Pope and other key aspects of Catholicism, so they were deemed heretics by the Catholic Church. This apparently didn't matter much to most people living in the French town of Beziers. Catholics and Cathars had lived there together for many years in relative harmony. On July 22, 1209, they were celebrating the annual Feast of Mary Magdalene together, a religious holiday observed by various Christian religions.

Suddenly, the festivities were cut short when an army of "Crusaders" sent by Pope Innocent III showed up outside the walls of the town. The military leader of the army was Simon de Montfort, a French nobleman highly motivated by the Pope's promise that he could keep the land of any heretics he killed.

The Crusaders were accompanied by an official representative of the Pope, a French Cistercian monk named Arnaud Amalric (also variously referred to as Arnald Amalric and Arnauld-Amaury). De Montfort demanded that the leaders of Beziers turn over the town's Cathar heretics to him. They refused.

The Crusaders attacked. According to accounts written decades later, as the attack began, a soldier asked Amalric how they would be able to tell which Beziers townspeople were Catholics and which were Cathars. Amalric supposedly answered (in French): "*Kill them all. God will recognize his own.*"

Some sources give the alleged quote as "Kill them all, for the Lord knows his own" or as "Kill them all. The Lord knows his own." It eventually came to be most commonly paraphrased as: "Kill them all and let God sort them out."

https://naturallawinstitute.com/2018/06/the-origins-of-kill-them-all-and-let-god-sort-it-out/

The Pope supposedly, a god fearing man, however, since the times of popes, none of the popes seems to care about anything or anyone except to control the masses for the Vatican's bidding of Catholicism.

Who will god sort out? Those of the Evil-wrongdoers named herein. All of the liars, thieves, pirates, amoral and unethical wo/mankind, who do know for what they do, act it deliberately. For a prize, God will sort us all out; those i, expose!

The Trial Would End With A New Beginning

i, recall sitting there in disbelief that all of i, facts and evidence, that is indisputable, placed on the record, was not brought out at trial because dick-em was working for ass-wipe niners gang. Ass-wipe niner's hard work to suppress i, facts and evidence paid off as i, beleive ass-wipe paid dick-em to throw i, under the bus.

All of the games played on i, by the Chatsworth court clucks, bitch-mlo, robin and ass-wipe niner, ass-wipe's attorn'eys top-ramin, weiner-dog and dick-em, whom were all definitely working towards the same goal and it was not on i, behalf. It is especially the hired piece of shit attorn'er dick-em's betrayal, that i, witness first hand.

It did not even take a few weeks, days or even hours to realize what truly transpired at this k.u.n.t. kangaroo court room of margaret lynn Oldendorf aka, bitch-mlo.

Not even 30 to 45 seconds when bitch-mlo read the decree, as the final decision, which was only for approximately $23,000.00 against ass-wipe and robin niner. It was a breach of rental agreement and not a breach of contract or fiduciary duty, yet in i, support.

i, was sitting there and then when i, do realize after a few seconds that this was the end of this juncture of the court action, i, focused around as i, looked about and wondered where i, attorn'ey had gone while ass-wipe and robin shook hands with top-ramin. i, realized that dick-em and weiner-dog were gone out in the hall.

i, got up out of the chair, walked to the courtroom door and as i, cracked it open, i, looked out and seen dick-em and weiner-dog hugging each other, slapping high fives and jumping for joy. i, heard them both say, yah we did great in there, and you were awesome, and did you see how the [~~judge~~] read the judgment and the look on adam daniel's face...."

i, was sickened and once again begun to get angry. The feeling of betrayal begun to slowly seep back into i, veins like lava oozes out of the center of its volcano and onto the ocean waters. It was appalling to i, and i, opened the door a few more inches.

Anger, Disbelief, Abandonment, & Betrayal
By then, both dick-em and weiner-dog were still embracing as if they just had a new baby or won the lotto together. If, i, didn't know any better and at that time, it appeared as if they both were having orgasms while holding each other in their arms embrace.

It was, at this point, that i, cleared i, throat very loud, so they could here i, was there and both of the lovers stopped jumping, hugging, and tap dancing like little ballerinas and looked over at i, watching their display of affection.

They both stopped and gathered themselves as if they were wiping the (sperm, seed (archaic, dialect), spunk (taboo), scum (US, slang), seminal fluid, or come/cum (taboo), as in jism or jissom (taboo), as spermatic fluid) that ejaculated out of their penis heads, all over their faces.

As the etheric white prostatic fluids dripped down their mouths on to the courthouse floor; their mouths were wide opened and it was not because they did not want to spill a drop. i, could not believe that i, just witnessed their display of betrayal. So much corruption as i, stand in dismay with a friend watching them fu** me over.

i, slowly and completely flung the courtroom doors wide open and as i, walked closer to where they were, the only thing on, i, mind was to grab that piece of shit richard thomas miller (dick-em) by his throat, pound i, fist onto his face like a jackhammer on steroids and as hard and as many times i, could.

Is it Gods intervention or just a coincidence?
Next i, seen i, self actually visualizing picking dick-em up over i, shoulders as i, rushed him to the edge of the third level banister at the opened rail and fling him over and down onto the first floor whereby his head would of surely split open all over the floor as i, was prepared to watch the blood ooze from his ears until his body became lifeless as i, watch all of the deputies come to dick-em's rescue.

i, recall an arm was placed onto i, shoulder and a voice that said **STOP**, as someone tried to stop i, from stepping into i, act of no return. Although i, most likely would have been out of the clink by today 2025, it is not i, intent to harm anyone, as i, have become a better man than all of the prostatic pubic serpent and not a one of them can hold a candle to the voluminous character and wisdom i, have achieved to date from all of their evil-wrongdoings. Se la vie.

CHAPTER 3, III, THREE

At that point, it actually solidified i, total comprehension, right after the trial was over, and witnessing the infectious display of conspiracy to commit malpractice, i, realized the worst thing that i, ever had done, was hired this attorn'ey dick-em or any attorn'ey.

Vow To Do And Be Better Than Ever B-4

It was at this point forward i, vowed to never ever hire another attorn'ey as long as i, live and i, vowed to learn everything about *l.a.w.* and the *l.e.g.a.l.* system, which i, have learned are two different animals. They sound to be the same, sound similar as mainstream public believe them to be, yet they are not the same.

i, am told by some very well known law abiding scholars, that to discover what is true is to achieve realization by first hand experiences. It is to learn how to govern i, own life. i, own life can only be governed by and through experiences of the past that shape the present and future to live on i, own terms.

This life all wo/mankind experience should not be wasted on this idea that govern mentals are the lord of all lord or that the pope is or ever has been the only living mankind that has the keys to the kingdom of Jesus Christ, David or God almighty.

After this trial day, was over, i, continue to vow and stand on i, heart and soul that no one can do better for i, than i, can do for i-self. This is not to say, that i, can do brain surgery on i, self better than a brain surgeon.

However, law is not brain surgery nor is the legal statutory schema. It sometimes feels like brain surgery when a wo/mankind goes to deal with the courts or govern mental agents that have an agenda to not allow you or i, to leave without losing something they so much need to feed the corporate satanic machine.

L.a.w. is not difficult however, l.e.g.a.l. is said to be more difficult than brain surgery. It is meant to be this way, in order to control, obfuscate, and hypothecate the wealth of all wo/mankind into the matrix machine. To write complaints, verses writing a claim.

Using notices to protect your rights and property verses begging the machine agents to not steal or allow you to keep a portion of your own labour (offspring, land or bank accounts) or else you will lose it all.

These tactics are coercion, extortion and not lawful. However, when you have a B.A.R. card, this card is a license to lie, steal, cheat, rape, with immunity of impunity. So if you want to protect your rights and shut down fraudulent court issues without getting besieged or be detained, then all wo/mankind need to read more; your court life depends on it.

Thankful For God's Intervention
i, do not know how i, stopped from fulfilling this angered daydream, other than at this very miniscule of that moment in time, i, cousin and other friends saw what i, seen, and they knew i, was beyond furious, and as i, was in motion to do just what i, was thinking of doing, i, friend grabbed i, shoulder and said "*STOP*"! and "*They are not worth it. Don't do it..., leave them alone..., they will get theirs.*"

i, friend knew i, was not in i, right mind, and i, to this day, knows that i, was beyond the point of no return in i, mind. Had i, not been stopped, had god not intervened at that minuscule of that moment, i, may still be in jail to this day, doing lots of time for wasting i, life on such a scumbag attorn'ey who truly are the lowest slime like slugs on this planet.

As i, came back to reality, from that daydream of satanic ecstasy, dick-em walked over to, i, with many witnesses present, as he shut his mouth, as some of us walked to the elevator. Then, while we were all in the elevator, going downstairs, dick-em had the nerve to say, "*I want a transfer off of this case...*"

It is no wonder attorn'eys have a bad rapp; all of dick-ems guilt was expressed in those witnessed actions and by his own words "*I want a transfer off of this case.*"

i, thought "no problem you can go wherever you want however, i, was going to make certain dick-em would not receive one more pennies from i, as i, am certain ass-wipe niner gave him enough outside of the courtroom for both of us?

SATAN'S 6TH MINION OF THE BITCH M.L.O. CHATSWORTH CRIMINAL GANG OF 2007 – 2025

Ronald George Niner, The Man Who Spermed Scott Alan Niner; how far will a father's fear of desecrated name go to save his name-sake?

Ronald George Niner
Satan's 6th Minion
(Sperm-donor)
C.E.O.
Creative Graphic Services

Ronald George Niner better known as "sperm-donor" is a man who was revered, once appreciated, well liked by i, Adam-Daniel- or daniel –adam from the family borsotti, until sperm-donor turned his moral and ethical satanic tail between his satanic legs, and abandoned his belief. If this was his belief, then it is something that was not and could not have been under any good God that i, know of today.

By sperm-donor allowing his bad judgment to thwart what is true about his son, ass-wipe, niner, and by knowing everything that i, stated and was making i, stand upon, what ass-wipe and robin niner had done, sperm-donor tried to save his family name. It is over what is amoral, unethical and what is wrong verses what is right.

It is not so much that sperm-donor was or is a bad man, because i, do not think sperm-donor *was*. It is more that sperm-donor allowed his better judgment of what is true and under god's commandments, to be thwarted by sperm-donor's son ass-wipe niner's actions. Rather than letting ass-wipe learn the lesson of life the way that most honest moral and ethical wo/mankind learn wisdom; the way of life's trials and tribulations on his own. Sperm donor aided and abetted his son, ass-wipe niner as the orchestrator, in the shadows, whereby even his family did not know in the beginning that ass-wipe was committing adultery, using cocaine(N.A.) and other bad things ass-wipe was capable of and actually doing. This is an indication why ass-wipe ripped i, off and went out with i, money and started its own business as previously stated Dangling Carrot Creative. The business was started with god fearing, yet corrupted money.

Although, the entire niner family do know enough about ass-wipe's temper growing up, if ass-wipe has ever truly grown up concerning ass-wipe having to control everything and have everything ass-wipe's own way, it will be revelational.

i, do not know when of course ass-wipe's family became conversant to ass-wipe's plot to take advantage of i, as man, thrown his ex-wife robin under the bus of adultery, and abuse (as robin told i, personally) regardless of the fact to steal, lie, and abscond a disabled man's money. It does not matter when the niner family knew because the niner family allowed themselves to be drawn into ass-wipe's unscrupulous, amoral tornado of lies and deceit.

It Was God's Gift To Us All

When i, received, as the remedy of a settlement from the 03rd day May 2001 accident, the funds were supposed 2-B set up N-2 an account for i's future medical and other life-altering needs. Robin Niner being i, conservator, representative Payee for i, Social Security Disability, monthly living funds, should have known as robin's husband, ass-wipe had acted the parts of the fiduciary responsibilities equal to robin. The law is precise on fiduciary duties. Do not mix and mingle another wo/mankind's assets with your own assets and do not steal. Do not enter into contracts with infants, disabled, drunken or coerced wo/mankind.

Instead of talking to i, and working things out, sperm-donor became involved by assisting ass-wipe along with jim/james, the eldest brother to hide assets, commit unlawful transfers of business assets, bank accounts, titles; who knows what else.
Sperm-donor even had gone as far as getting up on a witness stand to perjure himself in order to assist his little boy ass-wipe and daughter in-law robin to lie and cheat i, out of the money that sperm-donor was not willing to give ass-wipe.

i, know why sperm-donor did not loan ass-wipe any money which was a family issue. Yet, they all made it a public issue when they individually and collectively conspired to steal from i, a once severely disabled man by aiding ass-wipe's deliberate deceit.
It was about September October 2005, scott alan niner, hereinafter, renewed as "ass-wipe" begun to have trouble within his family. At the time leading up when ass-wipe began to cheat against robin niner, ass-wipe was breaking away from the family business because jim or james niner, the older brother, had and was receiving all of the control over their business creative graphic services.

James Niner do play a small roll in these niner events, as stated B-4, however, i, shall leave james to himself for now and his belief in god and not bring him in only to say, james should have shut his big fat mouth to his brother ass-wipe and sperm-donor after james escorted i, as a witness to i, attorn'ey's for i, final settlement.

Reminder Of An Earlier Issue
At the time, i, was supposed to receive i, settlement from the attorn'ey james wilson vititoe, hereinafter, "Do-we, Cheat-em & Howe," or "DCH", there was a meeting set up to finalize i's settlement from the 2001 incident. It was DCH who had made many attempts to abscond most of the judgment from the 3rd of May 2001 accident. i, will leave this chapter out for another real life tale, of his-story. It became clear, sperm-donor threw all of his own decent principles out the moral window when he became more involved with i's fight for what is true and right to expose ass-wipe niners for all of their attempts to get away with crimes. Crimes against honorable moral and ethical compass are as it is against a disabled man, which is a blindness of love to jesus and god.

Sperm-donor proved he had only one thing in mind. That was in order to protect sperm-donor's own family name; he would have to go along with ass-wipe's plan. Although, i, do to this day semi-respect sperm-donor niner for what he has achieved for him, and his entire niner family. On a society level, for business intent, sperm-donor do aid and abet ass-wipe and robin niner to steal, lie and cheat i, out of over 90% of all the future funds that were to assist i, to this very day after rehabilitation.

Justification Is The Wrath Of God

No wrongs make anything a right, especially when wo/mankind give up God for a moment to gain something for self as sperm-donor did in order to save his name sake from being a deadbeat within society. Ass-wipe can never be saved until he repents to what is true openly.

This does mean to come clean that what he do to i. i, say that sperm-donor was able to temporarily protect ass-wipe's name from legally but not lawfully paying for the crimes. By forking out money for ass-wipe's attorn'eys, top-ramin, for unlawful transfer of the business, Dangling Carrot Creative, the hiring attorn'ey James Thomas King hereinafter, (Jack-off) the fraudulent stage and to violate god's commandments was set.

Readers this is a place for you to write your notes, ideas, for self or the author:____

If you know this ass-wipe niner and want to send i, your stories, send to care of: Disabled Justice 5152 Sepulveda Boulevard, Suite 175 Sherman Oaks California [91403] :) i might compensate you?

SATAN'S 3RD TRONE IN THE SAGA OF SCOTT ALLAN NINER'S CRIMINAL GANG OF 2007 – 2025 2ND APPELLATE DISTRICT COURT OF APPEAL

300 S. Spring Street 2nd Floor, North Tower Los Angeles, CA 90013

Not completely knowing at this point nor understanding what an *Open Court of Record* truly is nor how the statutory scheme worked, i, was forced to file an appeal, at the appellate court [93] where i, uncovered more corruption.

Based on the domino effect of the first Satan's trone that fell, the rest of the corruption that transpired at the Second District Court of Appeal was caused by none of the defendant niner's or their

---

[93] **APPELLATE COURTS:** Some appellate courts, particularly supreme courts, have the power of discretionary review, meaning that they can decide whether they will hear an appeal brought in a particular case. And a case in Trial Court typically involves the presentation of evidence and witness testimony and deals with questions of fact and questions of law. • An Appellate Court, in contrast, reviews decisions of the Trial Court, on appeal, and deals only with questions of law.
In contrast, an Appellate Court is wherein a party files against the decision of a lower court. Appellate jurisdiction is the power of an appellate court to review, amend and overrule decisions of a trial court or other lower tribunal. Most appellate jurisdiction is legislatively created, and may consist of appeals by leave of the appellate court or by right.
https://search.yahoo.com/yhs/search?hspart=pty&hsimp=yhs-ext-ff_freetestnow&param1=20220527&param3=speedtest_%7EUS%7Eappfocus1%7E&param4=%7Efirefox%7E%7E&type=yhs-ext-ff_freetestnow_appfocus1_ff&grd=1&p=what+does+the+appellate+courts+main+purpose+

attorn'eys. It is a fact that none of the niner's filed any answers or any of the appeal papers at all. By lack of interaction with the appeal, it placed the fallen corrupted domino of i, denial to overturn the corrupt superior court bitch-mlo (margret lynn oldendorf) court action PC040224.

In contrast, to what most wo/mankind think, an appellate court is wherein a party files against the decision of a lower court when there is some mistakes made by either deliberate act or inaction. It could be a blatant mistake of discretion or the lower court actors made grave error, in wanton, by mistake or malicious act.

Appellate Courts Believe It Can Do:
In the statutory world, which most citizens and residents reside, the appellate courts, particularly supreme courts, have the power of flexibility to review; meaning that they can decide whether to hear an appeal brought in a particular action at l.e.g.a.l. and not l.a.w. within an *open court of record*. An action at a Trial Court typically involves the production of evidence by witness authentication and deals with questions of fact and questions of law. Whereas, an Appellate Court, in contrast, will review decisions of the lower nisi prius trial court, on appeal that deals with questions of l.a.w only in word but not substance.

Appellate jurisdiction is the power of an appellate court to review, amend and overrule decisions of a trial court or other lower tribunals when not done by a *trial by jury*. Most appellate jurisdiction is legislatively created, and may consist of appeals <u>by leave</u> of the appellate court or by right. However, usually only by bench trials because a true *Open Court Of Record* do not encompass a bench trial because that is by consent and in the statutory l.e.g.a.l. world and not a world of l.a.w. .

Open Court Of Record Not Statutory
Yet, with a wo/mankind that files an action at an *open court of record*, there is no appeal. The reason there is no appeal necessary is all of the facts have already been determined and the only thing to figure out is why did the evil-wrongdoer who caused another wo/mankind harm, going to or not going to compensate for the harm evil-wrongdoer do cause wo/mankind who is forced to push a claim.

Usually there is no reason to call forth a *trial by jury*, however, when an evil-wrongdoer has a lawful excuse in contrast to legal excuse, why the wrongdoer did not stand in honor and handle the action on the private side of life, then the only necessary hearing to bring forth is a *trial by jury*. Otherwise there is no need for an entire long drawn out court actions of today like a statutory schema because the only purpose for a statutory scheme administratively is to waste time, money, and to fall into the trap of the corporate courts. The corporate courts' agents love controversy.

This is why we always hold an *Open Court of Record* as a court of record. It is in honor and stands on all the facts presented. When the wrongdoer(s) do have a lawful excuse why they do not bring forth compensation for their harm to another wo/mankind, there might be opportunity to receive a jury of one's peers. Anything less than an *Open Court of Record*, by a *trial by jury* of one's peers is nothing less than a fictional statutory, non lawful court. This works in an administrative process, which is not l.a.w. nor is it constitutional. [94] Constitutions do not affect a wo/man.

Simplicity The Key To All Things

Govern mentals do seem to not want simplicity within their system and definitely not with any of govern mental operated courts of every type. Almost all mainstream courts are based on statutory schema that need to run their proper way in order to control the wealth of all citizens, residents, agents, employees and their like kind of enslaved mind's to the statutory schema. Not living wo/mankind.

When Simple Simon do say, or to say, "why put off tomorrow what can be resolved today" do not work for i. Resulting, when a wo/mankind file their action at l.a.w., each has to have all facts placed on the claim already so there is no need to prove any questions of l.a.w. because the facts are indisputable and there is only one thing 2-B determined. What is to determine, is how much or what will bring a harmed wo/mankind back to whole?

---

[94]**1215.ORG**: Go to 1215.org for the definitions of a Court of Record, and the difference between a judge, a magistrate and a court.

To stand on honor with any court issue all i, and you want to do, is finalize the honorable notices and proffer the proof of claim, and not complaint. To fulfill the out of court lawful action is truly simplicity. It is a k.i.s.s. method. (see definition); There are many different types of govern mental agencies and other corp(s)orations with offices within this structure where the Second District Court of Appeal building is operating. The agents truly do operate on people's (remember in this *living missive* "people" mean wo/mankind) lives as they dissect every red cent or wealth they can as an unmoral and unethical servitude to their court agent's whim.

Although, this corp(s)oration or so-called state of California dejure lawful courthouse-ship for the second district is what most people think a savior to when the lower court [~~judge~~]s pubic serpent go off kilter from what the facts and evidence prove. It is not dejure by right of lawful court doing a public service, rather caters to the special interests and protects the pubic serpent regardless of whether they are wrong. It is when serpent do things maliciously, or make ignorant or plain old dumb mistakes that the Second District will step in to correct mistakes made by lower courts. It is one step below a supreme court's to the underworld of satanic machines created by agents and not god. Rather it is the fall guy syndrome for govern mentals that are paid to protect certain special interest corp(s)orations whereby any appellate court may or may not get involved.

When the machine changes its ways and becomes lawful again, let i, know as i, might change i, ways of living. Until then, God has supreme judgment over all things. i, do not consent to ever going to a jurisdiction for a state/federal enclave.

Open Court Of Record Is Law For Mankind

With an *Open Court of Record* there are no [~~judge~~]s to judge, no commissioners to make rulings, and no attorn'eys allowed to litigate or pro-se-cute anything. The only process has all been final and the only designation necessary by a court cluck or a magistrate is to keep the decorum of the court safe and to witness the facts and evidence brought forward by the one who do file a claim. It is the lawful court, which has no court actors rather a wo/mankind that is separate from the magistrate designated thereto hold it, that sits unbiased to either side and can only witness all the facts and sign the decree as a witness only. This is a simple *open court of record.* Similar to a notary in how they witness the wo/mankind signatory as in who they say they are and not the contents of the paperwork.

This is not the same as a pubic serpent whereas calling themselves a commissioner or [~~judge~~]s, pro-se-cuter, or an attorn'ey at law (which truly means an attorn'ey at legal) and tries to determine everything from the start to finish of almost all court hearings, motions or cases today and is timelines as l.a.w. is not ever l.e.g.a.l..

Contrast Between Claim And Complaint
A Court of record, a Court not of Record is a key component as stated in contrast to a claim and a complaint. The *Open Court of Record* is not a process of today when a statutory schema is introduced because someone signed away their rights to contract. There is a disconnect as how to file and where to file a proper court action. It is ignorant to a legal verses law that takes on the roll as citizens, residents and agents verses a wo/mankind. No wo/mankind can ever have a nexus in the l.e.g.a.l. realm.

When a statutory schema action, goes to an appeals court, there are fewer cases overturned where the Court finds in favor of a wo/mankind that does not have an attorn'ey. This reason is not because the non-attorn'ey did not bring forth good facts, case law, codes or statutes presented. The most common reason is that the non-attorney did not have an attorn'ey. The claims court does not have appeals compared to a complaint court. However, no matter what type of case a non-attorney do file, the court agents have an arsenal of case law, rules, and codes to deny a non-attorney regardless of how correct the paperwork is. The statutory courts only have nexus with a statutory court process that is never the true law. The court system is and always has been evolving to what it is of today 2025. The non-claim court is done in order to overwhelm the people by statute, codes, rules regulations and acts that is meant to fluster the average wo/mankind's understanding of what to do and when to do it. It is done by justification.

It is pubic serpent are hired as Bank Authorized Representative B.A.R. members that operate like doctors doing surgery on all wo/mankind's rights, titles, interest's estates, usage and control of land and property; which rites and rights are property.

Notice To The Reader To Research
i, case alone, along with many others i, will write about herein is for the reader to review the case numbers on line, are memorialized at the back of this *living missive*.

i, do this for the public to read and to back i, facts, written herein, whereas the courts just flat out deny i, and many other wo/mankind that handle their own court actions. Heaven forbid where a non-attorn'ey can be shown to actually do better than a licensed practicing attorn'ey regardless of their year's experience. Do not forget attorn'eys practice l.e.g.a.l. whereas wo/mankind actually apply and instruct law and never practice what they already know is true, to the law.

What Appellate Courts do, is give wo/mankind a place where wo/mankind can lodge their personal views of what wrongs the lower court's final decree was and rebut the mistakes of the lower courts. It is not in the best interest of the appellate court actors to overturn a usurped jurisdiction when the pubic serpent was not authorized by the wo/mankind that originally filed the court action at a lower court.

These f.u.k.c.-ing courts are not operating in compliance with a lawful *open court of record*. All courts, not just one of them, all of them, act as authority over the people's property, when govern mentals were originally set up, or to appear as they act unbiased.

Yet, end results are almost always to steal, take, things while court actors conspire with other wo/mankind that act as agents to acquire, wealth by theft yours and i, property, rights, and freedoms from you and i, as wo/mankind.

The sad part of all this is you and i, as wo/mankind are used as labor to fund the very existence of such institutions by theft. The l.e.g.a.l. courts are not in sync with l.a.w. There is always an opportunity gone by when one wo/mankind can prove their allegations to stand up to reverse what is the new age raping of people by deception.

Just Do Not Consent And You Are Fine

The only way that any actors of any federal or state court can get jurisdiction over a wo/mankind is by consent, of the governed. It is by contract or sheer stupidity by those who do contract themselves N-2 a jurisdiction of said unscrupulous courts.

It is all city, county, state and federal agents actually believe they own every wo/mankind as their slave. These pubic serpent that work for these agencies actually believe that any wo/mankind that has a berth/birth certificate, a passport, driver's license, credit cards, mortgage, credit report, bank accounts, marriage license, carry federal reserve notes or anything that connects a wo/mankind to such commercial corporate entity, is their slave.

Slaves, not in color, language, education, male or female, rather like animals that know not for their hierarchy to god. This includes being born on North American states or naturalization, whereby one takes an oath to any states united.

Courts are not what we perceive them to be, not for you and not for [me] i. What most ignorant people comprehend is that city, county, state and federal agencies run the whole country and what is to be is to be. All courts are run by alleged pubic serpent who is supposed to serve all public. What a pubic serpent really do is run a monopolistic matrix in order to serve citizens to the corp(s)orations as a meal on any given day.

It does not matter what time of day these blood thirsty agents and sucking leaches get hungry. If it is you they hunger for, since you find yourself in their bailiwick (courthouse-ships) or their sights, you are going 2-B breakfast, lunch, brunch, or dinner. Some are just a midnight snack without care for law or your rites/rights.

Even when you have not done anything unlawful and you have never harmed another wo/mankind or any property of any wo/mankind, rather you find yourself subject as a target by govern mentals or an associated agents abuses its position or clout.

This is similar to Martin Luther King, John Fitzgerald Kennedy, Abraham Lincoln, Jesus Christ, Gandhi, Donald John Trump, or i, adam-daniel of the family borsotti. It is that agents do not like when any wo/mankind speak out as to what is true, as i do. It has to be done for all wo/mankind need to learn how and why to stand up.

Most wo/mankind know when we speak a language that is true, in opposition of what agents do not like, for whatever reason, agents transform into satanic ritualistic serpents, that require new blood (property or money) to set a model to transfuse or just to make a point as example of how to be a good slave so other slaves won't follow you.

i, as Donald John Trump was used as an example and still am and may be used again as an example in the future. i, do what i, do and say without any reservations of fear, no matter what. i, may be served on an unlawful platter once this *living missive* is finalized and to be served as another example. i, shall not fear as Jesus and God are always in i, heart.

To this day, i, have not ever hired an attorn'ey again in over 20-ish court actions to this day 2025 and i, will continue to share all of i, other court cases, trials and triumphs of this journey through DisabledJustice.org.

To prove that the statutory schema is and how disabled the justice court systems' agents truly are, there can be no fear for what might transpire, only spirited wo/mankind ready to stand tall on free will.

Courts Are Not A Place Wo/Mankind Belong
A Court is only for enslaved minds that are given titles, as the likes of: Citizen, Resident, Tenant, Person, Individual, Ens Legis, Employee, Infants, Indigents, Ignorant, Agents, ~~Sovereign Citizens~~ (which is actually an oxymoronic term).

It is all capitalized all titles such as police officer, ~~judge~~, (president, secretary, governor, mayor…) and those that do take on jobs knowingly or unknowingly who wreck havoc on an entire world of wo/mankind that are ignorant to facts stated.

The havoc is created when any or all govern mentals believe that they are bigger, smarter, and have more rights, titles, interest and control by superior authority and gun power to use as threat against any wo/mankind. This is already prevalent that already has begun.

Agents treat wo/mankind as nothing more than canon potter. The bottom line is that as long as all wo/mankind live life within the laws of wo/mankind, then there is no problem.

With all societal govern mentals that are good hard and honest working wo/mankind acting as agents that have been led to believe what is not true. That is govern mentals are in place for benefit of people. It can never be true when one looks at what govern mentals do?

If the power of the doctrines is by people and are made of people, then what happens when govern mentals get larger, take more wealth from the average people as wo/mankind? The end result is a difference between animals and law abiding wo/mankind that are the of age majority. Animals, hue-man or citizens are not respected.

Persons as “the people of….” are not respected. So, why should wo/mankind respect agents that create controversies for self gain as a fiction that does not exist?

Govern mentals that get too big ends up consuming itself which appears to be transpiring today 2025. Model of govern mental corp(s)rations using fear is unlawful but l.e.g.a.l. as is eminent domain.

Eminent domain takes private property by l.e.g.a.l. when one proves no right to take the greater of public domain verses a govern mental corp(s)orations. As long as a fiction agent compensates land owners reasonably everything is supposed to be lawful. All courts are the apex of abuse.

Just because agents place mandates or codes, regulations, ordinances down on paper does not give it credence. As a matter of rite and right, all wo/mankind must question everything.

When we fail to stand up we end up being rolled over on our stomachs, to be taken at will; not one, butt by all agents in the name of a fiction.

Satan's 7th - 9th Minions of The BITCH M.L.O. Chatsworth <u>Criminal Gang</u> OF 2007 – 2025

2ND APPELLATE DISTRICT COURT OF APPEAL Action # B21796 - 2011

Dennis Mayer Perlus
7th Satan's Minion
1st Blind Mouse
(Pubic Serpent)
B.A.R. #**57999**

Norvell "Fred" Woods Junior
8th Satan's Minion
2nd Blind Mouse
(Pubic Serpent)
B.A.R.# **35745**

Frank Y. Jackson
9th Satan's Minion
3rd Blind Mouse
(Pubic Serpent)
B.A.R.# **57384**

Three blind [~~judge~~]s mice - three blind [~~judge~~]s, mice

see how they act – against all of the facts,

They all ran after the money from power,

To do what they are told, whether unethical or amoral,

To suppress a disabled man's rights and beliefs,

Did you ever see such a horrific decree,

By these three blind [~~judge~~]s mice

three blind [~~judge~~]s mice

By: i, a man; Adam – Daniel;

Three Blind ~~Judges~~ Mice See How They Run
There is no difference between a titled Superior Court and A District of Appeal's Court. They are all a part of the same statutory schema that is set out to steal from wo/mankind. To take is to conspire to suppress all *free will* of wo/mans rites/rights.

These three blind mice that act as [~~judges~~], of the second district court of appeal, do as all of the rest who completely disregard i, adam-daniel-of family borsotti's lawful filings. i, as all wo/mankind require certain rites/rights to perceive the process of unbiased agents from the agencies, which is not an administrative court action. It is supposed to either be a lawful *open court of record* accordingly to common law court or law for mankind. However, i, was supposed to have a lawful *open court of record* at superior court. Once i, law in action was to get to appellate level, it is already at a l.e.g.a.l. statutory schema, administrative unlawful and not lawful court.

It was three blind mice that assisted to aid trial court employees as pubic serpent to deny i, trial court records, along with the lower kangaroo court titled; The Superior Court of Los Angeles, Chatsworth California. Whereas bitch-mlo, was the magistrate along with the court cluck, osana, pubic serpent, who refused to send all of the record on appeal. This is just another interference by agents to suppress i, lawful rights by refusing i, records from reporters and court cluck record.

The lower f.u.k.c.-ing court clucks from Chatsworth Courthouse-ship denied all of i, transcripts on appeal, and all of the f.u.k.c.-ing appellate court clucks denied i, even though ass-wipe and robin niner never replied to the initial appeal.

i, had an ADA Americans With Disability Act Representative to assist i, with the entire appeal. None of the f.u.k.c.-ing niner's showed, nor did any of their f.u.k.c.-ing pieces of shit attorn'eys; top-ramin nor weiner-dog. When anyone files an appeal and the other side does not respond to the appeal it is supposed to act as a default. Same thing when someone files a claim or a complaint with a summons and properly serves the other side, the timeline is set to reply. When the served party does not answer, show up or even send up a smoke signal, the opponent loses by evasion. However, for i, a man; adam – daniel of the borsotti family, the courts have different system that do not apply to a lawful court nor i.

The only thing the three blind mice did is blindly deny the appeal, and make it look like i, did not do i, part by making certain the record on appeal was available. Even though all three blind mice had full knowledge that i, was completely denied all court transcripts, record on appeal, and joint statement for the record on appeal. Therefore, i, do place in its place statement on appeal which it too was not replied to by ass-wipe, robin nor their attorn'eys top-ramin or weiner-dog. Who loses when an unrebutted affidavit stands true in commerce? Yes, the one who does not rebut.

The original reason given to deny i, appeal was that i, did not forward the complete record on appeal. This reason was preset by all court actors. The fact California Transcribers Board members denied i, for years, is proof by facts as evidence that all of the court actors all knew about the denial B-4 i, was denied the entire appeal.

It makes no sense other than what i, said previously, they are prejudice towards i, a disabled man because they gave the transcripts to other litigants who requested them. Think about it, a Pilate program was set up by Sacramento Court Reporters Board to assist wo/mankind that could not afford records on appeal. i, elect everything listed from A to Z inclusive on appeal.

Regardless, i, do file an opening brief, with no reply. When there is no reply, just like when there is not reply to an original claim or complaint filed, a default will ensue for evasion by acquiesce.

It definitely was no coincident, i, was refused all record on appeal, multiple times. i, had made multiple attempts to the superior court, Chatsworth Courthouse whereas the woman that act as magistrate, [margaret lynn oldendorf] bitch-mlo outright denied i. She denied Americans with Disability Act (ADA) and fee waiver denied. In addition, the California Court Reporters Board, TRF Pilot Project should have availed all transcripts on appeal denied i, without cause.

One Knows Regardless Of Knowing

There was only one main criterion to receive the pilot program. i, was already granted a fee waiver on the case; therefore, i, should have never been denied this requirement for i, appeal.

For the Court Reporters Board to deny i, to receive what many other wo/mankind have received when required them for their appeal can only mean *one* thing. i, was not denied transcripts because i, was not taken advantage of by the niner family, nor was i, denied because of the lack of being able to afford the record on appeal.

i, was denied because there is at that time and until this very day a conspiracy to deny i, everything i, applied for. Every motion to the court from this case forward; as i, have been denied to this very day 2025 as you, will read further on in the future of this *living missive.*

Even though i, was completely denied the court record on appeal, i, was still able to move forward by way of, oration at the appeal. So, the three blind mice moved forward on oration at the appeal. Do not 4-get i, do submit a statement record on appeal. Not one of the niner's, not ass-wipe, robin, sperm-doner's attorn'eys weiner-dog and top-ramin objected to the entire appeal. As you guessed it, none of the niner's ever showed, did not reply, and it was like a default; as in a slam dunk court ac tion. What, a slam dunk for i, a man's victory was a sure thing by their evasion is culpability to god and i.

Disability Advocate With His Own Agenda

i, had to hire an ADA advocate which i, did. Although it did take much of the stress off of i, similarly to the stress i, felt with the original lower court trial. The one big difference is that i, thought because the advocate was not a licensed attorn'ey, that i, was not going against, i, integrity to i-self to have an advocate assist i, with the appeal.

However, it turned out this was not a good thing because i, had hired an ADA advocate who was referred to me by a friend. i, truly had no idea what was going to happen at the appeal hearing. Not having ever done a court action, an appeal or even a trial, everything was a new avenue; another street turned onto and yet, to date, i, have not ever hit a dead end; only a cross to burden at every cross road.

Side Swiped Alternative Motives

Similarly to how i, felt when i, became overwhelmed at the superior court trial, if not more stressful than i, trial. As an appeal board consists of three blind mice who act as [~~judge~~] s. Remember, i, had no complete record. i, was putting all of i, faith, outside of i, in this ADA advocate. i, let go again of i, power. All he was to do is orate in front of the three blind mice appeal panel. Although, i, was still learning about the difference between *lawful* and *legal*, certain things were ad lived and realized as life unfolded. The manifestation of Christ to the Gentiles as represented by the Magi (Matthew 2:1–12). The advocate is not a Jesus Christ; is closer to Satan.

Being so overwhelmed and going through the motions of being used and lied to by i, best friend, abandoned and betrayed by the hired attorn'ey for the niner court action at Satan's No. 1 Trone (Chatsworth Courthouse), and preparing for the Appeals Court. When the court hearing began, all i, could do is allow the ADA advocate to orate the appeal while i, sat there continuously wiping the tears from i, eyes. i, guess, i, was still dealing with healing from TBI and PTSD reactions. Thinking i, was ready, but truly i, was not.

i, was unable to focus while watching the three blind mice sitting on the panel just attentively listening to the ADA advocate. The three blind mice even seemed very impressed by ADA advocate from Tex-ass. His name was Kenneth Allen Goldblatt, hereinafter, "Tex-Ass" had an ability to orate the federal disability laws and what i, issues were for the appeal truly was second best to none. i, was not in control of i, ability to stay focused enough and do i, best from allowing the water-works from flooding out the appeal's room which seemed like i, was a fire hydrant that had exploded.

Know Who You Hire B-4 You Hire Them

Turns out the ADA advocate had his own agenda, why he was assisting i. i, thought his duty was to i, the disabled man on the appeal. It was not until after the oration with the three blind mice that i, realized the Advocate Kenneth Goldblatt, was only there to help him. Kenneth Goldblatt's previous agenda to help i, was not disclose until the day of; actually right after oration as appeal concluded. i, obviously had no idea that this advocates' motive was to use i, case on appeal to set up all three blind mice in order 2-B able to sue them when they disregard law and the ADA by-laws. When "Tex-Ass" was finished orating at the appeal's court, the court cluck in her genuine manner, asked Tex-ass for his full name and contact information.

It was at this very moment when, Tex-ass did not just give the court cluck his information. Tex-ass had to elaborate as to what he does, and why he was there, which at this juncture he did do a fine job at orations on appeal. Tex-ass, started with giving the court cluck his name and number and then he followed with "*I sue judges…*" and no, he could not just stop there.

He went on and on, to the point where the court cluck began to show fear from what Tex-ass was expressing about how he is going to sue any judge who fucks with Tex-ass. This fu**ing over weight Texan i.e., Tex-ass that charged i, money to fly his oversized gluteus maximums and periformus lard ass out from Texas to California, and put him up in a down town Los Angeles, hotel, totally screwed i, over. He had the gall to demand to be placed in an upscale hotel so he did not need to drive to Appeals Court.

i, just stood there with i, mouth wide open in disbelief. Although, i, did make an attempt to stop him from going off on the appeals court cluck. i, tried to nudge and then pull tex-ass away from the cluck. i, even tried to down play what he was saying. i, was more embarrassed and discouraged when Tex-ass, told i, right in the front of the court cluck, "Shut up and go back to where you (i) came from. Because he was not going to be denied his egotistical arrogant rant to this appeal court cluck about his intension to sue these three blind mice/~~judges~~.

It was too late for any reconciliation of what he started, as the horse opened up his ass as Tex-ass released those words of threatening manner. It was as if i, was not there while tex-ass's could not stick its dick back in his pants because he had already shoved it in his own mouth and degraded i, and showed his true colors. This was when i, wanted to rip his gonads out through his throat with i, bear hands. What was going on with all of these men taking i, money, act as if they are assisting i, in the manner they swear they will fight for i. In the end, all they fight for is an opportunity to take i, money, received under the table payments to assist their own agendas, and in the end fu** i, over for their own personal ambition.

i, suppose that i, have big expectations for other wo/mankind's integrity, morals, ethics and their honorable word. When one says "*I will…*" i, actually believe them. i, did trust ass-wipe niner and robin with their agreement. Then i, do believe dick-em would fulfill what he said he would and then i, and others witness this butt fu**ing ass-wipes attorn'ey weiner-dog at the court house; the action was unscrupulously mis-interpretive by b.i.t.c.h.-MLO. Now i, deal with Tex-ass Kenneth Goldblatt with his own agenda to sue judges, using i, case as a proxy. i, do not change as i, do believe that there are some wo/mankind somewhere on this planet that know the true meaning of integrity, morals, ethics and actually follow through with not breaking their honor for anything or any fixed agenda.

It is not too much to expect the same integrity i, give to others, especially when paying for a service, to those who charge a fee to give it their all out best effort to stand in honor to i, to their self and especially to god. i, often wonder how wo/mankind can allow their own self worth to be thwarted by the love of money, greed, ego, pride, or a personal agenda over standing with good character to follow laws of god and laws of comity, reciprocity that of God's grace.

Neither paycheck nor oath to an agency can subvert the oath to god or to oneself. When one gives another wo/mankind their solemn word, which is what ass-wipe did with i, and goes against it, then brings others such as ass-wipe did.

Whether one gives their word to a wife it cheats on, its biological father, sperm-doner and its brother james niner, it proves that what ass-wipe do state was not to i, not to god or himself, but to Satan's devilish functions.

Tex-ass did exactly the same thing. i, do accept accountability as this taught i, to never place i, own power to others, when god gives the opportunity to become the age of majority;   a self revelation.

Only Satan will benefit truly from others lack of fulfilling the commandments, lack of integrity, morals and ethics. Only Satan can and will require repentance from ass-wipe and all others that do trespass against i, a man over this *living missive*.

i, cannot wait until i, learn of ass-wipe's repentance towards i, nor will i, hold i, breadth waiting for him to actually realize its wrongs and repent to his god satan.

SATAN'S 4TH TRONE THE SAGA OF SCOTT ALLAN NINER'S <u>CRIMINAL GANG</u> OF 2009 – 2025

UNITED STATES BANKRUPTCY COURT
ACTION # 2:11-BK -18734

Thomas Brian Donovan
Satan's 10th Minion
(Shit-for-brains)
The man who do <u>act</u> as U.S.B.K.
[Judge] Pubic Serpent
What is a bankruptcy any ways?

i, can tell you what a bankruptcy is not. A bankruptcy (BK) is not a place wherein wo/mankind can just wipe away all of their accumulated debts in a manner of receiving a fresh clean start. Also, a BK is not a place that all of one's sins will disappear from the face of earth. A BK is a thing that corp(s)orations do when the corp(s)orations want to wipe away an overwhelming level of built up Karma wherein the corp(s)orations desires a new start, on a clean slate, on the monopoly board called fictional world *within* the United States Corp(s)orational enclaves.

This United States *of* [and] or *for* America, including, but not limited to INC. is not a place of reality, rather it is an Alice in Wonderland, Wizard of Oz, Matrix, Dome like bubble which entails no wo/mankind in reality. It is a place only for agents to operate a doppelganger known as a fiction called hue-man, person, citizen, resident, employee, individual as every title created within govern mental enclaves.

Therefore, when a wo/mankind files for BK, it truly is not the wo/mankind rather it is the enslaved citizen, resident, agent, employee, individual, tax payer, or the all capitalized wo/man of straw called the straw wo/man. You see woman or man do not apply for the wo/mankind. A wo/mankind cannot be liable for a made up fantasy, camouflaged by its non-living corp(s)oration. Wo/mankind can only setoff and discharge any or all deadbeat-debtor's debts. It is that Jesus Christ already paid for all of our sins [95] forward for eternity. All Sins are known as debts.

Therefore, it is important to realize this previous passage and not abuse any agency knowingly or willfully. This man above: Thomas Brian Donovan, hereinafter, "Shit-For-Brains" or "Sfb" that acts as a conjured title, known by title of [~~judge~~] has a long lasting effect on those who he taketh advantage of forevermore.

---

[95] **PAID FOR ALL SINS:** It's true that God offers salvation to us as a free gift — and the reason is because Jesus Christ has already paid the price for it by giving His life for us. The Bible says, "For the wages of sin is death, but the gift of God is eternal life in Christ Jesus our Lord" (Romans 6:23).
https://billygraham.org/answer/if-jesus-died-to-pay-for-all-our-sins-as-the-bible-says-then-why-do-we-still-have-to-confess-them-and-commit-our-lives-to-him-in-order-to-be-saved/

In his name is the name of Shit-for-brains, he
who truly has no brains for what is to come as
God's wrath will surely cometh soon,
and until then, let us not assume nor presume,
that a man who appears a man, who may appear
disabled is that of a fable.

On Scott Alan Niner, or better known as ass-wipe's, bankruptcy action, in order to try to get away with not fulfilling ass-wipe's integrity to i, a man, which ass-wipe do his very best to not fulfill at every level. To this very day, ass-wipe and robin niner still owes, i, as man, all principal amount plus all of the interest for which i, aim to collect lawfully from ass-wipe or from his namesake.

This means that his offspring still owe i, compensation for the harm that his next to kin cause as a trespass against, i, a man. Do not forget, there is no statue of limits on trespass.

You see, in the land of shits and giggles, known as commerce, the fiction stays with the fiction. In the world of wo/mankind, a trespass never ends until damages are fulfilled to the one who is harmed by the evil-wrongdoer as a deadbeat debtor. Look at the history books.

Notice of Intent to Robin & Scott Alan Niner (Ass-wipe)
i, shall be filing notices for all of the compensation plus interest that Scott Alan Niner "ass-wipe" still owes to i, to this very day 2025, because ass-wipe and all others who file bankruptcy, named evil-wrogndoers, cannot name i, a man in the bankruptcy because a bankruptcy is never between a wo/man and another wo/man. (i, will share with readers fiction v. fiction and man v. man later, stay tuned).

What is sickening in i, heart as well it should be in all of the readers minds, as with today's' wo/mankind, that do not fully comprehend what L.A.W. is to compare what corp(s)orations are in a statutory colour of l.e.g.a.l. schema.   There never is a wo/mankind ever present when an attorn'ey is present. In other words, even when an alleged wo/mankind files at a state court, federal court, including and not limited to a bankruptcy, it is the ens legis fictitious Alice and Wonderland, Wizard of Oz character or actor and not the actual wo/mankind who it benefits. Rather a B.K. only pertains to the *all caps* [96] corp(s)oration which is the owned entity by the states united Inc. registered with every county which sounds like the wo/mankind's actual name, but in fact they are two separate animals all together.

The Fruitful Tree Is The Spoiled Apple

Therefore, i, say herein now and for all eternity, ass-wipe scott allan and robin niner, you, still owe i, from 2006, through to date plus all of the interest, which i, am coming to collect ☺ soon as a redemption by compensation for the harm you cause as a trespass against i, a man. Be prepared to pay the piper as i, hold a flute. The other issues are that, one by one, each Evil-wrongdoer do continue to individually and collectively conspire against i. However, none of them can ever get away from god's wrath [97] and Jesus's death made his blood available for all to come to him and redeem. As all repentance of all sins must be in the wo/man never from a corp(s)orations; as in the crimson stain. As to crimson stains so to the facts each evil-wrongdoer listed herein do trespass forever until the sins of their world cause from sperm-donor down the bloodline throughout eternity.

Therefore, there never is a statutory limit (statute of limitations) of time against god's laws. As long, as the dishonor is ongoing, harm is always current, and all of the Evil-wrongdoers are subject to present its sins. Sins are forever forgiven, when you believe, yet only when we find eternal life in Jesus Christ. Even Jesus Christ is as i, am man made in the image of god, therefore, as a man, i, too must fulfill i, journey into kingdom of heaven. You do not waive to what is true, through and throughout.

i, Shalt Not Forget Eventually Will Forgive

Remember for the reader, i, was already at the superior court at Chatsworth for a prove up hearing process to retrieve i, collections, liens, levies, as well as the garnishing of ass-wipes wages.

---

[96] **ALL CAPS:** All caps is all capital letters equal all fictions not real incorporated by mankind.

[97] "EXCEPT YE REPENT YE SHALL ALL LIKEWISE PERISH." (Luke 13.5) .

Apparently ass-wipe and his father sperm-donor hired a new attorn'ey James Thomas King, hereinafter; "Jack-off" to file the bankruptcy at the United States Bankruptcy Court.

The look on sperm-donor's face and body language said it all. As if filing a bankruptcy could stop, gods will from being fulfilled. Sperm-donor made certain that sperm-donor, was the man who walked the papers right up to the bitch-mlo's court cluck at the superior court Chatsworth courthouse-ship. Sperm-donor brought his gunslinger top-ramin to the court to try to place a stay on i, deliverance of god's wrath by i, gifted offer ahead of schedule.

It was as if sperm-donor needed to show i, that he was the one in control of what was going on with ass-wipe. That it is all along sperm-doner that has always been in control of the trespass against i, and that it was not only ass-wipe, but most likely orchestrated by ass-wipe and his sperm-doner father.

If sperm-donor could fix all his sons sins, even sperm-doner must truly know in its somewhat moral ethical and spiritual understanding that only God is God and Jesus is the path to ass-wipe's redemption of salvation through repentance. Public repentance is long overdue. However, a wrath of repentence is coming soon to their local environs through this missive.

Conversely, if the fruit, as in his son ass-wipe fell from the original sinful tree, as in sperm-donor, then sperm-donor should had restored his sons sins back to thee who he stole from, lied to, cheated on, and made ass-wipe's sins whole again.

Instead, sperm-donor acerbated the issues by adding to the sins B-4 his son who either lied to his mother, brother and father, or his father is where the same amoral, unethical and dishonorable tree the fruit fell from as in the original sinful tree.

i, do not truly believe this last passage about sperm-doner being as sinful, however, he is when he allowed the sins of ass-wipe to continue which makes sperm-doner an accessory to the original sins.

SATAN'S 11TH MINION IN THE SAGA SCOTT ALLAN NINER'S <u>CRIMINAL GANG</u> OF 2007 – 2025

ATTORN'EY REPRESENTS FRAUD
CASE # 2:11-BK -18734

James Thomas King
[Pubic Serpent]
Satan's 11th Minion
B.A.R. # 82087
(Jack-off)

Scott & Robin Niner's Bankruptcy Attorn'ey

What is interesting now, as i, do bring this character James Thomas King back into the limelight of this *living missive*, as i, shall elaborate even more on the sinful ways of wo/mankind that act as attorn'eys,[~~judge~~] and their like kind.

There is no moment wherein a limit of time goes by when a perpetrator who commits a trespass, as each evil-wrongdoer herein is held liable for said trespass. Once sperm-donor and top-ramin walked into the superior court where bitch-mlo's was acting as a court witness [~~magistrate~~] and showed the automatic stay from the bankruptcy court, it was forever imbedded in the annuls of god's wrath for redemption.

Sperm-donor glared i, down non-stop as if, sperm-donor had full power over everything his little baby boy who actually needed daddy to wipe ass-wipe's butt.

They thought he had won the action, by sperm-doner stopping the superior court collections process when filing an automatic stay. Boy were they all wrong. It was truly a remarkable disgusting display as i, watched a grown men, with haughty eyes, trying to make themselves feel as if they (his ass-wipe son and himself) have won against i, a disabled man.

When all they truly did, especially to this day, is desecrate god's laws; one of reciprocity, two deceptions upon all wo/mankind by filing a fraudulent bankruptcy action, among many other trespasses.

i, did not know at that time, what a bankruptcy truly does, nor did i, know what an automatic stay was. However, i, had learned many things i, did not know then, compared to now that i, do know which is why i, write this *living missive* uncut. Regardless, i, have endured much more to come here in, as this process of learning god's law verses Satan's legal unfolds. What is interesting, is law is simple, even a fourth grader can comprehend when a l.a.w. is applied compared to L.e.g.a.l.;

It didn't matter the outcome as i, was ready, willing and able to go all the way. All the way, meant i, would not stop exposing ass-wipe, nor any other evil-wrongdoer for the harm they deliberately cause against i. Heck, i, already made a concordat to god through vows to redeem i, spirit, once, able to fulfill integrity; thyself to god.

First Time For Something Scarce

Next issue was when the first day i, was at the United States Bankruptcy Court and "jack-off," the man that act as robin and ass-wipe's (hereinafter singular is also plural) attorn'ey made obscure statements at open court; interestingly that in i, mind was not reasonable. Jack-off's statements were that not only was jack-off re-presenting all ass-wipe's, he was also re-presenting i, on the same case through another attorn'eys name. How jack-off pulled this off, i, do not know but something was fishy in the depths of the [~~judge~~]'s smelly pubic serpent 's coli, even though it truly was gibberish-like diarrhea spewing from all of their orifices.

It did not make any sense and i, kind of shrugged it off at the time, because i, do not know the satanic ritualistic ways of the courts, their employees, nor the Bank Authorized Representatives (B.A.R.). They truly are linked by titles of attorn'ey. Nevertheless, it did dawn on i, several years later when i, discover that courts are not lawful. They do not operate the way 99 % of wo/man believes them to function.

Talking Among Buddies At Open Court

i, recall jack-off and thomas brian donovan (shit-for-brains) making statements at open court that jack-off volunteers pro bono [98] litigants for the bankruptcy courts under program. Shit-for-brains operates and donates his time, as well for the public as a pubic serpent. Oh i, could have thrown up all over the table right there on the spot, when i, heard this statement. Of course shit-for-brains nodded and continued to strip i, of all due process of i, rite/rights. It was not only i, rite/rights as a man who present self at the adversarial ass-wipe niner's court, i, was fully deemed disabled by Americans with Disability Acts & Amendment Act doctors. ADA actually means nothing to them as they believe ADA is moot?

i, know that when wo/mankind acts as some title, such as a ~~judge~~, they think that they have some ungodly power to do whatever they want without any repercussions for their actions. This is furthest from what is true. In the world of monopoly, commerce, whereas corp(s)orations, such as Superior, Federal or even District Courts are incorp(s)orated, their agent-pubic-serpent think they can do what they will. As long as wo/mankind give up their consent to allow court actors to get away with deceit, it is semi true avowal but not fully concerning consent.

i, began to challenge the unlawfulness of ass-wipe and sperm-donor's attempts to get away with unlawful conveyances. After some of the ongoing of the Bankruptcy were filed, niner's attorn'ey

---

[98] **PRO BONO:** short for Medieval Latin *probono* pubico "for the pubic good;" from *pro* (prep.) "on behalf of, for" (see *pro-*) + ablative of bonum "good" (see bene-).
https://www.etymonline.com/search?q=pro+bono
i, explaqination: is a legal term and has not place within law. It clearly means that one who donates time of a profession to others who cannot afford their services and is under **LEGAL**: lawbreakers exercise government artificial law…

jack-off, begun to hide the lies, shady transfers of assets, business titles, and positions from what i, to this day know Dangling Carrot Creative is i, business and not ass-wipes, nor sperm-donor's business. Because they created it off of their original theft and deceit against i.

Ass-wipe used all of the money that ass-wipe and robin absconded from i, by false pretenses to start the business, Dangling Carrot Creative at Santa Clarita California. It was then and to this day sham upon a court and against, i, a man.

At the first court hearing, ass-wipe did not show up, only his hired and alleged gun slinger attorn'ey, james thomas king aka "jack-off". At this first hearing, is where i, continue to learn how corrupt court actors are. i, learned there are zero morals, ethics, and what is wrong is actually what is right. Where there is just-us there is zero justice for any wo/mankind at all of the federal and state courts as well abroad. i, also learned that a corp(s)oration is always an all capital corporation attached to everyone's berth/birth certificates. The *collective* corp(s)oration wastes no time in grabbing up its slaves and forcing them into indentured servitude as *citizens*.

The seemingly harmless act of filling out a certificate of live birth ensures that you, a living breathing hue-man being, with a soul, are ushered into this corporate structure without any chance to challenge this action. Your par-ents have just signed their new born baby, birthed *into* the United States under Maritime Law and Universal Commercial Code (The Law Of The Sea) like a ship docking into the port of New York; then turned over to the Federal Govern mentals by way of a Certificate of Live Birth. This contract places its listed contents (you) as property *of* the United States Govern mentals.

You are born into servitude, and you are immediately considered to be collateral for the good faith and credit of the United States Govern mentals, U.S. INC. You are now part of the herd, a herd of hue-man chattel, enslaved from inception. And you have just been veiled in an artificial person-hood; you have been incorp(s)orated and given a STRAWMAN corporate name similar to your hue-man name.[99] (See the following website https://realitybloger.wordpress.com/tag/killing-your-strawman-the-path-to-freedom/and

[99] **BIRTH/BERTH CERTIFICATES, STRAW MAN**: "Supposedly, governments were invented to make human life easier and safer. But governments always end up enslaving humanity. That which we create to "serve" us ends up ruling us. The U.S. government by and for the people... now imprisons millions, takes half the national income by force, over-regulates, punishes, tortures, slaughters foreigners, invades countries, overthrows governments, imposes 700 imperialistic bases overseas, inflates the currency, and crashes future generations with massive debts. That which we create to serve us ends up ruling us. The problem with the "state as servant" thesis is that it is historically, completely false, both empirically and logically. The idea that states were voluntarily invented by citizens to enhance their own security is utterly untrue... The earliest governments and empires were in fact a ruling class of slave-hunters, who understood that because human beings could produce more than they consumed, they were worth hunting, capturing, breaking in, and owning... When cows are placed in very confining stalls, they beat their heads against the walls resulting in injuries and infections. Thus farmers now give them more room; not because they want to set their cows free, but rather because they want greater productivity and lower costs. The next stop after free-range is not freedom. The rise of state capitalism in the 19th century was actually the rise of free-range serfdom. Additional "liberties" were granted to the (human) livestock not with the goal of setting them free, but rather with the goal of increasing their productivity... When you look at a map of the world, you are not looking at countries, but farms. You are allowed certain liberties: limited property ownership, movement rights, freedom of association and occupation; not because your government approves of these rights in principle – since it constantly violates them – but rather because free-range livestock is so much cheaper to own, and so much more productive... State capitalism, socialism, communism, fascism, democracy... these are all livestock management approaches. Some work well for long periods... and some work very badly. They all fail eventually because it is immoral and irrational to treat human beings as livestock... Rulers have recognized that if they prevent you from fleeing the farm, you will become depressed, inert, and unproductive. A serf is the most productive when he imagines he is free. Thus your rulers must provide you the illusion of freedom in order to harvest you most effectively. Thus you are allowed to leave, but never to real freedom, only to another farm. Because the whole world is a farm. They will prevent you from taking a lot of money, they will bury you in endless paperwork, they will restrict your right to work... but you are "free" to leave. Due to these difficulties very few people do leave, but the illusion of mobility is maintained. If only 1 out of 1000 cows' escape, but the illusion of escaping significantly raises the productivity for the remaining 999, it remains a net gain for the farmer. You are also kept on the farm through licensing. The most productive livestock are the (so-called educated) "professionals". So the rulers fit them with an electronic dog collar called a license, which only allows them to practice their trade on their own farm. To further create the illusion of freedom, in certain farms the livestock are allowed to choose between a few farmers (politicians) that the investors present. At best they are given minor choices (votes) in how they are managed. (But) they are never given the choice to shut down the farm and be truly free. Government schools are indoctrination pens for livestock. They train children to "love the farm" and to fear true freedom and independence, and to attack anyone who questions the brutal reality of human ownership. Furthermore they create jobs for the intellectuals that state propaganda so relies on. The idea that democracy and some sort of social contract justifies the brutal exercise of violent power over billions is patently ridiculous. If you say to a slave that his ancestors "chose" slavery and therefore he is bound by their decisions, he will simply say 'If slavery is a choice, then I choose not to be a slave.' This is the most frightening statement for the ruling classes, which is why they train their slaves to attack anyone who dares speak it. Statism is an ideology, and all ideologies are variations on human livestock management practices. Nationalism is pimped-out bigotry, designed to provoke a "Stockholm Syndrome" in the

the other website:
https://beforeitsnews.com/power-elite/2012/11/killing-your-strawman-2-a-free-mans-chronicle-2440520.html)

i, did i, best to stand i, ground, and while still learning l.e.g.a.l. verses l.a.w. as i, go, what i, experienced is that a man that act as a [~~judge~~], Thomas Brian Donovan, "shit for brains" and jack-off were both playing games with i, at open court. Each begun to test, i, knowledge of the l.e.g.a.l. verses l.a.w.-ful system.

It, did not matter that i, was without a mollusk family, slime-ball, slithering-snake-like, skunk-smelling, leeching piece of shit legless lizard aka attorn'ey, who feed off of god fearing and law abiding wo/mankind. Nor did i, have anyone to support i, as a next friend.[100], Still, i, found out someone at the court or that shit-for-brains actor, had appointed a surrogate attorn'ey, on i, court action without i, knowledge.

Is A Wo/Man That Act As ~~Judge~~ Also A Medical Doctor?

i, do continue to bring up the facts of i, impairments, from berth/birth as well as disabilities caused by repercussions of the May 3rd 2001 accident. The BK court fully disregarded. This court, like all previous courts were all aware of the facts that robin niner was designated by social security administration and had l.e.g.a.l., l.a.w.-ful, moral and ethical ramifications acting as conservator, representative payee. She, along with robin's husband ass-wipe niner, whom all had fiduciary duties to perform and should have

---

livestock… You do not have to be livestock. Take the red pill. Wake up…" —Stefan Molyneux

[100] **Next friend:** In common law, a next friend (Law French prochein ami) is a person who represents another person who is under age, or, because of disability or otherwise, is unable to maintain a suit on his or her own behalf and who does not have a legal guardian. They are also known as litigation friends. When a relative who is next of kin acts as a next friend for a person, that person is sometimes instead desc... Wikipedia
What is a 'next friend' in a legal document?
But when a legal document refers a person's "next friend," it isn't talking about that person's social circle. Rather, the "next friend" is an individual appearing or appointed by a court to act on the behalf of a person lacking legal capacity, such as a child or a person who has been incapacitated due to illness or injury.
https://search.yahoo.com/yhs/search?hspart=pty&hsimp=yhs-ext-ff_freetestnow&param1=20220527&param3=speedtest_%7EUS%7Eappfocus1%7E&param4=%7Efirefox%7E%7E&type=yhs-ext-ff_freetestnow_appfocus1_ff&grd=1&p=legal+%22next+friend%22+

never entered into any business dealing concerning money with a disabled man ever.

When i, do question shit-for-brains, "sfb" kept its f.u.k.c.-ing slimy orifice shut and then jack-off made a comment about i, attorn'ey of record. Then when i, questioned them again, about "*what attorn'ey do i, have ~~re~~-presenting i…?*" they both looked at each other and then disregarded answering i, inquiry about the fact that there was a piece of shit attorn'eys name next to i, name on the court docket. Showing that something smelled worst than a skunk (Pepe Le Pue) on the downtown BK courthouse-ship and it was not i, as it was coming from sfb's bench.

Not only do shit-for-brains disregard all of i, medical evidence, all of the ADA requirements under Title II & Title III Amendment Acts, shit-for-brains completely disregarded all judicial canons of ethics. By making medical determinations about i, a man; that have documentation, clearly visible and some intangible, known disabilities; for shit-for-brains to make statements on record about actually doing his own diagnosis of i, without a medical license, is his detriment to all canons and to his trespass against i.

Once, shit for brains made self-determination that not only i, was not disabled, shit-for-brains (Thomas Brian Donavan) made it clear to say that i, was lying about i, disabilities, therefore, shit-for-brains would not grant any ADA accommodations. i, do object and challenged shit-for-brain, who is not a medical doctor, without any court appointed medical evaluations makes a medical butchery. i, questioned to see his medical credentials to make medical assessment about i. Shit-for-brains donovan aided and abetted ass-wipe's attorn'ey jack-off/james thomas king to suppress i, by way of trespass by way of conspiracy.

Deadbeat Debtor's Is Not For You, Hah?

Now, at that point, i, required and made it known at open court for a next friend and or an ADA advocate. Because i, was without understanding that fact that they had appointed a surrogate attorn'ey, continuously denied i, every requirement to bring ass-wipe in to the court for a 2004 (deadbeat) debtor's exam [101] and ADA issues. All shit-for-brains did was deny i, everything required far-reaching. All creditors have a right to question any deadbeat debtor (ass-wipe niner) under oath, about deadbeat debtor's assets, statements made on its bankruptcy and a whole host of other prove-ups. It is to commence under oath statements made by any deadbeat debtor, as herein ass-wipe, jim/james, sperm-doner and robin niner.

i, evidently am the exception to the rule, as i, knew ass-wipe and sperm-donor were hiding assets, and i, do have all right to bring them in for the 2004 exam. All creditors are supposed to be able to file a 2004 exam, even if they do not have any evidence. All anyone needs to ask is questions under oath such as: locating certain property, examining the deadbeat debtor's financial transactions, investigating whether they lied on their bankruptcy papers, hidden property, or otherwise committing bankruptcy fraud.

However, every normal wo/mankind that is with or without an attorn'ey gets lawful process of a 2004 (deadbeat debtor) examination except adam-daniel of the borsotti family. i, was litigating to protect i, right to seek the exam.

i, cannot say enough, whether or not any court actors says no, every creditor is allowed to discharge (remove) one or more of ass-wipe deadbeats debts.

It do not matter, that i, did not know how to write motions or any lawful or legal papers. Although i, was being taught by qualified research writers, and litigation experts, paralegals and some attorn'eys as i, go along. Over all of i, objections orally on record and on paper all demands were denied without cause.

---

[101] **What Is a 2004 Examination?**
Occasionally, the bankruptcy trustee, a creditor, or the debtor in a bankruptcy case will want to ask the debtor or another witness questions under oath. Or, a party might need documents that might be relevant to the issues in the bankruptcy case. A 2004 examination (authorized under Rule 2004 of the Federal Rules of Bankruptcy Procedure) works like a deposition. The witness is placed under oath and answers questions. A court reporter records and transcribes everything said. The witness might also be required to produce documents.
https://www.alllaw.com/articles/nolo/bankruptcy/2004-examination-in-bankruptcy.html

No Medical Doctorate, Or Oath Of Office, No Buenos
Even when i, proffered all i, medical reports, of all the injuries sustained, the facts that i, undergo over eight surgeries, rehabilitation at the Midlothian Virginia Brain Institute. With over 2000 documents, along with the Social Security Disability Doctors' reports, and other private doctor's medical records; Shit-for-brains made his self-determination instantly to refuse ADA and evaluated i, berth/birth and other medical conditions. Denied i, all basic litigation process as a creditor.

It did not matter, as the more i, filed, the more i, was denied. Not just one or two, but every single time and usually without any hearings, without ass-wipe, his ex-wife robin, his sperm-doner father nor their attorn'eys being present at open court. It seemed to be a repeat of the Superior Court Chatsworth California saga and nightmare from Satan's street.

Just like when richard-cranium, bitch-mlo denied i, to enforce ass-wipe to bring in all of his proof of statements. i, demand law, bitch-mlo and richard-cranium denied i, the right to all discovery B-4 trial. After their f.u.k.c.-ing, kangaroo k.u.n.t. ass trial and post judgment hearing all was denied at court. However, it was not a lawful open court because they closed everything lawful to i, to be able to receive due process.

Pubic Serpent Choose Who Wins Despite Facts/Evidence
As the mover of this action and also known creditor, i, move the power of court to force deadbeat debtor to prove all rights to receive a bankruptcy. Yet, for some reason, ass-wipe was being protected, not by some supernatural power or the lack of i, ability to move the court properly and definitely God would not support this deliberate suppression of i. However, i, did not know then how much all of the court agents were in on suppressing, i, every attempt.

Over time, the true spirit of the satanic courts would come to fruition at future court actions. Yet, what do manifest to this point, was discouraging, however, i, was not discouraged enough to quit and was ready to go all the way to the end, whatever that meant. i, am still on that road?

Forced To File Additional Adversary Action

i, was contemplating to file an adversary action but for what just to be denied again? i, was denied the regular bankruptcy that ass-wipe filed. The appeal i, filed was denied and both of them without any cause. The deadbeat debtor ass-wipe was never forced by trustee David L. Hahn who had no right in law or statutory world of courts, to deny i, or any creditor their day in court; a day to bring the bankruptcy through a normal juridical process as in 2004 [deadbeat] debtor test.

Do All Courts Talk To Each Other?

i, questioned i, right to receive lawful process from four separate courts. Each denied without cause and moving through all of the denials in i, attempts to bring to surface games ass-wipe suppressed. i, know i, repeat this issue, yet, to bring N-2 open court 2-B cross examined, all wo/mankind that file bankruptcy are subject to the creditors. To be able to bring them N-2 a deposition, a post judgment debtor hearing, or a 2004 debtor exam is denied by all of the pubic serpents. What was i, doing wrong, i, thought? Why can i, not get the courts to make the deadbeat debtors prove their bankruptcy, to prove their statements true, to force the deadbeat debtor and defendant niners to prove everything they state at open court or on their under oath declarations, and other papers they swear to?

It was not just James Thomas King, aka, jack-off-pubic serpent, BAR # 82087 and shit-for-brains, to deny. i, can only sum up, it must be Satan's den called the United States Bankruptcy Courts, Superior Court of the State of… or the United States Circuit/District Courts… The problem is all of the corporate enclaves' agents continue to trespass upon all public wo/men from the low level clucks to and including, but not limited to The United States Supreme Court agents that all were fulfilling the conspiracy no doubt. The l.e.g.a.l. system created Devil's trones. These dens where all citizens and agents act a title are employed by such underworld fragments as flames from hell, and only act a part to destroy god's purpose for all mankind's comity, reciprocity, honor, integrity and gods graceful will.

Who knew jack-off, that is a part of the B.A.R. club, as usual would be like all the rest of the comrades to the club? Could it be so simple, that i, am not a B.A.R. member, thus, i, have no nexus to their satanic non oaths? Leaving i, with no l.a.w. ?

U.S. Bankruptcy Adversary Case # 2:11-ap-02293 Thomas Brian Donovan B.A.R. # 34106

Thomas Brian Donovan
Shit-for-brains

See what is a special poem for this fiction to follow:

Donovan receives another crack pop shot at
Adam -Daniel – of the borsotti family

"Oh what webs we weave, when we are unethical as far as
the eyes can see,

Another attempt to suppress, what is purely money to collect,

Although his name is not known, only a pebble from a stone,
That makes up the sea of pirates not alone,

Only god knows what is real for his is a story to foretell,
For the likes of the man above, will certainly see hell,

As i, will make certain to close the iron curtain on his name,
For what he has done to i, he should be forever shamed."

The man: who act as a [~~judge~~], ~~Thomas Brian Donovan~~ known as shit-for-brains, takes another crack-pop shot at a disabled man's heroic attempt to stand on impartiality, Juris Prudence, protected by Lady Justice, guided and overseen by Jesus Christ. It can only be evil-wrongdoers against true internal morals and ethics, and what is truly called l.a.w., that shit-for-brains has yet to realize he is guided by Satan. Satan and Jesus Christ do not mix!

The man that acts a bankruptcy serpent [~~judge~~], shit-for-brains, not only dismissed i, adversary court action, as fast as it was filed, this time it is dismissed <u>with prejudice</u> [102] meaning that i, could never bring back a case ever again within their statutory administrative schema. So, instead, i, bring it to this *open court of record*, herein.

Of course this is supposedly why most courts encourage litigants to go to the higher courts on appeal. What do you the reader think i, did? Of course to fulfill this original endeavor, i, filed an appeal because i, knew something was wrong in Denmark or at the United States Bankruptcy Court, California by this shit-for-brains.

Reflection As To What The Court Did

i, being flat out denied i, right by shit-for-brains to receive 2004-Debtor-exam and hearing to bring not only ass-wipe, sperm-donor, but in addition ass-wipes brother jim/james, or aka willie niner in.

Willie Niner received his nickname when he or the other niner klan made up the name as he is also known, to make a record under oath as to why he and his family were supporting ass-wipe and robin niner in their refusal to compensate a disabled man in his rite/right to his final decree at law. All i, required is for each woman and all three men to raise their hand and tell what is true, only true and nothing but what is true so help them god. i, do not think that is very much to ask, however, govern mental agents all seemed that i, was demanding too much from ass-wipe's family.

---

[102] **WITH PREJUDICE**: Generally **with prejudice** means that the case is over and cannot be brought back on any merits. However, it does have different connotations varying from Civil, Criminal and Common law,…" https://en.wikipedia.org/wiki/Prejudice_(legal_term)

The question is why are all agents protecting the likes of ass-wipe's family over i, rite/rights, titles, interest, estate and control of i, a man's ability to receive the same neutrality of any wo/mankind?

i, mean, the very purpose of a bankruptcy action is for any creditor which i, Adam – Daniel of the Borsotti family am, still to this day, a creditor because a trespass each wo/mankind has perpetrated against i, and i, estate was the same trespass then as is to this very day, which i, already discussed previously. No statute of limits.

Let's say for shits and giggles, that i, was not severely disabled at the time bitch-mlo, top-ramin, weiner-dog, richard-cranium, dick-em, sperm-donor, Three-blind-mice, tex-ass, shit-for-brains, jack-off nor robin niner or all other evil-wrongdoers cause fraud against i. As previously stated: "**Every** creditor and i, mean **every** creditor named on **every** bankruptcy has a right to be treated fair with impartiality." Every creditor has right to examine any deadbeat debtors statement of facts period except i.

It is text book bankruptcy as well text book state court procedures and for every post judgment court action, wherein a victor, as in i, as for every wo/man to receive discovery, request for production of documents, special and form interrogatories, subpoenas deuces tecum, depositions at the California state and federal equivalent to Freedom of Information Acts (F.O.I.A.) [103] Brady requisite.
Yet, i, was refused every single required normal due process, court etiquette, accommodations and as herein i, am once again refused to

---

[103] **FREEDOM OF INFORMATION ACT** pubic access to documents or other data in the possession of a government agency or pubic authority,…"
OR CALIFORNIA PUBIC RECORDS ACT: Is the freedom of Information Act (FOIA) for federal under USC?
The Freedom of Information Act (FOIA) provides that any person has the right to request access to state agency records or information except to the extent to which the records are restricted from disclosure by any exemptions contained in the Act. California's version of this Act is the state's **Pubic Record Act** (CPRA). 5 U.S.C. § 552, is the United States federal **freedom** of **information** law that requires the full or partial disclosure …"
https://search.yahoo.com/yhs/search?hspart=pty&hsimp=yhs-ext-ff_freetestnow&param1=20220527&param3=speedtest_%7EUS%7Eappfocus1%7E&param4=%7Efirefox%7E%7E&type=yhs-ext-ff_freetestnow_appfocus1_ff&grd=1&p=what+is+freedom+of+information+act+

receive from this court assistance of counsel, refused ADA accommodations, refused to bring all ass-wipe, sperm-doner and robin niner's criminal gang for these basic rules of bankruptcy 101 requirements. It is no wonder why people have zero to little faith in the American judicial system. This statutory system caters to the cult agents and their minions and all others that they want to unlawfully protect; not by canon, only through satan.

Where Have All The Good Serpent Gone?

i, know in i, heart, there are good public servant, agents, employees, and wo/mankind, that act as court clerks, commissioners, [~~judge~~]s, magistrates, advocates, and all titled wo/mankind somewhere within the city, county, state and federal court as govern mental systems. i, just do not know of any by name or reputation until i, heard about this one man that quit his job due to court corruption. It was too overbearing for his biblical moral and ethical heart, mind and soul.

i, was always told by a good old longtime friend, who knows L.A.W., that the statutory schema, known by codes, regulatory process; a man who has faith that not all wo/mankind that do act as [~~judge~~]s, commissioners, magistrates, court clucks, employees, politicians for a govern mental court system and all of the other hundreds of agencies that are set up by this foreign govern mentals called UNITED STATES OF AMERICA INCORPORATED, STATE OF CALIFORNIA; CITY OR COUNTY OF… are not all bad. Not all bad? That was a mouthful.

i, did and do i, best to want to believe that not all public servants are corrupt. i, have filed hundreds to a thousand of letters, correspondences, notices, affidavits, declarations, claims, complaints, conditional acceptances, offers and acceptances, objections, safe harbor offers, motions, responses, answers, questions, requests, demands, requirements, discovery, and i, have never received any honest, integrative, true replies.

i, have heard more than ambiguous, unintelligent and vague run around excuses. i, was shunned to other agencies or flat out denials, yet mostly, non-replies to crucial necessary information by just about every known agency to the monopolistic commercial govern mental world. i, list is as endless as their ellipsis. Regardless that i, stand on l.a.w. or that i, stand in honor and follow god's laws on the private side of commerce, i, require the same. It do not matter that govern mental agents do not follow God's laws, to deny i, always.

Maybe there is hope that there will only be one wo/mankind that will do the right thing and assist i, to expose what is true of these govern mentals; just as Jesus Christ do a very long time ago. Never 4-get, "*All we need is one…*" i, am optimistic that after this *living missive* is privately and publicly known, i, will receive at least one reply by a wrongdoer personally, as you can bet on it.

FYI: Jesus Turns The Tables Without Fear

The cleansing of the Temple narrative tells of Jesus expelling merchants, as money changers from the Temple and is recounted in all four canonical gospels of New Testament. The scene is a common motif in Christian art. If this happened, and i, do believe it do, then this man called Jesus was a very courageous man of God and was able to do things that few wo/mankind could or would do without feeling fear for his actions. Jesus must have enormous testes, amount of faith, and power to feel no repercussions for his actions against all money changers, known by some to work for the roman govern mentals and the rabbi's at the time; same as today?

i, continue to repeat, to disrupt agents ability to plunder, control, instill fear, to enslave minds, hearts and souls of many wo/men. It is i, intent to liberate the minds, body and spirits of those that have fallen short of the ultimate knowledge of the great books ever written as i, did. i, am always learning and adjusting in faith.

Although, i, am not anyone who is second to God, Moses, Jesus Christ, Gandhi, Nichiren Daishonin, or even Daisoku Ikeda or any tell-us-lies-vision evangelists. i, am a man with a name given by i, mother or father on this earthly level playing field, who is inspired through biblical teachings.

Inspired to learn and as i, realize, i, potential, i, believe i, feel similar to those who have come long B-4 i, above. Does this mean that i, as a man, of wo/mankind, cannot do i, part in assisting those other great spiritual realms to expose those who are evil-wrongdoers?

i, as well as you readers, already have the answer, regardless of where you stand on State in contrast to god, verses what is moral, ethical, right, wrong or indifferent. Look at what a congressional makeup is as it is affirmed in the not-so-recent past.

Congress Declares The Bible "The Word Of God"
I'm so thankful that there will always be one day in the year when people all over our land can sit down as neighbors and friends and remind ourselves of what our real task is. This task was spelled out in the Old and the New Testament. Jesus was asked, "Master, which is the great commandment in the law?" And He replied, "Thou shalt love the Lord thy God with all thy heart, and with all thy soul, and with all thy mind" This is the first and great commandment. The second is like unto it, "…thou shalt love thy neighbor as thyself. On these two commandments hang all the law and the prophets." It is stated "…Hang on the law and the prophets" Do this law mean Land Air and Water? L.A.W.?

Congress Declares The Bible "The Word Of God"
97th Congress Joint Resolution
[S.J.Res. 165] 96 Stat. 1211
Public Law 97-280 - October 4, 1982" Also see
https://biblehub.com/mark/12-30.htm

No Debunk, Just Take Things On Their Words
i, will add this section, everything govern mentals state must be true fact. Just like it is stated, Jesus is the son of God. Jesus cannot be God himself can he? It is the same that everything govern mentals

state is fact? i, do not want to burst any bubbles, however, the first commandment is "Thou shalt have no other gods before me." If this is true and i, do think this is true, just ask Moses. Jesus came after this commandment, therefore, Jesus cannot be THE god rather one of us of wo/mankind, just like we all are made in the image of God as it is stated; yet these are beliefs not facts? Or are they? i, suppose it is in hearts and souls of any beholder.

Is it not true that the statement is clear as it can be said so, it is written? **Genesis 3:5** "*For God doth know that in the day ye eat thereof, then your eyes shall be opened, and ye shall be as gods, knowing good and evil.*"

Although, i, am not a biblical scholar, nor will i, ever attest to being a scholar of anything. i, am a master, a gentleman and a scholar of i, own life. As you the reader is also a scholar and master of your own life as well. i, do know how to read and write and i, do know how to research and use archives to assist i, in differentiating between fact and fiction. i, do know from right and wrong, as in comity.

When Congress Declared The Bible "The Word Of God" well who am i, to question such authority. When govern mentals declare something it must be true? Although i, am being facetious; agents for agencies sometime get it right. No matter who declares anything, it is up to each one of us wo/mankind to question everything.

Research ourselves, and do not just take for granted that because it comes from any govern mental agent source, that it is fact that can be proven. Go out and research for you. Then after you do research, then you make a determination for you as to what is true. This is your personal realization B-4 learning.

This goes for everything even the difference between L.A.W. and L.E.G.A.L. When all results are in by you and no one else, then you stand on your findings. This is what i, share herein for your benefit of what is true. i, know i, do not lie. As i, always tell what is true even when i, lie. What do that say? It says i, am not always right, however, i, do not deliberately tell what is not true. You do research!

SATAN 12TH MINION IN THE SAGA OF SCOTT ALLAN NINER'S CRIMINAL GANG OF 2007 – 2025

U.S. Bankruptcy Trustee Case # 2:11-bk -18734
David L. Hahn No License #

David L. Hahn U.S. Trustee
[Pubic Serpent]
Satan's 12th Minion
(Un-Trustee-worthy)

This man David L. Hahn, seems to be instructed not to follow law against the niner criminal gang. It is by fact not paranoia, not by theory, nor by chance, as when any trustee do refuse to apply l.a.w., rather instructed not to follow l.a.w. by an evil minded wrongdoer, evidence to not allow a man to receive due process of Law, stifles basics of all judicial process. Injustice certainly is a conspiracy to commit crimes, at minimum to aid and abet ass-wipe's criminal gang.

Now, i, am certain that david l. hahn (if this is who he is) known herein by "Un-trustee-worthy", denied to reply to i, when un-trustee-worthy should have enforced statutes, codes, rules, regulations and sometimes acts. What is governing bankruptcy for i, as a man; i, as someone that is known also as creditor, the man that is harmed by ass-wipe criminal gang. Wonder who told un-trustee-worthy not to fulfill the 2004 deadbeat debtors exam hearing?

It Is i's, Business By Niner's Fraud And Default
When a bankruptcy case is filed, the United States assigns an alleged impartial trustee to each case. The trustee administers the action and liquidates any deadbeat debtor's nonexempt assets. It is Bankruptcy 101. It is not highway 101; it is 101as in the basics of bankruptcy period!

It is true david l. Hahn, Un-trustee-worthy, refused to enforce ass-wipe, robin, sperm-doner and brother jim/james or whatever willie niner's name is, to appear for questioning. The important issues herein are, it is not only for a wo/man that files the bankruptcy to come in, it was also i, right to demand all niner's. Even to this day (remember there is no statutory scheme in law of trespass) anyone that has their names associated with Dangling Carrot Creative, or what i, to this day know is truly i, business, to prove anything ass-wipe was saying under oath on B.K. papers, i, rights were stolen.

It is a known fact, by the record, and by all of ass-wipe's associated friends, that ass-wipe do have business relations. His friends who also know that scott alan niner is a liar, a thief, and that ass-wipe knows how to abuse the juridical system to get what he wants. i, know witnesses under discretion that know what i, say is true.

This means nothing in this judiciary system, especially what they have done to i, as a man, is lawful and is only under color of the l.e.g.a.l. system incorp(s)orated. In certain terms, if you are paying for an attorn'ey or you know pubic serpent in certain places, and of course, who you are paying under the table, you will get what you want, even if it is amoral, unethical not according to law. Because money talks and well, more than bullshit walks. So far, ass-wipe niner is the one that walked. Yet, he is not Scott-free...

As it was stated so elegantly by a man down town Los Angeles, the court is not for the lay wo/mankind who seeks justice, if you have money then you can buy your own justice...(See Disabledjustice.org) or go to Youtube: (at the 6:00 minute mark).**https://www.youtube.com/watch?v=bYcW4xiNqq8**

Although i, as a man will not stay too long or another moment to waste i, words, energy or more thoughts on David L. Hahn (un-trustee-worthy), i, kind of do not mind that he might sue i, for what i, do say as true. Because un-trustee-worthy is just another puppet in a bigger picture of scott allan niner criminal gang, this is nothing new to the public. Everyone who is above ground knows the basics of the good ol-boys and girls club. Of course that is how all judicial systems are rigged to the highest bidder. i, am pretty sure there is no dispute from anyone on this issue except those who are [~~judge~~] actors, named evil-wrongdoers herein.

Not only did i, require this trustee to bring ass-wipe in for the deadbeat debtors 341 hearing, i, actually proved with all facts and evidence that ass-wipe's father, sperm-donor, and willie or james/jim niner aided and abetted ass-wipe in the fraudulent scheme to rip off creditors; creditors, including and especially i, Adam – Daniel of the Borsotti family. But why would a trustee that is guaranteed to receive lots of money, from ass-wipe's listed company, honorably place his title and license in jeopardy? Trustees are able to do a lot, with all of their power, such as a trustee can look N-2 assets of a deadbeat debtor like niner criminal gang or any one that *knowingly* volunteers themselves into a govern mentals' venue. When one do not know then one do not have disclosure.

How Low Can You Go?
David L. Hahn, rather, un-trustee-worthy continued to refuse, i, many required correspondences, notices, motions, and demands for un-trust-worthy to follow the rules, statutes, codes and regulations pertaining to i, lawful right for all Niner's on behalf of all other creditors, including, but not limited, niners superior court attorn'eys top-ramin and weiner-dog.

Do not forget that ass-wipe named the niner's attorn'eys as creditors. After ass-wipe's attorn'eys did what they did to i, ass-wipe named his own attorn'eys so ass-wipe did not have to pay them for ripping i, off and doing to i, what all of the niner's had part in.

This action by ass-wipe is of no surprise knowing how unethical and unappreciative ass-wipe and robin niner were at that time. Ass-wipe, sperm-donor and brother allowed ass-wipe to name his own attorn'ey top-ramin and weiner-dog. It is by lying under oath, aids and assists theft against i, decree, it is known abuse against a man. This is niner's adult abuse of a once, severely disabled man.

Make This Issue Known Multiples

Once ass-wipe temporarily got what he wanted, which was to get away with taking advantage of i, taking advantage of his ex-wife robin niner, whom ass-wipe committed adultery against, he ripped off other people he was renting from.

One day i, might ask the scumbag attorn'ey's top-ramin and weiner-dog how they felt knowing what they do to a disabled man. So not only was ass-wipe working to defraud i, the govern mentals, his ex-wife, and many other listed creditors, ass-wipe bought a brand new S.U.V. and actually cited the new car on the bankruptcy too.

Why would someone do this listing, because it is a moral, honest, ethical, up righteous and outstanding citizen thing to do? Ass-wipe's father was God fearing, cared about integrity, loves his government and would always pay his taxes, his debts, friends and family. He always pays back money he borrows, and above all else, keeps his word to oral and written contracts!

This is not ass-wipe niner nor any of its accomplices when dealing with i. Think about this readers: Here ass-wipe used i, his wife, his father and family and his attorn'eys, then ass-wipe began to threaten i, even more to scarte i. Everyone already knew that he would get away with not even paying the attorn'eys for legally and not lawfully pulling off these godless crimes.

i, wonder how humiliated top-ramin, weiner-dog, sperm-doner and robin and even jim/james feel once they seen that ass-wipe were not going to pay them everything for all of their time, knowledge, and deceptive and harmful tactics against i; ?!@$#^*( )_[ ]\ + ; Is Ass-wipe 5150?

i, guess the real epitome of this joke, and i, am not laughing… is still on joseph ramin kerendian and thomas wanner aka top-ramin and weiner-dog. Because they did great work when hired to get [Thomas miller] dick-em to assist a thief and a liar to achieve ass-wipe's greatest accomplishment in life up to that point.

Reader: do not forget they incorporated i, one-time hired piece of shit attorn'ey for the trial, Richard Thomas Miller AKA Dick-em. Dick-em used its wife's disability to build i, confidence, compassion in Dick-em who assisted ass-wipe's attorn'eys, in the theft and i, trust; not to forget hundreds of thousands of dollars. Even worst, their refusal to hold strong to gods laws and i, original indenture is to their demise.

A Man Consecrated By False Pretense

i, am ethereally certain the two attorn'eys, top-ramin and weiner-dog should feel vindicated by laws of comity and reciprocity. The fact that ass-wipe and sperm-donor paid a sum certain, up front, B-4 the superior court action PC040224 trial commenced, i, will be shocked. Shocked that top-ramin and weiner-dog were 100 % fully compensated, by the niner criminal gang is of question to this day.

Unless the two attorn'eys are as dumb as i, think them to be, and allowed ass-wipe or sperm-donor to not pay them until after the trial was final, as this act of waiting until after the trial would vindicate their stupidity for receiving what all attorn'eys do deserve when they knowingly, with intent re-present a wo/mankind as a citizen or any unlawful compass, when they know they re-presented people who are liars, thieves, unethical/amoral. What about when an attorn'ey is knowingly amoral?

Is it the act for attorn'eys that accept court actions for the love of money, the thrill of the monopoly game, or just for the fact to not have a loss on their record. Is it so the attorn'ey can place another notch on their win/loss belt? i, do not know as i, am not attorn'er, however, it must be thrilling to re-present clients knowing they are not ethical or moral and try to get them off of crimes.

Yet, to fulfill the challenge to get a client to win at all costs may be another thrill. i, do like challenges to win at sports, cards, or games, but i, will not nor do i, gamble when dealing with another wo/man's livelihood, i, own morals and ethics or life. This is what gives attorn'ers a bad name. Attorn'ers do whatever they can to assist their wealth for another vacation, sending their minions off to college, or to possibly become like their pay-rents with a new house, yacht or whatever toys an attorn'er receive off of other wo/mankind's suffering.

It is beyond god's purpose. Is it enough for attorn'ers to feel vindicated under Satan's (courts) rules, as in they have to fight for the big "*W*"? As stated i, am not an attorn'ey or advise, which is different for each idiot; whoops i, actually meant attorn-ey idiom, my bad :)… As a satanic creature of an ens legis fictional world, the moral cost hardly seems fit.

Readers, Satan like attorn'eys, do not care where anyone comes from, how much money one holds, by fame or fortunes. Satan is a concept that resides in every pubic serpent, agent, titled person, especially, from all govern mental agencies. It is those who knowingly, with mal intent completely justify their means to an end result.

The result can be to over tax masses of wo/mankind that do not wish to play the monopolistic game. Therefore, Satan is not a devil; it is all rogue agents that know for what they do is against what is moral and ethical and do it in the name of the State or agency. This is a purpose created to obfuscate you and i.

Satan [104] is actually used as a metaphor a symbolic paragon of enlightenment for evil-ism, wisdom, egoism and liberty. Satanism truly is a devilish function that attained characteristic from within hearts, minds and souls of who do wrong as a trespass against other wo/mankind by justification. To achieve what is not lawfully right, to take, to inflict, to succumb to, nor justify by its own personal or professional means; in wanton, satan is intent behind the action of others not true.

A Message From Humility

This writing is about humility i, gain for being able to tell you, only if you believe in God, Buddha, or <u>devilish functions</u> of mankind; the

---

[104] **SATAN:** is and has always been used to depict the amoral unethical and ritualistic bad mannered characteristic from within a wo/mankind as a way to point fingers towards others who do not believe in what the mainstream of god fearing wo/mankind believe. (i, will save the elaborated version for i, next missive see pages 28-61 above)

traits of all experiences by preserving morals and ethics of mankind. Devilish Function is a temptation whether devilish, personal vendetta, glee or some other deadly cardinal sin.
Devilish function is created against logic, reason and common sense. Devilish Function goes beyond moral and ethical construct from experience, knowledge and journey from berth/birth, especially when against what is law regardless of biblical study.

Devilish function is all that truly exist from within one's own thoughts, words and actions. It is what transpires from and by those wo/mankind that are catalysts of some personal inner fear, hu-man trait, desire or wish driven by wrath, envy, lust, anger, greed, ego, pride, gluttony, or sloth.

Devilish function can be an order received by a boss and you fulfill this order regardless of what your inner self-determination is or was as you go against your inner moral and ethical soul. Maybe your devilish function is fulfilled in the name of ideology or as an order by a so-called inner voice that says "do not…" or "do it…" and you or i, do it anyways without worry or watchful care.

Devilish function is by thee who assisted in the effects of an imbalanced spiritual presence. Those who will answer herein and to their spiritual awakening; Devilish Function is Satanism at its finest. When you are a Satanist, similar to many agents for this United States and States United agencies, by proxy you do it by going against god's laws.

Most importantly because of the work that govern mentals do for and in the name of…. Each agent takes advantage, control or justifies the end means by states devilish function regardless of knowing for what the agent inflicts on others as they do as you do; as in each do it anyways.

Mode To Break The Mold
In the process of knowing the difference between right and wrong, i, do i, best to write this *living missive* and in all other areas of i, life to live within accordance of Gods purpose. God's purpose is whatever i, believe and know as true to what is in accordance to create value for society, stay true and expose all evil-wrongdoers.

SATAN'S 5th TRONE IN THE SAGA OF SCOTT ALLAN NINER'S CRIMINAL GANG OF 2007 – 2025

The United States Ninth Circuit of Appeal
Bankruptcy Appellate Panel

125 South Grand Avenue, Pasadena, California 91105

Any wo/mankind, as i, did not say any corrupted attorn'ey, which is familiar with state and federal court systems know all court systems operate on a hierarchy schema; not one that god is operating, unless you believe The State is your lord.

As most know B-4 anyone can get to the ninth circuit court of appeal, one must go through the lower courts first. The problem i, have with the court's pubic serpent is that they believe they are above all laws, statutes, codes, rules, regulations, ordinances, and acts regardless that they go against god's morals and ethics.

At Ones Own Peril To Act With Such Conduct
Besides the obvious that most wo/mankind that operate as pubic serpents, employees, agents, or officers, at all of the institutions; each do not follow god's laws. If each wo/mankind that work for these institutions do make an attempt to follow god's laws, verses to enforce under the guise of the institutional rules or regulations, there employees find themselves doing amoral and unethical acts at their own risk to God's wrath. One purpose of this *living missive* is to expose evil-wrongdoers. i, do know that there are a few, like

maybe a handful of good, honest, moral and ethical wo/mankind that act as public servants.

As agents or the like, that do their best to stretch all establishments rules, regulations for the sake of their own spiritual or monistic beliefs, i, feel your high regard. However, a very quick lesson that many wo/mankind either found out the hard way, by others stories or of their personal experiences; it is more productive, for their livelihood to follow their inner circle of satanic amoral, unethical process to protect machinery of the institute, than to follow god's laws.

Never-Ending Path, The World For Justice
i, found i-self continuously searching for what is true or what i, thought was due process, from said real lawful and integrative characters from within this ninth circuit court system.

After i, was denied at lower bankruptcy courts whereby i, received no cure, 2004 exam, no due process, zero respect, and in most cases, i, was mocked, abused, discredit, and discriminated against. (Back to 9th circuit soon); The discrimination was not for the color of i, skin, nor was it i, was perceived as a citizen(because i, am not), nor that i, have bluish-green eyes, brown hair, that i, was deemed disabled, or for i, spiritual beliefs. Nor could it ever be for i, character, as i, hold i-self to highest standards of Karma [105] through God's commandments.[106]

> For side note: when i, was at one of the court hearing at the Chatsworth Courthouse, at 9425 Penfield Avenue, Chatsworth California 91311

---

[105] **KAR·MA /ˈKÄRMƏ/**: In the Buddhist tradition, **karma** refers to actions driven by intention , a deed done deliberately through body, speech or mind, which leads to future consequences. The Nibbedhika Sutta, Anguttara Nikaya 6.63: Intention I tell you, **is** kamma. Intending, one does kamma by way of body, speech, & intellect.1. (in Hinduism and Buddhism) the sum of a person's actions in this and previous states of existence, viewed as deciding their fate in future existences: "a buddha is believed to have completely purified his karma" https://search.yahoo.com/yhs/search?hspart=pty&hsimp=yhs-ext-ff_freetestnow&param1=20220527&param3=speedtest_%7EUS%7Eappfocus1%7E&param4=%7Efirefox%7E%7E&type=yhs-ext-ff_freetestnow_appfocus1_ff&grd=1&p=what+is+KArma+

[106] **TEN PLUS COMMANDMENTS**:

> Cases/Accounts #: PC04224 – 2007 ; Not only was i, denied all lawful process, in the end, bitch-mlo(margaret lynn oldendorf) made fun of i, spiritual beliefs. It was at that time, i, made comments as an example, that i, not so much did not understand the legal process, as the denials by that court did not make any sense.

i, required answers to why bitch-mlo refused i, the basics of court process when i, do challenge by objections that bitch-mlo, who is nothing more than to be a witness for the public and not to ~~judge~~ over the action, would incorporate [melvin douglas sandvig] or richard-cranium, to refuse i, motion to compel and motion for reconsideration to compel all discovery.

Therefore, i, stated to bitch-mlo by saying: "just as if your honor would not understand "Nam Myoho Renge Kyo," which is a Buddhist term; she said "I do not know what that means…"
It means, (Devotion to the Mystic Laws of Cause and Effects through the teaching of sound by vibration that only comes from taking action).

Ikeda Sensei's Encouragement
At the very next hearing, bitch-mlo mocked i, Buddhist teachings. Whereas, bitch-mlo made certain that i, was listening when she stated mocking Buddhist comment using i, words and mocking Karma. (i, do have it recorded for facts and evidence when necessary) End of side note;
In the greatness of moral and ethical characteristic is how to defeat Devilish Functions with wisdom, courage, obstacles over devilish functions naturally arise to assail those that practice the correct teaching. Remember legal is all about defending, controversy and fighting. The law is all about integrity, honor, morals ethics, comity and reciprocity. L.a.w. is created by god and settles there to the end.

Here, Nichiren Daishonin teaches an important point for victory in Buddhist practice—for only by recognizing this truth and courageously confronting and triumphing over such obstacles, will it be possible for us to realize our own inner transformation. …

1. Those who let themselves be influenced by devilish functions will be drawn toward the evil paths of existence, while those who are intimidated by them will be prevented from practicing the correct teaching. In short, wisdom and courage are the foundation for victory in this struggle—the wisdom to see devilish functions for what they are and not be swayed by them and the courage to stand up to them without fear. (*The Teachings for Victory*, vol. 1, p. 100)

2. The Only Way to Liberate People From Suffering as Nichiren Daishonin indicates when he says, "If they [devils] did not [arise], there would be no way of knowing that this is the correct teaching," those who rigorously uphold and practice the correct teaching in this evil latter age will be assailed by storms of obstacles and devilish functions without fail.

The only way to liberate the people of the Latter Day of the Law from fundamental suffering is to firmly establish the means by which the Buddha nature inherent in all human beings can be manifested in each individual's life and in society.

This great path can be opened only by those who are able to establish the deep, strong faith necessary to defeat the fundamental darkness inherent in human life. That is because all obstacles and devilish functions are in essence manifestations of fundamental darkness. (*The Opening of the Eyes: SGI President Ikeda's Lecture Series,* pp. 9–10)

Back To The Story Of Impartiality
The reason those pubic serpent did not like i, nor were any of they going to follow the law, is that those pubic serpents, while on their job, holding their title as ~~judge~~ pubic serpent, are too arrogant, think they can get away with anything they choose and do not follow laws nor reciprocity.

As the only relationship serpent cater to is their own kind within their genre. Some of the pubic serpent known as wo/mankind that act to ~~judge~~ i, life style rather than to follow canons, Juris prudence by true lawful process; instead follow to create their schema.

i, do not like to ever ass-u-me (it needs no definition) or presume without facts backing everything up. i, do speak only proven facts. Unless it is by i, own belief or emotion which, cannot be backed up, what i, say is true through to you. Due to the fact that none of the pubic serpent would ever answer i, direct questions, i, now state that pubic serpent herein do follow their hierarchy and are of the type devilish function take control of their actions.

By their fear of loss of livelihood and satanic oath to the B.A.R. Association, each evil-wrongdoer is ruled by choice and not by character, not by fear, nor comity.[107] Ruled by oath given.

---

[107]**COMITY**: - **Courts Are One Sided With Prejudice**
There are certain standards that agents or public servants are supposed to deal with the public. This is not to differentiate between any type of wo/mankind verses a citizen, resident or one of their own agents.
Therefore, the courts must maintain comity and to serve all wo/mankind equally. It is a known fact, from i, experiences, and many other testimonies i have heard and experienced firsthand, the tactics of the govern ment agents and pubic servants is to not treat everyone the same as the next recipient at the courts.
When a common law recipient is at court, the pubic servants try to force the wo/mankind to fall into their trap of their statutory schema and do away with the true law.
The pubic servants use certain tactics that force authoritative and especially, prejudiced attitude toward members and are less patient and actually cause controversies with wo/mankind who present them at their own actions without the BAR carrying card members. For example, there is no leeway or understanding to answer questions even when it pertains to the statutory schema or the common law and the pubic servants throwing out threats of contempt when the wo/mankind make attempts to follow and enforce their rights to a trial by Jury, or to enforce the natural common law.
i, have not ever received any answers or justification to i, questions of "subject matter jurisdiction," In Personam Jurisdiction, argument based on real law. The courts never actually prove that any jurisdiction is lawful because most of the time, there is no injured party. (But this is a discussion for another time).
In cases where one is being accused the first issue is always jurisdiction and it seems that these courts since 1984 refuse to hear these issues and the pubic servants are unlawful to move forward.
The courts show bias and prove prejudice against all wo/mankind, with the [judge's] unfairness and disrespect for the true laws.
The courts and its pubic servants are there to serve the wo/mankind of these great nations and it is imperative that ALL pubic servants adopt this comity to treat all class of litigants whether a citizen, resident, or a wo/mankind and the court must and shall be forced to change, continue solid long-time laws that are set from hundreds of years as court policy and not just a statutory schema procedure.
There is an already identified population of wo/mankind and it is not the citizen, resident an agent nor is it a dog, cat, horse or mouse. It is the existing laws of the land that are predicated upon serving all wo/mankind who have been and are already identified having a generally common set of laws, rights, beliefs and expectations. Comity is the Key to a lawful judicial

SATAN 13TH MINION IN THE SAGA OF SCOTT ALLAN NINER'S <u>CRIMINAL GANG</u> OF 2007 – 2025

U.S. B.K Appeal: Case # **2:12-cv-10284** James S. Otero

James Samuel Otero
B.A.R. # **73992**
[Pubic Serpent]
Satan's 13th Minion
(Pubic-Sperm-ant)

The following several pages are one of many type of notices i, sent to over a hundred politicians, [~~judge~~] attorn'eys, Court Clucks, agents for state and federal agencies. In order to bring forth honor and to fulfill justice under God, the state and federal enclaves, i, offered safe harbor, comity and reciprocity that's dually owed.

The following action and appeal was filed at the Ninth Circuit Court of Appeal at Pasadena California BK: Case Niner 2:12-cv-10284 - SJO. The end result was a dismissal without cause and without one court hearing by i, or anyone's presence. Not one out of over one hundred evil wrongdoers showed up or answered i, notice.

Pubic-sperm-ant above obviously did not follow law, nor do any of the other ninth circuit pubic serpents follow true and honorable law. All they all do is suppress i, rights, dismiss i, actions with trumped

---

process for all wo/mankind everywhere across this globe, yet rarely practiced.

up bullshit made up to stop i, every attempt for justice. This is why i, do file and send pubic-sperm-ant the following lawful notice:

Start the quote:

"Samuel James Otero (Ret.),
United States District Court [Judge],
555 W. 5th St., 32nd Floor,
Los Angeles, California. 90013;
u.s. of A

Dear, **Samuel James Otero (Ret.), United States District Court ~~Judge~~,**

We come you, **Samuel James Otero (Ret.), United States District Court ~~Judge~~, or your successor,** to make a peaceable stand for our inalienable tangible and intangible rights and protections.

We are notifying you of an urgent matter needing your immediate attention. Pursuant to the 1849 Constitution of California and the 1789 Constitution for the United States of America, Trading with the Enemy Act, (**T.W.E.A.**) as only in times of war, the Emergency Banking Relief Act, (**E.B.R.A.**) which created enemies of the State, we are writing to notify you of data security incidences involving [several] California resident[s].

This notice provides updated information relating to multiple incidents previously reported to you, **Samuel James Otero (Ret.), United States District Court ~~Judge~~,** the California State, and Federal Government Offices between January 01, 2001 through to date January 01, 2022, on behalf of and for DANIEL ADAM BORSOTTI, the estate.

i, Daniel Adam of the family Borsotti (hereinafter "Beneficiary") a Private "Citizen of The United States of America" in *esse and sui juris* owing no allegiance to the present *de facto*, provisional emergency war powers military government established by Congress via "Emergency Banking & Relief Act", an act that first approved and conferred all national Proclamations of President Franklin Delano Roosevelt and then amended the "Trading With the Enemy Act" to apply to every artificial "person" subject to the military jurisdiction of the "United States" occupied by the army and the navy on March 9,1933.

Daniel Adam of the family Borsotti, as beneficiary, is also the Presumed Donor for the *de jure* Private "Citizen of the United States" Estate and the Private Business Trust **"DANIEL ADAM BORSOTTI", and Daniel Adam of the family Borsotti, beneficiary,** solemnly affirms and declares the following:

You received this invitation and are required to attend DANIEL ADAM BORSOTTI'S, Estate and Trust ***Appellate Division Hearing*** on or about January ______, 2022 at:

Stanley MoskCourthouse , 111 North Hill Street, Los Angeles California. 90012 Courtroom 67 on the 4th, floor at 8:30 a.m. to protect the interest of the United State of America or show cause why you believe exemptions apply to you.

Because we continuously demand the court's Jurisdiction to be solely an article III Court, which is a "Court of Record" and not an Article I Legislative or Article II Military Tribunal, We have been and continue to be denied the inalienable and constitutional protections that We merit and require.

To preserve and protect the Article III courts, and to keep you, **Samuel James Otero (Ret.), United States District Court ~~Judge~~,** in checks and balances, We demand with this invitation the presence of you to witness Article I, and Article II military tribunals, which you are cordially required to come to the aid of a friendly Private Citizen of the United States....

We continue to challenge you, as an agent for the **U.S. District Court,** the jurisdiction of this court and all courts as from our perspective the only issue within the realm of discussion is what trespasses you have done and this lack of jurisdiction via recorded entity, that is the following:

This hearing is for the complete re-storation of all the property for the DANIEL ADAM BORSOTTI, Estate **and** for an opportunity to show cause, if any, how and why **the U.S. District Court,** has an interest, to protect the UNITED STATES OF AMERICA INC. and the UNITED STATES entity created on May fifteenth, nineteen sixty-four, CERTIFICATE OF LIVE BIRTH, Local Registration District And Certificate Number B7053 18615 **known as DANIEL ADAM COHEN** which was amended by me on August eighth, nineteen ninety-five and Date Accepted For Registration on August twenty-second nineteen ninety-five from DANIEL ADAM COHEN to **Daniel Adam Borsotti** (by the STATE OF CALIFORNIA AMENDMENT OF BIRTH RECORD TO REFLECT COURT ORDER CHANGE OF NAME Amendment Number 95-0009573, State File Number 64-146992)

It seems to us that **Samuel James Otero (Ret.) and the United States District Courts,** have a duty to protect its interest in the title of the bonded entity DANIEL ADAM BORSOTTI and to come to the aid of a friendly Private Citizen of the United States...on behalf of the beneficiary who is not lost at sea, named here on and for the record as **Daniel Adam from the family Borsotti ("Beneficiary")** CERTIFICATE OF LIVE BIRTH, Local Registration District And Certificate Number B7053 18615 **known as DANIEL ADAM COHEN** which was amended by me on August eighth, nineteen ninety-five and Date Accepted For Registration on August twenty-second nineteen ninety-five from DANIEL ADAM COHEN to **Daniel Adam Borsotti** (by the STATE OF CALIFORNIA AMENDMENT OF BIRTH RECORD TO REFLECT COURT ORDER CHANGE OF NAME Amendment Number 95-0009573, State File Number 64-146992)

Beneficiary is not a slave under the IN GOD WE TRUST, USA INC.

Beneficiary has a covenant with God and therefore cannot trespass into any other jurisdiction but it does seem to us that all people have or should have certain inalienable rights to be protected from encroachment by you, the Los Angeles County, the California State and United States government, including, but, not limited to, local state and federal municipality from such misanthropists who have not come to understand their own failures, weaknesses and biases so much so that they excuse themselves when they engage in misguided behavior including, but, not limited to escheating, usurpation, theft of rights, title, and interest of property including, but, not limited to person, houses, papers and effects.

Samuel James Otero (Ret.) and the United States District Court Judge's job is as guardian to protect the life and estate from conspiracy to commit theft against Daniel Adam of the Family Borsotti as Beneficiary.

We invite, request and demand your appearance to see honorable justice, as we shall place you on the witness stand.

You are not only invited to this **Appellate Division hearing**, you have a duty to protect the estate, the people of Los Angeles County and California states, United States and United States of America, whether persons or private citizens' against foreign and domestic encroachment.

This invitation does not give you, **Samuel James Otero (Ret.), nor the United States District Courts** any authority to speak, to trespass upon inalienable rights of one of the people born on and who remains on the land such as this beneficiary, rather it demands you, to be present as you are duty bound to protect its own interest in the ens legis fictitious corporate Article I, of the 14th Amendment Citizen's trust, DANIEL ADAM BORSOTTI, Estate.

We accept your oath as originally written and intended with no deletions.

Caveat: if you do not believe in your Oath or believe it is not germane, we remind you herein that you are obligated militarily, lawfully, morally and ethically to defend the State, Municipality, the united states' Article 6 of the U.S. Constitution and entity estate:

The oath of office is SO important to American ideals, rights, liberty, and freedoms — and is the woven fabric of our society itself — that it is required of everyone who holds any civilian, law enforcement, or military office, from townships on up to the utmost levels of our government. It's even required of all immigrants who desire to become U.S. citizens. And is as follows:

Oaths:

From the Presidential Oath of Office, Civil Office Oath, Congressional Oath of Office, Federal Judiciary Oaths, The United States Oath of Allegiance (Immigration), U.S. Military Oath of Enlistment, U.S. Military Officers Oath, Officers of the National Guard of the various states (additional oath), and the checks and balances are that of such duties that must be adhered to in the times of war or peace and that of any strife, or we "all" would have allowed our duty to defend this country to fall short of each duty forsaken by thee.

All oaths common threads:

"***I do solemnly swear (or affirm) that I will faithfully execute***..." and or "...***shall be bound by Oath or Affirmation***..." and or "...***support and defend***..." and or "...***under the Constitution and laws of the United States***..." and or "...***against all enemies, foreign and domestic***...; and "...***I will bear true faith and allegiance***..." and or "...***the Constitution of the State (Commonwealth, District, Territory)***..."

<u>Checks and Balances:</u>
Whether presidential, military, congressional, state or supreme courts, to the county/municipality, judges, magistrates, commissioners, Policing Officers, County Clerks, **the United States District Courts,** even citizens have somewhat duties and in so doing, citizens whether public or private have full Constitutional authority to resist, reject, ignore, or challenge any code, law or rule which violates the Constitution and any other laws which remain Constitutional.

We believe that you, **Samuel James Otero (Ret.),** are required to represent your oath and protect the rights of the people against foreign and domestic insurrection.

If you received this invitation herein is because you are on a list of those entities whom have encroached unlawfully against the estate for DANIEL ADAM BORSOTTI, a CITIZEN of the United States and one of your duties is to protect and defend this CITIZEN and on behalf of the **Beneficiary** of such Estate.

My demands for this hearing is the demand to show cause over Jurisdiction, Equitable Rights, Subrogation, and Recoupment, i.e., to name you as you are one of the trespassers and remedy for "the complete re-storation of all of the estates tangible and intangible property demands you be present.

OUR AGENDA FOR THE HEARING

Proprietary, Private, Restricted, Priority, Confidential,
Borsotti's **Exclusive Equity** Hearing
The Complete restoration of all of the property
Right to Subrogation and Recoupment
Private Citizens Status
Military Occupied Courts
Straw man + Man of Straw ESTATE
Certificate of Live Birth (COLB)
Fraud, Constructive Fraud
Sign of a vindictive prosecution (refusal of habeas corpus)

The following list is extensive list of ***trespassers*** whom appear to have declared war against the Estate of DANIEL ADAM BORSOTTI, and the Beneficiary. This list is extensive, but, not exhaustive. We have included those who we believe are or should be accused of wrongdoing against the DANIEL ADAM BORSOTTI, Estate.

These misdeeds have occurred over a long span and to the best of our knowledge and belief of the Beneficiary Daniel Adam, of the family Borsotti we state they are as follows:

LIST OF COUNTY, STATE & FEDERAL AGENCIES WHO COULD AND SHOULD HAVE STOPPED THE PREJUDICES, DISCRIMINATIONS, DEPRIVATIONS AND

MALICIOUS PROSECUTION AGAINST DANIEL ADAM BORSOTTI, Estate.

1. **List of unceasing harassment by agents, employees, and contractors from the cities, Counties, California state and federal agencies which had duties to protect, stop, and bring justice to these deprivations, discriminations and not limited to:**

2. **CITY OF SANTA CLARITA AND ITS COURTS,**

3. **CITY OF VAN NUYS AND ITS COURT,**

4. **CITY OF CHATSWORTH AND ITS COURT,**

5. **CITY OF LOS ANGELES AND ITS COURTS,**

6. **LOS ANGELES POLICE DEPARTMENT,**

7. **LOS ANGELES SHERIFF DEPARTMENT,**

8. **PUBLIC DEFENDERS OFFICERS,**

9. **CITY OF SAN FERNANDO COURT,**

10. **ANTELOPE VALLEY AND ITS COURT,**

11. **STATE OF CALIFORNIA,**

12. **CALIFORNIA HIGHWAY PATROL,**

13. **CALIFORNIA DEPARTMENT MOTOR VEHICLE,**

14. **LOS ANGELES CITY ATTORNEYS OFFICE,**

15. **LOS ANGELES MAGISTRATES, COMMISSIONERS, JUDGES AND ADMINISTRATORS,**

16. **DEPARTMENT 95, JUDGE DANIEL JUAREZ**

17. **LOS ANGELES EXECUTIVE OFFICERS (COURT CLERKS),**

18. **LOS ANGELES BOARD OF SUPERVISORS,**

19. **PRESIDENT BARRACK HUSSEIN OBAMA**

20. **PRESIDENT DONALD JOHN TRUMP**

21. **LOS ANGELES COUNTY ASSESSORS,**

22. **DEPARTMENT OF JUSTICE,**

23. **LOS ANGELES COUNTY RECORDERS,**

24. **CALIFORNIA GOVERNOR JERRY BROWN JUNIOR**

25. **CALIFORNIA GOVERNOR GAVIN NEWSOM**

26. **CALIFORNIA ATTORNEY GENERAL KAMALA DEVI HARRIS,**

27. **CALIFORNIA ATTORNEY GENERAL XAVIER BECERRA,**

28. **CALIFORNIA SECRETARY OF STATE ALEX PADILLA**

29. **LOS ANGELES CITY AND COUNTY PROSECUTING ATTORN'EYS:**

30. **INTERNAL REVENUE SERVICE**

31. **LOS ANGELES COMMISSIONERS**

32. **DEPARTMENT OF GENERAL SERVICES ATTN: RISK MANAGEMENT**
33. **CALIFORNIA BAR LICENSED ATTORNEYS**

34. UNITED STATES DISTRICT COURT MAGISTRATES

35. CALIFORNIA COMMISSIONS ON JUDICIAL PERFORMANCE AND OTHERS…

Information: De Jure, Land and Soil Jurisdiction
County/State Federal Administrators - representative Contact list of trespassers upon request:

The State of California issued its own Bill of Rights in 1849 with a strong defense of property rights (1849) which the estate rights to be protected are solid and with the full faith and credit of the United States.

When any encroachment by any government, the United States Military and this includes YOU, **Samuel James Otero (Ret.) and the United States District Courts** to fulfill all oaths to the people public or private and it is paramount that YOU intervene while exercising such, equitable, common Law and inalienable rights.

Summary For James Samuel Otero:

What is written herein is what we are filing against you whom have received this invitation not only the entities in this matter are already or will be filed with the DOJ, as we demand to have you answer for your actions, and is why you should be present as we require you to reply to all of these allegations which we take seriously.

This previous list is just a few of the agents, agencies and perpetrators which Beneficiary preserves the right to amend by adding or redacting any name on the list.

Beneficiary accuses Deprivation of Unalienable Rights under Color of Law, Deprivation of Unalienable Rights under lack of Process of Law, Slander, Intentional Infliction of Emotional Distress, taking advantage of a man with known disabilities.

We accuse each and every perpetrator had lacked Jurisdiction to contract and Conspired by Trespasses in their personal and professional capacities against Beneficiary.

We look forward that you, Samuel James Otero (Ret.), be present and that you will represent your own interest, the interest of the **United States District Courts,** in this matter and should have protected the United States entity DANIEL ADAM BORSOTTI, Estate.

Further, this Friend of the Court sayeth no more and stands mute.
daniel adam of the family borsotti /s/ Borsotti, Daniel Adam, in esse and sui juris Private Citizen of the United States of America Private Citizen of the California State Specially and Privately residing in Exclusive Equity on the Land in Los Angeles County Presumed Donor for the Private Business Trust

"DANIEL ADAM BORSOTTI"
All Right Reserved Without Prejudice

End Quote

Above is an actual excerpt that was filed unscrupulous court actors with the many of the 27 separate court actions filed erroneously dismissed:
Place some notes if you like: ______________________________

____
____
____
____
____
____
____
____
____
____
____
____

SATAN 14TH MINION IN THE SAGA OF SCOTT ALLAN NINER'S CRIMINAL GANG OF 2007 – 2025

U.S. B.K Appeal: Case # 2:12-cv-10284 Bernal Jesus, Gilberto

Jesus Gilbert Bernal
B.A.R. # **147477**
[Pubic Serpent]
Satan's 14th Minion
(No-jesus-inhere)

Thinking With a Parasites Mind?
These two men; that are pubic serpents, pubic-sperm-ant and no-jesus-inhere who act B-4 the Ninth Circuit Court of Appeal Bankruptcy Appellate Panel (BAP) [~~judges~~], are as arrogant as they come.

As all of the other over confident so-called pubic serpent that are supposed 2-B ethical, lawful, have received and given their oath to the people of the united states of America, the wo/mankind of California or [Californification] Republic states; act like all of the others act as unethical pubic serpents.

By refusing i, a lawful court process, denied first hearing at open court, denied without cause, shows that it do not matter what or who files papers or court cases for i, agents all seem to shut i, down B-4 i, ever get 10% through i, court actions.

It were somewhere within the appeal at B.A.P., whereby pubic serpents, pubic sperm-ant and no-jesus-inhere, do write a decree as an unlawful ruling that show the true characters of these types of serpents. i, know that they are truly not of mankind, for example; most of the public has heard the term "…the people of…the united states" or "… the people of…California" which these terms are what all public has a lawful right to expect. We demand all wo/mankind together, to respect certain mannerism. These two serpents lack couth and honor from wo/mankind that go to court as i, as man filed i, appeal.

The people or i, choose to use the words wo/mankind instead of people on a whole because words mean things, and i, as mankind need to and should demand as the people once did certain respect from all pubic serpent B-4 all court actions. "Four score and several years ago…"[108], for the serpent to uphold their oaths. Even though Abraham Lincoln did use the previous terms, now days, it is usually used in a more sarcastic, idiotic manner as "*…four score and several years ago…*" as a score is 20 years and therefore, it is a term with little meaning…Lincoln stated: "in a larger sense, we cannot dedicate --consecrate --hallow --this ground"

i, have a right to demand true judiciary process and not a fake, statutory schema. When anyone brings the past forward, it truly does not apply to wo/mankind who were not there to have been a

---

[108]**THE GETTYSBURG ADDRESS**, Gettysburg, Pennsylvania, November 19, 1863: Four score and seven years ago our fathers brought forth on this continent, a new nation, conceived in Liberty, and dedicated to the proposition that all men are created equal. Now we are engaged in a great civil war, testing whether that nation, or any nation so conceived and so dedicated, can long endure. We are met on a great battle-field of that war. We have come to dedicate a portion of that field, as a final resting place for those who here gave their lives that that nation might live. It is altogether fitting and proper that we should do this.
But, in a larger sense, we cannot dedicate -- we cannot consecrate -- we cannot hallow -- this ground. The brave men, living and dead, who struggled here, have consecrated it, far above our poor power to add or detract. The world will little note, nor long remember what we say here, but it can never forget what they did here. It is for us the living, rather, to be dedicated here to the unfinished work which they who fought here have thus far so nobly advanced. It is rather for us to be here dedicated to the great task remaining before us -- that from these honored dead we take increased devotion to that cause for which they gave the last full measure of devotion -- that we here highly resolve that these dead shall not have died in vain -- that this nation, under God, shall have a new birth of freedom -- and that government of the people, by the people, for the people, shall not perish from the earth.
Abraham Lincoln, November 19, 1863;
http://www.abrahamlincolnonline.org/lincoln/speeches/gettysburg.htm

part of a certain events for wo/mankind of today rather for people of that time. The idea that certain people think it do affect the populace of today; similar to the declaration of independence, articles of confederations, and constitutions of California or the United State for America. The wo/mankind need to rethink what declarations, or cons-titutions truly are and what those doctrines truly mean within their own current relations. The past is what created today!

The con-stitutions and previous documents are trusts or contracts and are just what it sounds like a "con" stitution (a con by an institution) that the joke is actually on wo/mankind who thinks any constitution actually applies to people of today in 2025. When a wo/mankind come onto a court's property, as one's own self, how does a previous contract apply to i, or you?

The answer is very simple. Remember i, do tell you readers previously and further in this *living missive*, that the only wo/mankind that is bound by anything is only to god's laws.

Not manmade l.e.g.a.l. (legal) statutes, codes, rules, regulations, ordinances or acts unless what? one consents to contract, by fear of threat (which do not apply), or by ignorance of non-full disclosure of what is true. However, to uphold the sacred cow [109] as the masses of citizens, residents, or any other corp(s)oration created title, that are always treated like cattle, be ready to be herded into a coral for slaughter,[110] as a citizen, resident or titled entity.

The ideology of a con-stitutions, and most of all, a serpent's oath to laws of mankind are as solid as an oath to the sacred cow. However, the oath to god is forever binding, never wavering, always true and correct with only those who are conscience of such an oath to govern thyself by means for which commandments command.

---

[109]**SACRED COW**: is an idiom, a figurative reference to cattle in religion and mythology. A sacred cow is a figure of speech for something considered immune from question or criticism, https://en.wikipedia.org/wiki/Sacred_cow_(idiom)

[110] SLAUGHTER: Slaughter definition for this sentence means taken advantage by govern ment agencies treated as a slave with no rights and must give up 75 % of the labour made over their lifetime.

In other words, to all of you evil-wrongdoers who are listed herein and to those that have not reached this list herein, your political futures are short lived. Whether you thought you would never make it to this type of *living missive*; you can never be so arrogant to think that you will, or ever can get away with anything for which you think, say or do as an agent against true laws nor against another wo/mankind. (See ruling at back of missive)

There is a small booklet written by: Susan D. Settenbrino, JD New York, New York, which tells the story in her own words about "Judicial Bias & The Political Process A system of justice or a system for "Just-Us"?

I agree with Susan D. Settenbrino on at least one particular topic and from i, own experiences that "elected ~~judge~~s serpent need to please other parties to raise funds. Appointed [~~judges~~] need to please politicians and their supporters". Where do this intent leave wo/mankind that desire to vote by their choices and in order to keep all serpents within checks and balances? It is only a people that have correct power to decide who is in or continues their tenure period.

It is a fact that "the public generally votes for parties not candidates so there is NO incentive for a ~~judge~~ to serve the public" whereas a pubic serpent do not care as i, said B-4. i, shall state it again, the actors known by pubic serpent think they have full immunity with impunity. The serpent do to whomever what they desire without recourse or fear of loss of livelihood. It has to stop; it is time now!

i, Courts' Raison D'être To Fulfill This Living Missive

There are many statements made by many intellectually smart wo/mankind. We actually need *rational grounds for existence* to fulfill any logic, reason or common sense.

At this point of i, journey, i, must borrow some of those quotes in order to make a point. It does not take away from or add to a quotation as i, use the borrowed chart to make i, point, of reason to realize as follows:

CHECKS AND BALANCES

Executive Branch **(President carries out laws)** 	**Checks on the Legislative Branch** Can propose laws Can veto laws Can call special sessions of Congress Makes appointments Negotiates foreign treaties	**Checks on the Judicial Branch** Appoints federal judges Can grant pardons to federal offenders
Legislative Branch **(Congress makes laws)** 	**Checks on the Executive Branch** Can override President's veto Confirms executive appointments Ratifies treaties Can declare war Appropriates money Can impeach and remove President	**Checks on the Judicial Branch** Creates lower federal courts Can impeach and remove judges Can propose amendments to overrule judicial decisions Approves appointments of federal judges
Judicial Branch **(Supreme Court interprets laws)** 	**Check on the Executive Branch** Can declare executive actions unconstitutional	**Check on the Legislative Branch** Can declare acts of Congress unconstitutional

This chart i, do borrow from "UNCHECKED POWER GUIDE, By: Susan D. Settenbrino J.D. i, hope she do not get upset. i, do not know how to find the author or creator. i, apologize in advance and will stop printing upon lawful proof. However, it is a chart that tells a lie. A lie larger than life because govern mental is a creation of fiction on paper. Unless readers fall short of taking control of one's own life, on every level and realize the first form is people. Fictions have no nexus to man in blood or soul.

The chart actually tells tales of the dark side. Tales of lies and deceit because it only applies to fictions created by govern mentals and not for wo/mankind. Rather for all states united, ens legis fictitious entities that seem and appear to be real, however, truly are only created as paper puppets. It was stated in *"Unchecked Power Guide,"* i, borrow another quote by Anthony D'Amato; the quote depicts what pubic serpent known by [~~judges~~] do to the people at all court actions in general:

"The foundation of false orders is intellectual dishonesty." "What kind of judiciary system has this society produced where judges can misstate the facts of a case and then proceed to apply the l.a.w. to those fictitious facts." And *"Can anybody be safe in court if this practice is allowed to continue? When judges can listen to the evidence and then tell a contrary story, what remains of justice?*

The vaunted security we have in a free country and a just legal system turns to quicksand."

By: Anthony D'Amato

It is the quicksand from where all wo/mankind need a moral rope for survival. i, am a man that is throwing wo/mankind that rope to poetic justice. Back on page 41, 59, 198 talks about the example of pubic serpent's gone rogue. It is no different with the short following excerpts as follows:

SILENCE NO MORE!
<u>*Daniel Borsotti*</u> **v. [~~judge~~]** <u>*Fernando Manzano O'lguin:*</u> See Disabledjustice.org) or go to Youtube B-low: (at 6:00 minute mark).

<u>https://www.youtube.com/watch?v=bYcW4xiNqq8</u>

Sometimes it is who your attorn'ey is when they know a corrupt ~~judges~~ serpent that already has an oath as a B.A.R. member for a corp(s)oration.

Thus, it is who your attorn'ey knows and plays golf with, hangs out with, or it is ~~judges~~ blueblood good-ol-girls/boys club members who get prizes or benefits. As in…money talks and …

This is nothing new to the public, everyone that is above ground that has a pulse, knows the basics of the good ol-girls/boys club. Of course, it is how these judicial systems are rigged to the highest bidder, stated by the man on the streets of los angel-less.

i, am pretty sure there is no dispute from anyone on this last issue except those who are [~~judges~~] court actors that i, do expose. (When there is a dispute, write to i, at general delivery van nuys california) [91406] .

The next section is all about another abusive rogue serpent gone loose as a goose and as shady as a weasel dimorphic in a manner that they are all wo/mankind, however as agent not;

SATAN'S 6th TRONE CALIFORNIA STATE SUPERIOR COURT <u>CRIMINAL GANG</u> OF 2014 – 2025

The Superior Court, 42011 4th Street West, Lancaster, California 93534-7182

Michael Antonovich Antelope Valley Courthouse
Case # **91102QU** August 8TH 2013 Courtroom A-19

A beautiful structure erected out in the middle of the desert. It was built on lies and deceitfulness of govern mental agents such as the likes of [~~judges~~] pro-se-cutting attorn'eys, district attorn'eys agents, politicians, policy enforcers, in wanton, sweat equity of many innocent patrons, citizens, residents, PERSONS, people of… defendants, plaintiffs, pro-se's, and especially ignorant wo/men who know not l.a.w.s for which are not being applied towards wo/mankind.

It is how true knowledge is found in this *living missive* and not on some street corner, or in a vehicle code book, within the internal revenue service (I.R.S.) code, or any statute, code, rules, ordinance, regulation or acts created by govern mentals, whether legislative, executive, or judiciary branch; as it do not apply to wo/man. The true law is and always has been found written within and on the holy bible and other religious texts that have been passed down from generation of each and every wo/mankind throughout a free society.
For people as non citizens of the United States of America, it is as always has been found within the bibles, older *law* dictionaries

(which can be thwarted) and other writings. However, it is not what is true when placed within a newer type of dictionary such as Blacks, Webster's and court texts as addition to newer definitions that change meanings of words.

To change thinking process of a public, by re-training people into believing certain words mean certain things, is the ultimate outcome for serpent that work for govern mentals. The Daniel and Merriam Websters, Boviers, Older Blacks law, Ballentines, and many other disctionaries will depict the trueness of what law is compared to the newer dictionaries that have changed original intent over time. However, remember even dictionaries were written by lawyers and do not hold a candle to the bible and commandments. Commandments are always the go to laws of the land.

Older Dictionaries Tend To Be Truer
For a commentary on the use of dictionaries by the Supreme Court of the United States, see Keven Werbach's **essay**. Generally speaking, the older the dictionary, the more likely there is true meanings of the words. Newer dictionaries tend to be skewed to reflect policies of the powers-that-be rather than real law. For an extreme example of a dictionary that has succumbed to such pressure, see **dictionary.law.com** See **Dictionary Re-Definition** for a commentary about changing dictionaries to suit the wishes of government.

ONLINE : Webster's 1828 Merriam-Webster Unabridged**;** Burn, A New Law Dictionary**;** Williams Law Dictionary**;** Bouvier's Vol 1 A Law Dictionary**;** Bouvier's Vol 2 A Law Dictionary, Holthouse A New Law Dictionary**;** Bouvier, A Law Dictionary**;** Scott Military Dictionary**;** Abbott Vol 1 of 2**;** Abbott Vol 2 of 2**;** Rapalje Vol 1 A Dictionary of American and English Law**;** Rapalje Vol 2 A Dictionary of American and English LawBlack's Law Dictionary, 1st Ed.**;** Bouvier Vol 1**;** Bouvier Vol 2**;** Stroud 2 Vol 1Stroud 2 Vol 2**;** Stroud 2 Vol 3**;** Mozley Whiteley Law Dictionary**;** Stimson Vorhees A Concise Law Dictionary of Words Phrases**;** Thomson Dictionary of banking Cahill The Cyclopedic Law Dictionary**;** Black's Law Dictionary, 4th Ed., and a few others which are the original meanings of most of the real law as most of them start around the year from 1792 through 1903 and newer…

Go to **1215.org**:
https://www.1215.org/lawnotes/dictionaries/index.html and etymology at: https://www.etymonline.com/ will direct you to all original origin from whence words have come or been created for l.a.w. What i, do not like is how govern mentals deliberately change meanings of words to commit fraud upon wo/mankind in order to change a society's thinking, to create a dumbed down society. It is to benefit agents and agencies only and not the public.

CCK-Whore on the following page abused by clout shamefully act against i, a man is only one despicable act against i, as man;

SATAN'S 15TH MINION CAROL CHENKIN KOPPEL,<u>CRIMINAL GANG</u> OF 2007 – 2025

Carol Chenkin Koppel
[Pubic-Serpent]
Satan's 15th Minion
(CCK-W.H.O.R.E.)

Michael D. Antonovich Courthouse Case #
3 Counts of Contempt Charges
By Carol Shenkin Koppel B.A.R. # **59612**
Case # **91102QU** August 8TH 2013 Courtroom A-19

Lancaster Calif.: [A] (Retired) Superior. Calif.
Pubic Serpent/as woman
Assigned ~~Judges~~ Program, 455 Golden Gate Ave,
San Francisco, CA 94102

An assigned [~~judges~~] program means that a pubic serpent will float around from place to place, which means one courthouse-ship to ship; never truly setting any roots in one courthouse. Whereby they build camaraderie like relatives with the court clucks, similar to a family. It is like when a man and woman get married and have children. Instead, pubic serpent become like a wo/mankind who goes from partner to partner never truly setting any roots like a promiscuous relationship into one partner or courthouse. However, this cckoppel-whore was first retarded; i, mean retired, then begun floating from ship to ship on Assigned [~~Judges~~] Program.

This pubic serpent, cckoppel-w.h.o.r.e. floated her promiscuous w.h.o.r.e.-like strutting attitude into the wrong courtroom because when i, showed, up, this cckoppel-w.h.o.r.e. had no idea what she was getting herself into. i, have yet to hear from the cckoppel-whore who owes i, an apology to this day of 2025. i, am certain that cckoppel-w.h.o.r.e. forgot about i. Well, after all, the multiple incidents that she caused, besides the loss of i, freedom, personal time, stress, she had taken away in a moment of i, life.

This gave i, an experience that cckoppel-whore now will pay for the rest of its life. By making she or it famous by getting she picture onto the cover of a rolling stone. Well, not truly as that prestigious as that magazine, however, at least she is in this *living missive* and the Banner as on the Hall of Shame in the forthcoming volumes.

This court action at l.a.w. eventually had gone to their chief [~~justice~~] Thomas Robert White Supervising [~~judge~~], B.A.R. number 47251. The man that acts as pubic serpent chief [~~justice~~], acts as if i, was a lower level *person* instead of a man. As to give a title of no nobility (via 13th Amendment) yet a man nevertheless under god's laws of Moses, Jesus, gravity, inertia, cause and effect, reap what one sews, comity, reciprocity as stated B-4, God almighty.

When [~~Justice~~] White hereinafter "Whit-man" received i, claims against carol-chenkin koppel-w.h.o.r.e., whit-man immediately dismissed the action. The action was the benefit of one of i, eight court victories B-4, i, begun to receive more opposition from many pubic serpents.

The Following Factual Excerpts

After i, wrote whit-man and expressed of the trespass by one of its rogue pubic serpents, cckoppel-whore, i, do receive the following to prove i, always tell what is true, even when i, lie. See the trail…:

> In this second letter, you also asked that your case be dismissed. I was recently advised that on August 8, 2013, Judge Carol Koppel reviewed and reconsidered your matter and dismissed your case in the interest of justice. She vacated your finding of guilt and your sentence as well as the compliance date of August 15, 2013. The clerk was directed to send you a copy of her decision and an amended abstract was forwarded to the DMV (attachment: Order on Additional Proceedings).
>
> Finally, your most recent letters expressed concerns about your appeal. As the case has been dismissed, issues pertaining to appeal are no longer applicable.
>
> No further action will be taken on your case and the matter is deemed closed.
>
> Very truly yours,
>
> Thomas R. White
> Supervising Judge, North District

i, should tear this notice to pieces in favor of all people, but i, wont. You see, whit-man tries to stand in and on behalf for cckoppel-w.h.o.r.e.'s dishonor by actions which most definitely could have and should have been a huge lawsuit against all of them. The State of California for hiring this f.u.k.c.-ing, dumb-ass k.u.n.t. ass b.i.t.c.h. and yet, i, was not then nor have i, ever been one to prosecute for no reason. It is i, newfound journey to instill morals, ethics and true law back within society at the courts across this vast country that drives, i, not money, fame or power, only morals and ethics.

This was not quite the eighth victory dealing with infractions in a row that i, due receive while learning about *law* verses *l.e.g.a.l.* within the statutory schema. It was the second to last action i, do win B-4 all of the issues rising that i, was discriminated against by this State, Federal and the niner gang along with govern mentals linked to ass-wipe.

Ass-wipe made his threats in posts 2007, 2009, 2010 and then again 2014 and beyond. It was the following story that cckoppel-whore must read, or maybe she family are still alive and will read this. Read what their mother, grandmother, i, doubt daughter; her family who art still on this earth, will know what is true about their kin and what it do to i, a once severely disabled man.

Remanding Is Not Lawful When Ego Dictates It
i, was at a court hearing for an alleged speeding ticket on or about April/May 2013 and i, was exercising the rights, i, or many americans and especially wo/mankind believe all Americans, residents, citizens believe have certain rights to protect us. Many Americans believe that we all have rights to a court case, at common law, or constitutional law, and in order to make i, stand for i, rights, as any wo/mankind not only could or should. We all must stand tall when innocence and welfare of freedom is at stake. (i, shall express about rights later, yet, this is what i, knew back then)

The woman who acts as [~~judge~~], Carol Chenkin Koppel, aka Koppel-w.h.o.r.e./w.h.o.r.e.[111] was the type of woman that acts as a pubic serpent who floats around through courthouses. Because CCK-w.h.o.r.e. was retired and still making money on the side while CCK-whore was collecting her retirement, pension by obfuscation of the public hard earned labour, was double dipping.

While acting, like an actor on a movie set, as a sit in [~~judge~~], pubic serpent that is supposed to witness for courts and wo/mankind, it met up with i, a man, that was on his journey to freedom. A true meaning of the word whore is to prostitute (it is done sexually which is the same thing as working in commerce) oneself in order to receive compensation (see i, definition herein of w.h.o.r.e. Foot note 77&112). What i, soon realized is cck-w.h.o.r.e. exercised complete overbearing ignorance and belief that she could take advantage of i, a man for several reasons:

1. The W.H.O.R.E. is Without Honor by Openly Refusing i, Evidence, 2. Refusing, i, belief in i, right to apply the State constitutions, **3.** For abusing its authority, which she did not have,

[111] **W.H.O.R.E.** : Without Honor Openly Refusing Evidence

because i, never did consent to any jurisdiction, **4.** For refusing the united states constitution, **5.** for denying i, the right to exercise all of the potential remedy proffered to i, as a man, **6.** For unlawfully kidnap i, personal property (i, body) **7.** For unlawful search and seizures, of i, property, **8.** For having shackles placed all over i, body and placed into the state stockade. **9.** It gave orders, like Nuremburg, to its other pubic serpent that goes by the names of deputy sheriffs and **10.** Do trespass against i, life, freedoms and i, joy. No, not pursuit, to actual freedoms of movement when and where i choose; so i, thought.

i, thought the states and united states con-stitutions applied to i, as a man. i, thought that i, was going to be protected when i, stood behind the podium/lector and made comment that i, shall stand on dry land back behind the lector. Boy was i, wrong and right all at the same time.

However, a people as in wo/mankind and not one of the people of… for which i, thought at the time, i, was and where true *law* stands. As i, now know that it is not *law*, rather it is the l.e.g.a.l., under colour of legal as in the statutory schema. i, do since then learn that all court actors operate today by certain made up codes and acts like parliament that do not apply to i, nor you, unless you contract and consent into/INTO the jurisdiction and venue. (i, shall explain later for readers into next volume).

i, Walk A Mile For A Camel, Not Injustice

i, had traveled many miles to file, several different types of papers at the Lancaster courthouse-ship, 42011 4th Street West, Lancaster, California 93534-7182, which were jurisdictional challenges. Certain types of common law lawful recipes[112], which courts truly do not adhere to today because they are operating in a fraudulent venue, not operating by common law nor con-stitutionally.

---

[112] **LAWFUL RECIPES**: are types of papers written that are common law in fact and legal in theory. By Common law in fact is by the facts presented as it can only be determined by a *trial by jury* of one's peers and not by the theory or biases of individual ~~judges~~ who work towards changing the common law by their overbearing egotistical or personal views of changing a prior ~~judge's~~ decision based on some new theory, when facts are clear, evidence is verified by a wo/mankind who do witness willing to state under oath at open court and standing on such law…
law (and sometime maxims of law) is the only way any wo/mankind can receive true justice.

Case precedence is not controlling as each *law* action is unique. There is never two people, citizens, residents, individuals or wo/mankind, or acts exactly alike. There also is never the exact same circumstance that can lawfully set a precedence that lasts longer than ink that dries on a check that is in the mail.

Thus, a false case law to be used with your newly filed issues and court action cannot apply. Prior cases where a previous pubic serpent, who witnesses a magistrate or commissioner has ruled, shall ever control higher than a *trial by jury*.

There is no action more lawful than that of an *open court of record*. However, this was one of i, first few cases i, did win B-4 i, became known for i, tenacity to stand on what i, believe to be true law within court venues. i, was prepared, ready for the court action, filed all of i, pre Motions Hearing and practiced multiple times for the day of the hearing.

Serpent's Sail Caught by Promiscuous Wind

While the cckoppel-w.h.o.r.e. was floating around as a womankind acting as a [~~judicial officer~~] court witness, i, just so happened to cross paths with this cckoppel-w.h.o.r.e. at the time i, was testing i, newfound knowledge of *law*.

This floating pubic serpent, for the record, acted truly as a w.h.o.r.e. = Without Honor Openly Refusing Evidence as a w.h.o.r.e. that floats around by the wind on a sail. Offering its services similar but not quite like what most people say a whore is compared to a w.h.o.r.e., disrupting wo/mankind lives. By flaunting alleged powers, offering personal non-ethics and non-morals, to the highest bidder, like a two bit w.h.o.r.e., instead the highest bidder herein for she is the corp(s)oration. All courts are incorporated and controlled by banking cartel for which CCkoppel-whore fortaketh an oath not to abuse, or dishonor pubic servitude. It is well known that all govern mentals swear oaths not to the actual public, rather only unto the banks corporate controller of all pubic serpent that act as attorn'eys, ~~judges~~, commissioners, politicians and the likes of the B.A.R.

i, as a man, do not have any duty, like the cckoppel-w.h.o.r.e., to the people of California nor to the people of the united states *for* or *of* america. Therefore, i, cannot be disbarred, nor can i, be held in any l.e.g.a.l. contempt for exercising gods *laws* that are not in dispute with any other *laws*. God's *laws* which are the highest *laws* and shall always be adhered to over any corporate, statutory, codified, regulatory, agent created rule from depths of Satan's dominions on mother earth.

Dressed For Success To Honor

i, was at the first hearing, there about June/July 2013, for the pubic serpent so-called arraignment for which is the hunt of a witch or as Donald John Trump calls it "a witch hunt." They are same minds of Salem leaders who accept no facts or evidence. i, was dressed well, in a beautiful zuitesuite, with silver cuffs and a striped tie that had the stripe angled to the left patterned with the bar dexter "\" [113], and shiny no-scuffed well established shoes with i, small back pack hanging over i, shoulder.

The only thing out of place to differentiate i, from a lawyer, attorn'ey or barrister was that i, was carrying a backpack and i, never take on any titles other than that of man.

i, had all of i, notes, papers, questions and responses ready to place the policy enforcer (highway patrolman policy enforcer) hereinafter [officer] "Sadanko"[114] on the witness stand. To enforce i, right, to truly apply l.a.w. and i, was not going to take any prisoners, especially no overbearing unlawful pubic serpent that wanted to challenge i, ability to stand on law. Why no prisoners? Because i, was a learned man with i, newfound knowledge of l.a.w., i, was determined to exercise all rights of i, which truly is the rights of any and all wo/mankind as god's *free will.*

---

[113] **BAR DEXTER "\"** : It goes back to English heraldry. When the Colonists declared their independence from England, everyone in America became sovereign under the common law. In the USA until around 1970 ties were patterned with the bar dexter "\", representative of sovereignty or nobility (Constitutional Preamble people). During the 1970's ties had mostly neutral patterns "X". During the 1980's ties phased into patterns with the bar sinister "/", representative of subjectiveness or non-nobility (Constitutional 14th Amendment citizens). The easiest place to find sovereign ties is in thrift stores where old folks' clothing gets donated. I've noticed that lately bar dexter ties are occasionally being sold. **HERALDRY** : is a discipline relating to the design, display and study of armorial bearings, as well as related disciplines, such as vexillology, together with the study of ceremony, rank and pedigree. Wikipedia

[114] OFFICER SADANKO: officer Sadanko was form Cheech Marren and Tommy Chong "Up In Smoke..." Tell-us-lies-vision and theatre comedy shows.

This was actually a minor step in i, growing pains of learning about the court processes and in how to handle i-self at court settings. i, tell you, i, am always very respectful, dressed for success, used all the proper verbiage, such as “your honor…” answered questions directly, sat down when asked, did not disrespect anyone nor talk down to any pubic serpent or court clucks. i, gave all respect the lawyers, attorn’eys, ~~judges~~, and lay-wo/mankind should receive when they return reciprocity. i, thought everyone deserved to be treated as i, want to be treated. Because of their years of study and receiving their B.A.R. Cards as a B.A.R. Associate, they shall not treat i, less than i, demand; same R.E.S.P.E.C.T. by, Tina Turner. When a court cluck said “*all rise*” i, rose, and “*you all may be seated*” i, had taken a seat. i, was a good enslaved mind as i, friend said to act in accordance with their system. One cannot ever lose nor diminish any rights or authority to another wo/mankind when showing the utmost respect to their genre.

However, he did not speak in i, tong, but you get the picture. Rights of a wo/mankind cannot be stolen, given, nor taketh away lawfully or honorably. i, truly did what attorney do as i, was taught by William Thornton that has dedicated over 30 years to his teaching tools on Common Law at 1215.org.
Bill’s website trained i, as the website is set up to allow all wo/mankind to train them. When in doubt go to 1215.org for all you need to know is how to, where to, when to and why to make a stand for justice. However, in their D.O.J. (Deprivation for just-us) statutory system, instead of justice, it is only for the corp(s)orations to prepare against natural non-mainstream, institutionalized lawyer degree. No wo/mankind is treated respectfully as B.A.R. carrying members.

i, remember back 2013 at room A-19 at Lancaster California. When i, do walk onto the floor of that courtroom, there is a deputy sheriff, a court cluck and i, do not recall any court reporter, at that time. i, am reminded of the complete disregard for the l.a.w. the pubic serpent expressed. i, recall that i, am a man, with all of i, full rite/right given to i, at berth/birth from God. It is through the tenacity of Jesus Christ that i, too and you can and should hold all those pubic serpent, agents, as employees or any wo/mankind that take a title, liable for what they say and do. It is i, and with hope,

you readers know one's self worth. It is you who can actualize the part we all attribute when we apply true law of god, no matter where we are, and no matter what threats by those who place their own kind above others.
Those pubic serpents who think they can do and say anything to anyone without any repercussions for their actions and inactions is a thing of the past. This is a new world of wo/mankind instilling our world order to enforce morals and ethics for all agents that we pay to be honorable.

Caveat:

CAROL CHENKIN KOPPEL: cckoppel-w.h.o.r.e.: and all derivations

DANIEL ADAM BORSOTTI: government created fiction/surety

Adam daniel of the borsotti family: i, a man:

Court Clerk: Court Cluck

i: a man; adam daniel- of the borsotti family, shall state of i, personal firsthand knowledge under oath to god and do place hereinafter what i, recall of i, interactions with carol chenkin koppel-w.h.o.r.e. without having to resort to records that were made at the time of the hearings and is as follows;

The court cluck stood up, made she statement: "*Court is now in session…, All rise for the honorable Carol Koppel presiding, you may be seated…*[115]"

> Carol Chenkin Koppel (CCK-w.h.o.r.e.)… i, call case number # 91102QU; The People of the State of California verses DANIEL ADAM BORSOTTI…

i, was ready, when *the* name was to be called up to the podium and i, also was ready to stop short of the revolving doors and refused to

---

[115] It was difficult to rise and sit but i, do it out of respect of a friend who was training i, ways of the courts.

enter onto the wet deck of the ship where the (courtroom podium) was stationed.

(CCKoppel-W.h.o.r.e.): "*please come on up here and sit at the defendant's table*"

Once, the name **ADAM DANIELS…** was called, i, stood up fast, as i, do hop onto i, feet with a slight pop, because i, heart was racing thousand miles per seconds as it always did when at the courtrooms, whereby drama plays out upon most wo/mankind who do not know the ways of the courts yet.

i, do state:

i, a man: "i, am not the ens legis fictitious corporate entity,… i, am here in that matter as a man."

(cck-w.h.o.r.e.): Mister Borsotti, are you Mister Borsotti? I would like you to come over here to stand at the Defendants table (she motioned through swinging doors) where you need to be seated…

i, a man: no thank you, i, am fine over here...right here and i, can hear you just fine from over here and…

(cck-w.h.o.r.e.): no please sir I, want you to come over at the table!

i, a man: i, do not want to get my feet wet, so i, will stay over here on dry land…[Which was outside of the vestibule] (the swinging doors) on the public side of the courtroom…

(cck-w.h.o.r.e.):i, insist that you sit up here…and you will not get wet over here sir, i, assure you it is dry… stand inside over here at the defendants table!

i, a man: no mam, thank you, i, will stay here i, can hear you just fine…can you hear me? And i, am not that name, you can address me as adam…

(cck-w.h.o.r.e.): bailiff will you please escort Mister Borsotti to the table…

i, a man: it is against my better judgment, however, as you place me under threat and duress, i, will move to the table by your extortion tactics…

Whereby i, set my backpack onto the table, got out all of my papers, and was almost ready to begin…

(cck-w.h.o.r.e.): okay we have Mister Borsotti here and the officer is here, and so lets begin…

i, a man: First i, have already set a… today for a motions hearing on certain issues that need to be dealt with B-4 any action begins…

(cck-w.h.o.r.e.): No! Mister Borsotti, I will run this court according to what I, say and there is no motions hearing set on calendar, therefore, I have read the charges to you, do you understand the charges?

i, a man: i, do not understand anything herein as i, am not practicing law, i, do not understand what charges you are referring to and i, challenge jurisdiction and uhm… B-4 anything can move forward jurisdiction[116]must be proven on the record…

(cck-w.h.o.r.e.): What don't you understand about the charges? You have been cited for VC 22349 of the

---

[116]**JURISDICTION CHALLENGE**: The adjudicator's jurisdiction is of high importance. If the adjudicator does not have jurisdiction to determine the dispute, their decision will be null and invalid, and a court will not enforce it.
A jurisdictional challenge is when a Respondent makes a submission challenging the adjudicator's jurisdiction to determine a dispute.
Common jurisdictional challenges include: there is no contract; the contract is not a construction contract; non-compliance with the adjudication procedure; the adjudicator's appointment is invalid; no dispute has crystallized; the dispute crystallized is different from the dispute in the Notice of Intention to Refer; and the dispute has already been decided in a previous adjudication;
When a jurisdictional challenge is submitted the adjudicator will ask the other party to respond to it. Normally jurisdictional challenges are focused on legal points and a solicitor should assist a party with drafting or responding to a jurisdictional challenge. What is a jurisdictional challenge and what happens if one is raised? Morton Fraser MacRoberts

Vehicle code excessive speed traveling 75 miles per hour (MPH) in a 55 MPH zone. How do you plea?

i, a man: i, do not ever plea because i, do not beg for anything, and i, already told you, i, do not understand any of these proceedings…

i, a man: Secondly the constitution states that you are obligated and have certain duties to uphold all my rights, especially concerning the jurisdictional challenges… Article …, Section … Clause… it clearly states,…"

(cck-w.h.o.r.e.): Mister Borsotti, I do not want to hear you mention the constitution in my courtroom …

A long pause…

i, a man: Yah, ahh, but Article …, Section … Clause …. [117]

---

[117] When you do a counterclaim does that mean their claim is no longer active?
Yes. They temporarily lose jurisdiction because in the first cause of action the question of jurisdiction is the issue. Once jurisdiction is challenged, jurisdiction cannot be 'assumed', it must be proven to exist. They must prove they have jurisdiction before they may proceed.

"However late this objection has been made, or may be made in any cause, in an inferior or appellate court of the United States, it must be considered and decided, before any court can move one further step in the cause; as any movement is necessarily the exercise of jurisdiction. Jurisdiction is the power to hear and determine the subject matter in controversy between parties to a suit, to adjudicate or exercise any judicial power over them; the question is, whether on the case before a court, their action is judicial or extra-judicial; with or without the authority of law, to render a judgment or decree upon the rights of the litigant parties. If the law confers the power to render a judgment or decree, then the court has jurisdiction; what shall be adjudged or decreed between the parties, and with which is the right of the case, is judicial action, by hearing and determining it. 6 Peters, 709; 4 Russell, 415; 3 Peters, 203-7" Cited by STATE OF RHODE ISLAND v. COM. OF MASSACHUSETTS, 37 U.S. 657, 718 (1838)

This cite has been verified.
If they proceed without proving their jurisdiction to the counterclaiming court, then the proceedings from that point onward are void.

"Where a court has jurisdiction, it has a right to decide any question which occurs in the cause, and whether its decision be correct or otherwise, its judgments, until reversed, are regarded as binding in every other court. But if it act without authority, its judgment and orders are regarded as nullities. They are not voidable, but simply void, and form no bar to a remedy sought in opposition to them, even prior to a reversal. They constitute no justification, and all persons concerned in executing such judgments or sentences are considered in law as trespassers."

(cck-w.h.o.r.e.): I told you do not mention the constitution in my courtroom one more time or I will hold you in contempt that is your second warning;

Longer pause…

i, a man: Ah… but article …. Section… Clause….. Clearly states… that you have an obligation, and duties to prove jurisdiction onto the record when challenged it even says from the United States Supreme Court cases…. X, Y & Z"

(cck-w.h.o.r.e.): bailiff "***REMAND HIM***…."book him for three counts of contempt…

The bailiff came over to i, as i, stood there in i, Zoot suit, grabbed me abruptly, turned me around and handcuffed i, hands behind i, back;

Then he started to open up i, backpack;

i, a man: i, do not consent to searches…

After rummaging through i, personal belongings, deputy arrested i, and begun physically taking i, against i, will somewhere to another area where other deputies, began the process to actually book i, into jail. Then the other deputies eventually attempted to finger print i, and throw i, ass in a jail cell.

i, did not allow them to finger print i, and threatened to get physical with i, as the deputies wanted to grab i, hands and roll the fingers on the electronic prints.

i, was not prepared for this, however, i, adapted very quickly to being arrested even though, i, have never been arrested for three counts of contempt. i, had learned from many online gurus about stories of what to do and not to say and do. i, was a little bit prepared, however, nothing is the same until one actually is going

---

Elliott v Peirsol, 1 Pet. 328, 340, 26 U.S. 328, 340, 7L.Ed. 164 (1828)

through the real life issues that play out in the present. Stay tuned. (i, shall share those experiences another time in this *living missive*).

The Nice Deputy With A Heart
As i, sauntered into the elevator, i, realized that we were going down several levels into some place that was not going to be fun. As i, could not wonder if i,was not going down into the depths of judicial hell, i, did know that god is always with i;

As the elevator doors opened, i, looked out and seen a young lady who had on Deputy sheriff's uniform hereinafter Deputy #1, and one man Deputy #2, in uniform who were both already waiting for i, as if i, was a celebrity.

As i, paced over to the two deputies, the tough guy deputy who roughed i, up a little bit in the court room, said book him for three counts of contempt.

The young lady Deputy #1 asked, i,

Deputy #1: "what did you do?"

i, was silent for a moment in pause, and then after a few seconds…,

i, said "well i, was there contesting a speeding ticket, and i, had already filed for a motions hearing, B-4 the actual case can move forward, i, and everyone has a right to a motions hearing on certain issues.

CCKoppel-whore [~~Judge~~] denied i, a motions hearing, which i, filed several weeks ago and i, demanded it B-4 we move forward…. i, have all the proof i, filed for the motions hearing i, said…

CCKoppel-whore: [~~judge~~] said we are here for the charges and will not hear any motions hearing… move on…

Then i, said that the constitutions states at article … section… clause…. And she told i, if i, mention the constitution one more time, that she would remand me."

At that time, without hesitation, the man **deputy #2**, said "Gosh fu**ing dam it, I am sick and tired of her doing this…" she is wasting our time, and she needs to stop…"

Then, **deputy #2** continued… sorry I have to book you in…"

i, said "you do what ever you need to do, but i, do not consent to this process, nor do i, consent to you, taking i, picture or finger prints, searching i, backpack…and i, will not sign anything."

The young lady **Deputy #1** begun to go through i, backpack and empty out some of i, belongings onto the table**. Deputy #1** grabbed my papers out first, then she got a hold of i, current American Red Cross Badge and lapel buttons and said "look serge, he is a American Red Cross instructor…"

Deputy #2, said "I am sorry…" as he gave i, that look that he truly was in disgust and apologetic and instructed **Deputy #1** to just continue to go through i, backpack…. As **Deputy #2** just shook his head in disgust.

After about two minutes, as i, sat handcuffed on the bench, **deputy #3** came over and said "let's go" and i, got up and followed **deputy # 3** over to a community cell;

When **deputy #3** had taken off the handcuffs and said go in there, as he pointed to this jail cell where there were about eight or nine prisoners sitting, talking, eating sandwiches and drinking milk and orange juice.

i, know that it was very loud, then as i, was entering into the holding tank, it became silent. So silent to the point one could hear a pin drop or a mouse flatulate. i, walked over to sit down on the bench.

Here i, am all dressed up in zoot suit and tie, clean shaved, trimmed hair slicked back, wearing i, finest cologne reeking and appearing like Rico Suave. i, wondered why it became so quiet whereas prior to entry it was very busy and loud as if they were partying and i, became the trepidation of their party. They were all men, some more dressed than others, nevertheless all alleged criminals. As i, sat there they all looked over at each other, while looking at i, and i, am pretty certain they thought i, was a cop, or an informant or someone not like they. Not one of them said one word for five minutes, which seems a long time.

Then i, decided to make a statement, "who wants this sandwich and milk" one guy said thanks man. Then all of the other guys look at each other again and then one of them gave the head nod and the other one said what are you in here for?

i, said you would not believe it if i, told you what happened to i. i, then said very loud, who wants to learn about the constitutions and common law? As i, begun to educate them on common law and issues of jurisdictional challenges, it was not more than 30 seconds, a deputy hollered i, name and said you come over here.

So, i, got up and walked out of this cell and followed the **deputy # 2** who said you are going over here into this cell.

They must have been watching and listening to what i, was saying and were not going to have someone like i, educate other mankind in the true *law*. The fact that i, was vegan, did not have anything to drink, nor eat, up to that point, as i, was left by i, self in a single cell, for about four plus hours.

i, became board after about 15 minutes and began moving back and forth in the cell, practicing some dance moves i, had learned and mimicking some of the martial arts forms i, knew from years previous training.

i, do stay in this single cell until i, name was called again.

Deputies Try To Intimidate i,

Periodically one deputy would walk by the cell to check on i, maybe because it did not have any cameras like the other holding tank, or because they wanted to see if, i, was scared or just to intimidate i. Then another deputy and another then finally after several hours, **Deputy # 1**, came over to i, with a whole bunch of handcuffs and chains in hand. i, thought… "What are they going to do with those"? It actually looked like when a tow truck pulls a wrecked bus out of a ditch.

i, said, "What is with all of those chains and cuffs"?

Then **deputy# 2** came over with i, backpack on his shoulder and said put your hands behind your back, and he begun to place multiple handcuffs and chains all across i, body.

He placed them crisscrossed around i, waist up to i, shoulders and down to i, ankles then around i, waist. And then i, was told to sit down and wait. Then a third deputy walks up and said "let's go daniels".

i, could barely step without falling, let alone stand from all of the extra weight and because of the feeling of imbalance as the cuffs on both wrists and ankles were all over tightened; so tight that i, could barely breath normally, not to mention, with each step they were cutting into i, skin; It made i, a bit nervous of the unknown.

i, have never been treated with such benefit. i, felt like i, was some crazed maniac, Unabomber or the guy from Silence Of The Lamb. It was as if they were afraid i, was going to eat their heart or brains while we walked to wherever we were going. As i, inched i, steps out of the cell, **deputy # 3** walked over and guided i, back into the elevator and upstairs where we were going.

As the elevator moved upward, it eventually stopped at one floor and another deputy stepped in. Then we continued up to the fourth level. i, asked the deputy for some water because i, mouth was full of cotton like stickiness, like when you smoke marijuana and get cotton mouth. It was so bad i, lips were sticking to each other to the point i, was unable to get i, words out clearly. The only problem is that i, was not having any munchies or fun.

Time For Tarnished Judicial Armageddon

As i, was shuffled into a darkened, quiet and creepy looking courtroom, i, almost fell because of i, ankles and hands locked down right behind i, waist and not having eaten, or drank anything for over five hours. It is not good for someone who is vegan with hypoglycemia that usually needs to eat something at the least every two to three hours.

The dark, damp, cold and weary deck on the courthouse-ship which was truly not set up for public view, i, wondered what the heck? Where am i, and why is it so dark with little to no lights, and where are the court reporter and other court actors?

As i, looked around the court dungeon, i, observed one highway patrolman sitting at where they usually called the Plaintiff's table. Then i, was escorted over to where the courts call the defendants side or table. i, do see a woman who later disclosed she as a court cluck of this wearied dreary dark courtroom. Then i, saw that woman who acts as a [~~judge~~] k.u.n.t., CCKoppel-w.h.o.r.e. who had thrown i, into the original stockade.

They definitely left the room very dark on purpose. It took i, a while to focus to where i, could see everyone. The few mankind who act as soldiers, were standing right behind i, and on each side of i, in what i, believe was an attempt to intimidate i. There was no reason to intimidate i, because i, could not reach i, hands more than one inch from i, waist, and i, feet could barely take a ¼ " step at a time.

i, a man: No one said a word, so i, spoke up and said can someone get i, a glass of water.

(cck-w.h.o.r.e.): Shut up and sit down and start your case.

i, a man: i, told that f.u.k.c.-ing k.u.n.t. ass w.h.o.r.e… are you kidding i,…? How can i, do i, trial without any papers, or a pencil?

i, need i, papers and a pencil and the backpack…

(cck-w.h.o.r.e.): i, said you start your case or else i, will find you guilty and you can spend the night in jail…

i, a man: With cotton mouth, no papers, no pencil, hands strapped down to body, forced to sit and not move one inch, which i, could barely move a muscle. i, was going to have to wing it on all of i, practice, studying and the role play that i, worked with a mentor of common law.

After looking around the room again, at everyone in their proverbial places, all of a sudden, i, realized that there was some man sitting over where jurors would sit all by himself just watching and taking notes on his pad or booklet.

i, a man: i, do begin with the basics, asking for names rank and serial numbers of the highway peon patrolman.

(cck-whore): just begin asking your questions we already know who he is…

i, a man: but i, do not know and i, have certain questions that need to be asked to establish jurisdiction…

(cck-whore): JUST GO ON AND ASK OR ELSE I, WILL FIND YOU GUILTY…

i, a man: i, said officer (we will call him Sedanko) Sedanko you claim i, was speeding is that correct? Then B-4 he answered…

i, a man: Then i, continued to ask all of the normal questions such as his place of work, how long has he been on the force, about the last time he had his radar and sonar calibrated, what was the weather like…. Visibility, what time of day, and do he have any wo/mankind who do witness besides himself that i, was indeed speeding?
Other questions like did i, injure anyone, how does he know it was i, car he got on radar not the larger vehicle which was on the road and passing, i… and Sadanko would not answer with more than…

(Sedanko) its on the ticket, or its in the record, and making statement to I, like "you know why you are here…" and " don't ask me, I do not recall…or it is not relevant…"

i, a man: do you have any evidence that proves i, was in fact speeding?

(Sedanko) its on the ticket, or its in the record, and making statement to I, like "you know why you are here..." and " don't ask me, I do not recall...or it is not relevant..."

(cck-w.h.o.r.e.): Do you have any other questions for this officer...?

by this time, CCK-w.h.o.r.e. was getting ansie, and was telling i, to hurry up.

and continued as she kept hurrying i, up by tapping on her bench, telling i, she has heard enough, and do you have any more questions for this officer.

She also stated he has already answered that or he does not have to answer this or that...

CC-w.h.o.r.e. was acting as the officer's pro-se-cuting attorn'ey, which there was not anyone else, such as an public pretender defender or an attorn'ey for the state at the f.u.k.c.-ing k.u.n.t. ass kangaroo courthouse-ship hearing.

i, a man: i, said without i, notes, and evidence which i, need them in order to examine the witness, without them i, cannot do a good examination.

Because i, had already done some discovery months prior, and could not do the action without i, papers and notes,

i, kept winging it until i, said some things that truly set off the CCKoppel-w.h.o.r.e..

(cck-w.h.o.r.e.): that is going to be it with your questions if you do not move this case forward;

i, a man: Officer what is the code that you cited that i, had allegedly broken the law and cause an injury to another wo/mankind or property?

(Sedanko) it is on the ticket;

i, a man: Officer Sadanko could you tell the court and i, what the code says exactly word for word or even paraphrase in order for you to cite someone for a law you say that has been broken;

(Sedanko): its in the code book of civil procedure under vehicle code; That is correct you were speeding…

i, a man: Can you cite the code or read it from memory or from the book?
Then Sadanko picked up the code of civil procedure book 2008 edition, and tossed it over on the [defendant's] table where i, was shackled and said you read it… It was at that very point that i, said:

i, a man: officer Sedanko, you stated that you have been in lawenforcement for over 15 years?

Sedanko: that is right fifteen years…

i, a man: i, repeated it, so you have been a law enforcement officer and you call yourself a law enforcement officer and you don't even know the laws or codes for which you state to enforce;

(cck-w.h.o.r.e.): **THAT IS IT**, we are through. I am not going to allow you to sit here and desecrate this well established and well decorated officer…. We are through, I am going to call and end to this trial and I, will rule on this tomorrow;

At this point, the woman who acts as ~~judge~~, pubic serpent, CCK-w.h.o.r.e., Carol Chenkin Koppel (alleged pubic serpent) on loan or rent, was practically spitting and sputtering and gasping for air, as she began to foam at the mouth like a rabid dog with rabies… or a bitch in heat and a b.i.t.c.h. or as what i, thought she almost blew a fuse…

so i, said:

i, a man: mam please calm down, please calm down… you are going to give yourself a heart attack and i, do not want that on i, conscience;

(cck-W.h.o.r.e.):As the w.h.o.r.e. continued to gasp for air and shorten her heart rate in a more Manageable and calming; manner, CCK-w.h.o.r.e. said "we are through, you are finished, you do not have any more time to ask any more questions;

i, am man: i, have rights to continue i, am not finished and you refused i, personal evidence and papers for this action…i, just do not want you to have a heart attack so i, do object…

(cck-w.h.o.r.e.) i, am going to demand that you come back tomorrow morning unless you won't return and at that point, I will place a warrant out for your arrest. Then you can spend the night in jail and i, will rule tomorrow you must be back here at 10:00 a.m. tomorrow in the courtroom A-19.

i, a man: yah yah Yah… sure I, do not care whether i, sleep here or at home… i, can use a good rest by now anyways…

i, a man: i, do not care whether i, spend the night in jail or not, you decide, but i, will be here at 10:00 a.m. no matter to i, you make the call…

What was most interesting was, at the time, i, was being released by the deputies, as the night officer **Deputy #4,** had i, backpack in his hand and wanted i, to sign it out, which i, declined to sign anything so he then asked i,

(Deputy #4) "what were you in for? Because they have to confirm what reason if you know to acknowledge the contract which I, did I, best not to contract with anyone there and that is true;

i, a man:	Three counts of contempt;
(Deputy #4)	Nope, it says here you were a failure to appear…
i, a man:	Now i, did not think too much of it then nor as time had gone on, i, do realize that i, was used for a much larger scheme than what i, was led to believe; i, told what is true to the deputy #4, and he reaffirmed that it was *failure to appear* even though i, was already there and it was for alleged three counts of contempt of court;

On The Following Day
It was on that very next day, i, was able to bring two wo/mankind, who do witness on i, behalf, to the f.u.k.c.-ing, k.u.n.t. ass w.h.o.r.e's dungeon for what it stated was for the results of the unlawful trial without a pro- se-cuter attorn'ey, no public pretender defender (PPD) offered and not a trial by a jury of one's peers.

Cckoppel-w.h.o.r.e.'s attitude and contrary to the previous day, when i, was able to have zero witnesses present, zero motions hearings, no constitutions cited, zero of i, own discovery i, brought with i, and the refusal of a PPD at this f.u.k.c.-ing, w.h.o.r.e.'s, k.u.n.t. ass nisi prius, draconian star chamber courtroom;
Once, the f.u.k.c.-ing, k.u.n.t. ass CCK-whore seen i, was not alone, it then changed its demeanor just a bit, however, the end result was going to be the same.

Guilty On No Facts
The w.h.o.r.e. found i, guilty of speeding, was forcing an abstract to the DMV, to suspend the driver's license even though i, had already <u>*rescinded*</u> the california state issued driver's license several years prior. The fact that the DMV acknowledged receipt of the license rescission and i, was not driving and do not need a State issued driver's license when not in commerce is beyond draconian courts unlawful acts. With no evidence, no injured party, no witnesses accept the man who act as officer itself. The issues that officers

have is they cannot be a witness alone against another wo/mankind ever. The State, which is fiction, not real, cannot have one of its minions to state any facts on record and find anyone else guilty of anything lawfully. And this w.h.o.r.e. Carol Koppel abused position. This is why pubic serpent as officers, whether policy enforcer, attorn'er, or court officer, all by titles, are always one and the same accuser and is why a conflict of interest occurs. One officer cannot ever be a lawful witness regardless of what type of court. It is within every l.a.w. and l.e.g.a.l. rather under color of l.e.g.a.l.: statutes, codes, rules, regulations, ordinance, constitutions or bible ever known, to the federal or state courts can be the judge, jury and executioner. To Juris prudence when a pubic serpent is the accuser and the only witness; it sets l.a.w. on its f.u.k.c.-ed up k.u.n.t. ass head without lawful due process.

The Received Rude Awakening

What happened, was not that i, was taught anything lawful. i, received what i, thought was going to be a rude awakening by courts on what to not do and how the courts truly operate. i, realized very quickly that it played out scenes like in a movie, wherein i, seemed to be in a bubble, in the Wizard of Oz screenplay, fabricated by the Alice and Wonderland character. Falling deep into the rabbit whole, i, was spit back out of the matrix monopolistic nightmare by that f.u.k.c.-ed up cckoppel-whore.

What truly happened was that i, begun to study more and learn how to follow the tips on the website **1215.org** even more and then ended up receiving a doctorate degree. Then i, begun to reverse and expose CCKoppel-w.h.o.r.e. and the likes of every courthouse witness-w.h.o.r.e. throughout Southern California. i, discovered what and who CCKoppel-w.h.o.r.e. and these State, County, of California and federal govern mentals truly are.

Carol Chenkin Koppel is nothing more than a floating serpent w.h.o.r.e. who act like a pubic agent, that used mercenaries with guns and badges dressed up like on Halloween, believing and acting as if they have lawful authority. All created by fictitious incorporated govern mental actors, to obfuscate all common law rights, estates, use and control that implement a non-realistic monopolistic game, backed by a system of agents as ignorant wo/mankind. A system not of reality of wo/mankind, whereby each agent rape, kidnap, threaten, deprive, withhold, steal, extort and abuse all natural rights as *free will* of a man. In wanton commit trespass.

Instead of i, losing all rights and a tarnished name within society, after the court action was over, i, begun to write to the Commission on Judicial Performance that had gone nowhere. i, sent claims of what cckoppel-w.h.o.r.e. did to i, to the california governor, attorn'ey general, president of the united states, and sent copies of the appeal that i, filed to the chief justice of the Lancaster Courthouse-ship. Herein again is what whit-man (Thomas Robert White) sent back to i, as follows:

> In this second letter, you also asked that your case be dismissed. I was recently advised that on August 8, 2013, Judge Carol Koppel reviewed and reconsidered your matter and dismissed your case in the interest of justice. She vacated your finding of guilt and your sentence as well as the compliance date of August 15, 2013. The clerk was directed to send you a copy of her decision and an amended abstract was forwarded to the DMV (attachment: Order on Additional Proceedings).
>
> Finally, your most recent letters expressed concerns about your appeal. As the case has been dismissed, issues pertaining to appeal are no longer applicable.
>
> No further action will be taken on your case and the matter is deemed closed.
>
> Very truly yours,
>
> Thomas R. White
> Supervising Judge, North District

This is the actual copied excerpt from Supervising ~~Judge~~ white after i, sent i, claim of what is true to the chief justice, governor, Commission and many others. This justice white knew i, meant business. The only way this man, who acts as a justice, would be able to get away from a huge lawsuit against cckoppel-w.h.o.r.e. and its courthouse along with the california enclave was to make a choice to get that fukc-ing cckoppel-w.h.o.r.e. to drop all issues dealing with i. Considering all of the evidence and i, actual ability to file a direct suit against the carol chenkin koppel k.u.n.t. ass, w.h.o.r.e., l.e.g.a.l., b.i.t.c.h. and all of the state of california actors for hundreds of millions, they concealed any further issues. Of course, the Commissions on Judicial Performance are a laughing joke. This is a waste of tax-payers labour and should be abolished. (i, will explain to you later on)

The only honorable thing to do was to dismiss everything. However, the harm by way of trespass had already been committed against i, and it is continued to this very day even (12) twelve years hereafter by the woman carol chenkin koppel.

i, Do Invite CCKoppel – W.h.o.r.e.To The Party

i, do invite the k.u.n.t. as serpent cckoppel-w.h.o.r.e., to the original party some years thereafter to make certain that f.u.k.c.-ing by k.u.n.t. ass w.h.o.r.e. did not feel left out of the invitation list of all of its draconian satanic-like comrades, who do act similar to all the other state and federal satanic minions by way of trespass.

As i, do for all other pubic serpent, i, invited Carol Chenkin Koppel to the *Amicus Curiae Hearing, set for Wednesday January 30th, 2022, 8:30 a.m., Stanley Mosk Courthouse Room 67.*

Of course, none of them replied nor were any of them present for this party. i, do not blame them for not showing up for their piece of the pie, cake, or pre hors d'oeuvres before they became the main course meal. However, i, do hold each responsible for trespass each do commit against i. As mankind of God's green earth, there is no statutory limit that runs against one who do commit trespass. There are no statutes of limitations on trespass. A trespass do still continue against i, a man adam-daniel from the borsotti family to this day in the year of our lord Jesus Christ of God's 2025.

The actual facts of what i, do state about:

None prosecuting attorn'ey,

None Defense Attorn'ey (PPD)

None reporter;

All the reader needs to do is read the following actual excerpt sent to i, by the evil-wrongdoer Carol Koppel Chenkin w.h.o.r.e. to see facts for yourselves. i, have a right as all wo/mankind have *free will* as rights to make the record and the fact that f.u.k.c.-ing k.u.n.t. as l.e.g.a.l. w.h.o.r.e. knew it, as in Carol Koppel – w.h.o.r.e. was in big trouble when and not if facts were ever to get to the public, as it was released for all the world to read.

It has become a reality for i, to be able to know that all of the trespass by this b.i.t.c.h. will soon enough become a reality and for the world to know what happened, not only to i, as a man, rather to hundreds of thousands of wo/mankind and most likely millions over 150 years. i, am able to do it through this *living missive*. For the pubic serpent is not a reality. E. Harris the court cluck, can attest to it all! (See below):

Cck-Whore Autograph Acknowledges De Ceit.

There is and never was a need for the DMV to receive something like an amended abstract it has no jurisdiction over.
"*i, a man; adam – daniel of the borsotti family, always tell what is true even when i, lie*" However, i, have all facts without dispute. When i, seek you shall find, what is true from i, to you never mind;

Superior Court of California
County of Los Angeles

ADDITIONAL PROCEEDINGS						Clerk: E. Harris
Defendant's Name: Daniel Borsotti						Case Number: 91102QU
Date: 8-8-13	Dept. A19	Judge: Koppel	Prosecutor: None	Defense Atty. None	Reporter: None	Inter. / Language

Upon review and reconsideration of the totality of the trial proceedings, the court hereby vacates the finding of guilty. The sentence is vacated and the citation is hereby ordered dismissed in the interest of justice. Date of August 15, 2013 is vacated.

Clerk to send a copy of this decision to the defendant.

Amended abstract sent to the DMV.

Regardless of what this b.i.t.c.h. cck-w.h.o.r.e. says or do, i, realized the fraud upon the people as wo/menkind cause i, to rescind the state issued driver's license back on or about February 2010. A drivers license i, do not need to live i, life amicably.

When i, do begin to learn what is true about this fictional ens legis corp(s)orations STATE OF CALIFORNIA AND UNITED STATES INC. that are allowed to operate through agents on a whole as managing govern mental agencies. This was about 3 years prior to this fictional witch-hunt against i, a man. Whereby i, was not even within or without the States jurisdiction. When a wo/mankind is not contracting with each individual agency the wo/mankind are not and is not bound by their f.u.k.c.-ed up codes, rules, ordinances, regulations or acts period.

When someone or agent tells you different, let them know if you move against me, you are liable to i, a trespass against [my] life as i, am not within your jurisdiction.

All wo/mankind have the free will and right to contract. However, just because one accepts a driver's license or other state coerced issued contracted license does not give the govern mentals full power to enslave any wo/mankind on every level from State to Federal. This is not involuntary voluntary servitude. This is god's world!

Readers: The author wants to give you some more writing note space as i, do believe you have questions that cannot wait until you finish this living missive to put to paper for the future memorial:

Chapter 4, IV, Four

SATAN 16th MINION OF THE MELVIN DOUGLAS SANDVIG
CRIMINAL GANG OF 2007/2014 – 2025

[Pubic Serpent] Case # PS016624, Melvin Douglas Sandvig
B.A.R. # 101320

Melvin Douglas Sandvig
[Pubic Serpent]
Satan's 16th Minion
(Richard-cranium)
B.A.R.#101320

Superior Court of California, Chatsworth Courthouse,
North Valley Division
Daniel - Borsotti V. Scott Allan Niner 2014 Case # **PS016624**

It was about November/December 2008, when i, first encountered this short, balding and very low voice speaking man; who act as a [~~judge~~] pubic serpent, [Melvin Douglas Sandvig], hereinafter "richard-cranium", who is supposed to have taken an oath as a public servant, that turned dis-honorable.

Not only dishonorable, downright, dirty and unethical; a pubic serpent from Chatsworth Courthouse-ship. Maybe i, should have said just a puppet on a corruption of strings. As most pubic serpents that are ready to do satan's bidding for corp(s)orations known by

UNITED STATES OF AMERICA INC. and THE STATE OF CALIFORNIA INC. and others on the public side of commerce. Maybe it is caused by threats of war ass-wipe niner pledged by its $60,000.00 reward to ruin i, life. Niner did pledge actual Federal Reserve notes to wreck i, life. What an egotistical idiot would make outlandish felony threats towards another wo/mankind? Terrorist threats would have of landed i, in prison, but not any of the Niner?

It just so happened that this Superior Court of California Chatsworth Courthouse action number **PS016624**, is the second encounter i, dealt with richard-cranium, whereby richard-cranium acted in union with ass-wipe to suppress i, rights. Rites to freedom, to live free unencumbered from fear, free of other wo/mankind threats, free from collusion, extortion, and conspiracy which is why i, needed to receive the temporary restraining order (TRO) against ass-wipe. Scott Alan Niner and his family or as they are now known as herein; ass-wipe niner's criminal gang.

It was about this time 2014, in the process of receiving i, remedy for fraud robin and ass-wipe perpetrated against i, life. When ass-wipe begun his campaign to reap more havoc against i, life, by way of threats and his claim to spend as much money as it will take to ruin i, to desecrate i, name within society, to get i, thrown in jail.

Ass-wipe had made open threats to harm i. Scott was going to hire bad agents, employees and pubic serpent to come after i, to take away i, home, i, car, i, livelihood, and inevitably bankrupt i, life. For i, standing up for i-self, for utilizing the only form of fictional remedy that a society offers to wo/mankind to seek justice for one which is supposed to be for all.

Its citizens, residents, foreigners when they are on the land and even people of California and of the United States of America; impartiality with or without the incorp(s)oration is justice for all. Ass-wipe niner even went as far to state, that i, need to find and follow *his* God and that *his* god is the only god that will *redeem*, i, life. That i, Buddhism teachings is inferior to ass-wipe's god. It is amazing how ignorant, egotistical and arrogant ass-wipe is.

Was it Richard-cranium or Divine Intervention?
It was at this time, Richard-cranium along with a man; below who act as [~~judge~~] Lloyd Clark Loomis, hereinafter, "Clue-less", which both, Richard-cranium and clue-less denied i, the motioned restraining order for no apparent cause.

i, was just flat out denied without cause, without a hearing without any rights to bring in other wo/mankind who do witness certain facts and evidence to prove ass-wipe's threats. i, know that b.i.t.c.h.-mlo hired on Richard-cranium for the PC04224, 2007 court action whereas, Richard-cranium denied i, the rights to receive discovery and to depose ass-wipe niner, for the basics of discovery and due process of law.

At this point, although i, was apprehensive and having gone through everything i, had by ass-wipe niner family, i, did not know of any unethical, amoral, unlawful or illegal acts that did occur by the pubic serpent other than what i, do state.

However, to i, then, as i, still believed, past tense, all attorn'eys had faith in that the judicial system was a lawful place where wo/mankind can bring their grievances, to be witnessed by unbiased woman and men that act as public servants.

Some of the pubic serpents were known by the people of… to call forth from a society as in <u>*Trial by Jury*</u>, to determine both law and fact; as in jury nullification. Although that was so long ago. How the courts were set up to hear cases and for a republican form of government.

This idea was the public trial by jury to determine, not what they were told to rule by some pubic serpent known as an f.u.k.c.-ed up k.u.n.t. ass ~~judge~~, but with the juries' own good conscience, by morals, ethics, reason logic and common sense of honorable aptitude.

As readers convert and come to their own determination, after having heard everything that i, have gone through, even though much of what is written comes from i, side of what i, do interpret.

Thee serpents who were to have sworn an oath and were supposed to be bonded against any harm that might come to i, or you, is where the shit hits the road to determined by said readers.

Regardless of whether i, claim to be a member of the public or a free man, a trespass is trespass a most egregious sin. It does not matter what their title, when wo/mankind trespass on i.

i, a man, believe in divine intervention. i, as man also know that thee who lives with the least interaction with govern mentals and interact with wo/mankind from within or without the united states as citizen or many other titles, by way of the serpent, is i, and your own prerogative. Walk light when trust is placed wrongly.

We are the freest "of" "in" or "as" a society. For deliberate negligence, in general, for others that like to live free of govern mental constraints, should not be forced to be subject as a <u>people of … California</u> and or as <u>people of … the United States of America</u>. No wo/men can ever be subject unless harm is caused by another wo/man.

i, did set for a motioned hearing with Richard-cranium only because Richard-cranium was placed onto the court docket for i, court action. Although due to the biases previously caused by Richard-cranium against i, as a man, Richard-cranium was duty-bound to recues itself from acting anywhere on, or near i, court actions ever. Was this on purpose or by divine intervention?

At least one thing i, have learned, when it come to govern mentals and court actions, nothing is by divine intervention. Everything that the court clucks and pubic serpents do is methodical, on purpose, and with intent. Mostly mal intent, even so, intent is always present.

All i, was working towards is a permanent or even temporary injunction against ass-wipe because of all of the overwhelming facts and evidence i, have to support the (TRO) Temporary Restraining Order and injunction. Much of the evidence came directly from ass-wipe's personal email to i, *personal emails*. Some of the facts as evidence also came from the horses ass-wipe himself orally.

See Ass-Wipes Emails Below:
i, will be adding ass-wipe niner's email posts that are in contrast to i, purpose for standing up for i, self. It is for what i, do know what is fair, just, moral, ethical and rite/right. Not only for i, facts as to what is true, i, do this for all wo/mankind, for i, healing and god's interest. You see, when a criminal does a crime and gets away with it, or a criminal thinks she/he gets away with their crime, a criminal loses, all perpetrated against lose, and the public loses. Maxim of Law: "*At time of war laws are silent*" They cause a known war!

> **"Necessity has no law."** [Plowd. 18, and 15 Vin. Abr. 534; 22 id. 540]
> "In time of war, laws are silent." [**Cicero**]

Non-moral commandment, being l.e.g.a.l. is a condition that universally prevails in official systems of the world today. Meaning, that no lawful basis exists upon which anything can be created, or be made to emerge, upon which basis allegiance and obedience can be legitimately demanded over god's laws.

Acting under law of necessity, i.e. lawlessness, allows complete total right of everyone to disregard any and all alleged assertions of any l.e.g.a.l., verifiable, and presumed legitimate jurisdiction over anything or anyone.

Anyone acting against anyone under such non-law is self-confessing to be a naked criminal aggressor, and con man who has forfeited all credibility and right to demand allegiance, obedience, or compliance with any jurisdiction she/he might assert.

If you, as a real being, are in real law and it is impossible for an attorn'ey or ~~judge~~ to recognize or access it, you are not (and cannot be made subject to by them) in their jurisdiction. The crucial issue is then how to notice them of your position and standing.

A person created under de jure law, with the person's identifying name appearing as prescribed l.a.w. and according to the rules of English grammar, is a l.e.g.a.l. fact.

A corrupted "alter ego" version of that name, manufactured under the l.e.g.a.l. fiction of "right of presumption" will have "credibility" only so long as the presumption remains unchallenged. The rule of the world is that anything and everything skates unless you bust it. So readers, go bust those [~~judge~~]s ass-ets.

Therefore, in order for one to be held accountable, a criminal or accused must be brought forth in a lawful fashion. As the l.e.g.a.l. is not l.a.w. therefore, no fiction can be held accountable unless it is by the LAW of mankind. This is not the same as the courts of and created by the govern mentals.

Regardless of whether it be THE UNITED STATE, UNITED STATES, United States Inc. or The United States of America, the same laws apply, however the l.e.g.a.l. is not the same with each power. One being by the people for the people, one being by the govern mentals for the govern mentals, and the other being by God and for all wo/mankind.

Please stay tuned as this *living missive* gets more interesting as i, and you the reader risk forward with what is true in i, heart and with hope you concurrently.

The Need For Transparency

Up to now, there is zero transparency from within or without dealing with any state or federal govern mental created court systems. When pubic serpent do whatever she/he wants, or thinks it can get away with, it sets an untrusting worthlessness towards a public and in return, non-trust is received from public; tenfold.

When govern mentals get too far out of control in abusing their positions, powers, and inability to act in honor to public, eventually a public rises up to set all agents of said systems in checks and balances. Are we there yet? God knows. It was even written onto those fraudulent documents called the Articles of Con-federations,

Constitutions of.... Declarations of... treaties of... and just about every oath alleged taken by said pubic serpents.

1. "Courts must publicize their operation and decision process."
2. "~~Judge~~s must disclose their assets and conflicts of interest."
3. "Outsiders must be able to find out what is happening within the court system."
4. "A free media with access to judicial proceedings and documents along with an active civil society to publicize lapses and work for reform,"

   Please read the authors stuff below; research Susan please; by: Susan Rose-Ackerman

i, do follow the thoughts and actions of raison d'etre [118], as a wo/mankind, or organization. Raison d'etre is the most important reason for existing in the way that a wo/mankind do anything and everything in life. However, the difference between a person, organization and wo/mankind is that wo/mankind created government, organizations and corp(s)orations, which created citizens, residents, persons, plaintiffs, defendants, individuals, ens legis fictions of every type.

Therefore, the hierarchy of status is always God, then wo/mankind. The rest of them are inferior. i, serpent, agents for... or employees of... [~~judges~~], commissioners, magistrates, politicians, and any other title is all inferior to i, as a man and you as a wo/mankind. This is very difficult, a reality for almost 99% of the wo/mankind, persons, citizens, residents and their like kind to grasp. It is actually very difficult for pubic serpents to grasp as all pubic serpents are all inferior, yet they are and we must continue to remind them, we created all of them before God and not as gods.
It will take some time, and i, as in wo/mankind am working on educating the world of these realities. It actually will not take long when we are able to use the satanic forms of media to get words out to the public at large. Just imagine how quickly this new, or rather

[118] RAISON D'ETRE: To stand strong on one's thoughts, words, actions and belief structure as a way of life.

original, knowledge will spread across the globe. Like a healing plandemic of medicine created remedy for all wo/mankind, all over this god's green earth, to be in harmony all at one time.

Questions for readers are, will Satan allow god's true messages to be received across this globe? i, do have a small answer to this question, which is: how come after several thousands of years since Moses, Jesus, Daniel, Peter, Paul and Mary, and a John Lennon song: "*…Imagine all the people, living life in peace….*" have been shared, taught reproduced, and instilled across this globe, do wo/mankind still not get the big picture? Because there are too many or actually only a few that have control of mass media that thwart any narrative in order to control the youthful minds of wo/mankind. Wherever there is electronic devices, agents have their agenda to fulfill B-4 a last battle between good and evil before the all-knowing "Day of Judgment."

SATAN 17th MINION OF THE MELVIN DOUGLAS SANDVIG CRIMINAL GANG OF 2007/2014 – 2025

[Pubic Serpent] Case # PS016624
Lloyd Clark Loomis **B.A.R. # 85239**

Lloyd Clark Loomis
[Pubic Serpent]
Satan's 17th minion
(Clue-less)

The few things i, can say about this man, Lloyd Clark Loomis hereinafter "Clue-less" who act as a pubic serpent is not for or against Clue-less. It is that whether it is clue-less to trueness of *law* of this nation and world; clue-less should have known what he was doing is going against god's l.a.w. The unlawful statutory schema is not laws of reciprocity. Clue-less as a man caused a trespass upon i.

Clue-less will be forever, like all other evil-wrongdoers, enshrined herein as clue-less who maliciously, with deliberate intent do suppress a once severely disabled man's rights to an unbiased lawful process. Clue-less will go down in this *living missive* as his-story of aiding, abetting and conspiring with Richard-cranium and many other known evil-wrongdoers named herein who assisted ass-wipe's criminal gang.

Reciprocity is the key to any true nation. It is the *l.a.w.* of God, karma, and Ten Commandments. One reaps what one sews and God's laws and karma is the bedrock of all true *law* for all 50 states and should be for the entire world.

People for years have sustained a level of what one reaps one sews. However, it seems that somewhere several years ago, govern mental agents, especially, the pubic court serpents, stopped caring about breaking all the rules, *laws*, for which use to control the pubic serpents. Imagine a world where l.a.w. is applied equally to all wo/mankind regardless of status, genre and who you work for.

When any number of wo/mankind work together to suppress any groups or even one wo/mankind, it is time to get rid of those evil-wrongdoers.

What clue-less did was follow his colleagues in their reign of terror and suppression against i, as man. Suppression comes by way of aiding and abetting ass-wipes' family (which includes robin niner [and not scott's blood sister robin]) and his brother, jim/james or Willie" but more so his father sperm-donor.

Had Robin Niner not allowed ass-wipe to coerce she to steal, lie and cheat to cause havoc and attempt to annihilate i, adam-daniel of family borsotti's, name, livelihood, and i, pursuit for life; this *living missive* would not be written.

The lack of compensation for trespass, by way of harm, ass-wipe's statement of "*any means necessary...*" as stated in its email posts to i, directly caused trespass of others.

Ass-wipe Niner said it himself and i, Quote:

> *" From:*
> *scott1@danglingcarrotcreative.com*
> *Subject: www.santaclarita.com/Modules/ShowDocument.aspx?documentid=5076*
> *Date: Sat, 1 Nov 2014 16:58:01 -0700*
> *To: ~~yourmotivator1@live.com~~ [that post No Longer a viable email]*

" I will make things happen within the city and with your neighbors......... I'm done fucking around with you. You better hope your within compliance. Otherwise, as I said in the email, this is only one SMALL step that i'm going to take to make sure you leave me alone. You will be too busy trying to keep your life as it is right now, your life as it is right now.......I refuse to continue this as I'm getting married in two weeks......That's your deadline to personally make a commitment to me to move on with your life, legal or not but if you continue to involve yourself in my life.......... I won't stop until every aspect of your complete ignorance is exposed to everyone, everywhere including the government and your family. I will only tell the truth, as I have always done........your just a thief and only take advantage of people as you always have cause you don't have the intelligence to do anything on your own.....only by being a cheat and a liar....

> *TWO WEEKS..........ONE RESPONSE and it goes away, if not........GAME ON........I'm not worried cause my entire life is by the book, ethical, honest, and true. I pay the IRS exactly what is due and don't twist the truth, they can explore, look all they want and so can you....... the laughs on you cause I live my life honestly and by the book, can you say the same?..........*
>
> *why don't we see...................*

Instead of spending 60k on an attorney fighting your completely fraudulent law suits, I'm willing to spend 60k to expose you to the truth to the government etc. etc. and others to put you where you belong.

Last Chance to stop this Danny..........Hope you choose the right way.......or my 60k is going to make sure you end up where you belong.....with criminals...... "

i, end this quote;

i, am not going to comment much about what ass-wipe sent 2014. Threats speaks for itself. When one does an analysis of what ass-wipe sent to i, ass-wipe was trying to make himself convinced that what he wrote is true (which truth is not what is true). It is only in his own mind to justify his past, present and future until repentance.

Ass-wipe's statements cannot be true, for the facts that he committed adultery, was a family nuisance, which is why he left the family business, was doing crack cocaine with his mistress, and taking advantage by lying to a once severally disabled man.

There are others who ass-wipe was had business with who he did not pay, the fraudulent transfers of property, business assets to his family, changing names to protect the guilty, as to what he owed, and unlawful conveyance; the fraudulent bankruptcy he filed … on and on…. not to speak of the thoughts of ass-wipe also defrauding his creditor(s).

The assertions and refusal to completely paying attorn'eys and i, am pretty sure that he must have given something to dick-em as dick-em is not the type of attorn'ey to throw i, under the bus without receiving a payout to suppress i, ability to due process, and commit malfeasance, malpractice which contradicts many writings not to withhold herein.

Yet, clue-less, thereby allowed his own best judgment, no not his best judgment, because his best judgment cost another man his day in court, his right 2-B free from terrorist threats and live without fear, not to ~~judge~~ i, as a man before facts and evidence was allowed to be brought forward; denial of a *trial by jury* to move i, TRO action forward, appeal in order for judicial system to work like it is supposed to for many moons.

Clue-less, along with bitch-mlo, richard-cranium, ass-wipe, top-ramin, weiner-dog and dick-em, sperm-doner, (ex-wife) robin niner and others who do conspire like all the pubic serpent agents as paid suppression-ists' to assist ass-wipe niner from being brought to justice is the travesty to, of and from this alleged justice system.

All clue-less needed to do was to invoke the TRO which means "Temporary…" so i, could receive a reprieve from terrorist tactics ass-wipe niner commited. Clue-less should have and he could have done the right action, and at the same time, clue-less by taking orders from richard-cranium, had overridden true law, Juris prudence, and the alleged oath to public to this point.

The fact Richard-cranium and bitch-mlo already stopped i, to receiving all pre-trial discovery. When each worked together to refuse or recall when osana f.u.k.c.-ing, k.u.n.t ass court cluck and the courtroom cluck w.h.o.r.e.-s played a run-around game to suppress i, ability to receive Subpoenas Duces Tecum, set the scene for conspiracy to suppress law and judgment and is attest to their trespass against i.

Instead clue-less did lose his morals and ethical compass as clue-less allowed himself 2-B swept up N-2 the group of conspirators' along with all the others herein this *living missive* known as evil-wrongdoers.

Clue-less is not the first one to follow in the footsteps of devilish functions and as the reader will read; he is not the last one either. (Let us venture forward because it gets f.u.k.c-ing, b.i.t.c.h., k.u.n.t. ass w.h.o.r.e. crazy worse B-4 it ever gets morally and ethically any better) i, would like to place notice herein to express i, definitions of words herein are at the back of this missive.

They are created to receive a unique reaction, for continuous healing, and to light a spark for readers whom should know by now, this *living missive* is all about exposure of evil-wrongdoers. These actions by i, are accumulative, not malevolent that deserve nothing less than spirited exposure.

See Online Actual Court Summary Docket:
Online Services , Case Access **CASE NO. 19CHCV00766**
CASE INFORMATION

Case Information | Register Of Actions | FUTURE HEARINGS | PARTY INFORMATION | Documents Filed | Proceedings Held

Case Number: PS016624
DANIEL BORSOTTI VS SCOTT A NINER

Filing Courthouse: Chatsworth Courthouse

Filing Date: 11/12/2014
Case Type: Civil Harassment (General Jurisdiction)
Status: Judgment by Court-Petition denied 12/24/2014

FUTURE HEARINGS

Case Information | Register Of Actions | FUTURE HEARINGS | PARTY INFORMATION | Documents Filed | Proceedings Held

None
PARTY INFORMATION

Case Information | Register Of Actions | FUTURE HEARINGS | PARTY INFORMATION | Documents Filed | Proceedings Held

BORSOTTI DANIEL - Petitioner In Pro Per

NINER SCOTT ALAN - Respondent

Documents Filed

Case Information | Register Of Actions | FUTURE HEARINGS | PARTY INFORMATION | Documents Filed | Proceedings Held

Documents Filed (Filing dates listed in descending order)

12/10/2014 Proof of Service
Filed by Petitioner In Pro Per

12/09/2014 Notice (OF INVALID RULING NOTICE OF ACTION AFFIDAVIT OF DANIEL A. BORSOTTI; IN SUPPORT OF ACTION FOR CONTEMPT; POINTS AND AUTHORITIES)
Filed by Petitioner

11/12/2014 OSC & Temporary Restraining Order (BY JUDGE MELVIN SANDVIG)
Filed by Petitioner In Pro Per

11/12/2014 Pet for Injunctive Ord-Harrassment

Proceedings Held

Case Information | Register Of Actions | FUTURE HEARINGS | PARTY INFORMATION | Documents Filed | Proceedings Held

Proceedings Held (Proceeding dates listed in descending order)

12/24/2014 at 08:30 am in Department F51, Lloyd C. Loomis, Presiding
Pet for Injunct Prohbit Harassment - **TRO is denied.**

12/03/2014 at 09:00 am in Department F46, Susan Lopez-Giss, Presiding
Pet for Injunct Prohbit Harassment - **Continued by Plaintiff**

12/03/2014 at 08:30 am in Department F51, Lloyd C. Loomis, Presiding
Pet for Injunct Prohbit Harassment - **No Stip/Matter tranf. to other Dept**

12/02/2014 at 08:30 am in Department F51, Lloyd C. Loomis, Presiding
Ex-Parte Application - **Denied**

Register Of Actions

Case Information | Register Of Actions | FUTURE HEARINGS | PARTY INFORMATION | Documents Filed | Proceedings Held

Register of Actions (Listed in descending order)

12/24/2014 at 08:30 am in Department F51, Lloyd C. Loomis, Presiding
Pet for Injunct Prohbit Harassment - **TRO is denied.**

12/10/2014 Proof of Service
Filed by Petitioner In Pro Per

12/09/2014 Notice (OF INVALID RULING NOTICE OF ACTION AFFIDAVIT OF DANIEL A. BORSOTTI; IN SUPPORT OF ACTION FOR CONTEMPT; POINTS AND AUTHORITIES)
Filed by Petitioner

12/03/2014 at 09:00 am in Department F46, Susan Lopez-Giss, Presiding
Pet for Injunct Prohbit Harassment - **Continued by Plaintiff**

12/03/2014 at 08:30 am in Department F51, Lloyd C. Loomis, Presiding
Pet for Injunct Prohbit Harassment - **No Stip/Matter tranf. to other Dept**

12/02/2014 at 08:30 am in Department F51, Lloyd C. Loomis, Presiding
Ex-Parte Application - **Denied**

11/12/2014 Pet for Injunctive Ord-Harrassment

11/12/2014 OSC & Temporary Restraining Order (BY JUDGE MELVIN SANDVIG)
Filed by Petitioner In Pro Per
http://www.metnews.com/index.htm ;

https://www.lacourt.org/judicialofficers/ui/SearchResult.aspx?wb48617274=E26606E5

End Quote: Summary Court Docket

The next names are from lists of previously stated wrongdoers to be revealed. All of the evil-wrongdoers at this time were all named herein as: quality loan service corporation (annia quintana & rochelle matkin), nationstar mortgage llc(jay bray and robert stiles), jp morgan chase llc(jamie dimon), and the revealed true names of:

mccarthy & holthus(john thomas), auction.com(jeffrey friedman), federal home loan mortgage corporation/freddie mac(david brickman & mark grier), coldwell banker(charlie young, phil boroda, & major von brunk) only to name a few…

Because of the facts that all of the court pubic serpent were causing a trespass individually and collectively as in a R.I.C.O. act, that i, could have filed, this *living missive* is the affidavit for such a future claim. i, was forced to file to recues Richard-cranium from ever handling i, court action at any time in the future.

See the following disgusting bullshit that no wo/mankind should have to deal with. Although i, do skip four years and misplace this recusal, i, deliberately will go back on track after i, make i, point to readers as all readers are the *trial by jury*.
The next quote is similarly different to the previous facts used;

i, quote:

"RECUSAL, DISQUALIFICATION OF MELVIN D. SANDVIG (CHIEF ADMINISTRATOR) [JUDGE] FOR CAUSE Title 28 U.S.C. § 455(a); C.C.P. § 170.3(b)(2)(A), C.C.P. § 170.3(a)(1), 170.3(c)(1); **EXHIBITS 1-10**

Date: January 16, 2020
Time: 8:30 a.m.
Dept. F-47

Affidavit regarding Recusal, Disqualification for cause

I, Daniel-Adam..., ("Your Affiant" or "Claimant") Sui Juris, hereafter "i", "me", or "my", over the age of majority, competent to testify, having information and belief, on Los Angeles county soil aver, teste, promise under penalty of perjury per the laws for California, and the united States of America, as God as my witness only the following is true:

I recues, and/or disqualify [Judge] Melvin D. Sandvig ("Administrator..." or "MDS") Pursuant to 170.1(a)(6) (iii) on the grounds that he has ruled unfairly against me several times and at present time your Affiant has an Appeal filed, against a ruling made by [Judge] Melvin D. Sandvig, in the appellant Court (See Exhibit "A" 2nd District court of Appeal complete file on October 17th, 2019) A person aware of these facts might reasonably entertain a doubt that the Judge would be able to be impartial.

Your Affiant makes this affidavit on the CITY OF LOS ANGELES, COUNTY OF LOS ANGELES, on January 15TH, 2020; And ...

[**continue quote**]

VERIFICATION

I, Daniel Borsotti, declare that I am the Claimant in the above-entitled action. I have read the foregoing Demand for "Recusal of Judge" and know the contents thereof.

All of the information contained in the Application is true of my own personal first hand knowledge, except as to those matters which shall be upon oral argument in front of a panel of three judges, and as to those matters, I believe them to be true.

I declare under penalty of perjury that the foregoing is true and correct and that this declaration was executed at Los Angeles, California.

I hereby certify that I filed the foregoing with the Clerk of the Court for the above-numbered and -entitled cause of action and served a true and correct copy on all participants in the case by mailing by

First-Class Mail, postage prepaid, or have dispatched it to a third party commercial carrier for delivery within three (3) calendar days to the following participants:

[Autograph]:
By: <u>Adam- Daniels, as man</u>
<u>List of person to be served:</u>

Notice to principal is notice to Agent:

Auction.com, Jeffrey Friedman, 1 Mauchly, Irvine, California. 92618; J.P Morgan Bank, James Dimon, 1111 Polaris Parkway, Columbus, Ohio. 43240; McCarthy & Holthus, LLP, John Thomas, Firm Headquarter, 411 Ivy Street, San Diego, CA 92101; Quality Loan Service Corporation, Rochelle Matkin, Annia Quintana, 2763 Camino del Rio S, SAN DIEGO, CALIFORNIA. 92108; Freddie Mac, David Brickman, c/o Corporate Secretary, 8200 Jones Branch Drive McLean, Virginia 22102; Coldwell Banker Corporate Headquarter, Charlie Young, 175 Park Avenue, Madison New Jersey. 07940; NATIONSTAR MORTGAGE, LLC, Jay Bray, Robert Stiles, 350 Highland Drive, Lewisville, Texas. 75067;

By: adam-daniel of the family borsotti

End Quote

No [~~Judge~~] Can Review Its Of Demand For Recusal?
Even the court's own rules states that no ~~judge~~ serpent can review its own recusal, especially with so much actual proof backing up all statements against said wo/mankind that act as pubic serpent.

i, Filed Amicus Curiae Hearing, to bring forth Richard-cranium (melvin douglas sandvig) to be present on Wednesday January 30th, 2022, 8:30 A.M. Stanley Mosk Courthouse Room 67, whereas i, invited Richard-cranium to the party. i, was refused.

Refused as usual for any pubic serpent ever to be present and for the actual incourt inquiry when all court actors clearly knows each do cause a trespass at hand against i, a man. It is not the first nor the last recusal. (See future refuses to recuses).

A Summary Of The Years Of Bias
Quote:
i, have a summary of fraud upon i, and the trespass showing a long history of biased by Richard-cranium as follows:
Melvin Douglas Sandvig admitted to the Truthfulness of the Fact that the following are Governing Rules of this Case;

Your Affiant repeats, re-alleges, and incorporates by reference the foregoing paragraphs as if those paragraphs were fully set forth herein;

Your Affiant states and Melvin Douglas Sandvig admitted to the truthfulness of the fact, In the name of God, with the gaze of Our lord, that Daniel-Adam Steve's son; Cohen/Borsotti is appearing specially and not generally, vi et armis [119];

Your Affiant states and Melvin Douglas Sandvig admitted to the truthfulness of the fact that your Affiant is claiming, exercising and invoking ALL RIGHTS, including but not limited to God granted Rights, inalienable rights, human Rights, and all Rights guaranteed and protected by the united States Constitution, the California Constitution, the Universal Postal Union Treaty and other unspecified International Treaties;

Your Affiant states and Melvin Douglas Sandvig admitted to the truthfulness of the fact that the undersigned is the Appellant in the case FOR WHICH Melvin Douglas Sandvig is the subject sub-judice [120];

Your Affiant states and Melvin Douglas Sandvig admitted to the truthfulness of the fact that the undersigned is the [Plaintiff] man in the trial court case that this appeal derives from;

Your Affiant states and Melvin Douglas Sandvig admitted to the truthfulness of the fact that the undersigned adapts and incorporates herein by reference, as if fully set forth herein, the entire

---

[119] "with force and arms —used of a trespass to person or property which is the immediate cause of damage" https://www.merriam-webster.com/dictionary/vi%20et%20armis
[120] ***sub judice,*** **: "before a judge or court : not yet judicially decided" https://www.merriam-webster.com/dictionary/sub%20judice**

SUPERIOR COURT OF CALIFORNIA, COUNTY OF LOS ANGELES , Civil Unlimited Jurisdiction, Case PC04224, BORSOTTI v. NINER, including but not limited to, And

2007 Superior Court California, Case No.: PC040224;

A. 2014, Superior Court California BORSOTTI v. NINER Case No.: PS016624;

B. 2015 United States District Court Case No.: CV-04112 JAK (AFM) (C.D. Cal. May. 16, 2016) BORSOTTI v. MELVIN D. SANDVIG

C. 2017 Superior Court California Court Case No.: BORSOTTI v. NATIONSTAR MORTGAGE LLC, et. al., PC057982;

D. 2018 Superior Court Case No.: PC058470 BORSOTTI v. QUALITY LOAN SERVICE CORPORATION et. al., whereas Melvin Douglas Sandvig Recused himself from any impropriety; And

E. 2019 Superior Court Case 19CHCV00766 whereas Subject Melvin Douglas Sandvig is the subject to, including and not limited to, and appeal for discrimination, bias, alleged fraud upon the court, revenge etc…

Your Affiant states and Melvin Douglas Sandvig admitted to the truthfulness of the fact that the incorporation by reference is not limited to, all Minute Entries, Rulings, Calendared hearings, Transfers/Referrals by court and/or clerk, removals, and Orders, the entire docket listed above;

Your Affiant states and Melvin Douglas Sandvig admitted to the truthfulness of the fact that the undersigned submits the following facts, law and authority, including but not limited to, as JUDICIAL NOTICE [450- 460] EVD. CODE 201, as basis for and in support of this pleading;

Your Affiant states and Melvin Douglas Sandvig admitted to the truthfulness of the fact that the instant case is governed by, inter alia [121], the Federal Rules of Civil Procedure and, inter alia, the Federal Rules of Evidence and, inter alia, the United States Code and, inter alia, the united States Constitution of 1787 and, inter alia, the amendments thereto including the original 13th Amendment and, inter alia, the California Constitution and, inter alia, the Treaty of Paris of 1781 and, inter alia, the Hague Convention and, inter alia, the Universal Postal Union Treaty and, inter alia.

ALL other human rights treaties and, inter alia, the Affidavit Memorializing Conversations Regarding Self Disqualification of Judges in COUNTY OF LOS ANGELES , and inter alia, the Affidavit of Nihil Dicit and of Tacit Agreement filed on or about the same time MDS's Oath of Office was signed, all estoppels on government agencies and/or agents, and others and, inter alia. These Rules and Laws have not been abrogated as to evade as of January 16th, 2020 issues.

Your Affiant states and Melvin Douglas Sandvig admitted to the truthfulness of the fact that he has been recused in a prior case involving the undersigned.

F. Your Affiant states and Melvin Douglas Sandvig admitted to the truthfulness of the fact that he acted without jurisdiction in hearing the case sub judice [122], due to self recusal in 2014, Superior Court California BORSOTTI v. NINER Case No.: PS016624; 2017 Superior Court California Court Case No.: BORSOTTI v. NATIONSTAR MORTGAGE LLC, et. al., PC057982; 2018 Superior Court Case No.: PC058470 BORSOTTI v. QUALITY LOAN SERVICE CORPORATION et. al., whereas Melvin Douglas Sandvig Recused himself from any impropriety; And.

Your Affiant states and Melvin Douglas Sandvig admitted to the truthfulness of the fact that the prior recusal of Melvin Douglas

[121] inter alia "among other things" https://www.merriam-webster.com/dictionary/inter%20alia
[122] *sub judice,* : "before a judge or court : not yet judicially decided" https://www.merriam-webster.com/dictionary/sub%20judice

Sandvig establishes proof of the bias and prejudice of Melvin Douglas Sandvig against the undersigned;

Your Affiant states and Melvin Douglas Sandvig admitted to the truthfulness of the fact that he has a bias and a prejudice against the undersigned;

Your Affiant states and Melvin Douglas Sandvig admitted to the truthfulness of the fact that he HAS A BIAS AND A PREJUDICE IN FAVOR OF THE DEFENDANTS, due to ACTIONS TAKEN AGAINST Claimant by Sandvig's unscrupulous actions to deny Claimant all of the previous stated rights, including but not limited to all of the above and are as fully stated herein; And

Your Affiant states and Melvin Douglas Sandvig admitted to the truthfulness of the fact Sandvig Has A Bias And Prejudice In Favor Of case outcomes that include favorable verdicts for the BANKS, SERVICERS, TRUSTEES, BROKERS, including but not limited to, AUCTION.COM; FEDERAL HOME LOAN MORTGAGE CORPORATION and other Defendants;

End Quote.

(**For the Reader**, i, move forward to next pubic serpent whom should have cut her short and curlie-cues B-4 they became ingrown against i, a man's future of ongoing trespass) i, as i, always do i, best to stand by and with honor. Whether you readers think i, have anger issues, or am writing to belittle anyone. i, am not! i, did not start out this way as i, will end on a greater notation as god as i, witness. It will take time as all one's healing for each wo/man is based on their own time and issues. The wo/mankind whom have come to know i, and work with i, know i, am who i, say i, am.

FYI: i, do what i, say i, will do, and fulfill most if not all of i, integrity by assisting i, self in healing, assisting other wo/mankind though their personal growth, endeavors, triumphs, and tribulations to overcome for self, with the notion to build a strgon everlasting honorable foundation towards Jesus Christs, life and death, god's purpose, and for creating value for and within society. Whether it is your idea, or what you think is the right path, it works the only way i, know for healing.

SATAN 18th MINION OF THE SUSAN L. LOPEZ CRIMINAL GANG OF 2007/2014 – 2025

[Pubic Serpent] Case # PS016624
Susan L Lopez-Giss B.A.R.# **61675**

Susan L. Lopez-Giss
[Pibic Serpent]
Satan's 18th Minion
(Suzie-que)

Play Pass The [Litigant] Man Buck Game
i, am not going to expose too much on this woman who acts as a pubic serpent, Susan Lopez-Giss hereinafter Suzie-que like most of the other pubic serpent is a pawn in a process of denying i, the right to a Temporary Restraining Order against ass-wipe niner.

This was the court action that melvin douglas sandvig recused himself and passed i, onto a pubic serpent named suzie-que by impasse. Regardless of history by richard-cranium for conflict of interest; to even touch any action of i, shows bias of richard-cranium to act on i, new court action.

Therefore, in the interest of deprivation for just-us (D.O.J.), and to protect ass-wipe niner, this action was transferred first to richard-cranium, then clue-less, thereafter to miss suzie-que and then back to Clue-less, whereby, clue-less was instructed to dismiss the action regardless of all of the facts and evidence i, brought forward. Clueless did as he was instructed to do by Satan.

However, Susie-que could not even touch this action attached either to i, as a man, even with clue-less's or richard-cranium's p.e.n.i.s. [~~dick~~] if she wanted to. (See excerpt)

> **12/03/2014** at 09:00 am in Department F46, Susan Lopez-Giss, Presiding
>
> Petition for Injunct Prohbit Harassment - Continued by **[Plaintiff]** the court

It was not a very long meeting when i, was passed over to suzie-que's courtroom. However, i, do not know what game was being perpetrated against i, as, i, do know that suzie-que was a pubic serpent that had taken over bitch-mlo's old court room.

She just transferred i, action back to clue-less as suzie-que was not willing to, nor could it have any jurisdiction over i, as a man. However, i, do bring i, court action for a trespass seeking a TRO against all of the multiple threats by ass-wipe niner. Maybe the intent was to stress i, out to place i, in old courtroom whereby i, won, however, there is no poetic justice.

Suzie-que could have and should have done the proper and honorable thing which was to move the TRO forward and then allow a full judicial and lawful process forward against ass-wipe. Susie-que did not do that honorable act. Instead suzie-que just followed like all of the other pubic serpents. Take orders from your superiors, whom are directed by the B.A.R. who work for a hierarchy of corp(s)orations whom take orders from top bankers. By the way, kudos to you suzie-que for following orders like Nuremburg.

Pubic Serpent Follow Orders From Superiors
Remember the Nuremburg trials; we learned no lawful moral or ethical wo/mankind can claim they were just doing their job. It is wo/mankind that is the perpetrators against all other wo/mankind when thee whom is the one who cause harm to another knowingly, willfully, and with/without intent. To do so in the name of a job, is on the evil-wrongdoer, not a fiction agency as a satanic culprit.

It is not state or federal governments, nor is it a police department, politicians, or any other titled pubic serpent, such as FBI, CIA, IRS, (L.A.P.D.) POLICE OFFICER, or any other alphabet soup group acronymic agent working for their agency, that can claim "*I, was just doing my job…*", or "*I am doing as I am told…*," for what a paycheck? (God will be the final judge). However, in the mean time, i, am here to assist god in an effort to ease God's duty a little bit. As with this concept, pubic agents think they do the same when invoking their l.e.g.a.l. system.

This is not the 8th, 12th, 17th or 18th century. This is the 21st century, whereas by now, if a wo/mankind does not know the difference between right or wrong, lawful, as what is harmful to another wo/mankind, or legal verses law, then those who do so, do commit a trespass upon and against another wo/mankind by self-ignorance.

To justify is to be able to think B-4 acting and it is okay to act as a puppet on a string; just remember your string is being strung by a puppet master which is completely on the one who strings themselves to justification of the job or alleged superior orders.

Even a puppet needs a master to pull its strings. When a puppet or its master cares less for their own redemption, is not of i, concern, as it is i, concern with the trespass against i, that which i, have received from those f.u.k.c.-ing arrogant, amorally illiterate, ethically uncaring, and monopolistic machinery k.u.n.t. ass w.h.o.r.e.'s [123] who just care about themselves, a paycheck and duty to satan.

For their pay day, ego or fame, each puppet or its master receives a prize for their bad deed against their fellow wo/mankind's wellness on a whole. This idea to not care, and do mal intent justifying it for the paycheck, as the prize, is a trespass. However, it is said and i, shall repeat, that it is not for i, to ~~judge~~ critic others for it is supposed 2-B up to god in the end to bring those to justice on their final judgment day. i, do believe, and at the same time, morally and

[123] **W.H.O.R.E.:** Without Honor Openly Refusing Evidence…

ethically, god wills critic all satanic minions, at that moment, of their end for eternal retribution of souls.

This would be including, god will critic i, for telling what is true, at the expense of time i, place into those who cause i, harm, for i, not moving on with i, life, regardless of facts that i am supposed to be a good moral and ethical religious practitioner of the commandments.

Just because i, believe i, do what is right for others to learn and for i, own healing, as stated B-4, some have said it is for i, selfishness. This too is under scrutiny by god's critic of what i, do regardless of whether i, feel it is with good intent and not for others to judge i, only i, do to i.

It does not matter whether a pubic serpent believes in god or not, nor if they even care what is right or wrong. What matters is that when any pubic serpent-agent, or a wo/mankind acts for an agency, when each commits trespass, there is harm. A wrong is committed and the agent cannot justify but do in the name of agency.

Lifelong Believers Read From The Heart

For those who do believe that god is the original source of all things, i, offer this excerpt from a friend. i, do not know where it comes from, but i, do like it and it works to get the point across and is as follows:

> *"Each man receives his eternal retribution in his immortal soul at the very moment of his death, in a particular judgment that refers his life to Christ: either entrance into the blessedness of Heaven — through purification or immediately, — or immediate and everlasting damnation"* [124]

i, as a man will not allow those who cause an intentional and resolute disruption of i, life, to freedom and i, pursuit of i, happiness

---

[124]https://www.catholiceducation.org/en/culture/catholic-contributions/where-does-the-soul-go-after-we- die.html#:~: text=If%20we%20have%20died%20with%20venial%20sins%20or,our%20soul%20will%20then%20be%20welcomed%20N-2 %20Heaven.

to get away with what trespass each have perpetrated against i. As i, do believe that i, being a caretaker of this earth, it is i, duty as a mankind to do, i, part to assist god with god's duties; god set high standards for he-self as well as i;

Therefore, i, write this *living missive* from i, heartfelt care, compassion, and comprehension that once, i, do expose all of those for what they do, i, have fulfilled i, part to create value for this world. It is easy to do the right thing, as herein on mother earth.

Whereby, i, shall then allow father time to give i, final redemption opportunity whereby each perpetrator will either ascend to heaven or descend back down to their forever burning, wherever that place for perpetrators.

Therefore, suzie-que, did not do much wrong other than refuse to do what she should have done in her own best understanding when the facts and evidence were brought forward at i, open court. Suzie-que read the papers i, do file. Suzue-que had actual excerpts of the post emails from ass-wipe niner and all other facts.

Suzie-que was there not to be bias, to not do as richard-cranium and other serpent's who act as a court officer instruct. Suzie-que's only duty is to witness those facts and evidence and to move the action forward N-2 a temporary restraining order to a future hearing for the permanent injunction. That was it. It is a no brainer.

The no brainer is that this serpent suzie-que has no moral aptitude to do the correct and honorable action and sign the order for TRO against ass-wipe niner's gang by their extortionist and terrorist threats. (We now move over to the Federal District Court Action) Stay tuned as i, move from one Satan's <u>trone</u> to another trone.

A place where satan takes and internal seat by unstable wo/mankind or devilish function that has crossed over from l.a.w. into the l.e.g.a.l. unstable fiction.

SATAN'S 7TH TRONE UNITED STATES DISTRICT COURT CRIMINAL GANG OF 2015/2016 – 2025

(Federal Docket CV 15-04112 JAK)

300 North Los Angeles Street Los Angeles California 90013

The following on (page 235) posts are taken from the emails from Yahoo.com and will be in quotes to keep them unaltered as precise word for word and i, replies which were filed onto a federal court action (Federal Docket CV 15-04112 JAK (AFM), Certified Mail 7014 1820 0000 9210 4186), Federal Court Certified Mail 7014 1820 0000 9210 3080), C/CA Non Response to All Affidavits… This Document" Los Angeles County…" thereafter the denial was final… read on:

The United States District Court has a long history with i, federal court actions. However, the history, i, have is not healthy as all of the previous court actions spoken about herein. i, now know the system is not broken, within itself. It is the pubic serpent that need to go and take a long vacation away from courts, like forever into purgatory for repentance, whereby each wo/mankind that act as pubic serpent may be held accountable. So far on earth, they reign their terror abroad.

i, am not and never have been an ens legis fictitious corporate entity, a person, citizen, resident, or berth/birth certificated entity, individual nor have i, nor will i, be an agent, representative, pubic serpent, govern mental employee. The court actors are hypothecating, subjugating and abrogating the wealth of wo/mankind. i, continue to expose them for their trespass regardless of their titles of pubic serpent.

Courts Trust Their Parent Corp(s)orations

It is a trust that i, do not have since awaken to fact that all capital named trust entities are created 10 to 15 days after every berth/birth of all offspring. Agents for corps create a belief they own all citizens by a indoctrinated Birth Certificate.

i, am, therefore i, am, when i, do walk onto any land where govern mental incorp(s)orated buildings are erect. The man that can and i, do set all agents up for a default. i, do know that it is not i, fault for unknowing to acquiesce to their system. Their system is not taught at any of the public schools. Although, the fact that i, have not advanced past the fifth/sixth grade, i, do not have a public education or indoctrinated mind is not programmed as an average U.S. citizen;

Why did govern mentals not give full disclosure through public schools for the future for all wo/mankind, to know what is true of their enslavement, by judiciary, executive and legislative corporate system; a fraud comes full circle from god.

Who have such innocent minds than the youth of this world? From kindergarten through grade twelve into college, very few youth and adults actually know how govern mental agencies operate? As a matter of *l.a.w.*, i, have not ever received professional training to know how to operate in l.e.g.a.l. B-4 i, enter a courtroom for any action that i, do file or was created to obfuscate i, labour for the past 60 plus years. Sure i, have gone onto the internet watched many gurus. i, have learned how to drag self through a system that until recently, i, realize has been unlawful.

Regardless of the fact that i, do not reach past the 5th to 6th grade of mainstream public unified schools, is not the reason for ignorance of the law. The fact that a high percentage of wo/mankind recognizes nothing about l.e.g.a.l. or l.a.w. is a test to deliberate fraud that is perpetrated against the public by govern mentals.

Although, many wo/mankind who do act like [~~judges~~] and [magistrates] have always denied i, any lawful court process as a man, as i, do always continue to search for a lawful court. i, can tell you i, do not find the lawful court until May 24th 2023. (i, shall share with the reader so keep on keeping on reading).

A trust is a trust not only as an entrusted indenture between one or more wo/mankind or corp(s)oration, to another, the pubic serpent cannot see, hear or act lawful towards i, as i, am not one of their trust owned property.

When pubic serpent for corp(s)orations, refuse to answer i, questions as an alleged owned surety, in their understanding, it suppresses law. i, cannot be a *man* at their venues. At the same time, a surety, as an offspring, is deception when agents for States believe it is parent of all citizens that have no B.A.R. card or by title of a fiction.

i, was frustrated, fed up with disregard of court actors to uphold i, rights to present all of i, facts and evidence. As man that do witness i, demand a *trial by jury* of i, peers and not as peers of a foreign species. What is a foreign species between a citizen, resident, person and wo/mankind? It is contrasted as a title is not a wo/mankind. It presumes it is a pay-rent philosophy of ownership by a title.

Why i, filed an action at the U. S. District Court against 29 evil-wrongdoers is for the following reasons. Govern mentals only trust an entrusted rogue trustee.

The agent as pubic serpent is a trustee. When a wo/mankind is present at the corrupt star chambers, thus, a wo/mankind at court, enforce their right to its own *free will*, the enslavement is stripped from the agents as trustees and transferred back to the sovereign as wo/mankind on the spot. Transfer is from title back to wo/mankind.

Action Against 29 Corp(S)orations Or Pubic Serpent

That means 29 wo/mankind who have taken on titles for state and federal govern mental have maliciously with intent cause to bankrupt, i, to take away i, freedom, to defame i, character, to steal i, land, take away all of i, material worth, do rape i, kidnap i, as in i, wealth and to desecrate an honorable man. They try to integrate a man through a system into Satan's den where forever damnation reigns and is not what God created. It is wo/mankind on earth that allows themselves be taken advantage of. It is the ones who have signed, sealed and delivered their names forever into and onto the stones of hell of incessant suffering that i, worry about.

Honorable repentance are acts by wo/mankind who learn true law verses l.e.g.a.l. schema, no longer allows agents to take advantage of their old ignorant ways, which is similar to god accepting repentance into the lord's kingdom while still on earth. There is a waiting list for repentance. It is a redemption process not for 29; It is twenty-nine agents, and persons who are about to learn what true law is believed to look like. It is not for the faint hearted and i, am ready, willing, and always able to stand on law. i, also stand on what is true backed by facts and evidence which has been long overdue for i, as a man adam- daniel of borsotti family. (Stay tuned for a future of facts as the next 25 actual court actions i, was forced to file for i, rights).

It was June 2015, i, was forced to file action at l.a.w. with the United States District Court United States District Court, Master File: Case # CV-15-04112 with more than hope, that this federal court will honor i, right because the lower nisi prius [125] courts at the State level, operate as f.u.k.c.-ing[126] (kangaroo courts), completely refused to follow any natural law of wo/mankind. It is by those that do not object to the lesser of l.a.w. known by L.e.g.a.l.,[127] that incorp(s)orate the statutes, codes, regulations or acts of the similar structure that refuse all l.a.w.

i, do know that a pubic serpent either do not know what a claim is or looks like as they usually only see complaints that are filed by either plaintiffs or defendants. A man who do file a claim verse all evil-

---

[125] **NISI PRIUS**: The most clear and true definition of a nisi prius court is only the one that is found at: https://www.1215.org/lawnotes/lawnotes/nisiprius.htm

[126]**FUKC**; F.U.K.C.: Forever Under Kangaroo Court (when adding ing, ed, es, or just s, it acerbates the word "fukc"

[127]**LEGAL**; L.E.G.A.L., Lawbreaker, Exercising Government Artificial Law or any added pronunciations such as ing, es, ed, etcetera

wrongdoer that cause a wo/mankind harm by another wo/mankind is always lawful not legal. Also, the pubic serpent were baffled when they read i, claim because it is actually a claim for which relief can be granted and not a bullshit complaint asking mommy or daddy to fix i, problems.

It Is Not Mighty Mouse To Save The Day

i, do state as true the following paragraphs were written by, i, own hand with personal firsthand knowledge and i, do change the font herein to show readers what is written is actually taken verbatim from a claim filed at the United States District Court Case # CV-15-04112 down town Los Angeles as i, know it to be true and is 99% to 100% verbatim after ass-wipe niner begun his threats;

> On July 29th 2015, i, Daniel Borsotti placed i, seal on a document which explains everything that transpired by the orchestration by Scott Allan Niner and the rest of his criminal gang.
>
> A copy can and will be available for any future trial for which it is necessary to bring forth all facts and evidence to substantiate all claims made herein by i: a man; Daniel-adam-of the borsotti family.
> For the purpose of saving grace and space, i, shall reference the title of such written, *living missive* and verified papers as:
>
> "…NOTICE TO ALL STATES COURTS AND THE UNITED STATES, A Perfected Claim of Obligations by Daniel Borsotti, THIS DOCUMENT IN ITS ENTIRETY IS A Claim Under which Relief Can Be Granted…." CERTIFIED BY NUMBER RE 497 881 929 US, Security (15 USC) USSEC Tracer Flag Not a point of Law
>
> Scott Allan Niner made threats directly to the man Daniel A. of the family Borsotti as follows **in quote**:

1. Allegation 1:
It is the understanding of the Affiant Daniel Borsotti : Scott Allen Niner sent the Emails Enclosed herein to Daniel Borsotti as a direct and targeted threat to violate the natural and in a lien able right of this sovereign man to be free of Mixed War, trespass, conspiracy, coercion, extortion, robbery by agents of corporations and governments (sic) and their owner(s) . **Without timely response this is affirmed; And,**

From: scott1@danglingcarrotcreative.com
Subject: www.santa-clarita.com/Modules/ShowDocument.aspx?documentid=5076
Date: Sat, 1 Nov 2014 16:58:01 -0700
To: yourmotivator1@live.com

I will make things happen within the city and with your neighbors.........I'm done fucking around with you. You better hope your within compliance. Otherwise, as I said in the email, this is only one SMALL step that i'm going to take to make sure you leave me alone. You will be too busy trying to keep your life as it is right now, your life as it is right now.......I refuse to continue this as I'm getting married in two weeks......That's your deadline to personally make a commitment to me to move on with your life, legal or not but if you continue to involve yourself in my life..........I won't stop until every aspect of your complete ignorance is exposed to everyone, everywhere including the government and your family. I will only tell the truth, as I have always done........your just a thief and only take advantage of people as you always have cause you don't have the intelligence to do anything on your own.....only by being a cheat and a liar.

TWO WEEKS..........ONE RESPONSE and it goes away, if not........GAME ON........I'm not worried cause my entire life is by the book, ethical, honest, and true. I pay the IRS exactly what is due and don't twist the truth, they can explore, look all they want and so can you.......the laughs on you cause I live my life honestly and by the book, can you say the same?..........

why don't we see...................

Instead of spending 60k on an attorney fighting your completely fraudulent law suits, I'm willing to spend 60k to expose you to the truth to the government etc. etc. and others to put you where you belong.

Last Chance to stop this Danny..........Hope you choose the right way.......or my 60k is going to make sure you end up where you belong.....with criminals......

http://www.santa-clarita.com/Modules/ShowDocument.aspx?documentid=5076

From: scott@danglingcarrotcreative.com
Subject: Contacting Daniel for motivating assistant!
Date: Sat, 1 Nov 2014 16:31:00 -0700
To: yourmotivator1@live.com

I just received papers Danny. It's so sad that your life has turned into such a distorted view of the facts. And your god is mistaken. As you will see. With your building without permits, taking advantage of elders, trying to get something that you did not gain yourself, getting free money from fake lawsuits, basically, living your life trying to get something for nothing by lying, deceiving, taking advantage......instead of truly advancing your intelligence and learning how to truly help, advance others in your life. You are selfish, only think about yourself. I am now done sitting back, letting you do what you do which is full of lies and complete distortion of the truth.

Instead, I'm about to truly show you what it takes to lead a honest, truthful life, which I do, both with the government and personally with everyone I come in contact with. It's so sad you have to do this and that I now have to stop this exposing to everyone exactly what you are all about. Lies, Deceit, getting something for nothing. I'm about to embark on a path that only exposes the truth, does not lie, does not make things up, only exposes you for who you are to the government, your friends, your family and god willing, and yes God, not Buda, yourself. YOUR HEADING NOWHERE DANNY. And believe it or not, even after everything you have tried to do to me.....it makes me sad that GOD is not in your life and you have to learn from things the hard way as if he was.......you would better understand intelligence and how to treat people with human dignity and honest intentions.

Unfortunately for you Danny, I can't spend anymore time sitting back, letting you make false claims, lie to the courts, to your family and friends, I have to expose all of it. It has always been at my disposal, but I wanted to spare you the embarrassment and being exposed for the true person you are. I cannot sit idly by at this point and let it to continue as you have disrupted several years of my life and I'm not going to take it any longer. You should have though that one day, I might just have enough and you would have stopped trying to lie, get something for nothing etc. etc. and live your life the right way, true, honest etc. etc.

We are there now Danny. I'm sorry, I won't let you continue to be a part of my life, I gave you space to get real with yourself, instead, you continue. I won't be a part of it any longer.

If you have a change of heart about your actions, please let me know, but you have two weeks to respond or I will continue so that your time is consumed with your illegal activities, Tax evasion problems, illegal building and residence situation and so on so forth. I will now expose you for who you are and what people think of you and won't stop until you are so tied up with your true illegal activities that I will be a thing of the past.

Two weeks from today, then the only thing exposed about you is the truth.......NOT lies like you tried to tell about ME. The TRUTH PREVAILS ALWAYS! So you better really think about everything you have going on in your life.....I will spare no expense to expose it to the world........ And yes, I know that different from you cause I will only expose the truth, not try to MAKE SHIT UP to get something for nothing.

GET A LIFE, EDUCATION and a CONSCIOUS.
Scott Niner
Dangling Carrot Creative
27520 Avenue Mentry
Valencia, Ca. 91355
661-295-6610 xt. 111

Proof of Allegation 1 :

There is no evidence contrary to this allegation;

Affiant believes no evidence exists ; Affiant denies evidence exists; Affiant will accept only wet ink autograph counter affidavit by real men with first hand knowledge point for point and the decision of a lawfully convened sheriffs jury of my peers to investigate and understand all players and affidavits and vacate this affidavit as proof this allegation is false. This is the syntax and the grammar for the avoidance of the contempt and perjury of "this document" and this court. And;

All respondent Corporations and Offices In Default for the dishonor of real men for non response

Your Dishonor Creates the funds under HJR 192 Pubic law and Pubic Policy for the Default and Dishonor of Agents and Officers as real men by Non Response to Affidavits constituting Contractual Obligations. And;

Federal Docket CV 15-04112 JAK (AFM)

)

Certified Mail 7014 1820 0000 9210 4186

) Federal Court

Certified Mail 7014 1820 0000 9210 3080

) C/CA

Non Response to All Affidavits "This Document") ss Los Angeles County

Obligation 1 :

This completes the one for one correspondence required under this agreement.

{(CON = 16) x (USC = 19) x (DEBTORS [Scott Niner] = 1) x ($10,000.00)}=$3,040,000.00

Itemized Ledgering for the man shall be accomplished by multiplying: Number of Constitutional Violations (CON) times $10,000.00 [18USC241/242] by the number of

Title 18/15 Violations, then multiplying by the number of defaulted respondents (DEBTORS) resulting in Obligations of this Allegation.. See affidavit in the Nature of Notice of Understanding and Lawful Intent Page 26 Constitutional ledgering Page **59** Proof of Notice and Service page **63**

2. Allegation 2

It is the understanding of the Affiant Daniel Borsotti, Scott Alan Niner states directly in these Emails included herein The Intent to spend $60,000.00 in currency of the United States in the first Email; Then ups the anti to Sparing No expense in pursuit of the illegal activity of manipulating persons and government to put Daniel in jail and bankrupt Daniel Borsotti as a direct and targeted threat to violate the natural and in a lien able right of this sovereign man to be free of Mixed War, trespass, conspiracy, coercion, extortion, robbery by agents of corporations and governments . **Without timely response this is affirmed; And,**

Proof of Allegation 2

There is no evidence contrary to this allegation; Affiant believes no evidence exists; Affiant denies evidence exists; Affiant will accept only wet ink autograph counter affidavit by real men with first hand knowledge point for point and the decision of a lawfully convened sheriffs jury of my peers to investigate and understand all players and affidavits and vacate this affidavit as proof this allegation is false. This is the syntax and the grammar for the avoidance of the contempt and perjury of "this document" and this court. And;

All respondent Corporations and Offices In Default for the dishonor of real men for non response

Your Dishonor Creates the funds under HJR 192 Pubic law and Pubic Policy for the Default and Dishonor of Agents and Officers as real men by Non Response to Affidavits constituting Contractual Obligations.

Federal Docket CV 15-04112 JAK (AFM)
)
Certified Mail 7014 1820 0000 9210 4186
) Federal Court
Certified Mail 7014 1820 0000 9210 3080
) C/CA
Non Response to All Affidavits "This Document") ss Los Angeles County

Obligation 2 :

This completes the one for one correspondence required under this agreement.

{(CON = 16) x (USC = 19) x (DEBTORS [Scott Niner] = 1) x ($10,000.00)}=$3,040,000.00 Itemized Ledgering for the man shall be accomplished by multiplying: Number of Constitutional Violations (CON) times $10,000.00 [18USC241/242] by the number of Title 18/15 Violations, then multiplying by the number of defaulted respondents (DEBTORS) resulting in Obligations of this Allegation.. See affidavit in the Nature of Notice of Understanding and Lawful Intent Page 26 Constitutional ledgering Page **59** Proof of Notice and Service page **63**

3. Allegation 3

It is the understanding of the Affiant Daniel Borsotti Scott Alan Niner states directly Nov 2014 in these Emails included herein he is doing this to "show Daniel Borsotti how the Justice system really works" and in fact ups the anti stating he will spare no expense to bring Daniel under control of the god of Scott Alan Niner. **Without timely response this is affirmed; And,**

Proof of Allegation 3 :
There is no evidence contrary to this allegation; Affiant believes no evidence exists; Affiant denies evidence exists; Affiant will accept only wet ink autograph counter affidavit by real men with first hand knowledge point for point and the decision of a lawfully convened sheriffs jury of my peers to investigate and understand all players and affidavits and vacate this affidavit as proof this allegation is false. This is the syntax and the grammar for the avoidance of the contempt and perjury of "this document" and this court. And;

All respondent Corporations and Offices In Default for the dishonor of real men for non response
Your Dishonor Creates the funds under HJR 192 Pubic law and Pubic Policy for the Default and Dishonor of Agents and Officers as real men by Non Response to Affidavits constituting Contractual Obligations .

Federal Docket CV 15-04112 JAK (AFM)
)

Certified Mail 7014 1820 0000 9210 4186
) Federal Court
Certified Mail 7014 1820 0000 9210 3080
)ss C/CA
Non Response to All Affidavits "This Document") Los Angeles County

Obligation 3 :
This completes the one for one correspondence required under this agreement.

{(CON = 16) x (USC = 19) x (DEBTORS [Scott Niner] = 1) x ($10,000.00)}=$3,040,000.00 Itemized Ledgering for the man shall be accomplished by multiplying: Number of Constitutional Violations (CON) times $10,000.00 [18USC241/242] by the number of Title 18/15 Violations, then multiplying by the number of defaulted respondents (DEBTORS) resulting in Obligations of this Allegation.. See affidavit in the Nature of Notice of Understanding and Lawful Intent Page 26 Constitutional ledgering Page **59** Proof of Notice and Service page **63**

4. Allegation 4
It is the understanding of the Affiant Daniel Borsotti: Scott Niner states directly NOV 2014 in the Emails sent to Daniel Borsotti: THE METHODS by which Scott Allen Niner intends to use in the machinery of the Local, City, State, Federal, International government(s) and Collection Agencies (IRS) to attack Daniel Borsotti through DANIEL A BORSOTTI trust within the United States and the State of California. **Without timely response this is affirmed; And,**

This is a violation of the natural right for a sovereign man to be free of Mixed War, Trespass, conversion, Robbery, Racketeering extortion, by agents of corporations and government(sic) under color of law. This is a dishonor in the bankruptcy of the united States and your dishonor creates the funds under HJR 192 pubic Law and pubic Policy..

Proof of Allegation 4 :

There is no evidence contrary to this allegation; Affiant believes no evidence exists ; Affiant denies evidence exists; Affiant will accept only wet ink autograph counter affidavit by real men with first hand knowledge point for point and the decision of a lawfully convened sheriffs jury of my peers to investigate and understand all players and affidavits and vacate this affidavit as proof this allegation is false. This is the syntax and the grammar for the avoidance of the contempt and perjury of "this document" and this court. And;

All respondent Corporations and Offices In Default for the dishonor of real men for non response

Your Dishonor Creates the funds under HJR 192 Pubic law and Pubic Policy for the Default and Dishonor of Agents and Officers as real men by Non Response to Affidavits constituting Contractual Obligations .

Federal Docket CV 15-04112 JAK (JCD)

AFM AFM)

Certified Mail 7014 1820 0000 9210 4186

) Federal Court

Certified Mail 7014 1820 0000 9210 3080

)ss C/CA

Non Response to All Affidavits "This Document") Los Angeles County

Obligation 4:

This completes the one for one correspondence required under this agreement.

{(CON = 16) x (USC = 19) x (DEBTORS [Scott Niner] = 1) x ($10,000.00)}=$3,040,000.00

Itemized Ledgering for the man shall be accomplished by multiplying: Number of

Constitutional Violations (CON) times $10,000.00 [18USC241/242] by the number of Title 18/15 Violations, then multiplying by the number of defaulted respondents (DEBTORS) resulting in Obligations of this Allegation.. See affidavit in the Nature of Notice of Understanding and Lawful Intent Page 26 Constitutional ledgering Page 59 Proof of Notice and Service page 63

5. Allegation 5

It is the understanding of the Affiant Daniel Borsotti: Scott Niner states directly NOV 2014 in the Emails sent to Daniel Borsotti : The Entities, Persons, Corporations, and governments by which Scott Niner intends to employ accessible assets in the machinery of the Local, City , State, Federal, International government(s) and Collection Agencies (IRS) to attack Daniel Borsotti incarcerate him, force him to bankruptcy at the will of Scott Alan Niner and others. **Without timely response this is affirmed; And,**

Proof of Allegation 5 :

There is no evidence contrary to this allegation; Affiant believes no evidence exists ; Affiant denies evidence exists; Affiant will accept only wet ink autograph counter affidavit by real men with first hand knowledge point for point and the decision of a lawfully convened sheriffs jury of my peers to investigate and understand all players and affidavits and vacate this affidavit as proof this allegation is false. This is the syntax and the grammar for the avoidance of the contempt and perjury of "this document" and this court. And;

All respondent Corporations and Offices In Default for the dishonor of real men for non response

Your Dishonor Creates the funds under HJR 192 Pubic law and Pubic Policy for the Default and Dishonor of Agents and Officers as real men by Non Response to Affidavits constituting Contractual Obligations .

Federal Docket CV 15-04112 JAK (JCD)
AFM)
Certified Mail 7014 1820 0000 9210 4186
) Federal Court
Certified Mail 7014 1820 0000 9210 3080
)ss C/CA
Non Response to All Affidavits "This Document") Los Angeles County

Obligation 5:

This completes the one for one correspondence required under this agreement.

{(CON = 16) x (USC = 19) x (DEBTORS [Scott Niner] = 1) x ($10,000.00)}=$3,040,000.00 Itemized Ledgering for the man shall be accomplished by multiplying: Number of Constitutional Violations (CON) times $10,000.00 [18USC241/242] by the number of Title 18/15 Violations, then multiplying by the number of defaulted respondents (DEBTORS) resulting in Obligations of this Allegation.. See affidavit in the Nature of Notice of Understanding and Lawful Intent Page 26 Constitutional ledgering Page 59 Proof of Notice and Service page 63

6. Allegation 6

The Method [Illegal use of money and influence rather than lawful use of the courts] by which Scott Niner intends to employ accessible assets in the machinery of the Local, City , State, Federal, International government(s) and Collection Agencies (IRS) to attack Daniel Borsotti through DANIEL A BORSOTTI trust within the United States and the State of California force him to bankruptcy. **Without timely response this is affirmed; And,**

Proof of Allegation 6 :
There is no evidence contrary to this allegation; Affiant believes no evidence exists ; Affiant denies evidence exists; Affiant will accept only wet ink autograph counter affidavit by real men with first hand knowledge point for point and the decision of a lawfully convened sheriffs jury of my peers to investigate and understand all players and affidavits and vacate this affidavit as proof this allegation is false. This is the syntax and the grammar for the avoidance of the contempt and perjury of "this document" and this court. And;

All respondent Corporations and Offices In Default for the dishonor of real men for non response
Your Dishonor Creates the funds under HJR 192 Pubic law and Pubic Policy for the Default and Dishonor of Agents and Officers as real men by Non Response to Affidavits constituting Contractual Obligations.
Federal Docket CV 15-04112 JAK (JCD)
AFM)

Certified Mail 7014 1820 0000 9210 4186
) Federal Court
Certified Mail 7014 1820 0000 9210 3080
)ss C/CA
Non Response to All Affidavits "This Document") Los Angeles County

Obligation 6:
This completes the one for one correspondence required under this agreement.

{(CON = 16) x (USC = 19) x (DEBTORS [Scott Niner] = 1) x ($10,000.00)}=$3,040,000.00

Itemized Ledgering for the man shall be accomplished by multiplying: Number of Constitutional Violations (CON) times $10,000.00 [18USC241/242] by the number of Title 18/15 Violations, then multiplying by the number of defaulted respondents (DEBTORS) resulting in Obligations of this Allegation.. See affidavit in the Nature of Notice of Understanding and Lawful Intent Page 26 Constitutional ledgering Page 59 Proof of Notice and Service page 63

7. Allegation 7
It is the understanding of the Affiant Daniel Borsotti Scott Alan Niner Specifically singles out the Buddhist philosophy of Daniel Borsotti for ridicule and threat by "a Scott Allen Niner. approved GOD". This is a violation of the First amendment directly and many others, a mixed war conspiracy to limit the rights and privileges afforded to Daniel Borsotti..**Without timely response this is affirmed; And,**

Proof of Allegation 7 :
There is no evidence contrary to this allegation; Affiant believes no evidence exists; Affiant denies evidence exists; Affiant will accept only wet ink autograph counter affidavit by real men with first hand knowledge point for point and the decision of a lawfully convened sheriffs jury of my peers to investigate and understand all players and affidavits and vacate this affidavit as proof this allegation is false. This is the syntax

and the grammar for the avoidance of the contempt and perjury of "this document" and this court. And;

All respondent Corporations and Offices In Default for the dishonor of real men for non response
Your Dishonor Creates the funds under HJR 192 Pubic law and Pubic Policy for the Default and Dishonor of Agents and Officers as real men by Non Response to Affidavits constituting Contractual Obligations .
Federal Docket CV 15-04112 JAK (JCD)
AFM)

Certified Mail 7014 1820 0000 9210 4186
) Federal Court
Certified Mail 7014 1820 0000 9210 3080
)ss C/CA
Non Response to All Affidavits "This Document") Los Angeles County

Obligation 7:
This completes the one for one correspondence required under this agreement.

{(CON = 16) x (USC = 19) x (DEBTORS [Scott Niner] = 1) x ($10,000.00)}=$3,040,000.00
Itemized Ledgering for the man shall be accomplished by multiplying: Number of Constitutional Violations (CON) times $10,000.00 [18USC241/242] by the number of Title 18/15 Violations, then multiplying by the number of defaulted respondents (DEBTORS) resulting in Obligations of this Allegation.. See affidavit in the Nature of Notice of Understanding and Lawful Intent Page 26 Constitutional ledgering Page 59 Proof of Notice and Service page 63

8. Allegation 8

It is the understanding of the affiant Daniel Borsotti Scott Allen Niner DEMANDS from Daniel a change of religious philosophy by a date certain or he will **Without timely response this is affirmed; And,**

Proof of Allegation 8 :

There is no evidence contrary to this allegation; Affiant believes no evidence exists ; Affiant denies evidence exists; Affiant will accept only wet ink autograph counter affidavit by real men with first hand knowledge point for point and the decision of a lawfully convened sheriffs jury of my peers to investigate and understand all players and affidavits and vacate this affidavit as proof this allegation is false. This is the syntax and the grammar for the avoidance of the contempt and perjury of "this document" and this court. And;

All respondent Corporations and Offices In Default for the dishonor of real men for non response
Your Dishonor Creates the funds under HJR 192 Pubic law and Pubic Policy for the Default and Dishonor of Agents and Officers as real men by Non Response to Affidavits constituting Contractual Obligations .
Federal Docket CV 15-04112 JAK (JCD)
AFM)

Certified Mail 7014 1820 0000 9210 4186
) Federal Court
Certified Mail 7014 1820 0000 9210 3080
)ss C/CA
Non Response to All Affidavits "This Document") Los Angeles County

Obligation 8:
This completes the one for one correspondence required under this agreement.

{(CON = 16) x (USC = 19) x (DEBTORS [Scott Niner] = 1) x ($10,000.00)}=$3,040,000.00 Itemized Ledgering for the man shall be accomplished by multiplying: Number of Constitutional Violations (CON) times $10,000.00 [18USC241/242] by the number of Title 18/15 Violations, then multiplying by the number of defaulted respondents (DEBTORS) resulting in Obligations of this Allegation.. See affidavit in the Nature of Notice of Understanding and Lawful Intent Page 26 Constitutional ledgering Page 59 Proof of Notice and Service page 63

9. Allegation 9
This is a specific and credible threat. Any reasonable man would take these emails directed at them at face value as the source of the thousands of hours of work Daniel Borsotti has endured at the hands of agents of Scott Allen Niner employed by the State, Cities and Counties of California. **Without timely response this is affirmed; And,**.

Proof of Allegation 9 :

There is no evidence contrary to this allegation; Affiant believes no evidence exists; Affiant denies evidence exists; Affiant will accept only wet ink autograph counter affidavit by real men with first hand knowledge point for point and the decision of a lawfully convened sheriffs jury of my peers to investigate and understand all players and affidavits and vacate this affidavit as proof this allegation is false. This is the syntax

and the grammar for the avoidance of the contempt and perjury of "this document" and this court. And;

All respondent Corporations and Offices In Default for the dishonor of real men for non response
Your Dishonor Creates the funds under HJR 192 Pubic law and Pubic Policy for the Default and Dishonor of Agents and Officers as real men by Non Response to Affidavits constituting Contractual Obligations .
Federal Docket CV 15-04112 JAK (JCD)
AFM)

Certified Mail 7014 1820 0000 9210 4186
) Federal Court
Certified Mail 7014 1820 0000 9210 3080
)ss C/CA
Non Response to All Affidavits "This Document") Los Angeles County

Obligation 9:
This completes the one for one correspondence required under this agreement.

{(CON = 16) x (USC = 19) x (DEBTORS [Scott Niner] = 1) x ($10,000.00)}=$3,040,000.00
Itemized Ledgering for the man shall be accomplished by multiplying: Number of Constitutional Violations (CON) times $10,000.00 [18USC241/242] by the number of Title 18/15 Violations, then multiplying by the number of defaulted respondents (DEBTORS) resulting in Obligations of this Allegation.. See affidavit in the Nature of Notice of Understanding and Lawful Intent Page 26 Constitutional ledgering Page 59 Proof of Notice and Service page 63

10. Allegation 10:

It is the understanding of the Affiant Daniel Borsotti : The Emails contained herein below taken at face value are requisite acknowledgment by Scott Niner and Conveyance of and to Daniel the Consideration by Scott Niner of the Ability, Access to and the Understanding that Scott Niner has agents thereof to exercise creation of records out of thin air and CAN IN FACT INFLUENCE the persons in the machinery of corporations, government(s), the courts and the BAR in a private targeted manner. This is malice aforethought. This is a tort **Without timely response this is affirmed; And,**

Proof of Allegation 10:

There is no evidence contrary to this allegation; Affiant believes no evidence exists ; Affiant denies evidence exists; Affiant will accept only wet ink autograph counter affidavit by real men with first hand knowledge point for point and the decision of a lawfully convened sheriffs jury of my peers to investigate and understand all players and affidavits and vacate this affidavit as proof this allegation is false. This is the syntax and the grammar for the avoidance of the contempt and perjury of "this document" and this court. And;

All respondent Corporations and Offices In Default for the dishonor of real men for non response

Your Dishonor Creates the funds under HJR 192 Pubic law and Pubic Policy for the Default and Dishonor of Agents and Officers as real men by Non Response to Affidavits constituting Contractual Obligations .

Federal Docket CV 15-04112 JAK (JCD)

AFM)
Certified Mail 7014 1820 0000 9210 4186
) Federal Court
Certified Mail 7014 1820 0000 9210 3080
)ss C/CA
Non Response to All Affidavits "This Document") Los Angeles County

Obligation 10:
This completes the one for one correspondence required under this agreement.

{(CON = 16) x (USC = 19) x (DEBTORS [Scott Niner] = 1) x ($10,000.00)}=$3,040,000.00 Itemized Ledgering for the man shall be accomplished by multiplying: Number of Constitutional Violations (CON) times $10,000.00 [18USC241/242] by the number of Title 18/15 Violations, then multiplying by the number of defaulted respondents (DEBTORS) resulting in Obligations of this Allegation.. See affidavit in the Nature of Notice of Understanding and Lawful Intent Page 26 Constitutional ledgering Page 59 Proof of Notice and Service page 63

11. Allegation 11
It is the understanding of the Affiant Daniel Borsotti : The Emails contained herein below taken at face value are requisite acknowledgment by Scott Niner of the intent use the financial, associative and other resources of Ronald Niner and James Niner to execute the influence of the persons and machinery of governments and the courts and others within and without his family and associations to assassinate the character of Daniel Borsotti and Bankrupt him without valid affidavits of

obligation. **Without timely response this is affirmed; And,**

Proof of Allegation 11 :
There is no evidence contrary to this allegation; Affiant believes no evidence exists ; Affiant denies evidence exists; Affiant will accept only wet ink autograph counter affidavit by real men with first hand knowledge point for point and the decision of a lawfully convened sheriffs jury of my peers to investigate and understand all players and affidavits and vacate this affidavit as proof this allegation is false. This is the syntax and the grammar for the avoidance of the contempt and perjury of "this document" and this court. And;

All respondent Corporations and Offices In Default for the dishonor of real men for non response
Your Dishonor Creates the funds under HJR 192 Pubic law and Pubic Policy for the Default and Dishonor of Agents and Officers as real men by Non Response to Affidavits constituting Contractual Obligations .
Federal Docket CV 15-04112 JAK (JCD)
AFM)

Certified Mail 7014 1820 0000 9210 4186
) Federal Court
Certified Mail 7014 1820 0000 9210 3080
)ss C/CA
Non Response to All Affidavits "This Document") Los Angeles County
Obligation 11:
This completes the one for one correspondence required under this agreement.

{(CON = 16) x (USC = 19) x (DEBTORS [Scott Niner] = 1) x ($10,000.00)}=$3,040,000.00 Itemized Ledgering for the man shall be accomplished by multiplying: Number of Constitutional Violations (CON) times $10,000.00 [18USC241/242] by the number of Title 18/15 Violations, then multiplying by the number of defaulted respondents (DEBTORS) resulting in Obligations of this Allegation.. See affidavit in the Nature of Notice of Understanding and Lawful Intent Page 26 Constitutional ledgering Page 59 Proof of Notice and Service page 63

12. Allegation 12

It is the understanding of the Affiant, Daniel Borsotti, Scott Alan Niner states directly Nov 2014 in these emails he is tired of "fighting" Daniel Borsotti's lawful Brady Requests for information and instead of Answering the interrogatories Served by Daniel, lawfully in the courts and Scott Allen Niner states the intent to use an unlimited amount of United states currency in the pursuit of illegal activity in the targeted exercise of the machinery of government and other means to attack Daniel Borsotti. This shows Malice and Intent. **Without timely response this is affirmed; And,**

Proof of Allegation 12 :

There is no evidence contrary to this allegation; Affiant believes no evidence exists ; Affiant denies evidence exists; Affiant will accept only wet ink autograph counter affidavit by real men with first hand knowledge point for point and the decision of a lawfully convened sheriffs jury of my peers to investigate and understand all players and affidavits and vacate this affidavit as proof this allegation is false. This is the syntax

and the grammar for the avoidance of the contempt and perjury of "this document" and this court. And;

All respondent Corporations and Offices In Default for the dishonor of real men for non response
Your Dishonor Creates the funds under HJR 192 Pubic law and Pubic Policy for the Default and Dishonor of Agents and Officers as real men by Non Response to Affidavits constituting Contractual Obligations .
Federal Docket CV 15-04112 JAK (JCD)
AFM)

Certified Mail 7014 1820 0000 9210 4186
) Federal Court
Certified Mail 7014 1820 0000 9210 3080
)ss C/CA
Non Response to All Affidavits "This Document") Los Angeles County

Obligation 12:
This completes the one for one correspondence required under this agreement.

{(CON = 16) x (USC = 19) x (DEBTORS [Scott Niner] = 1) x ($10,000.00)}=$3,040,000.00
Itemized Ledgering for the man shall be accomplished by multiplying: Number of Constitutional Violations (CON) times $10,000.00 [18USC241/242] by the number of Title 18/15 Violations, then multiplying by the number of defaulted respondents (DEBTORS) resulting in Obligations of this Allegation.. See affidavit in the Nature of Notice of Understanding and Lawful Intent Page 26 Constitutional ledgering Page 59 Proof of

13. Allegation 13
It is the understanding of the affiant Daniel Borsotti, Scott Allen Niner States directly he has made the conscious choice not to pay a lawyer $ 60,000.00 to answer the legal and lawful presentments by Daniel to Scott Allen Niner and follow this other path. **Without timely response this is affirmed; And,**

Proof of Allegation 13 :
There is no evidence contrary to this allegation; Affiant believes no evidence exists ; Affiant denies evidence exists; Affiant will accept only wet ink autograph counter affidavit by real men with first hand knowledge point for point and the decision of a lawfully convened sheriffs jury of my peers to investigate and understand all players and affidavits and vacate this affidavit as proof this allegation is false. This is the syntax and the grammar for the avoidance of the contempt and perjury of "this document" and this court. And;

All respondent Corporations and Offices In Default for the dishonor of real men for non response
Your Dishonor Creates the funds under HJR 192 Pubic law and Pubic Policy for the Default and Dishonor of Agents and Officers as real men by Non Response to Affidavits constituting Contractual Obligations .
Federal Docket CV 15-04112 JAK (JCD)
AFM)

Certified Mail 7014 1820 0000 9210 4186
) Federal Court
Certified Mail 7014 1820 0000 9210 3080

)ss C/CA
Non Response to All Affidavits "This Document") Los Angeles County

Obligation 13:
This completes the one for one correspondence required under this agreement.

{(CON = 16) x (USC = 19) x (DEBTORS [Scott Niner] = 1) x ($10,000.00)}=$3,040,000.00 Itemized Ledgering for the man shall be accomplished by multiplying: Number of Constitutional Violations (CON) times $10,000.00 [18USC241/242] by the number of Title 18/15 Violations, then multiplying by the number of defaulted respondents (DEBTORS) resulting in Obligations of this Allegation.. See affidavit in the Nature of Notice of Understanding and Lawful Intent Page 26 Constitutional ledgering Page 59 Proof of Notice and Service page 63

14. Allegation 14
It is the understanding of the Affiant Daniel Borsotti Scott Allen Niner States directly in the enclosed emails he will in in fact will use this Unlimited amount of money to prevent Daniel Borsotti from filing ANY further requests for information or Brady requests of him . **Without timely response this is affirmed; And,**

Proof of Allegation 14 :
There is no evidence contrary to this allegation; Affiant believes no evidence exists ; Affiant denies evidence exists; Affiant will accept only wet ink autograph counter affidavit by real men with first hand knowledge point for point and the decision of a lawfully convened sheriffs jury of my peers to investigate and understand all

players and affidavits and vacate this affidavit as proof this allegation is false. This is the syntax and the grammar for the avoidance of the contempt and perjury of "this document" and this court. And;

All respondent Corporations and Offices In Default for the dishonor of real men for non response
Your Dishonor Creates the funds under HJR 192 Pubic law and Pubic Policy for the Default and Dishonor of Agents and Officers as real men by Non Response to Affidavits constituting Contractual Obligations .
Federal Docket CV 15-04112 JAK (JCD)
AFM)

Certified Mail 7014 1820 0000 9210 4186
) Federal Court
Certified Mail 7014 1820 0000 9210 3080
)ss C/CA
Non Response to All Affidavits "This Document") Los Angeles County

Obligation 14:
This completes the one for one correspondence required under this agreement.

{(CON = 16) x (USC = 19) x (DEBTORS [Scott Niner] = 1) x ($10,000.00)}=$3,040,000.00
Itemized Ledgering for the man shall be accomplished by multiplying: Number of Constitutional Violations (CON) times $10,000.00 [18USC241/242] by the number of Title 18/15 Violations, then multiplying by the number of defaulted respondents (DEBTORS) resulting in Obligations of this Allegation.. See affidavit in the Nature of Notice of Understanding and Lawful Intent Page 26

Constitutional ledgering Page 59 Proof of Notice and Service page 63

15. Allegation 15

It is the understanding of the Affiant Daniel Borsotti Scott Allen Niner States directly in the emails he shall use this $60,000.00 and then unlimited funds and resources in the machinery of government for the express purpose to buy influence to attack Daniel Borsotti..**Without timely response this is affirmed; And,**

Proof of Allegation 15 :

There is no evidence contrary to this allegation; Affiant believes no evidence exists ; Affiant denies evidence exists; Affiant will accept only wet ink autograph counter affidavit by real men with first hand knowledge point for point and the decision of a lawfully convened sheriffs jury of my peers to investigate and understand all players and affidavits and vacate this affidavit as proof this allegation is false. This is the syntax and the grammar for the avoidance of the contempt and perjury of "this document" and this court. And;

All respondent Corporations and Offices In Default for the dishonor of real men for non response

Your Dishonor Creates the funds under HJR 192 Pubic law and Pubic Policy for the Default and Dishonor of Agents and Officers as real men by Non Response to Affidavits constituting Contractual Obligations .

Federal Docket CV 15-04112 JAK (JCD)
AFM)

Certified Mail 7014 1820 0000 9210 4186

) Federal Court
Certified Mail 7014 1820 0000 9210 3080
)ss C/CA
Non Response to All Affidavits "This Document") Los Angeles County

Allegation 1:
It is the understanding of the Affiant Daniel Borsotti : Scott Allen Niner sent the Emails Enclosed herein to Daniel Borsotti as a direct and targeted threat to violate the natural and in a lien able right of this sovereign man to be free of Mixed War, trespass, conspiracy, coercion, extortion, robbery by agents of corporations and governments (sic) and their owner(s) . **Without timely response this is affirmed; And,**

" From: scott1@danglingcarrotcreative.com
Subject: www.santa-

clarita.com/Modules/ShowDocument.aspx?documentid=5076
Date: Sat, 1 Nov 2014 16:58:01 -0700
To: yourmotivator1@live.com

I will make things happen within the city and with your neighbors.........I'm done fucking around with you. You better hope your within compliance. Otherwise, as I said in the email, this is only one SMALL step that i'm going to take to make sure you leave me alone. You will be too busy trying to keep your life as it is right now, your life as it is right now.......I refuse to continue this as I'm getting married in two weeks......That's your deadline to personally make a commitment to me to move on with your life, legal or not but if you continue to involve yourself in my life..........I won't stop until every aspect of your complete ignorance is exposed to everyone, everywhere including the government and your family. I will only tell the truth, as I have always done........your just a thief and only take advantage of people as you always have cause you don't have the intelligence to do anything on your own.....only by being a cheat and a liar.

TWO WEEKS..........ONE RESPONSE and it goes away, if not........GAME ON........I'm not worried cause my entire life is by the book, ethical, honest, and true. I pay the IRS exactly what is due and don't twist the truth, they can explore, look all they want and so can you.......the laughs on you cause I live my life honestly and by the book, can you say the same?..........

why don't we see...................

Instead of spending 60k on an attorney fighting your completely fraudulent law suits, I'm willing to spend 60k to expose you to the truth to the government etc. etc. and others to put you where you belong.

Last Chance to stop this Danny..........Hope you choose the right way.......**or my 60k** is going to make sure you end up where you belong.....**with criminals......**"

It is the understanding of the Affiant Daniel Borsotti, Scott Alan Niner states directly in these Emails included herein The Intent to spend $60,000.00 in currency of the United States in the first Email; Then ups the anti to Sparing No expense in pursuit of the illegal activity of manipulating persons and government to put Daniel in jail and bankrupt Daniel Borsotti as a direct and targeted threat to violate the natural and in a lien able right of this sovereign man to be free of Mixed War, trespass, conspiracy, coercion, extortion, robbery by agents of corporations and governments . **Without timely response this is affirmed; And,**

Allegation 2:
http://www.santa-clarita.com/Modules/ShowDocument.aspx?documentid=5076

From: scott@danglingcarrotcreative.com
Subject: Contacting Daniel for motivating assistant!
Date: Sat, 1 Nov 2014 16:31:00 -0700
To: yourmotivator1@live.com
I just received papers Danny. It's so sad that your life has turned into such a distorted view of the facts. And your god is mistaken. As you will see. With your building without permits, taking advantage of elders, trying to get something that you did not gain yourself, getting free money from fake lawsuits, basically, living your life trying to get something for nothing by lying, deceiving, taking advantage...... instead of truly advancing your intelligence and learning how to truly help, advance others in your life. You are selfish, only think about yourself. I am now done sitting back, letting you do what you do which is full of lies and complete distortion of the truth.

Instead, I'm about to truly show you what it takes to lead a honest, truthful life, which I do, both with the government and personally with everyone I come in contact with. It's so sad you have to do this and that I now have to stop this exposing to everyone exactly what you are all about. Lies, Deceit, getting something for nothing. I'm about to embark on a path that only exposes the truth, does not lie, does not make things up, only exposes you for who you are to the government, your friends, your family and god willing, and yes God, not Buda, yourself. YOUR HEADING NOWHERE DANNY. And believe it or not, even after everything you have tried to do to me.....it makes me sad that GOD is not in your life and you have to learn from things the hard way as if he was.......you would better understand intelligence and how to treat people with human dignity and honest intentions.

Unfortunately for you Danny, I can't spend anymore time sitting back, letting you make false claims, lie to the courts, to your family and friends, I have to expose all of it. It has always been at my disposal, but I wanted to spare you the embarrassment and being exposed for the true person you are. I cannot sit idly by at this point and let it to continue as you have disrupted several years of my life and I'm not going to take it any longer. You should have though that one day, I might just have enough and you would have stopped trying to lie, get something for nothing etc. etc. and live your life the right way, true, honest etc. etc.

We are there now Danny. I'm sorry, I won't let you continue to be a part of my life, I gave you space to get real with yourself, instead, you continue. I won't be a part of it any longer.

If you have a change of heart about your actions, please let me know, but you have two weeks to respond or I will continue so that your time is consumed with your illegal activities, Tax evasion problems, illegal building and residence situation and so on so forth. I will now expose

> you for who you are and what people think of you and won't stop until you are so tied up with your true illegal activities that I will be a thing of the past.
>
> Two weeks from today, then the only thing exposed about you is the truth.......NOT lies like you tried to tell about ME. The TRUTH PREVAILS ALWAYS! So you better really think about everything you have going on in your life.....I will spare no expense to expose it to the world....... And yes, I know that different from you cause I will only expose the truth, not try to MAKE SHIT UP to get something for nothing.
>
> GET A LIFE, EDUCATION and a CONSCIOUS.
>
> Scott Niner
> Dangling Carrot Creative
> 27520 Avenue Mentry
> Valencia, Ca. 91355
> 661-295-6610 xt. 111 "

End of quote from pages 132 through 148: (for the original filing see: the United States District Court action 15-04112 JAK (JCD) AFM;

End Quote

One Just Cannot Make This Shit Up
The above passages are directly from the actual claim and email posts from Scott Alan Niner which were all filed at the U.S. District Court Federal Docket CV 15-04112 JAK (JCD)AFM. Ironically the action i, do file, like almost every other action, was dismissed immediately without cause, without any discovery, without a *trial by jury*, without even one hearing. i, was never allowed to enter the courtroom to move this court action forward. An immediate fraud and conspiracy between Scott Allan Niner, all the previous evil-wrongdoers herein as 29 named wo/men that do trespass against i.

The quoted excerpts were copied uncut and forever instilled in this *living missive* for the purpose to show all readers not only did ass-wipe make statements about i, personal life, the $60,000.00 question is how would ass-wipe know anything about i, life? When dealing with alleged Internal Revenue Service, building permits, code violations, that is private information; it is interesting that ass-wipe placed these things in an email using those same subjects as threats and each one of them do come true. There are no coincidences to these threats and fruition that do transpire.

All the threats from Scott Alan Niner (ass-wipe) and his minions have all come true. Not only was the City of Santa Clarita coming after i, so was every other govern mentals agency that ass-wipe made comments to in his terrorist threatening post emails. Yet, none of these facts and evidence was enough for bitch-MLO, richard-cranium, clueless, nor suzie-que to grant a TRO and completely dismiss the action with prejudice without any hearings, without any replies by ass-wipe without one thing filed through discovery. This is why i, reiterate each act.

i, have not exaggerated any of the statements about any of the evil-wrongdoers herein this *living missive*. i, have many records, oral and other records that actually prove all attempts by ass-wipe and all of the others who do fulfill their threats.
Do not forget ass-wipe stated that he or it is the alleged God fearing man, who never lies, never commits adultery and is always honest one who never takes advantage of anyone, always lives his life by the book and is willing to open his tax records to the IRS. What about i, and all of the creditors at ass-wipe's bankruptcy that he was to open all books at 2004 [deadbeat] debtors examination.

Remember ass-wipe paid attorn'ey and pubic serpent, James Thomas King (Satan's 10th Minion), known by this *living missive* as "Jack-off" to suppress i, every move to bring ass-wipe's criminal gang to justice. Whereas Thomas Brian Donovan (shit-for-brains) assisted with his hiding of what is true from the public record. They should have known, that i, will not quit until what is true is exposed. i, wonder what book ass-wipe was talking about in his posts emails; "by what book"? The book of Satan's Minions in how to lie, cheat, steal, rape, and commit adultery, do crack cocaine with an alleged new wife or w.h.o.r.e. (as Robin Niner told i,) and defraud the public and a disabled man by deceit, threats, extortion and coercion. And actually hire others with a form of currency to conspire to the same?

i, really do not care what reason that ass-wipe sent the post emails because ass-wipe finally, after several years of i, attempt to receive justice through the courts that do aid him to commit crimes against i, and others. i, need, i, wish, and it is God's will to tell i, story. i, as a man have no reservations only to tell what is true to finally foretell to the world as exposed.

i, feel that none of the courts will allow i, to receive justice. It appears by the totality of all records the courts all protect ass-wipe, and all of the evil-wrongdoers named herein by aiding and abetting; colleagues, conspiring with a known cocaine addict, thief and adulterer. [128] After all, ass-wipe had his paid liar suppressors, most likely pay off the wo/mankind who act as [~~*judge*~~]s in all of the courts, to abuse all of, i, due process, administrative process, and every known attempt to receive a fair opportunity to receive discovery, to bring forth *trial by juries* in all of the court actions which were all denied. Actually all but one bitch-MLO (ibidem Chapter 1) were dismissed without cause. (i, shall allow the words to flow effortlessly from heart to, soul).

YouTube Saved Many Lives

So, in 2010 i, begun a moral and ethical campaign to tell i, side of the story in order to heal i, broken heart and make a great effort to apply god's teachings as: "…forgive us our debtors, sins and trespasses as we forgive those who trespass against us…" because i, needed to be heard, and i, am determined to tell what is *true* and nothing but what is *true*, so help i, god as i, witness; therefore, i, did

[128] **ADULTERY**: is extramarital sex that is considered objectionable on social, religious, moral, or legal grounds. Although the sexual activities that constitute adultery vary, as well as the social, religious, and legal consequences, the concept exists in many cultures and shares some similarities in Christianity, Judaism and Islam. Adultery is viewed by many jurisdictions as offensive to public morals... https://en.wikipedia.org/wiki/Adultery

some videos on You Tube as you readers can research for yourself, if you like? [129]

Furthermore, i, knew that in order to fulfill i, integrity to god on that one day, where as i, was crouched down into a tightened curled up ball; the day that Robin Niner ripped out i, heart when she sold i, friendship and told i, she would not support i, and that Scott's father sperm-donor made Robin a deal, for a final divorce decree that she would not give up for our life-time of unforeseen connection, especially for our god's graceful forever endless friendship[?]. Please do not forget the scene that once Robin left the house, i, was abandoned at i, land 27508 Sycamore Creek Drive, Rancho Santa Clarita California province where i, stayed in the empty master bedroom where Taz-man (the crazy dog) was trying to comfort i, by licking i, face from the tears practically flooding the home.

Money, Betrayal, Kills The Heart
i, had never felt such betrayal in i, entire life that felt like razor wire soaked in Carolina Reaper mixed with hydrochloric acid being ripped through i, body.

It was more hurtful than when the time i, pair-rents abandoned i, several times as a child, not the time where i, was in a fight searching for robin's Beagle Brandy. When i, alleged friend left i, to be pulverized by three young guys as Theodore ran away leaving i, there alone. After it was all over, i, ended up with a chipped front tooth forever. Yet, it was not as bad in 1995 when i, abandoned i, belief in God and that there was no god in Jesus Christ, as i, do only study Buddhism several years thereafter. Regardless i, do learn a tremendous amount of knowledge about spirituality.

No one can ever tell another child or wo/mankind what it feels like when one's own most precious relationship, when one feels they have a lifelong best friend, that alleged camaraderie would be betrayed for a decree of $1,200.00 for twelve months times ten years($144,000.00). Also, one blue Jeep Cherokee and medical benefits, a cell phone fully paid; over one's best friendship as a betrayal reward.

---

[129]**DISABLEDJUSTICE.ORG** :... multiple youtube pre-recorded factual videos

i, was determined as i, am forever determined to this day, 2025 to continue to speak from i, heart, continue to seek justice, to re-lease all the negative internal stress. If not for i, then for other wo/mankind that are not as mentally, emotionally, and spiritually sound as i, am. This is why i, have continued with the non-stop filing of court actions to receive justice on March 24 2023; on a certain future day.

It was there about that period when ass-wipe finally reviewed all of the YouTube video posts that ass-wipe assisted with i, to create. i, endeavor is with hope that people will review them, contact i, also to share their own stories to the world without fear of these types of govern mentals and private Satanists.
i, story has not wavered from day one to this day 2025. In order to tell what is true to the world, which i, as a man has always and do continue to the day i, perish. To always tell 1,000 % of what is true with no made up conjecture. This is the way it is and shall be on land of prophets and is how it should be for every wo/mankind.
i, will never waiver as “i, always tell what is true even when i, lie !”
:) -

Court Action # PS016624
Youtube: "Disabledjustice" Jan 31, 2010 through March 10th 2010; Go to Utube

https://www.youtube.com/watch?v=vulC__g7lsU
https://www.youtube.com/watch?v=dT1S2usB-oE
https://www.youtube.com/watch?v=37cDBQ2gxww
https://www.youtube.com/@danielborsotti6555

After the Temporary Restraining Order Court action # **PS016624,** was previously filed 2014, then erroneously dismissed, it appeared that govern mentals either placed i, on a certain list or i, was already there. A list that no one truly wants to be on, however, it seems as if, i, as a mankind made it to the [~~judges~~] number one most wanted man list.

Ass-wipe niner already made it clear what he was going to expend, how much money that he would put towards the annihilation of i, good name…, i, car…, i, house…, i, freedom…, and within society.

His threats all, not one or two but all of ass-wipe's terrorist threats are fulfilled one by one as each do trespass to this day.

i, know that scott ass-wipe niner does not have enough brains nor clout to pull off what was happening to i, as i, personally know that ass-wipes father ronald george niner (sperm-donor) and jim/james niner know many influential people in the Santa Clarita Valley and throughout many sectors of political and media forums.

Not only personally, but the Niner business Creative Graphic Services is very well known as well and did a lot of media and advertisements, issuing for many businesses in Santa Clarita California and throughout the entire movie, music, sports and many others types of industries. From the local police department and other city agencies too many media and other agencies to list.

Yes, it is the elders of the niner family who to this day are very well connected with influential people throughout California and beyond. Therefore, if ass-wipe was going to pull anything off, it would certainly and most likely, not just be his $60,000 he pledged to ruin i, life, but rather its statements of endless resources to ruin i, but it most likely would be with the assistance of his family or someone who might have knew his father sperm-doner.

A Side Note:
A man is a man of one's word, regardless of whether threats are amoral, unethical l.e.g.a.l., unlawful, what is right or wrong. When a wo/mankind fulfills a pattern by follow through to its actions, this reality is the effect of the cause. Ass-wipe niner's criminal gang fulfilled all threats and is the cause and effect. This *living missive* is the effects of ass-wipe and govern mentals avowal of war against i. It is also a war on wo/mankind compared to 14th Amednment citizens, residents as slaves that can only be born or naturalized "*in*" the 50 States United Corporations.

All Registration Is Subject To The Corp(s)oration
When wo/mankind consent to govern mental registration, it matters not what it is, govern mentals can trace, track, and control everything that is registered. Govern mental agents believe they

own you as a registered issue enslaved title. Do not forget that all wo/mankind, known by agents created this path for i, to expose.

i, expose all evil-wrongdoers since 2007 niner case, with the TRO action of 2014, of ass-wipes threats via posts, thereafter i, was pulled over six to eight times. i, know to this day, these unwarranted incidents of being harassed and intimidated, erroneously tailed and eventually pulled over, along with i, truck being stolen off of i, land by both local Santa Clarita, Los Angeles County and California state sheriffs abroad, which is of no coincidence. This is the **"...my 60k** *in currency of the United States and sparing no expense of manipulating persons and government to make sure Daniel ends up where you belong.....* ***with criminals......*** *in jail and bankrupt... to violate the natural and in a lien able right of this sovereign man; to be free of Mixed War, trespass, conspiracy, coercion, extortion, robbery by agents of corporations and governments..."*

However, back in 2014 until 2018/19/2025, i, learned of the constitutions, declarations of independence, House Joint Resolutions, such as House Joint
Resolution 192 ("HJR 192"), Pubic Law 89-719, Executive Orders 6073, 6102, 6111 and 6260, 7 12 U.S.C. § 95b,8 and UCC § 3-603. 9, UCC 1-207, and UCC 1-308, many Uniform Commercial Codes. i, will not go deep into all of those previous by-laws; frankly they do not apply to a wo/mankind only citizens.

Those previously stated codes, that are not by-laws rather l.e.g.a.l. system antics that only affect citizens, residents, card carrying members who consent to a driver's license, or take on certain titles, contract into a system that does not give full disclosure to the public in how the govern mentals truly operates and controls the codes to enslave allpeople; although it is obvious.

i, learned about Common Law, Maritime, Admiralty, Civil and the Family, Probate, Small Claims, Criminal law, unlawful Detainers and how the gold had or was being stolen from the people by the United States Govern mentals 1933. In addition, i, learned how many of the presidents have sold out the American people, from the time of Abraham Lincoln, to Franklin Delano Roosevelt, the stories of John Fitzgerald Kennedy, Ronald Reagan, and i, experienced firsthand and can remember both George Bushes, Clintons, Obama, Trumpets, through to date.

i, speak from i, experience not from opinions for 1. i, have never voted ever in i, entire lifetime, for any office, such as governors, mayors, presidents nor any elected officials, and 2. i, am not a political man and "*…frankly Scarlet, i, do not give a damn…*" who is in office, because all politicians seem to become corrupt.

If they weren't corrupt B-4 they ran for their office, they become skunks that stink up their public service and become the problem; the problem of why this once, great land of America is in shambles of today. It is the alleged politicians wreak havoc on their own citizens and residents.

From what i, have witnessed on i, own, many alleged great wo/men, sell out their souls for a pay off or certain prizes to devilish functions. Devilish functions cater to the way this country has come to know the wisdom of doctor wayne dyer: "when we keep doing what has always done, we will never get a different result". As insane as it sounds, it is insane.

i, do know whether it is a child, married couple, car, dog or cat, appliance, credit cards, or compensation for one's labour, when registered with any commercial federal or state govern mental agencies it is enslaved. This includes any corp(s)oration. It is owned and controlled by the entity for which it is registered to no matter what anyone thinks, or refutes to this subject that i, state is true.

Public Notice Is Not Hidden Or Is It?

i, do believe that the public have been given many notices, tips, and forecasting of what is to happen in the present, future and from as far back as time in memorial. The alleged loss of all of the wealth backing the American people that were supporting America at fort Knox, is said that it may have grown feet told to the public in the Wizard of Oz movie, which told a tail of govern mental corruption by the "… follow the yellow brick road…" as the gold was being stolen from the American people. This idea is a minor piece of the big theater. It matters not whether it is true or not at this point. Do not 4-get all corruption is by pubic serpent as, "there is no such a thing as a living government.

There are multiple movies that depict what govern mentals foretells for the future of wo/mankind. Actually, it is more so meant for persons, residents, citizens, individuals and the wo/mankind that unknowingly contract themselves and offspring to the state and federal govern mentals. This is scary to know, however, it is better to know than not to know. With knowledge, all wo/mankind can do something to protect their present and futures, in darkness all receive enslavement.

Thought From The Author
i, will add for you readers (wo/mankind) that do witness these *living missives*, with certain thoughts B-4 moving on: when a wo/mankind give up their rights to property[130] for the belief in security that public serpents, agents or employees of a govern mental will morally and ethically protect them from harm, they lose who they are and where they came from is desecrated by loss of ancestral crimson-stain.

Back To Reality Of Ass-Wipe And i,
The results to allow govern mentals to protect self, family and property expose the people that do a disservice to society on a whole. To ever place trust outside of themselves, forces all wo/mankind to become enslaved by the lack of desire to think for self, to take control of their own lives, and to dream the impossible dream, is lost through complacency, laziness, trust, ignorance and loss of respect. Regardless of i, past experiences while exercising i, traveling habits, while directing a automobile up and down the roadways, highways, and byways, it was about 1st week B-4 January 2015 whereby Niner's witch hunting threats truly begun to rev up towards i. This is what began to destroy all i, disposition in life.

i, was traveling down the highway minding i, own business when i, was pulled over for alleged speeding. This occurred at least five times within several weeks. Because i, had already rescinded the

[130] **PROPERTY**: What is One's own… Body, Spirituality, land, possessions, persona

driver's license several years prior, i, was very careful on the road rarely ever traveling five miles an hour over the posted limits. Then i, became more and more careful, vigilant, and aware of the speeds and knee-jerk reactions on the roadways. i, begun to question govern mental's acts and intrusions into i, life on a higher level than ever B-4.

This was when, i, began to be fed up with govern mentals using their policy enforcers known as California Highway Patrol, Los Angeles Police Department, and Los Angeles Sheriff's Deputies which consists of a standing army. It seemed more than a coincident that i, begun to be harassed, intimidated and coerced more often. It began to instill fear, threats and intimidation in order to get i, back into compliance. i, do not suspect when i, rescinded i, drivers license as much as ass-wipe niners threats, extortion and ransomed offers to the agencies for his cause.

However, i, realized that the system in what is stated as executive branch, which enforces on behalf of the legislative branch, follows the judiciary branch orders. It is and has always been set up to enforce policies, tax the public legally under colour of true l.e.g.a.l. schema, to steal property and rights of the public and not for protection of laws or property as previously stated and alleges by a con-stitution.

With each incident i, began to study *everything* i, could get i, hands on. Of course, the internet was i, greatest source of learning because anything such as needing a motion, to research a code, statute, rules or regulation, or case findings, all one needed to do was Google certain related words and a website, or documents, other patron's blogs would appear on the screen. The use of the internet for law is born for the average lay-wo/man. Of course, i, also used attorn'ers and paralegals, however, they would only teach to keep i, enslaved to their unlawful statutory way.

As time moved on, so with it, i, cars were impounded on several occasions. One time the Sherriff's of Santa Clarita came to i, house at 27508 Sycamore Creek Drive Santa Clarita California [91355], and stole i, truck right off of i, driveway. Regardless that is was on private property and agents made i, go through horrific processes, that stole a lot of i, hard earned labour (compensation for i, sweat) to retrieve those personal properties. A sheriff asked… "*what is your car worth*"? i, told him … "*it is worth $100,000.00 to i.*" The man just laughed it off and stole i, property anyways. (i, shall expose this pirate for the state later on)…

Another time, i, was traveling on the highway at Santa Clarita, and the truck was impounded and then days later it was released with zero charges as allegedly there was a glitch between the DMV and Triple AAA insurance. At that time all i, had to pay was for the impound. i, stood i, ground and eventually a sergeant at the Santa Clarita Sherriff's station released i, truck without any charges. However, it took i, days, a lot of study, writings, paperwork, orations and stressful trips to the station.
Then i, begun to receive multiple code violations on i, home and land; one for i, trashcans being on the driveway, or that i, grass was too brown and it was in the years of the great drought. Another code violation was because, i, had a white pickup truck on the driveway and it was not registered nor did it have a non operations slip on it, which is not against the *law*. However, it is against govern mental's codes, regulations, acts and enslavement mentality or the Niners threats?

Another time, sheriffs were tailing i, all the way towards i, home/land, and then stopped across the street and just sat there to watch i. This happened many times for several months. Next the Internal Revenue Service begun to audit i, and try to get i, to follow their protocol which i, knew i, did not owe them anything, nor could i, have owed them what they were making up. They were doing an unwarranted audit out of the blue. Actually it was all stated in ass-wipe niners terrorist threats in his emails.

i, do not even need to go to the level that, i, was being sought after, and it was apparent that ass-wipe niner's criminal gang had much to do with what was transpiring. Ass-wipe's terrorist threats were all coming to fruition one after another. At that time, i, did not put two and three together.

It was as if, i, was on Americas most wanted list and all of the agents had access to i, entire life. The amount of time and effort i, place to not contract, to stand alone, to not follow the Satanic, ritualistic monopoly United States Of America Inc. and State Of California Inc. i, might have receive many doctrines. However, i, do have A.A., B.A., PHD and Masters Degrees all by the School Of Hard Knox.

There is much more to come readers, please move onto Volume number Two, II, 2 "*Disabled Justice Lacking Equity Witihn The Justice System i, Am Not A Police-Man...*" to be continued:

Use the following lines for taking notes and for questions to ask author: ______________________

Table Of Contents

Notes

Disabled Justice,
Lacking Equity Within The Judicial System, "i, am not an attorn'ey" ....Page 1
Volume 1, One, I, Integrated God....Page 3
Tradenames.........Page 4
Legal Is Not Normally Moral or Ethical....Page 5
The Mission of Author /The man: Adam – Daniel Of The Borsotti Family....Page 6
Disclosure Of Right ....Page 7
B-4 We Begin; There Are Lots Of Things You Need To Know....Page 9
Political Porn Through The Courts....Page 10
May The Birds Of Paradise Fly Up Your Nose ....Page 12
Somebody Is Always Watching You ....Page 13
Introduction By I, A Man/Nam Myoho Renge Kyo....Page 14
Lord's Prayer ....Page 16
Govern Mentals Caught In Its Own Dragnet ....Page 19
Temporarily Skip To The Effect ....Page 20
The Healing Do begin/Screech, Smash, Bing, Bang, Boom ....Page 21
Like Mighty Mouse ....Page 22
Blinded By The Light ....Page 24
James Wilson Vititoe....Page 25

CHAPTER 1, I, ONE,

The Road To Recovery ....Page 25
This Caveat Is For The Wrongdoers/ Reassure What You Read Is True......Page 26
Healing Is A Process So I, Continue/For And On The Record....Page 28
Bible, Koran, Ideology, Philosophy, Etcetera....Page 30
Who Is This Precarious & Tenacious Man? ....Page 31
Wo/Mankind Are The Pubic Serpent ' Masters ....Page 32
Look Back To Move Forward....Page 34
Retain Da Power You Always Have To The End / You Should Have Give Up
Your Day Job ....Page 36
To Do Wrong Is Easy To Do Right Is Not....Page 38
To Continue Is Easy To Stop Is Difficult....Page 40
Message To The Public At Large/ Pubic Serpent Are Known Criminals ......Page 41
This Living Missive Has Multiple Benefits....Page 43
I, Will Make You Famous....Page 44
Intermission ....Page 45

i, Swear To Tell The Truth....Page 46
Wo/Mankind Vs Corporate / The Schools Of Devilish Functions ....Page 47
Volunteering Names Has Many Meanings ....Page 49
What Appears On Papyrus, Is Not Always True / Consensual Sex/Commerce By Consent ....Page 50
Harm To Another Wo/Mankind Or Property....Page 52
How Did We Get Here?....Page 53
Complacent, Lazy Or Ignorant ? ....Page 54
Back To The Founding Papers ....Page 55
Transform From Wo/Mankind To Bar Agent....Page 57
Knowing The Game Is To Function On The Board....Page 58
Wo/Mankind Transform N-2 Sharks ....Page 59
What Is 2-B Famous....Page 60
Notice Of Intent....Page 61
Borne /Berthed On North American Land/ The Age Of Majority ....Page 62
Always Give Notice B-4 You Enter Court/Court Of L.E.G.A.L....Page 63
Court Of Law/Courts Are Games With Certain Rules....Page 67
Direct Message To The Readers....Page 67
Until Death Due Do Us Part....Page 68
I, Said Many Times B-4 As I, Say It Hereinto....Page 69
Words From The Author ....Page 70
With Friends Like Them, Who Needs Enemies....Page 71
2000 through 2025/ Promiscuous With Another Woman ....Page 72
Is The Brother The Same....Page 73
A Falling Out With Family/ A Call For What Reason....Page 74
Sometimes Friends Are Better Than Lovers....Page 75
A Wolf In Sheep's Garments....Page 76
The Final Deal ....Page 77
What You Know Can Set You Free ....Page 78
Time To Consummate The Deal /Let Cancer Heal On Its Own....Page 79
Robin Elizabeth Lillian ~~Nigretto/Osborne~~ Niner ....Page 85
The Infamous Foreclosure Statement....Page 81
Brotherly Love....Page 82
Signing The Escrow Papers....Page 83
Get Away To Heal i, Body, Mind, Emotions & Spirit....Page 84
Men Of Martial Arts 2000 Calendar....Page 85
Deceit From The Start ....Page 86
Trespass Has No Statute Of Limitations....Page 88
Betrayal Started Its Engine....Page 89

Search For Honest Attorn'ey, Yah Right!..Page 90
Unlawful Detainer To File..Page 91
Betrayal Feels Worse Than Death Appears.......................................Page 92
Time To Get A Lawful Degree/Forgiveness Not Easy, Is Necessary & Proper..Page 93

CHAPTER 2, II, TWO
Law Of Wo/Man Vs. Pubic Serpent /R.I.C.O. & Corporate Corruption.......Page 95
Pubic Serpent Do Not Act In Honor..Page 96
To Dis-Cover Is To Unearth What Is New.......................................Page 97
Hidden No Names Saints...Page 99
A Freed Mind Is Freed Spirit &A Fearful Mind Is Fearful Spirit ....Page 100
A Memory From The Lane.. ....Page 102
Outside Of Court Is Where Honor Is ....Page 103
What Is A Court?/ What Is An Actor...Page 105
Tell-Us-Lies-Vision Is Not What Is True..Page 106
Ignorance Of The Law Is The Excuse..Page 107
Bait & Switch Monopoly..... ....Page 109
Full Disclosure What Is That? ....Page 110
SATAN'S NUMBER ONE TRONE CHATSWORTH CRIMINAL GANG...Page 113
Satan's 1st Minion Bitch-MLO Margaret Lynn Oldendorf.......................Page 114
Transfer Was Imminent And Do Issue ....Page 115
I, Thought Officers Were Bound To Honesty.....................................Page 116
I, Recall The Subpoena Runaround...Page 117
Bring In Another [Judge]Pubic Serpent ....Page 120

SATAN 2ND MINION OF BITCH-MLO CRIMINAL GANG/ JOSEPH KERENDIAN...Page 124
What Was The Achievement For? / It is Called Unlawful Conveyance ....Page 126
Sleep Well Satan Sleep Well ....Page 129

SATAN'S 3RD MINION OF THE B.I.T.C.H.-M.L.O/THOMAS EDWARD WANNER...Page 129
Crazy Mad Woman Downstairs ....Page 131
She Sold Friendship For Divorce Decree..Page 132
Averting Answers To The Questions..Page 133

SATAN'S 4TH MINION B.I.T.C.H.-MLO/DAVID WOODRUFF MEDIATOR..........Page 135
Court Is A State With Many Actors..........Page 136

SATAN'S 5TH MINION B.I.T.C.H.-MLO CRIMINAL GANG/ RICHARD MILLER..........Page 138
Great Lawyers Ask Important Questions..........Page 140
Where Do They Go To Lunch Dick-Em?..........Page 142
Stoned Out Of One's Mind..........Page 143
Combative Attorn'ey Game Over For Your Action/ End Of This Chapter Of Trial..........Page 144
Kill Them All And Let God Sort Them Out..........Page 145
The Trial Would End With A New Beginning..........Page 146
Anger, Disbelief, Abandonment, & Betrayal..........Page 147
Is it Gods intervention or just a coincidence..........Page 148
CHAPTER 3, III, THREE
Thankful For God's Intervention..........Page 149
RONALD NINER THE MAN WHO SPERMED SCOTT ALLAN NINER..........Page151
It Was God's Gift To Us All..........Page 152
Reminder Of An Earlier Issue..........Page 153
Justification Is The Wrath Of God..........Page 154

SATAN'S 3RD TRONE SAGA SCOTT NINER CRIMINAL GANG 2007-2025..........Page 155
Appellate Courts Believe It Can Do/ Open Court Of Record Not StatutoryPage 156
Simplicity Key To All Things..........Page 157
Open Court Of Record Law For All Mankind..........Page 158
Contrast Between Claim & Complaint..........Page 159
Notice To The Reader To Research..........Page 160
Just Do Not Consent And You Are Fine..........Page 161
Courts Are Not A Place Wo/Mankind Belong..........Page 162

Satan's 7th-09th Minions Niner Gang/Perlus Woods, Jackson..........Page 163
Three Blind ~~Judges~~ Mice See How They Run..........Page 164
One Knows Regardless Of Knowing..........Page 166
Disability Advocate With His Own Agenda/Side Swiped Alternative Motives..........Page 167
Know Who You Hire B-4 You Hire Them..........Page 168

SATAN'S 4TH TRONE SAGA NINER CRIMINAL GANG/THOMAS DONAVAN..........Page 170
Notice Of Intent Robin & Scott Niner (Ass-Wipe) ....Page 173
The Fruitful Tree Is The Spoiled Apple/ I, Shalt Not Forget Eventually Will Forgive ....Page 174

SATAN'S 11TH MINION JAMES KING /SCOTT NINER CRIMINAL GANG/ Attorn'ey Re-Presents Fraud Action For Niner Criminal Gang.....Page 176
First Time For Something Scarce..........Page 177
Talking Among Buddies At Open Court..........Page 178
(Footnote) BIRTH/BERTH CERTIFICATES, STRAW MAN ....Page 189
Is A Wo/Man That Act As Judge Also A Medical Doctor?..........Page 181
Deadbeat Debtor's Is Not For You, Hah?..........Page 182
No Medical Doctorate, Or Oath Of Office, No Buenos/Pubic Serpent Choose Who Wins Despite Facts Evidence..........Page 184
Forced To File Additional Adversary Action / Do All Courts Talk To Each Other?..........Page 185

SATAN'S 10TH MINION IN THE SAGA OF SCOTT NINER'S <u>CRIMINAL GANG</u> OF 2007–2025/ U.S. Bankruptcy Adversary, Case # 2:11-Ap-02293, Thomas Brian Donavon B.A.R. # 34106..........Page 186
Reflection As To What The Court Did..........Page 187
Where Have All The Good Serpent Gone? ....Page 189
FYI: Fear Jesus Turns The Tables..........Page 190
Congress Declares The Bible "The Word Of God"/ No Debunk, Just Take Things On Their Words ....Page 191
<u>**Genesis** 3:5</u>/ Congress Declared The Bible The Word Of God..........Page 192

SATAN'S 12TH MINION DAVID L. HAHN; NINER'S<u>CRIMINAL GANG</u> OF 2007-2025 ....Page 193
It Is I's, Business By Niner's Fraud And Default ....Page 194
How Low Can You Go? ....Page 195
Make This Issue Known Multiples ....Page 196
A Man Consecrated By False Pretense..........Page 197
A Message From Humility..........Page 198
Mode To Break The Mole..........Page 199

SATAN'S 5TH TRONE IN SAGA OF SCOTT NINER'S <u>CRIMINAL GANG</u> OF 2007 – 2025 /At Ones Own Peril To Act With Such Conduct..........Page 200

Never-Ending Path, The World For Justice..Page 201
Ikeda Sensei's Encouragement ....Page 202
Back To The Story Of Impartiality ....Page 203

SATAN'S 13TH MINION, JAMES SAMUEL OTERO SCOTT NINER'S CRIMINAL GANG OF 2007 – 2025/ U.S. Bankruptcy Court Action 2:12-Cv-10284..Page 205
Checks And Balances ....Page 210
Our Agenda For The Hearing ....Page 211
Summary For James Samuel Otero ....Page 214
SATAN'S 14TH MINION, JESUS GILBERT BERNAL SAGA SCOTT NINER'S CRIMINAL GANG OF 2007 – 2025/ Thinking With A Parasites Mind..Page 216
i, Courts' Raison D'être To Fulfill This Living Missive/CHECKS & BALANCES.. ....,,..Page 219
Silence No More! *Daniel Borsotti* V. [Judge] *Fernando Manzano O'lguin*..Page 221
SATAN'S 6TH TRONE CAROL KOPPEL CRIMINAL GANG OF 2014 – 2025.... ....Page 222
Older Dictionaries Tend To Be Truer /See Examples..........................Page 223

SATAN'S 15TH MINION CAROL C. KOPPEL, CRIMINAL GANG OF 2007 - 2025 / Michael D. Antonovich Courthouse Case # **91102QU** August 8TH 2013 Courtroom A-19..Page 224
The Following Factual Excerpts..Page 226
Remanding Is Not Lawful When Ego Dictates It...............................Page 227
I, Walk A Mile For A Camel, Not Injustice.....................................Page 228
Serpent 's Sail Caught By Promiscuous Wind..................................Page 229
Dressed For Success To Honor..Page 230
Caveat; Carol Chenkin Koppel (Cck-W.H.O.R.E.)..........................Page 232-235
The Nice Deputy With A Heart ....Page 237
Deputies Try To Intimidate i...Page 239
Time For Tarnished Judicial Armageddon......................................Page 240
On The Following Day/Guilty On No Facts.....................................Page 246
The Received Rude Awakening...Page 247
I Do Invite CC Koppel -W.H.O.R.E. To The Party.............................Page 249
CCK-Whore's Autograph Acknowledge de ceit..................................Page 250

CHAPTER 4, IV, FOUR

16TH MINION OF MELVIN D. SANDVIG <u>CRIMINAL GANG</u> OF 2007/2014 – 2025..Page 252 - 253
Was It Richard-cranium Or Devine Intervention..............................Page 254
See Ass-Wipes Emails Below / Necessity Has No Law? [Cicero]...........Page 256
The Need For Transparency ....Page 257
SATAN'S 17TH MINION THE LLOYD C. LOOMIS <u>CRIMINAL GANG</u> OF 2007 – 2025/Lloyd Clark Loomis, Pubic Serpent ....Page 259
Ass-wipe Niner said it himself and i, Quote................................Page 261-262
See Online Actual Court Summary Docket....................................Page 264-266
No [~~Judge~~] Can Review It's Of Demand For Recusal?..........................Page 269
Summary Of The Years Of Bias...Page 270-273
SATAN'S 18TH MINION OF THE SUSAN L. LOPEZ <u>CRIMINAL GANG</u> Of 2007- 2025 / Susan L. Lope Giss /Play Pass The [Litigant] Man Buck Game...Page 274
Pubic Serpent Follow Orders From Superiors..................................Page 275
Lifelong Believers Read From The Heart.......................................Page 277
SATAN'S 7TH TRONE UNITED STATES DISTRICT COURT CRIMINAL GANG OF 2015/2016 – 2025-(FEDERAL DOCKET CV 15-04112 JAK...Page 279
Courts Trust Their Parent Corp(S) Orations......................................Page 280
Action Against 29 Corp(S)Pubic serpent ....Page 281
It is Not Mighty Mouse To Save The Day..Page 283
One Just Cannot Make This Shit Up..Page 315
Youtube Saved Many Lives ....Page 317
Money, Betrayal, Kills The Heart ....Page 318
Court Action # PS016624..Page 319
All Registration Is Subject To The Corporation...................................Page 320
Public Notice Is Not Hidden Or Is It? ....Page 322
Thought From The Author / Back To Reality Of Ass-Wipe And ......Page 323-325
Table Of Content & Words and Phrases ....Page 327 - 361
Definitions Words & Phrases..Page 334 – 346
List of Evil Wrongdoers...Page 347
Satan's Trones..Page 348
References ....Page 350
L.A.W. Of Man Vs. Pubic Serpent & Corporate Corruption..................Page 351
Jesus Turned The Tables Over On The Merchants Forever...................Page 354
Evil-Wrong Doers List Herein Is Forever-Ending ....Page 355 – 356
List Of Denials Any Of These Familiar With You ??? ....Page 357

DEFINITIONS, WORDS & PHRASES

[ ] : Between brackets depict silence/invisible as it is not there they are used to alter or provide additional context to quotes

~~0000000~~ : Line through anything lessens the effect or is replaced anew

2-B : To be

4-get : Forget: forget something or omit accidentally or on purpose

4-U : For you (is short version for making space)

B-4 : Before : prior to a place and time

L8 : Late

L.A.P.D. : Los Angeles Police Department (agents)

"N" or "n" : when N or lower case n is by itself is defined as "and"

N-2 : In to or Into

T8-N : Taken

U : You

UCC- 3-402 (b) :Uniform Commercial Code: an authorized representative who signs an instrument is not personally liable on the instrument if the representative's signature shows explicitly the signature is made on behalf of a represented person identified in the instrument

W8-N : Waiting

X : Time

AB INITIO : From the beginning

ADHOCRACY : opposite to and cuts across bureaucratic lines To solve issues

ADMINISTRATIVE: is an executive court that administrates for the state and federal courts as a fictional court only not lawful dejure courts

AGE OF MAJORITY: Not always of the full lawful age of consent as an Adult

AMMIT : Demon rather than deity, due her role to 'devourer the dead

ANCESTRAL : next to kin, posterity, heritage and reverse or throw back

ANDROCRACY : Rule or supremacy of men, governed by hierarchy of men

ARREST : Taken away without consent, (a-rrest) as in take a knap

ASS : Donkey, jack-ass, anus of a wo/mankind, or ass-face

ATONEMENT : reparation for harm evil-wrongdoer cause another wo/man

ATTORN'EY : a wo/man that throws its sponsor under the bus for the BAR one appointed by another to act in her/his place

ATTORN'ER : turn over, transfer homage or allegiance, to another lord

B.A.N.D. : Barraters, Ante-chambered Nasty Dragnet

BANK-STERS : Wo/mankind that act as agents for bank institutions

B.A.R. : Bank Authorized Representative for banking agents

B.K. : Bankruptcy or BANKRUPTCY

BLOOD-SUPPER : "Do this," Jesus said institute the Supper, "*in remembrance of me.*" Jesus' words in the Gospels, echoed by Paul, make remembering critical to meaning of Supper.

BROK-STERS :broker who cares less for buying/selling and more for fees

BULWARK : Courtroom , department, division Satan's den

CALIFORNIFICATION : State agents fornicating unlawful rights all over people

C.E.O. : Careless Experienced Official/Corrupt Executive Oppressor

C.F.O. : Chief Financial Offender

CHAPTERS: as causes of actions for one continuous court case

CITIZEN: is always a slave under the 14th Amendment

CLAIM : is by wo/mankind against another wo/mankind only!

C.L.I.T. : Court Liar Initiating Trouble

CLUCK : Court or any type of Clerk as in a chicken that clucks

C.O.C.A.I.N.E. : Corrupt Opportunist Creates An Irrelevant Nixed Equity

COMITY : kindliness by refined nations to value each other laws/usage
COMPLAINT :not law; asks mommy/daddy to fix things by Complain[t]ing
CONS-TITUTIONS :con artists who makes body of rules, customs, or laws
COPYRIGHTS © : is right to copy subject for lawful juridical Claim It is not defined under U.S. Copyrights purpose
CORPS. : Corporation / Corp(s)oration as in a dead ens legis fiction
CRIMSON STAIN : Through him is belief God raised from the dead, glorified, so your faith and hope are in God" (1 Peter 1:18–20). Sin is like a crimson stain, indicative of blood guilt
CUCARACHAS : Spanish for a satanic parasitic action needing extermination
C.U.S.I.P. : Committee on Uniform Securities Identification Procedures
CUSIP : Unique identifying security code—to identify securities
DEADBEAT-DEBTOR : Is wo/mankind that refuse to stand on honor to reconcile harm to another wo/mankind
DEFENDANT : Party against whom a lawsuit has been filed or who has been accused of, charged with an offense backed by facts
DE FACTO : to 'de facto', meaning 'in fact' or 'in practice'
DEJURE : Pursuant to rightful entitlement or *claim*; by right; "by law"
D.O.J. : Deprivation On-behalf- for-Just-Us
DOPPELGANGER : a double created at berth/birth verified by proof certificate
DRAGNET :A moral net drawn through society for catching titled agents
DROIT : "a right, a legal claim to one's due," in the l.e.g.a.l. and law
DUMB : mute, still, refuse or unable to speak, person w/out intellect
ENS LEGIS : Creature of law; artificial being, contrast natural

person Applied to corps., deriving its existence entirely from law

EVIL WRONGDOER : Tort-feasor in law, Trespasser, to make do with mal intent

F.A.C.E. : Fraudulently Acquired Court Experts (if acronym's present)

F.B.I. : Federal Body Inspector or Federal Bureau of Investigation

F.E.A.R. : False Expectation Appears Real: fear, FEAR, with a **(.)**

FEASOR : Evil-wrongdoer, trespasser, literally "committer of a tort"

GESTALT : Organized whole perceived more than a sum of its parts

GOVERN : To Control self Or Others by Threat or Consent

GOVERNMENT : Fictional State/Federal masked by Agents; not real

HABEAS CORPUS : bring a wo/man B-4 a court to determine lawful status

HEARSAY : is an outside of court statement by third party assumed truth

H.F.T.T. :(Hold For Tax Tank) held in a stockade for tax on i, body

HUE-MAN : Colour of man, unreal "hue" Fiction diminished wo/man

I : "I" is corporate title & "i" is the living wo/mankind

IAALS : Institute Advancement American Legal System

IN : All capps/lower case, creates "inside" of "into" a fiction

INDIVIDUAL : As a noun, term denotes …a … natural person … and …., may in proper cases, include artificial person

ISSUE(s) : offspring created by god through a wo/mankind as host/ess

ISSUER :send out authoritatively, offers to private and public

JANE/JOAN : ane/Joan refers to Tricia … Taylor regardless if misspelled

John Henry Doe : Foreign Situs Trust

JOHN HENRY DOE : Cestui Que Vie ESTATE Trust

JOHN H. DOE : Public Transmitting Utility

JOINDER : A Wo/Mankind in "Joinder" to a "person" becomes the "walking dead" legally speaking;

JUDGE : There is no such thing as a [~~judge~~] for *any* court as only God is the one judge of all wo/mankind

JURY NULLIFICATION : The act of nullifying by state power over U.S. Gov. & is not only true law

K.I.S.S. : Keep It Simple Señor/Señorita

K.U.N.T. : Kruption Understands Nothing True

L.A.W. : God's Law; Land, Air, Water: Law is not the same as legal

LAWFUL RECIPE : papers written that are common law in fact, legal in theory

X, Y, Z or B-4-LAW : any word B-4 the main topic is diminished by its use i.e.; Case-law, Criminal-law, Probate-law is not the "law"

L.E.G.A.L. : Lawbreakers Exercise Govern-mental Artificial Law

LIBERTY : First of persons; of communities, state of being free from arbitrary, repressive, or autocratic rule or control

LICENTIA DOCENDI : Freedom, in both a good and bad sense depends on intent

LITIGANT(S) : to dispute, quarrel, strive, carry on a suit not a wo/mankind

LIVING MISSIVE : The action as process of exposure by an superior authority

LOS-T ANGEL-LESS : is truly the province of LOS ANGELES

MAL : malicious intent, on purpose, knowingly to cause harm

MAN : is second to god on the hierarchy of the totem pole

MAN-DATE : two men fishing/camping; night out shoot pool/throw darts

MAXIMS : Axiom, statement of a self-evident truth, of law; no doubt

MAGISTRATE : a wo/mankind acts as a public witness for the courts only

MENT(A)L : The mind as in mental as in deranged wo/mankind as agents

MISTER : A conventional title of courtesy B-4 a man's Christian name

M.O. : Modus operandi: picky way or method of doing something

MOLES RELEASE: An informant such as parent at birth/berth informs on issue

MOGEL(s) : commercial tycoons, entrepreneur, industrialist, capitalist

MOOT : Uncertainty, facts and evidence withheld from jury is fraud

MORTAL : Earthly

MR. : Acronym of Master name to refer to a man without a higher or honorific or professional title;

MSO : Manufacture Statement of Origin

NET : is equal to the internet

NEXUS : That which ties or binds together there is no parity

NOM DE GUERRE: fictitious person's name engaged in act, plainly "war name"

NUNC PRO TUNC : Now for then; turning back god's honorable clock

OSIRIS : Name of a principal god of Egypt, judge of the dead

OXYMORON : Abstract figure in which absurd or vague terms are united

PACER : Public court records online search by name instant results

P.E.N.I.S. : People Exercise Nonsensical Inept Shit

PEOPLE : Always distinct as wo/mankind; never a group of fictions

PARITY : equality or equivalence of rank or status

PERSON : Individual, Artificial LEGAL, partnership, association, corporation, of one kind or another legally generated and does not include the sovereign

PHALLUS : a man's penis

PLAINTIFF : A <u>person</u> that brings l.e.g.a.l. action against another <u>person</u>, such as in a civil lawsuit or criminal proceedings

POLICY ENFORCER : wo/mankind that act as l.e.g.a.l. enforcer of public welfare, can be police, sheriff, patrol, marshals; every type of agent, that enforces for every type of policy, code, rule or control & not always l.a.w.-ful

P.P.D. : Public Pretender Defender (one who pretend to defend)

PRAECIPE : an legal document order; generally involving the instigation of some form of swift and peremptory action

PRETENDER-DEFENDER :Wo/mankind that pretends to defend with honor of oath to public's best interest. Instead acts in conflict to protect the City, County , State or Federal Enclaves

PRETERMIT : omit to do, mention, abandon or continuous act for a time:

PROPERTY : not restricted to personal, rites/rights/writes, i, intangible(s)

PROTHONOTARY : principal clerk of a court, like a chief cluck of agency

PRO-SE-CUTER : wo/man that work for courts with interest against public "bring to a court of law, seek to obtain by l.e.g.a.l. process"

PUB[L]IC : (singular/ plural) serpent who work for corps. Not wo/man

PUBLICAN : tax-gatherer for the Roman government; tax collector

PURGATORY : form of lay retribution for spiritual cleansing after death

(S) MENT-AL : Added "**s**" means plural agents that work for establishments

RAISON D'ÊTRE : "rational grounds for existence."

R.E.M.I.C. : real estate mortgage investment conduit (remic) in commercial real estate financing is to pool loans and issue mortgage backed securities (MBS) or commercial mortgage backed securities (CMBS).

RECIPROCITY : Joint openness, equality of right amid diverse powers

REGAL RETINUE : Your peers, as in those that follow, Attendance in court

RITE/RIGHT : Religious, solemn ceremony act/ morally good, justified, or acceptable, free will as is rights

ROBEING : robe, long garment worn to the ground (rob short for theft)

RESIDE IN : one who live inside the matrix, or fiction not real…

SAFE HARBOR : give shelter to, secured zone, prospect to not be held liable

SATAN'S MINION : Adversary, one who opposes, obstructs, or acts as an adversary darling

SATAN'S VILLE : A place nobody likes and unlawful govern mentals dwell

SERPENT : limbless reptile; tempter in Genesis iii.1-5, "snake" a sly, treacherous person, one who exploits a position of trust in order to betray it.

SHIP : Every time "Ship" is attached to a word its pirating

S.H.I.T./POOP : Start High On Top/People Obstructing Other People

S.L.U.T. : Student Lawyer Under Training

SMUDGETHICS : Sarcastic statement and Ethics which means smeared ethics,

SOVEREIGN-CITIZEN : Oxymoronic term created by agents of Satan's underworld as govern mentals

SPONSOR : is a wo/mankind that hires a representative for court actions

STOCKADE : jail, prison, infirmary, lockup, detention, the big house

STRAW-WO/MAN : Ens legis fiction created by govern mentals in place of living wo/mankind meant to tax, enslave, as surety for life

SUIT (LAWSUIT) : Band of followers; a retinue, company; matching clothes obligation (of a tenant) to attend court; attendance at court

TAKINGS CLAUSE : a clause in the Fifth Amendment to the

U.S. Constitution stating that private property cannot be taken for public use without just compensation

TENANT : resident, occupier, govern mental or Corproate slave

TEFLON ROBE : Corrupt Judges Caught Exposing themselves to deception

TESTICULAR SACK : Is known as brains or lacking brains thereof by wo/mankind

TICKET : Notice informs wo/man of fines imposed for an illicit act

TOME : Digest or another volume as in *living missive*

TOTEM POLE : Hierarchy from top, God, wo/man down to pubic serpent

TRADENAME/ ™: is actually trade name not conducive to Trademark under the USPTO Trademark and Patent Office

TRIAL BY JURY : controls by jury nullification; always determines both law and facts; can hold pubic serpent with contempt and deny codes, statutes, rules, regulations nullify l.e.g.a.l. process

TRONE : seat taken by unstable sovereign or devilish function

TRUE : What is fact witness by two or more wo/mankind in god

TRUTH : On personal belief that is not backed by fact or evidence

TRY : Try or trying is not fulfilling and is half way to failure

UNTERMENSCH : Germans refer to non-Aryan people deemed sub-human

U.S.S.C. : united state supreme court

VEXATIOUS : pubic serpent(s) that individually or collectively sustains multiple denials against same wo/man's rights to a subject matter otherwise should have moved to a final self-determination or by trial by jury

VOLUME : a series; Claims of Action, wanton series of claims within one lawsuite with multiple causes of action

W.A.R. : War, war, war-ant is Without Authority Rebuttal

W.H.O.R.E. : Without Honor Openly Refusing Evidence

WO/MANKIND : Woman & Mankind; is made in the image of God and on a hierarchy totem pole analogy is under God above all Govern mentals;

W/OUT : short term: with/out ; without, devoid of, or, exclusive of…

For any other words, terms, phrases, or their like kind, a more comprehensible list of words and phrases can be found on Disabledjustice.org under terms and definitions;

WORDS AND PHRASES

All acronyms have the same meaning regardless of UPPER CASE or lower case; the meanings do not change as is defined herein. When it is not defined herein the meanings of all words do not necessarily mean the same as street vernacular, common English language or legal jargon; you must ask the author when there is a question in fact;

The use of the capital "I" is a fiction and the lower case "i" describes a living woman or man unless the "I" is used at the beginning of a sentence; All i, "t's" dotted and "i's" crossed is a metaphor for deliberately scrutinize everything thing i, say and write with unusual extraordinary bias;

Every "person" is a debtor by default, and every man or woman that suffers "joinder" to a "person" becomes "Surety" in the debt – money system of bondage, sacrificing their living energy via the fictional "transmitting utility," feeding the parasitic banking cabal which espouses the Roman motto: "*He who would be deceived, let him be….*"

When Titles are used: Such as naming a PERSON, PLACE OR THING, known by California, Los Angeles, New York, Donald John Trump,

When an "**s**", "**ed**" "**ing**" or any other . The "-ing" form is used in progressive verb tenses with auxiliary verbs (helping verbs). These are in active voice

The "**-ing**" and the past participle is bolded in the example sentences below. Notice that the "**-ing**" adjective refers **to** a thing and the past participle ("**-ed**") adjective refers **to** a person. The **"-s"** is added to add woman or man singular or plural such as with govern mental "**s**" = agent for the agency;
When adding "Ship" to the end of a word such as Courthouse-"***ship***" it depicts that venue out on the great oceans in maritime or admiralty jurisdiction, and not necessarily with control of jurisdiction over any wo/mankind;
The use of the word "do" whereas it might be better stated as "does" and the word "go" sometimes replaced by "goes" and visa vie and is left on purpose for the term in its present tense verses past tense; there is no rhyme or reason it is how the author writes and portrays to the readers his intent.

Any Quotations that are copied and pasted in this living missive, do take on many of the definitions unless otherwise stated herein;

Whenever certain words and phrases are used with/without a period (.) in-between each letter the meaning is the same for the acronym as if it does have a separator between each word for example: whore can mean the same as the acronym: w.h.o.r.e. which acronym is defined as (Without Honor Openly Refus-ing/ed Evidence) therefore fukc means the same as f.u.k.c. : Forever Under **Kangaroo Court**; whether added an "ing" "ed", "s" with a dash (-) go to the progressive verb definitions;
Cocaine is used as the acronym unless it states (N.A.) next to the words as follows: cocaine (na) ….. or cocaine is followed by a dash (-) between another word it resorts back to the acronym;
The Little Engine That Could: The unwavering courage to never give up on self Jesus or God
i, can tell you what adam - daniels is not;
See example:
adam-daniels is not a hue-man being who will take any S.H.I.T., (Pubic-serpent Obstructing Other People) P.O.O.P., from any power hungry agent, wo/mankind, citizen, or resident that is F.U.K.C.-ing(Forever Under Kangaroo Court) like K.U.N.T.-s (Korruption Understands Nothing True) piece of woman or mankind who acts as a C.L.I.T.(Court Liar Initiating Trouble) as an agent, pubic serpent ,

employee, individual hired F.A.C.E.(Fraud Acquired Court Experts) or P.E.N.I.S.-s(People Exercising Nonsensical Inept Shit) such as residents or citizens that are W.H.O.R.E.-s(Without Honor Openly Refusing Evidence) for any GOVERN MENTAL(Agent That Works For State/Federal Agency) private entities or D.O.J.(Deprivation For-Just-Us) agents, titles or their breed.

Outer Limits Of No Return: is to fulfill an act that has repercussion for eternity; to kill someone thus it would be final compared to hurt someone which is not final.

In The Pudding: The best way to know if something is true or not is to experience it firsthand.

Maxims of law: Some of them can be traced to early Roman law. Much more common in scope than the l.e.g.a.l. as ordinary rules of law, truly known by l.e.g.a.l. maxims. These maxims generally create a l.e.g.a.l. policy which I, state is not law. At least not under god's laws. The natural court is that of one by trial by jury. The States maxims are not the same and are supposed to be considered in deciding all cases. However, not with an Open Court Of Record.

Movers of the courts: can be woman or man, or ens legis fictions

Culpability by evasion: default with no repercussions to redress

https://www.reuters.com/legal/government/pervasive-judicial-misconduct-raises-question-whos-charge-here-2021-10-06/

Copywrited material; can only be what the author creates for this Living Missive. For example: when author creates a quote, writes personal firsthand knowledge or what author can prove by two or more witness, and not limited to borrowing from actors, musicians, artists or copies a pictures, the pictures are not copywritten unless it is of the author, or author receives authorization. Copied material form websites, internet is not copyrighted by this author, however auther uses it for this living missive as everything in this living missive is created as a court claim for which relief shall be granted;

FYI: taken "February 3, 2012. REUTERS/Chip East (UNITED STATES- Tags: CRIME... Purchase Licensing Rights ,opens new tab Read more (Reuters) - House Democrats announced

opens new tab last Wednesday that they would reform judicial integrity procedures after an investigation found that more than 130 federal judges have been violating laws and ethics rules by participating in cases involving companies in which they or their family members owned stock.

Over the last decade, judges improperly failed to disqualify themselves from 685 cases nationwide, according to the September 28 report by the Wall Street Journal. Sixty-one judges or their families even traded those stocks while the cases were playing out in court.

The video player is currently playing an ad. You can skip the ad in 5 sec with a mouse or keyboard 00:03Harvey Weinstein pleads not guilty to new sexual assault charge

The findings come on the heels of Reuters' "Teflon Robe opens new tab" investigation last year, which found that thousands of state and local judges across the country violated ethics rules over the past 12 years, including lying to state officials and making racist statements.

At least 5,206 people were directly affected, but most of the offending judges largely escaped punishment or accountability, even for shocking conduct like illegally jailing people and sexual abuse, Reuters found."

Readers Use the following lines for your notes: ________________

____

____

____

____

____

____

____

LIST OF EVIL WRONGDOERS

Satan's Minion List:

When a minion is out of chronological order does not have any intent or meaning for this living missive. See the list of Satan's minions for this missive as follows:

1. Scott Allan & Robin Niner, Satan's Married Minions (ass-wipe) Niner
2. Margaret Lynn Oldendorf, Satan's 1st Minion (B.i.t.c.h.-mlo)
3. Joseph Ramin Kerendian, Satan's 2nd Minion (Top-ramin)
4. Thomas Edward Wanner, Satan's 3rd Minion (Weiner-Dog)
5. David Earl Woodruff, Satan's 4th Minion (Mediator-prator)
6. Richard Thomas Miller, Satan's 5th Minion (Dick-em)
7. Ronald George Niner, Satan's 6th Minion (Sperm-doner)
8. Dennis Mayer Perlus, Satan's 7th Minion (1st Blind-mouse)
9. Norvell Fred Woods Junior, Satan's 8th Minion (2nd Blind-mouse)
10. Frank Y. Jackson, Satan's 9th Minion (Third Blind-mouse)
11. Thomas Brian Donovan, Satan's 10th Minion (Shit-for-brains)
12. James Thomas King, Santa's 11th Minion (Jack-off)
13. David L. Hahn, Satan's 12th Minion (Un-trustee-worthy)
14. James Samuel Otero, Satan's 13th Minion (Pubic-sperm-ant)
15. Jesus Gilbert Bernal, Satan's 14th Minion (No-jesus-inhere)
16. Carol Chenkin Koppel, Satan's 15th Minion (C.C.K.-whore)
17. Melvin Douglas Sandvig, Satan's 16th Minion (Richard-carnium)
18. Lloyd Clark Loomis, Satan's 17th Minion (Clue-less)
19. Susan L Lopez-Giss, Satan's 18th Minion (Suzie-que)

i, do ask the reader to find this phrase and send it to i, in order i, can be certain that Jesus actually do know what he was doing when Jesus allegedly died for our sins.

SATAN'S TRONES

1. Satan's 1st Trone Chatsworth Courthouse-ship: Pages 122,
2. Satan's 2nd Trone San Fernando Courthouse-ship: Volume No.2
3. Satan's 3rd Trone, Second Appellate District Court Of Appeal: Page 168,
4. Satan's 4th Trone, United States Bankruptcy Court: Page 187,
5. Satan's 5th Trone, United States Ninth Circuit Of Appeal Page: 220,
6. Satan's 6th Trone, Michael Antonovich Antelope Valley Court: Page 245,
7. Satan's 7th Trone, United States District Court: Page 308,
8. Trone is being written as these previously distributed, in progress court actions

A message for moral and ethical wo/mankind:

Do not allow the information herein to flood into your mind and spirit of what the State of California and The United State for America Stand for.

The govern mentals are hired to subvert your rites/rights which is and always have been made up, as stated, for the purpose to enslave, dumb down and to control all wo/mankind that know no better than to follow the govern mental agent's authoritarianism as sheep, w8-n for the slaughter.

Do not 4-get the drugs You have T8-n
You wo/mankind must wake up out from your Psychotropic like state of Psychosis, from the LSD as the elixir you have been fed your entire life through mainstream education, the tel-us-lies-vision, (ignorant peers).

And over time the drug of ignorance, begins to wear off and your reality becomes more focused on what you are doing and the path of your life befalls strange; although you think you know?

i, am not on drugs, but you readers are if you think the States and United States Inc. are real. The agents have you on their LSD and you do not even know it because you are oblivious on the ride of shiny objects for which you follow, seek, or know no better, even though you do know for what you do, and do it anyways!

Please readers place your notes of your personal issues on following lines as the author wants to hear from you personally:______________________________

REFERENCES

God Almighty: www.just pray.prayer
Jesus Christ: www.jesuschrist.god
William Thornton: 1215.org

Adam – Daniel: Disabledjustice.org
DisabledJusticeasking@proton.me

William Wagener: OnSecondThought.tv ;
https://williamwagener.blogspot.com/2010/06/blog-introduction-from-william-wagener.html

Clint Richardson: http://www.strawmanstory.info/
Robert Eugene Schaefer: "Land Patent Claims"
Youhavetheright.com

History: https://www.youhavetheright.com/history/
William Thornton: " 1215.ORG ": THE FINAL SOLUTION, TO PROPERTY TAX, BY JOE STEVENS, DECEASED, REVISED & REVIVED, BY AUGUSTUS BLACKSTONE:

https://www.1215.org/lawnotes/lawnotes/landpatent/land-patents-allodial-title-blackstone.pdf
Henry Ronald Gibson: "Suits In Chancery"
https://americanmeetinggroup.com/ron-gibson/

Encouraging a more peaceable posterity
The American Meeting Group community is made up of friends who want to learn how to protect what was intended for them, and to help make our families and communities a safer, better place for everyone. https://americanmeetinggroup.com/about/

Greg Paul & Jon Little: " Law For Mankind / SovereignsWay "
https://thesovereignsway.com/
https://www.youtube.com/watch?v=6fkNTVbPfwE

Jennifer Goodwin: https://laworlegal.com/event
Kevin Werbach's LOOKING IT UP: The Supreme Court's Use of Dictionaries in Statutory and Constitutional Interpretation (1994).

L.A.W. OF MAN

vs.

PUBIC SERPENT & CORPORATE CORRUPTION

THE MARGARET LYNN OLDENDORF
CRIMINAL GANG OF 2007 – 2025

NOTICE OF RELATED CASES:

Superior Court Chatsworth Calif.	Case # PC04224 -2009
Margaret L. Oldendorf	BAR # **116069**
Superior Court Chatsworth Calif.	Case # PC04224 -2009
Joseph Ramin Kerendian	BAR # **186343**
Superior Court Chatsworth Calif.	Case # PC04224 -2009
Thomas Edward Wanner	BAR # **195300**
Superior Court Chatsworth Calif.	Case # PC04224 -2009
ATTORNEY	BAR # **666-666**
2nd District Court of Appeal	Case # B21796 - 2011
Dennis Mayer Perlus	B.A.R. # **57999**
Fred Woods	B.A.R. # **35745**
Frank Y. Jackson	B.A.R. # **57384**

THE SCOTT & ROBIN NINER CRIMINAL GANG OF 2006 – 2025

(Scott Allan Niner & Robin Elizabeth Lillian Nigretto/Niner)

United States Bankruptcy Court Thomas Brian Donavon	Case # 2:11-bk -18734 B.A.R. # **34106**
U.S. Bankruptcy Adversary Thomas Brian Donavon	Case # 2:11-ap-02293 B.A.R. # **34106**
[Attorn'ey Represents Fraud] James Thomas King	Case# 2:11-bk -18734 B.A.R. # **82087**
U.S. BankruptcyTrustee David L. Hahn	Case # 2:11-bk -18734 No License #
U.S. B.K Appeal: S. James Otero	Case # 2:12-cv-10284 B.A.R. # **73992**
Michael D. Antonovich Court Carol Shenkin Koppel	Case # 3 counts Contempt B.A.R. # **59612**

THE MELVIN DEAN SANDVIG CRIMINAL GANG OF 2007 & 2015 – 2025

Superior Court Chatsworth California Chatsworth

[Pubic Serpent] Lloyd Clark Loomis	Case # PS016624 B.A.R. # **85239**
[Pubic Serpent] Melvin Dean Sandvig	Case # PS016624 B.A.R.# **101320**
[Pubic Serpent] Susan L Lopez-Giss	Case # PS016624 B.A.R.# **61675**

Statement by the Author for the rest of the world

i: a man; Adam - Daniel: Borsotti; state as true:

i, claim the woman and man who wrong i, continue to rob, rape to conspire against i, estate;

i, say, each woman and man above continue to trespass by way of barratry and continue to not follow real law;

i, say, each woman and man above trespass by way of theft of i, property;

i, say, the woman and man above aid to hypothecate; subrogate; and abrogate i, estate and private property;

i, say, the woman and man above deny i, a lawful trial by jury;

i, say, the women and the men: who act as public servants, do conspire to refuse i, to present i, own case causing a trespass on i, case by way of barratry, champerty, maintenance that cause vexatious trespass;

i, say, the men: herein; did sin of omission to conspire with other women and men to subterfuge jurors' when jurors ask "is there a law…" and jurors were not told what is true;

i, say, each man and woman above *trespass* by way of to conspire with other man and woman to wrong i, and do *trespass* by way of extortion, kidnap, unlawful detainment, robbery, threat, theft, and murder i, trust by unlawful means;

i, state: to receive full answerability for all writings within this Living Missive as i, claim for which relief shall be granted;

i, say this living missive is the cause govern mentals commit sin, that cause all wo/mankind to lose their lawful courts of record;

By: i, a man Adam Daniels

JESUS TURNED THE TABLES OVER ON THE MERCHANTS FOREVER

All within this one page is created by information so it was said so it was written. Now i, write it in i, own personal language:

As the story is written, Jesus Christ entered the grounds of the courtyard, as a temple of God, to cast and drive away all those who were selling and buying pigeons, doves and other animals. Some animals were for sacrifice, others for breeding; in wanton, those who cared less for morals and ethics were creating commerce while at the house of god. Jesus forbid it!

Fast 4-ward to 2025, is it not the same thing when the church has been feathered out and the Courts have taken the place of ecclesiastical forum?

It is time that you readers as i, a man do what Jesus Christ had the courage, tenacity and wherewithal to turn the tables on corrupt wo/mankind that ACT as magistrates, ~~judges~~ and commissioners.

[Pubic Serpent] **Margaret Lynn Oldendorf**
Calif. B.A.R. # 116069
[Pubic Serpent] **Thomas Brian Donavon**
Calif. B.A.R. # 34106
[Pubic Serpent] **Carol Shenkin Koppel**
Calif. B.A.R. # 59612
[Pubic Serpent] **Melvin Dean Sandvig**
Calif. B.A.R. # 101320
[Pubic Serpent] **Daniel Juarez**
Calif. B.A.R. # 168936
[Pubic Serpent] **Kamala Devi Harris**
Calif. B.A.R. # 146672
[Pubic Serpent] **Tani Gorre Cantil-Sakauye**
Calif. B.A.R. # 114470
[Pubic Serpent] **James Samuel Otero**
Calif. B.A.R. # 73992

List above is of Merchants i, turn tables on thee who trespass against i, a once disabled man. So it was said, as it is now, so it is written 4-ever.

EVIL-WRONG DOERS LIST HEREIN IS FOREVER-ENDING

i, noticed this list of claims against all evil-wrongdoers, as "***NOTICE OF RELATED CLAIMS…***" which are of interest to assist i, and require all readers to look in to all of the [wo] man names and case/account numbers herein;

As each relate to trespass by way of conspiracy to commit extortion, theft, threat, barratry, champerty, maintenance and to this day 2025, are all unresolved claims and each is a *trespass* against i, a man and a trespass on i, case:

1. Los Angeles Calif.: Samuel James Otero
   [A] U.S. District Court
   Pubic Serpent as man

2. Chatsworth Calif. : Melvin Douglas Sandvig
   [A] Calif. State Court
   Pubic Serpent / as man

3. Pasadena/Burbank: Margaret L. Oldendorf
   [A] Calif. State Court
   Pubic Serpent /as woman

4. Sacramento Calif. : Gavin Newsom
   [A] California Governor
   Pubic Serpent /as man

5. Los Angeles Calif.: (2 times) Daniel Juarez
   [A] Calif. State Court
   Pubic Serpent / as man

6. Los Angeles Calif.: Thomas B. Donovan
   [A] U.S. Bankruptcy
   Pubic Serpent / as man

7. San Fernando Valley: Paul Andrew Cohen
[A] A Citizen /Resident
Ward of the State as man

8. Beyond the 50 states: J.P. Morgan Chase, [A] C.E.O
as Title Jamie Dimon/as a man

9. Chatsworth Calif.: Pubic Serpent
[A] Court Administrator
Jefferey M. Harkavy/as man

10. Sacramento Calif.: Pubic Serpent
[A] Attorney General
Kamala Devi Harris/as woman

11. Valencia Calif.: Trespass by deceit
[A] Co-Conservator
Scott Allan Niner/as man

12. Sacramento Calif.: Pubic Serpent
[A]Chief Justice
Tani G. Cantil-Sakauye/as woman

13. San Diego Calif.: Private Contractor
[A]Q.Loan Service Corporation
Annia Quintana/as woman

14. Los Angeles Calif.: Surety/ Ens Legis
[A](A.B.N.)Estate /Trust
DANIEL ADAM BORSOTTI

15. Santa Clarita Calif.: Representative/Payee
[A] Abuse Fiduciary duty
Robin Nigretto/Niner/a woman

i, preserve all rights and remedies to add any new evil-wrongdoers upon more discovery once i, am aware of their correct and accurate name, depending on their actions/inactions of said recipient;

by: i, a man; daniel-adam of borsotti family .

LIST OF- DENIALS
ANY OF THESE FAMILIAR WITH YOU ???

1. i: a man; Adam-Daniel -Borsotti have been denied :
2. To Present Self As Private Counsel …
3. Lawful Administrative Process…
4. Enforcement to investigate interlopers stop interfering with i,
   Evidence, facts and tangible proof…
5. Physical Access To The Courts and kiosk (state, federal, county recorders, all agencies)
6. All Discoveries (in over 25 cases)
7. Freedom Of Information Act
8. Access Court Transcripts
9. Right to present Facts and Evidence
10. Required Authentication Of The Record by opposing man and woman
11. Verification Of R.P.O.I. (Real Party Of Interest)
12. To Present Self As A Man instead of Citizen, Plaintiff, Defendant, Corporation, ens legis… Fiction
13. Rites To Private Property…(rites and body are property…)
14. Access into the court federal buildings
15. Woman/Man Who Do Witness
16. A Court Of Record…
17. January 20th Transcripts and other dates, (of all 25 cases) to present for appeal DENIED!
18. A Complete Investigation Of the claims of Fraud …
19. W-4's , 1099's, 1099- OID's,
20. Investigation of identity theft…
21. Investigation of embezzlement…
22. Investigation of forged documents…
23. Investigation of Fraud upon the courts by (attorn-eys, judges,
    commissioners, family, bankters, foreclosing l.e.g.a.l.-mills…)
24. Habeus Corpus, when locked up as political prisoner …
25. Constitutional ledgers … (not a leg to stand on justify denials…
26. Freed from Being A Political Prisoner

27. This is why i, am compelled to place a crucifixion of the strawman up on lights! This list was only the first of many denials…

2025 to be continued…: See Volume Two, 2, II

Dear readers;
i, leave this section of *fibrous substance* for your thoughts, as to a summation of what you have read. i, ask of you as i, do ask of Jesus Christ; place your conception of what you think, feel, and have read on the following lines: ______________________________

When you are finished, i, encourage you to send it to i, personally;